A **FIELD** Guide
to Contemporary
Poetry and Poetics

Revised Edition

A FIELD
Guide to Contemporary Poetry and Poetics

REVISED EDITION

STUART FRIEBERT
DAVID WALKER
DAVID YOUNG

OBERLIN COLLEGE PRESS

Publication of this book was made possible by support from the Ohio
Arts Council.

Library of Congress Cataloging-in-Publication Data
Main entry under title:

A FIELD guide to contemporary poetry and poetics—revised ed. /
Edited by Stuart Friebert, David Walker, David Young.

A collection of essays which originally appeared in FIELD
magazine.
 1. Poetics—Addresses, essays, lectures.
I. Friebert, Stuart, 1931-   II. Walker, David, 1950-
III. Young, David, 1936-

LC: 97-066616
ISBN: 0-932440-77-0 (pbk.)

CONTENTS

3. The Image: A Symposium

4. Poetry and Values

5. Portraits and Self-Portraits

PREFACE

One of the hallmarks of *FIELD* magazine has always been its attention to what poets have to say about poetry. Since the first issue in 1969, alongside poems and translations we have featured essays on contemporary poetry and poetics by working poets. The editors' hope has been that in asking poets to speculate about matters important to them, a useful perspective could be opened up, specifically on questions about the craft and values of poetry in the latter part of the twentieth century, and more broadly on the creative process itself. Particularly in the early years of *FIELD*, serious attention to issues of contemporary poetics was relatively rare; the explosion of interest in literary theory tended to focus on narrative fiction or on the poetry of the past, and much of what was written about recent poetry tended to be arid and tendentious. Inviting poets to explore questions that immediately concerned them would, we hoped, serve as a way of enlivening and deepening the conversation.

The results were immediately gratifying. William Stafford and Denise Levertov agreed to discuss their own process of composition; Donald Hall and Robert Bly, the psychic origins of poetic form; Gary Snyder, the relation between poetry and community in a time of ecological challenge. Galway Kinnell and Adrienne Rich explored the representation of the self and sexuality in poetry, Miroslav Holub investigated the relationship between poetry and science, Russell Edson contributed a meditation on the nature of the prose poem, and a group of seven poets composed a symposium focused on the poetic line. These and many other essays evoked enthusiastic responses from poets, teachers, students, and other readers alike. A number have been reprinted in collections from such publishers as New Directions and the University of Michigan Press, as well as in textbooks and other anthologies. Though we would not claim credit for the resurgence of interest in what poets have to say about aesthetics, history, politics, and writing—as indicated by the success of recent collections of essays by Robert Hass, Adrienne Rich, Seamus Heaney, Eavan Boland, and Czeslaw Milosz, for instance— we do believe our encouragement has provided a catalyst for important thinking about crucial matters.

The first edition of *A FIELD Guide to Contemporary Poetry and Poetics* collected many of the best essays from the first ten years of the magazine. Despite positive reviews and respectable sales, its commercial publisher was about to let it go out of print just a few years after publication, when, fortunately, Oberlin College Press was able to step in and assume distribution. This revised and expanded edition reprints almost all of these now-classic essays (a few had to be dropped for considerations of space) and augments them with further dazzling performances, including Sandra McPherson on telling secrets, Shirley Kaufman and Larry Levis on the use of place in contemporary poetry, Laura Jensen on poetic form, a second symposium on the image, and three poets writing revealingly about their own insomnia, backache, and myopia. The resulting collection provides a rich and stimulating perspective on the state of contemporary poetry, as seen through the eyes—or over the shoulders—of the poets themselves.

All the poets included have been doubly generous: first in agreeing to write so thoughtfully and openly about matters of concern to them, and then in granting us the right to reprint their work. A few have asked to revise their essays slightly, but most remain as first published, topical references and all; each essay has now been dated to indicate its historical context. We are also grateful to the series of associate editors of the magazine who helped us develop this material over the years, to the late, lamented NEA-sponsored residencies which allowed many of these writers to spend time at Oberlin trying out their ideas, and to the Ohio Arts Council for supporting this new edition.

David Walker
May 1997

1 The Process of Writing

William Stafford

A WAY OF WRITING

A writer is not so much someone who has something to say as he is someone who has found a process that will bring about new things he would not have thought of if he had not started to say them. That is, he does not draw on a reservoir; instead, he engages in an activity that brings to him a whole succession of unforeseen stories, poems, essays, plays, laws, philosophies, religions, or— but wait!

Back in school, from the first when I began to try to write things, I felt this richness. One thing would lead to another; the world would give and give. Now, after twenty years or so of trying, I live by that certain richness, an idea hard to pin, difficult to say, and perhaps offensive to some. For there are strange implications in it.

One implication is the importance of just plain receptivity. When I write, I like to have an interval before me when I am not likely to be interrupted. For me, this means usually the early morning, before others are awake. I get pen and paper, take a glance out the window (often it is dark out there), and wait. It is like fishing. But I do not wait very long, for there is always a nibble—and this is where receptivity comes in. To get started I will accept anything that occurs to me. Something always occurs, of course, to any of us. We can't keep from thinking. Maybe I have to settle for an immediate impression: it's cold, or hot, or dark, or bright, or in between! Or—well, the possibilities are endless. If I

1

put down something, that thing will help the next thing come, and I'm off. If I let the process go on, things will occur to me that were not at all in my mind when I started. These things, odd or trivial as they may be, are somehow connected. And if I let them string out, surprising things will happen.

If I let them string out. . . . Along with initial receptivity, then, there is another readiness: I must be willing to fail. If I am to keep on writing, I cannot bother to insist on high standards. I must get into action and not let anything stop me, or even slow me much. By "standards" I do not mean "correctness"—spelling, punctuation, and so on. These details become mechanical for anyone who writes for a while. I am thinking about what many people would consider "important" standards, such matters as social significance, positive values, consistency, etc. I resolutely disregard these. Something better, greater, is happening! I am following a process that leads so wildly and originally into new territory that no judgment can at the moment be made about values, significance, and so on. I am making something new, something that has not been judged before. Later others—and maybe I myself— will make judgments. Now, I am headlong to discover. Any distraction may harm the creating.

So, receptive, careless of failure, I spin out things on the page. And a wonderful freedom comes. If something occurs to me, it is all right to accept it. It has one justification: it occurs to me. No one else can guide me. I must follow my own weak, wandering, diffident impulses.

A strange bonus happens. At times, without my insisting on it, my writings become coherent; the successive elements that occur to me are clearly related. They lead by themselves to new connections. Sometimes the language, even the syllables that happen along, may start a trend. Sometimes the materials alert me to something waiting in my mind, ready for sustained attention. At such times, I allow myself to be eloquent, or intentional, or for great swoops (treacherous! not to be trusted!) reasonable. But I do not insist on any of that; for I know that back of my activity there will be the coherence of my self, and that indulgence of my impulses will bring recurrent patterns and meanings again.

This attitude toward the process of writing creatively suggests a problem for me, in terms of what others say. They talk about "skills" in writing. Without denying that I do have experience, wide reading, automatic orthodoxies and maneuvers of various kinds, I still must insist that I am often baffled about what "skill" has to do with the precious little area of confusion when I do not know what I am going to say and then I find out what I am going to say. That precious interval I am unable to bridge by skill. What can I witness about it? It remains mysterious, just as all of us must feel puzzled about how we are so inventive as to be able to talk along through complexities with our friends, not needing to plan what we are going to say, but never stalled for long in our confident forward progress. Skill? If so, it is the skill we all have, something we must have learned before the age of three or four.

A writer is one who has become accustomed to trusting that grace, or luck, or—skill.

Yet another attitude I find necessary: most of what I write, like most of what I say in casual conversation, will not amount to much. Even I will realize, and even at the time, that it is not negotiable. It will be like practice. In conversation I allow myself random remarks—in fact, as I recall, that is the way I learned to talk—, so in writing I launch many expendable efforts. A result of this free way of writing is that I am not writing for others, mostly; they will not see the product at all unless the activity eventuates in something that later appears to be worthy. My guide is the self, and its adventuring in the language brings about communication.

This process-rather-than-substance view of writing invites a final, dual reflection:

1) Writers may not be special—sensitive or talented in any usual sense. They are simply engaged in sustained use of a language skill we all have. Their "creations" come about through confident reliance on stray impulses that will, with trust, find occasional patterns that are satisfying.

2) But writing itself is one of the great, free human activities. There is scope for individuality, and elation, and discovery, in writing. For the person who follows with trust and forgiveness what occurs to him, the world remains always ready and deep, an inexhaustible environment, with the combined vividness of an actuality and flexibility of a dream. Working back and forth between experience and thought, writers have more than space and time can offer. They have the whole unexplored realm of human vision.

A sample daily-writing sheet and the poem as revised:

15 December 1969

[handwritten draft]

Shadows

I

Out in places like Wyoming some of the shadows

are cut out and pasted on fossils.

There are mountains that erode when
clouds drag across them. You can hear the tick

~~the tick~~ of the light breaking edges off white stones.

At a fountain on Main Street I saw

our shadow. It did not drink but

waited on cement and water while I drank.

There were two people and but one shadow.

I looked up so hard outward that a bird

flying past made a shadow on the sky.

There is a place in the air where our house
used to be.

Once I crawled through grassblades to hear

the sounds of their shadows. One of the shadows

moved, and it was the earth where a mole

was passing. I could hear little

paws in the dirt, and fur brush along

the tunnel, and even, somehow, the mole shadow.

In churches their hearts pump sermons

from wells full of shadows.

In my prayers I let yesterday begin

and then go behind this hour now.

SHADOWS

Out in places like Wyoming some of the shadows
are cut out and pasted on fossils.
There are mountains that erode when
clouds drag across them. You hear the tick
of sunlight breaking edges off white stones.

At a fountain on Main Street I saw
our shadow. It did not drink but
waited on cement and water while I drank.
There were two people and but one shadow.
I looked up so hard outward that a bird
flying past made a shadow on the sky.

There is a place in the air where
our old house used to be.

Once I crawled through grassblades to hear
the sounds of their shadows. One shadow
moved, and it was the earth where a mole
was passing. I could hear little
paws in the dirt, and fur brush along
the tunnel, and even, somehow, the mole shadow.

In my prayers I let yesterday begin
and then go behind this hour now,
in churches where hearts pump sermons
from wells full of shadows.

                                            (1970)

Denise Levertov

WORK AND INSPIRATION: INVITING THE MUSE

Poems come into being in two ways. There are those which are—or used to be—spoken of as *inspired*; poems which seem to appear out of nowhere, complete or very nearly so; which are quickly written without conscious premeditation, taking the writer by surprise. These are often the best poems; at least, a large proportion of those that I have been "given" in this way are the poems I myself prefer and which readers, without knowledge of their history, have singled out for praise. Such poems often seem to have that aura of authority, of the incontrovertible, that air of being mysteriously lit from within their substance, which is exactly what a poet strives to attain in the poems that are hard to write. But though the inspired poem is something any poet naturally feels awed by and grateful for, nevertheless if one wrote only such poems one would have, as it were, no occupation; and so most writers, surely, are glad that some of their work requires the labor for which they are constitutionally fitted. For the artist—every kind of artist, and, I feel sure, not only the artist but everyone engaged in any kind of creative activity—is as enamored of the process of making as of the thing made.

There is nothing one can say directly concerning the coming into being of "given" or "inspired" poems because there is no conscious process to be described. However, in considering what happens in writing poems which have a known history, I have come to feel convinced that they are not of a radically different order; it is simply that in the "given" poem *the same kind of work* has gone on below, or I would prefer to say beyond, the threshold of consciousness. The labor we call conscious is, if the poem is a good one, or rather if the poet knows how to work, not a matter of a use of the intellect divorced from other factors but of the intuitive interplay of various mental and physical factors, just as in unconscious pre-creative activity; it is *conscious,* in that we are aware of it, but not in the sense of being deliberate and controlled by the rational will (though of course reason and will can and should play their modest part too).

The two manifestations of this underlyingly identical process can both occur in the composition of a single poem. Either sections of a poem emerge "right" the first time, while other sections require much revision; or, as I hope to demonstrate, many drafts and revisions can prepare the way for a poem which at the last leaps from the pen and requires little or no revision, but which is emphatically not simply a final draft and indeed bears practically no resemblance to the earlier "versions" which make it possible. In such a case, conscious work has led to the unpredictable inspiration.

I have chosen to tell the history of three poems—"The Son," I and II, and "A Man"—as examples of what happens, of how the laboriously written poem evolves and how the labor can sometimes lead to the entire "given" poem. The choice of these particular poems was determined by my happening to have kept all the worksheets for them and also by the fact of their close connection with each other.

The first of the three to be written was the first "Son" poem. The earliest note for it says simply, "Nik as a presence, *Who he was.*" This was a reference to an unpublished poem written almost seventeen years before—in the spring of 1944, just before the birth of my son. I did not publish this poem because I came to feel it was too wordy, just not good enough; but I shall quote it now as part of the story of these later poems:

> One is already here whose life
> bearing like seed its distant death, shall grow
> through human pain, human joy, shall know
> music and weeping, only because
> the strange flower of your thighs
> bloomed in my body. From our joy
> begins a stranger's history. Who
> is this rider in the dark? We lie
> in candlelight; the child's quick unseen movements
> jerk my belly under your hand. Who,
> conceived in joy, in joy,
> lies nine months alone in a walled silence?
>
> Who is this rider in the dark
> nine months the body's tyrant
> nine months alone in a walled silence
> our minds cannot fathom?
> Who is it will come out of the dark,
> whose cries demand our mercy, tyrant
> no longer, but alone still, in a solitude
> memory cannot reach?
> Whose lips will suckle at these breasts,
> thirsting, unafraid, for life?
> Whose eyes will look out of that solitude?

> The wise face of the unborn
> ancient and innocent
> must change to infant ignorance
> before we see it, irrevocable third
> looking into our lives; the child
> must hunger, sleep, cry, gaze, long weeks
> before it learns of laughter. Love can never
> wish a life no darkness; but may love
> be constant in the life our love has made.

My note saying *"Who he was"* referred to my memory of this poem, but I had not actually read the poem in several years, so it is to its general sense of questioning rather than to the specific words of the poem that I was harking back.

Next on the same piece of paper is the note, *"M.'s fineness of face—the lines—the changes out of boy-and-young-manhood. A life."* Out of these notes all three poems emerged.

The first draft of the first poem went like this:

> He-who-came-forth was
> it turned out
> a man.
>
> Through his childhood swiftly
> ran the current of
> pain, that men
>
> communicate or lie,
> the intelligence behind silence
> not always heard.

In hyphenating "He-who-came-forth," making these words into a name or title, I think I may have had American Indian names obscurely in mind, and with them the knowledge that in some cultures a true name is gained only after initiation; and that some Indians achieved identity only after the Big Dream which established their special relation to life. I may also have had sounding in me the echo of a poem of Robert Duncan's, in which he writes: "Wanderer-to-Come-to-the-Secret-Place-Where-Waits the Discovery-That-Moves-the-Heart," (from "The Performance We Wait For" in *The Opening of the Field*).

In the second draft the first stanza remained, as indeed it continued to do throughout, unchanged, but I seem to have felt a need to elaborate the image of the current running through childhood, the current of knowledge of the human condition, that men

communicate or lie, or one could say, communicate or die (or as
Auden put it, "We must love one another or die") but that this
communication, which at times has to fight its way through
silence, is a hard, hard task. But though my intention was to make
this clearer, I only got so far as to elaborate on the brevity of
childhood:

> Childhood is very short
> and shot through hastily with
> gleams of that current
>
> straining to its . . . .

This was obviously impossible; the words themselves were
straining; instead of waiting in that intense passivity, that passive
intensity, that passionate patience which Keats named Negative
Capability and which I believe to be a vital condition for the
emergence of a true poem, I was straining to *find words*; the word
had not found *me*. The word "straining," however, led me to my
third try, where, again preceded by the unchanged first stanza,

> He-who-came-forth was
> it turned out
> a man,

I continued:

> living among us
> his childhood sifted, strained out
> to retain
>
> all it held of
> pain, energy, lassitude,
> the imagination of man

Here the last words were intended to lead into another attempt at
giving a sense of that knowledge of the human condition, the seed
in the child of adulthood, of manhood, which I had tried to speak
of in the first draft. Again it was abandoned, with the continuing
sense that the words were not the right words. The fourth draft
begins to pick up a more concrete sense of the presence being
talked of, *how* he lives among us:

> Moving among us from room to room of
> *the soul's dark cottage*

in boots, in jeans, in a cloak of flame no-one
seems to see—

it is
the imagination's garment, that human dress
woven of fire and seagrasses—

how swift the current was,
'childhood,' that carried him here—

In this version appear details that immediately asserted
themselves to me as vivid and necessary and were retained—"in
boots, in jeans, in a cloak of flame"—but also an allusion I later
felt was extraneous, to "The soul's dark cottage," a quote from the
seventeenth-century poet Edmund Waller's wonderful couplet
which I have loved since childhood: "The soul's dark cottage, bat-
tr'd and decay'd,/ Lets in new light through chinks which Time
hath made." Also in this fourth draft the current, which in the
beginning had been the current of pain running through childhood, becomes itself the current of childhood, and the brevity of
childhood is expressed as the swiftness of that current. A variant
of this draft says:

How swiftly childhood's
little river carried him here!

and pain—or knowledge of pain, knowledge of suffering—is spoken of in an image quickly abandoned as seeming sentimental:

an injured dragonfly
cupped in his large gentle hands

In retrospect, I don't think this documentary image is *in itself* sentimental; but it has the effect of sentimentality in this context
because it is digressive and does not bring the occasion alluded to
directly enough into the poem, but lets it remain an allusion. Of
equal importance in the immediate decision to strike it out was
the sonically awkward juxtaposition of "injured" and "gentle." I
tried the substitution of "tender" for "gentle"—an injured dragonfly cupped "tenderly"—but no, the whole thing was going off on
a tack much too soft and pretty for what I wanted.

At this point I tried to get back to the human knowledge:

Man, whose imagination is not
intuition, whose innocence

cannot brace itself for the event
but is gone
over the edge, spared
no twist of joy's knife, never
missing a trick of pain

I was disgusted here with what seemed to me a cheap attempt to use these wellworn idioms; I felt it was gimmicky.

In the fifth draft I went back to the river image:

How swiftly the little river of childhood
carried him here, a current doubling back
on its eddies only as the embroidery of a theme,
a life's introduction and allegro!

Already heavy with knowledge of
speech and silence,
human perhaps to the point of excess,
of genius—

to suffer and to imagine

This version was abandoned because the musical allusion was, once more, a digression, an irrelevancy. In my sixth draft I went back yet again to write out all I had so far that seemed solid and right: the first stanza, "He-who-came-forth," and the second, which now changed to

Moves among us from room to room of *our life*

instead of "the soul's dark cottage," and from which the "cloak of flame" I had spoken of him wearing along with boots and jeans was now elaborated as:

This mantle, folded in him throughout
that time called childhood (which is
a little river, but swift)
flared out, one ordinary day,
to surround him—

—pulled out of his pocket along with
old candy wrappers
a cloak
whose fire feathers are

> suffering, passion, knowledge of speech,
> knowledge of silence . . .

Now here, with the becoming aware of those old candywrappers, I believe I was on the right track, but I didn't know it, for in a seventh draft I went back partially to "the Soul's dark cottage":

> Little shafts of day
> pierce the chinks in our dwelling.
> He-who-came-forth
> moves across them
> trailing fire-feathers. Slowly.

In the eighth draft the flame enwrapping him becomes a *fine* flame, and those shafts of light coming through the chinks become first "the harsh light we live in" and then "common light." I was getting close to a resolution. This process had been going on for some days by this time, and in order not to confuse you too hopelessly I have omitted reference to a number of variant words in some drafts. The eighth, and as it proved, final version, took place, as it had to, in a state where without further effort the elements I now had on hand seemed to regroup themselves, and the concrete evidence of the thing finally *seen*, instead of strained after, entered the picture. In this final draft I got back to my established particulars and was led, from the candywrappers, to see the curls of dust that gather in the corners of pockets, and to realize how treasures are transferred from one garment to another—and this cloak of flame was after all a treasure. Instead of any disquisition on the nature of the cloak of flame, I now felt I could depend on the context to imply this; that is, it is stated right away that He-who-came-forth has turned out to be a man, yet the jeans and boots and candywrappers suggest youth; and though the cloak of flame is something he has had from the beginning, it is only now that it is unfurled. The fact that "no one seems to see it" is modified to "almost unseen in common light"—have you ever looked at a candleflame in hard morning light, almost invisible? I now had a poem that seemed complete in itself though reduced from my original intentions—or rather, my dim sense of its possible scope; and some of my sense of its being complete came from my recognition of its sonic structure, the way certain unifying sounds had entered it: the *m* of *man* leading directly to the *m* of *moves, flame* echoing in *lain*, and the *err* sounds of *wrappers, transferred, curl, unfurled*, which bind the center of the poem, actually unfurling in the *f*'s, open *a*, *s*'s, *t*'s, and *i*'s of the last two lines.

THE SON

i

The Disclosure

He-who-came-forth was
it turned out
a man—

Moves among us from room to room of our life
in boots, in jeans, in a cloak of flame
pulled out of his pocket along with
old candywrappers, where it had lain
transferred from pants to pants,
folded small as a curl of dust,
from the beginning—

unfurled now.

The fine flame
almost unseen in common light.

Yet, in trusting that the image of the cloak of flame would pull
its own weight though unqualified, unsupported, and would
imply its meaning as a human and personal potential coming
into play, I had cut too drastically from the poem any sense of
the capacity for suffering inherent in this potential. I was eventually to come to the second "Son" poem by way of a realization of
this lack. But meanwhile, something familiar but always exhilarating occurred; the wave of energy which had built up during
the writing of one poem led me directly into another. The note
about the lines on a face and "A life," written on the same piece
of paper as "Who he was" but referring to a man in the middle of
life, was mnemonic for a complex of feelings I had long been
carrying.

My first try at this poem was dull and explanatory:

A man dreams and
interprets his dreams
A man makes
fictions, but he passes
from making fictions on into
knowledge, into
laughter and grief.

And in the margin I wrote, "the dreams of animals pass uninter-
preted." This was just an attempt to warm up, a casting about for
a clue. The second draft began by picking up from it:

> A Man is what
> imagines the world, imagines
> what imagines the world.
> He can weep
> for not having wept,
> he laughs
> helplessly at what is not, it is
> so funny.

But then this draft got involved in an irrelevant conceit:

> *Seven long years ago*
> *they stole little Bridget—*
> thy soul, man! O,
> what deep lines
> are dug in thy cheeks
> by all She has undergone,
> and you standing
> so still, you thought,
> on the one spot those
> seven minutes!

What had happened here was that the fact that seven years
before, certain troubles had occurred in the life of the man I was
writing about, and that their repercussions had continued ever
since, made me think both of the seven-year units of biological
growth and change of which I had read, and of the mythological
importance of the number seven. Seven years and a day is often the
period of trial in fairy tales; Thomas the Rhymer found he had
passed seven years in Elfland when he thought it was but a day; and
in the poem by William Allingham, a nineteenth-century Irish poet,
which I had quoted, or rather misquoted, little Bridget is stolen by
the fairies for seven years. My conceit identified her with the soul,
and tried to convey the idea that the soul's experiences, even those
that remain unconscious, mark the face with expressive lines,
though the consciousness may suppose that no change and development have been taking place. Both the conscious and unconscious living of the inner life, *living* it and not denying it, are essential to human value and dignity; yet we undervalue the inner life at
times when the outer life of action and achievement does not syn-

chronize with it; so that the man of whom I was writing had spoken
of himself in anguish as having been at a standstill for seven years,
because his outer life seemed baffled. The last lines of this draft:

> How fair the dark
> of thy deep look is,
> the beauty
> of thy being
> a man!

comment on the visible effects of inner experience, trying to say
that the endurance of suffering, the acceptance of the trials of the
soul, even though the life of action in the external world seems at
a standstill, is what gives a man his human beauty.

Feeling that the introduction of legend seemed (though in
fact it happened naturally) too recherché, especially since when
Bridget returns to the world she cannot live there but dies of sorrow at all that has changed during her absence, my third draft of
this poem tried to be more direct but was only prosy:

> 'Living a life' is what gives
> the beauty of deep lines
> dug in your cheeks
>
> Not what you have done but
> what seven years and seven
> or seven again gather
> in your eyes, in the

And at that point the poem was put aside for a day or so; I felt
baffled and dejected. But in this period of rest or at least of inac-
tion, the force of creative intuition had a chance to take over. All
the explicit elements I have mentioned retired into some quiet
place in my mind; and what emerged, complete save for a single
word, was the poem "A Man" as it now stands.

A MAN

> 'Living a life'—
> the beauty of deep lines
> dug in your cheeks.
>
> The years gather by sevens
> to fashion you. They are blind,
> but you are not blind.

Their blows resound,
they are deaf, those laboring
daughters of the Fates,

but you are not deaf,
you pick out
your own song from the uproar

line by line,
and at last throw back
your head and sing it.

Instead of the alien presence of Little Bridget, instead of abstract references to seven-year units, I was given a vision of "the years" embodied as figures that I think are at once more personal and more universal. The facts about them revealed themselves as I envisioned them—their blindness, their deafness, their brutal laboring persistence. In the third stanza I first wrote them down as "craftsmen," but I looked again and saw they were female figures, resembling the fates, the norns, and also the muses;* and then I suddenly knew that they were not the fates themselves but the years, the daughters of the fates. When the vision is given one, one has only to record. And with visions, as with dreams, comes some knowledge of what it is one is seeing. If one is a poet, then the envisioning, the listening, and the writing of the word, are, for that while, fused. For me (and I hope for the reader) this poem *bodies forth* the known material that led to it. Its images could not have been willfully created as mere illustrations of a point. But in mulling over what I knew I felt and thought I had stirred up levels of imagination, of things I did not know I knew, which made it possible for the poem to emerge in metaphor and find its songlike structure.

There was a lapse of some weeks between these two and the writing of the second "Son" poem. A friend's criticism and my own rereading of "The Disclosure" made it clear to me how insufficient it was, how I had not implied but withheld some of its proper content. I felt the remedy to be a second part, a continuation, rather than a refashioning of what I had already written. I found myself, while I pondered the problem, contemplating a woodblock self-portrait my son had made not long before. What I had before me was not only the print but the actual block

---

*I may have had some unconscious recollection of the Days in Emerson's poem of that title.

of wood with its carved-out surface. Looking at it, I came to re-
alise that "The Disclosure" told only that the boy had begun to
wear his heirloom, manhood, and said nothing of his nature.
This particular boy-becoming-man moved me for special reasons, after all; reasons which had nothing to do with his being
my son, except in so far as that meant I knew something about
him. What I was moved by was the capacity for suffering that I
had become aware of in him, the suffering for instance of the
painful silences of adolescent shyness in a rather conscious and
not merely frustrated way; and by the way such experience was
beginning to be made over in creative acts. No doubt the writing
of "A Man" had intensified this realization for me. This time the
first image, which again remained the central image of the poem
although in this case the words changed, was concerned with the
woodblock.

> Knives bring forth from the wood
> a man's face, the boy's face in his
> mind's eye, weeping.

This was immediately followed by some lines that were discarded
and never reappeared in subsequent drafts:

> His horseplay,
> his loud laughter—their vibrations
> still shake some nervous bell
> down under, hung in a fern tree—

The idea here was that his childhood was still so recent that the
vibrations of it had only reached Australia, and still had enough
force to swing a bell there. I am ignorant in scientific matters and
perhaps had misunderstood something I had read about the movement of soundwaves and their long life; and my abandonment of
this image was a result not only of recognizing its digressive-
ness—its focussing attention on a side-issue—but of my sense
that perhaps it was in any case merely fanciful.

The next draft brought in the action of making the woodblock:

> He hacks a slab of wood with
> fine knives and there comes into being
>
> a grim face, his vision of his own face
> down which from one eye

rolls a tear—his own face
in the manhood his childhood

so swiftly has led to, as a
small brook hastens
into the destiny of a river.

As you see, I had returned to the river image that had been so persistent in the first poem and yet had been dropped from it in the end. But the rhythms of this draft were wrong. In successive drafts, which I will spare you as the changes in them are small and confusing, the following revisions were made: "hacks" was excessive and became simply "cuts." "Fine" was omitted as an unnecessary qualification for "knives." The force of "hacks" goes into "violently," and the "fineness" of the knives into "precise," so that "violently precise" says both things together. "Grim" ("a grim face") became first "crisscrossed with lines of longing, of silences endured" and eventually "downstrokes/ of silence endured." On the same principle of condensation, synthesis, concretion, "his vision of" becomes "visioned" and "hastens" becomes the more active, particular, visually suggestive "rockleaping." The more vivid and specific a term is, the more extensive its possibilities of reverberation in the responsive mind. This is the essential meaning of William Carlos Williams' dictum that the universal is found only in the local. However, in one of the discarded drafts it was mentioned that the boy as a child had liked to draw fantastic inventions on graph paper; this was changed to "poster paints," which he had, of course, also used at one time, because in this instance the unique particular seemed likely to be relatively distracting, while poster paints are a widely shared and associative medium that nearly everyone remembers using or has seen their children use. A clause saying that the man's face in the woodblock was "incised as the boy's inward eye/ presages" was cut out as redundant.

THE SON

ii
The Woodblock

He cuts into a slab of wood,
engrossed, violently precise.
Thus, yesterday,
the day before yesterday,
engines of fantasy were evolved

in poster paints. Tonight
a face forms under the knife,

slashed with stern
crisscrosses of longing, downstrokes
of silence endured—
                        his visioned
own face!—
down which from one eye

rolls a tear.
                        His own face
drawn from the wood,

deep in the manhood his childhood
so swiftly led to, a small brook rock-leaping
into the rapt, imperious, seagoing river.

The resolution of the image of the "little river of childhood" into
the lines which end the finished poem came, once more, by way
of a clearer, deeper, *seeing* of the metaphor: once I knew and
recorded the way the little river, the brook, leaps over its rocks as
it nears a greater stream, I was given the vision of the great river's
rapt and majestic presence.

    To conclude, I wish to point out that the process I have
described does not take place in a condition of alert self-observa-
tion. When I looked through my worksheets I *remembered* what I
had been doing, what I thought I was after, in each case; but the
state of writing, although intense, is dreamy and sensuous, not ra-
tiocinative; and if I had thrown away the worksheets, I would not
have been able to reconstruct the history of the poems.

                                                            (1969)

Margaret Atwood

POETIC PROCESS?

I don't want to know how I write poetry. Poetry is dangerous: talking too much about it, like naming your gods, brings bad luck. I believe that most poets will go to almost any lengths to conceal their own reluctant, scanty insights both from others and from themselves. Paying attention to how you do it is like stopping in the middle of any other totally involving and pleasurable activity to observe yourself suspended in the fatal inner mirror: you may improve your so-called technique, but only at the expense of your so-called soul.

If allowance is made for the inevitable concealments and distortions, however, one may venture a few cautious statements:

1) Poems begin somewhere off the page. You hear pieces of them, sometimes the whole poem. When you have the equipment you write them down. If you start writing down too soon you may lose the rest of the poem.

2) Transcribing a poem changes it. The eye has preferences also. So does the typewriter.

3) Poets seem to do a lot of fiddling around on scraps of paper. It's practice of a kind and sometimes leads in new directions, but it's distinguishable from the real thing.

4) The real thing—the feeling of immersion, possession, something speaking through you, whatever it is—can produce wrong poems as well as right ones. But such judgments are for critics. Best for the poet not to worry too much about that, or about messages or usefulness or improving people's minds.

5) The only function publishing serves for the poet, as apart from the egoist and the careerist who usually follow him about, is to rid him of poems he has already written so he will have space in his head for new ones. The wastepaper basket performs the same service, but less effectively. Not until you've been confronted with your poem in the form of black spots on mashed and rolled trees do you realize what has all along been true: it isn't yours.

6) Being a poet isn't something you are or choose. It's something that happens to you at irregular intervals and with no guarantee it will happen again. You can disregard it when it does happen but you can't turn it on. All you can do is wait, and make doodles in the margins.

(1971)

Donald Hall

GOATFOOT, MILKTONGUE, TWINBIRD:

The Psychic Origins of Poetic Form

When we pursue the psychic origins of our satisfaction with poetic form, we come to the end of the trail. It is deep in the woods, and there is a fire; Twinbird sits quietly, absorbed in the play of flame that leaps and falls; Goatfoot dances by the fire, his eyes reflecting the orange coals, as his lean foot taps the stone. Inside the fire there is a mother and child, made one, the universe of the red coal. This is Milktongue.

1. Some Premises

First, in connection with oppositions:

1. Any quality of poetry can be used for a number of purposes, including opposed purposes. Thus, concentration on technique has often been used to trivialize content, by poets afraid of what they will learn about themselves. But concentration on technique can absorb the attention while unacknowledged material enters the language; so technique can facilitate inspiration.

On the other hand, a poet can subscribe to an antitechnical doctrine of inspiration in a way that simply substitutes one technique for another. Surrealism can become as formulaic as a pastoral elegy.

2. When a poet says he is doing *north*, look and see if he is not actually doing *south*. Chances are that his bent is so entirely *south* that he must swear total allegiance to *north* in order to include the globe.

3. Energy arises from conflict. Without conflict, no energy. Yin and yang. Dark and light. Pleasure and pain. No synthesis without thesis and antithesis. Conflict of course need not be binary but may include a number of terms.

4. Every present event that moves us deeply connects in our psyches with something (or things) in the past. The analogy is the two pieces of carbon that make an arc light. When they come close enough, the spark leaps across. The one mourning is all mourning; "After the first death, there is no other." This general-

ization applies to the composition of poems (writing), and to the recomposition of poems (reading).

5. The way out is the same as the way in. To investigate the process of making a poem is not merely an exercise in curiosity or gossip, but an attempt to understand the nature of literature. In the act of reading, the reader undergoes a process—largely without awareness, as the author was largely without intention—which resembles, like a slightly fainter copy of the original, the process of discovery or recovery that the poet went through in his madness or inspiration.

And then, more general:

6. A poem is one man's inside talking to another man's inside. It may *also* be reasonable man talking to reasonable man, but if it is not inside talking to inside, it is not a poem. This inside speaks through the second language of poetry, the unintended language. Sometimes, as in surrealism, the second language is the only language. It is the ancient prong of carbon in the arc light. We all share more when we are five years old than when we are twenty-five; more at five minutes than at five years. The second language allows poetry to be universal.

7. *Lyric poetry, typically, has one goal and one message, which is to urge the condition of inwardness, the 'inside' from which its own structure derives.*

2. Form: The Sensual Body

There is the old false distinction between *vates* and *poiein*. It is a boring distinction, and I apologise for dragging it out again. I want to use it in its own despite.

The *poiein*, from the Greek verb for making or doing, becomes the poet—the master of craft, the maker of the labyrinth of epic or tragedy or lyric hymn, tale-teller and spell-binder. The *vates* is bound in his own spell. He is the rhapsode Socrates patronizes in *Ion*. In his purest form, he utters what he does not understand at all, be he oracle or André Breton. He is the visionary, divinely inspired, who like Blake may take dictation from voices.

But Blake's voices returned to dictate revisions. The more intimately we observe any poet who claims extremes of inspiration or of craftsmanship, the more we realize that his claims are a disguise. There is no *poiein* for the same reason that there is no *vates*. The claims may be serious (they may be the compensatory distortion which allows the poet to write at all) and the claims may affect the looks of the poem—a surrealist poem and a neo-classic Imitation of Horace *look* different—but the distinction becomes trivial when we discover the psychic origins of poetic form.

I speak of the psychic origins of poetic *form*. Psychologists have written convincingly of the origins of the *material* of arts, in wish-fulfillment and in the universality of myth. We need not go over ideas of the poet as daydreamer, or of the collective unconsciousness. Ernst Kris's "regression in the service of the ego" names an event but does not explain how it comes about. But one bit of Freud's essay on the poet as daydreamer has been a clue in this search. At the end of his intelligent, snippy paper, Freud says that he lacks time now to deal with form, but that he suspects that formal pleasure is related to forepleasure. Then he ducks through the curtain and disappears. Suppose we consider the implications of his parting shot. Forepleasure develops out of the sensuality of the whole body which the infant experiences in the pleasure of the crib and of the breast. The connection between forepleasure and infancy is the motion from rationality to metaphor.

But to begin our search for the psychic origins of poetic form, we must first think of what is usually meant by the word "form," and then we must look for the reality. So often form is looked upon only as the fulfillment of metrical expectations. Meter is nothing but a loose set of probabilities; it is a trick easily learned; anyone can learn to arrange one-hundred-and-forty syllables so that the even syllables are louder than the odd ones, and every tenth syllable rhymes: the object will be a sonnet. But only when you have forgotten the requirements of meter do you begin to write poetry in it. The resolutions of form which ultimately provide the wholeness of a poem—resolutions of syntax, metaphor, diction, and sound—are minute and subtle and vary from poem to poem. They vary from sonnet to sonnet, or, equally and not more greatly, from sonnet to free verse lyric.

Meter is no more seriously binding than the frame we put around a picture. But the *form* of free verse is as binding and as liberating as the *form* of a rondeau. Free verse is simply less predictable. Yeats said that the finished poem made a sound like the click of the lid on a perfectly made box. One-hundred-and-forty syllables, organized into a sonnet, do not necessarily make a click; the same number of syllables, dispersed in asymmetric lines of free verse, will click like a lid if the poem is good. In the sonnet and in the free verse poem, the poet improvises toward that click, and achieves his resolution in unpredictable ways. The rhymes and line-lengths of the sonnet are too gross to contribute greatly to that sense of resolution. The click is our sense of lyric *form*. This pleasure in resolution is Twinbird.

The wholeness and identity of the completed poem, the poem as object in time, the sensual body of the poem—this wholeness depends upon a complex of unpredictable fulfillments. The satisfying resolutions in a sonnet are more subtle than rhyme and meter, and less predictable. The body of sound grows in resolutions like assonance and alliteration, and in near-misses of both; or in the alternations, the going-away and coming-back, of fast and slow, long and short, high and low. The poet—free verse or meter, whatever—may start with lines full of long vowels, glide on diphthong sounds like "eye" and "ay" for instance, move to quick alternative lines of short vowels and clipped consonants, and return in a coda to the long vowels "eye" and "ay." The assonance is shaped like a saucer.

The requirements of fixity are complex, and the conscious mind seldom deals with them. Any poet who has written metrically can write arithmetically correct iambic pentameter as fast as his hand can move. In improvising towards the click, the poet is mostly aware of what sounds right and what does not. When something persists in not sounding right, the poet can examine it bit by bit—can analyze it—in the attempt to consult his knowledge and apply it.

This knowledge is habitual. It is usually not visible to the poet, but it is available for consultation. When you learn something so well that you forget it, you can begin to do it. You dance best when you forget that you are dancing. Athletics—a tennis stroke, swimming, a receiver catching a football—is full of examples of actions done as if by instinct, which are actually learned procedure, studied and practiced until they become "second nature." So it is with poetry. The literary form of poems is created largely by learning—in collaboration with the unconscious by a process I will talk about later. Possible resolutions of metaphor, diction, and sound are coded into memory from our reading of other poets, occasionally from our reading of criticism, from our talk with other poets, and from our revisions of our own work, with the conscious analysis that this revision sometimes entails. New resolutions are combinations of parts of old ones, making new what may later be combined again and made new again.

When the experienced reader takes a poem in, his sense of fixity comes also from memory. He too has the codes in his head.

The new poem fulfills the old habits of expectation in some unexpected way. The reader does not know why—unless he bothers to
analyze; then probably not fully—he is pleased by the sensual
body of the poem. He does not need to know why, unless he must
write about it. The pleasure is sufficient. Since the poet's madness
is the reader's madness, the resolution of the mad material is the
reader's resolution as well as the poet's. The way in is the same as
the way out.

Whatever else we may say of a poem we admire, it exists as
a sensual body. It is beautiful and pleasant, manifest content
aside, like a worn stone that is good to touch, or like a shape of
flowers arranged or accidental. This sensual body reaches us
through our mouths, which are warm in the love of vowels held
together, and in the muscles of our legs which as in dance tap the
motion and pause of linear and syntactic structure. These pleasures are Milktongue and Goatfoot.

There is a non-intellectual beauty in the moving together of
words in phrases—"the music of diction"—and in resolution of
image and metaphor. The sophisticated reader of poetry responds
quickly to the sensual body of a poem, before he interrogates the
poem at all. The pleasure we feel, reading a poem, is our assurance of its integrity. (So Pound said that technique is the test of
sincerity.) We will glance through a poem rapidly and if it is a
skillful fake we will feel repelled. If the poem is alive and honest,
we will feel assent in our quickening pulse—though it might take
us some time to explain what we were reacting to.

The soi-disant *vates* feels that he speaks from the unconscious (or with the voice of the God), and the *poiein* that he
makes all these wholenesses of shape on purpose. Both of them
disguise the truth. All poets are *poiein* and *vates*. The *poiein*
comes from memory of reading, and the *vates* from memory of
infancy. The sensual body of the poem derives from memory of
reading most obviously, but ultimately it leads us back further—
to the most primitive psychic origins of poetic form.

3. Conflict Makes Energy

People frequently notice that poetry concerns itself with
unpleasant subjects: death, deprivation, loneliness, despair, if
love then the death of love, and abandonment. Of course there are
happy poems, but in English poetry there are few which are happy
through and through—and those few tend to be light, short, pleas-

ant, and forgettable. Most memorable happy poems have a por-
tion of blackness in them. Over all—Keats, Blake, Donne, Yeats,
Eliot, Shakespeare, Wordsworth —there is more dark than light,
more elegy than celebration. There is no great poem in our language which is simply happy.

Noticing these facts, we reach for explanations: maybe to be
happy is to be a simpleton; maybe poets are morbid; maybe life is
darker than it is light; maybe when you are happy you are too
busy being happy to write poems about it and when you are sad,
you write poems in order to *do* something. There may be
half-truths in these common ideas, but the real explanation lies in
the structure of a poem; and, I suggest, in the structure of human
reality.

Energy arises from conflict.

A) The sensual body of a poem is a pleasure separate from
any message the poem may contain.

B) If the poem contains a message which is pleasurable (a
word I have just substituted for "happy"), then the two pleasures
walk agreeably together for a few feet, and collapse into a smiling
lethargy. The happy poem sleeps in the sun.

C) If the message of the poem, on the whole, is terrifying—
that They flee from me, that one time did me seek; that I am sick,
I must die; that On Margate Sands/ 1 can connect/ Nothing with
nothing; that Things fall apart, the center will not hold—then pain
of message and pleasure of body copulate in a glorious con-
flict-dance of energy. This alternation of pleasure and pain is so
swift as to seem simultaneous, to be simultaneous in the complexity both of creation and reception, a fused circle of yin and
yang, a oneness in diversity.

The pain is clear to anyone. The pleasure is clear (dear) to
anyone who loves poems. If we acknowledge the pleasure of the
sensual body of the poem, we can see why painful poems are
best: conflict makes energy and resolves our suffering into
ambivalent living tissue. If human nature is necessarily ambivalent, then the structure of the energetic poem resembles the structure of human nature.

The sensual body, in poems, is not simply a compensation
for the pain of the message. It is considerably more important,
and more central to the nature of poetry. When we pursue the psychic origins of our satisfaction with poetic form, we come to the
end of the trail. It is deep in the woods, and there is a fire; Twinbird sits quietly, absorbed in the play of flame that leaps and falls;
Goatfoot dances by the fire, his eyes reflecting the orange coals,

as his lean foot taps the stone. Inside the fire there is a mother and
child, made one, the universe of the red coal. This is Milktongue.

4. Goatfoot, Milktongue, Twinbird

Once at a conference on creativity, a young linguist presented a model of language. Xeroxed in outline, it was beautiful like a
concrete poem. I looked for language as used in poems and
looked a long time. Finally I found it, under "autistic utterance,"
with the note that this utterance might later be refined into Lyric
poetry. It reminded me of another conference I had attended a
year or two earlier. A psychoanalyst delivered a paper on deriving
biographical information about an author from his fiction. He distributed mimeographed copies of his paper, which his secretary
had typed from his obscure handwriting; he began his remarks by
presenting a list of errata. The first correction was, "For 'autistic,'
read 'artistic' throughout."

The newborn infant cries, he sucks at the air until he finds
the nipple. At first he finds his hand to suck by accident—fingers,
thumb; then he learns to repeat that pleasure. Another
mouth-pleasure is the autistic babble, the "goo-goo," the small
cooing and purring and bubbling. These are sounds of pleasure;
they are without message, except that a parent interprets them as
"happy": pleasure is happy. Wittgenstein once said that we could
sing the song with expression or without expression; very well, he
said, let us have the expression without the song. (He was being
ironic; I am not.) The baby's autistic murmur is the expression
without the song. His small tongue curls around the sounds, the
way his tongue warms with the tiny thread of milk that he pulls
from his mother. This is Milktongue, and in poetry it is the deep
and primitive pleasure of vowels in the mouth, of assonance and
of holds on adjacent long vowels; of consonance, mmmm, and
alliteration. It is Dylan Thomas and the curlew cry; it is That dol-
phin-torn, that gong-tormented sea; it is Then, in a wailful choir,
the small gnats mourn.

As Milktongue mouths the noises it curls around, the rest of
his body plays in pleasure also. His fists open and close spasmod-
ically. His small bowed legs, no good for walking, contract and
expand in a rhythmic beat. He has begun the dance, his muscles
move like his heartbeat, and Goatfoot improvises his circle
around the fire. His whole body throbs and thrills with pleasure.
The first parts of his body which he notices are his hands; then his
feet. The strange birds fly at his head, waver, and pause. After a

while he perceives that there are two of them. They begin to act when he wishes them to act, and since the *mental* creates the *physical*, Twinbird is the first magic he performs. He examines these independent/dependent twin birds. They are exactly alike. And they are exactly unalike, mirror images of each other, the perfection of opposite-same.

As the infant grows, the noises split off partly into messages. "Mmm" can be milk and mother. "Da-da" belongs to another huge shape. He crawls and his muscles become useful to move him toward the toy and the soda cracker. Twinbird flies more and more at his will, as Milktongue speaks, and Goatfoot crawls. But still he rolls on his back and his legs beat in the air. Still, the sister hands flutter at his face. Still, the noises without message fill the happy time of waking before hunger, and the softening down, milktongue full, into sleep. The growing child skips rope, hops, dances to a music outside intelligence, rhymes to the hopscotch or jump rope, and listens to the sounds his parents please him with:

> Pease porridge hot
> Pease porridge cold
> Pease porridge in-the-pot
> Five days old.

Or himself learns:

> Bah, bah, black sheep
> Have you any wool;
> Yes, sir, yes, sir,
> Three bags full.
> One for my master,
> One for my dame
> And one for the little boy
> That lives down the lane.

The mouth-pleasure, the muscle-pleasure, the pleasure of match-unmatch.

But "Shades of the prison house begin to close/ Upon the growing boy." Civilized humans try gradually to cut away the autistic component in their speech. Goatfoot survives in the dance, Twinbird in rhyme and resolution of dance and noise. Milktongue hides itself more. It ties us to the mother so obviously that men are ashamed of it. Tribal society was unashamed and worshipped Milktongue in religion and in history. Among the out-

cast in the modern world, Milktongue sometimes endures in language, as it does in the American black world, and in the world of
poor Southern whites. In Ireland where the mother (and the Virgin) are still central, Milktongue remains in swearing and in the
love of sweet speech. Probably, in most of the modern world,
Milktongue exists only in smoking, eating, and drinking; and in
oral sexuality.

But Milktongue and Goatfoot and Twinbird have always
lived in the lyric poem, for poet and for reader. They are the
ancestors, and they remain the psychic origins of poetic form,
primitive both personally (back to the crib) and historically (back
to the fire in front of the cave). They keep pure the sensual pleasure that is the dark secret shape of the poem. We need an inter-
mediary to deal with them, for a clear reason: Goatfoot and Milktongue and Twinbird, like other figures that inhabit the forest, are
wholly illiterate. They live before words.

They approach the edge of the clearing, able to come close
because the Priestess has no eyes to frighten them with. The
Priestess, built of the memory of old pleasures, only knows how
to select and order. The Priestess does not know what she says,
but she knows that she says it in dactylic hexameter. Goatfoot and
Milktongue and Twinbird leave gifts at the edge of the forest. The
Priestess picks up the gifts, and turns to the light, and speaks
words that carry the dark mysterious memory of the forest and the
pleasure.

The poet writing, and the reader reading, lulled by Goatfoot
and Milktongue and Twinbird into the oldest world, become able
to think as the infant thinks, with transformation and omnipo-
tence and magic. The form of the poem, because it exists sepa-
rately from messages, can act as trigger or catalyst or enzyme to
activate not messages but types of mental behavior. Coleridge
spoke of meter as effecting the willing suspension of disbelief.
They are the three memories of the body—not only meter; and
they are powerful magic—not only suspension of disbelief. The
form of the poem unlocks the mind to old pleasures. Pleasure
leaves the mind vulnerable to the content of experience before we
have intellectualized the experience and made it acceptable to the
civilized consciousness. The form allows the mind to encounter
real experience, and so the real message is permitted to speak—
but only because the figures in the forest, untouched by messages,
have danced and crooned and shaped.

The release of power and sweetness! Milktongue also
remembers hunger, and the cry without answer. Goatfoot remem-

bers falling, and the ache that bent the night. Twinbird remembers the loss of the brother, so long he believed in abandonment forever. From the earliest times, poetry has existed in order to retrieve, to find again, and to release. In the man who writes the poem, in the reader who lives it again, in the ideas, the wit, the images, the doctrines, the exhortations, the laments and the cries of joy, the lost forest struggles to be born again inside the words. The life of urge and instinct, that rages and coos, kicks and frolics, as it chooses only without choosing—this life is the life the poem grows from, and leans toward.

(1973)

Robert Bly

REFLECTIONS ON THE ORIGINS OF POETIC FORM

After studying it a long while, I found something very unusual in Donald Hall's essay on the origins of poetic form. I'll go over the argument briefly. His idea is that three sensualities, all linked to the earliest weeks of our life, lie behind what we call "poetic form." They are the baby's enjoyment of making sounds, even when meaningless, which could be called mouth-sensuality, and in Milton become vast sonorities of vowels; the baby's natural kicking motions when it is joyful, which might be called dance-sensuality, and continues as the adult's love of dancing, and that powerful beat we notice in every line of Yeats; and finally, the pleasure of appearance-disappearance. A baby loves to see its mother's face appear, and then disappear, and appear again. That is very like the way the sound in a rhymed poem, for example, disappears, and then suddenly appears again at the last possible moment. This could be called appearance-disappearance sensuality, or match-unmatch. It's connected with hiding treasures and climbing into tunnels.

I think he's right that whenever we feel a poem has form (which he would like to call also a sensual body) these three pleasures or sensualities are all present. They are easy to see in the classic sonnet. Shakespeare's sonnets have a lovely play of vowels through each stanza; the dance sensuality comes in through the iambic beat, and, in his case, probably also in the musical rhythm over and above that, of the tune to which the poem was sung. Finally the rhyme words produce disappearance-appearance. Shakespeare in his sort of sonnet with its closing theme-couplet makes sure that the themes of the poem also perform the appearance-disappearance-appearance drama, to the great delight of the mind.

Two thoughts about present poetry occur then after these ideas become clear. The first is, what does this mean for free verse? As Whitman saw, the rhymed metered poem is, in our consciousness, so tied to the feudal stratified society of England that such a metered poem refuses to merge well with the content of American experience. We therefore have no choice but to write free verse, X. J. Kennedy and Yvor Winters notwithstanding. Whitman, Williams, Robert Duncan, Denise Levertov, Robert

Creeley have all seen that clearly. The next step would seem to be for the American poet to become much more conscious of these sensualities, and work to bring them into his free verse, in ways no other poets have done, or had to do, before him. Evidently Voznesensky's appearance-disappearance in assonance alone is fantastic, and assonance is clearly linked to the first sensuality also. H.D.'s "imagist" poems are impressive particularly for her return of vowels, so beautiful and so solid. But on the whole, recent American poets pay little attention to sound. If we are Puritans, that fact would help to explain the lack of attention.

I think the main originality of Hall's piece is that it is a convincing demonstration that poetic form can be understood not as an adult activity, but as an infantile pleasure. That view goes against the grain of a lot of critical assumptions. Many a poet defending himself from charges of doing nothing presents a picture of himself wrestling manfully with his craft alone hour after hour, adult discipline in his craft being impressive evidence of his serious adult attitude toward life. But that assumes the creation of poetic form involves adult activity. What if the delight in poetic form were actually a delight in and return to infantile sensualities? That also could explain the long hours "wrestling with his craft." (It helps explain too why the craft interviews in *The New York Quarterly* are so infantile.) If this new view is adopted, we see that what is childlike and infantile lies in the form, what is adult in the content. Content and form then make two poles, across which the magnetic energy of the poem arches. The fault with Ted Berrigan's group in New York and Bolinas is that they have brought the infantile into the content, where it doesn't belong. Then there is nowhere for the adult perceptions to go at all. This visualization of the poles also implies that content and form are opposite in charge, like the negative and positive poles of a battery. We notice immediately that it contradicts the Creeley truism that Olson enthusiastically adopted, namely, "Form is merely an extension of content." But I was getting sick of that proverb anyway. When everyone agrees that a given sentence is true, the chances are overwhelming that it is not. Form and content are magnetic opposites. Charles Olson wonderfully understood that American poetic form could not be an imitation of English form, and that the roots of form go back to the body and its breath, not to English metrical habits. It seems though that he wanted the form to be adult—he was interested in the time after the invention of the typewriter, rather than the primitive time before the baby or the aborigine has ever seen a typewriter.

His essay on projective verse makes the whole problem of form technical, post-industrial, needing ingenuity and a type-writer with a good spacer. I'm unjust to his intellectual liveliness, but there is some Puritanism, that is, dislike of childhood, in his essay. Russian poets don't seem to have that.

I'm sure all these generalizations are maddening to many, but I'll make a few more. X. J. Kennedy's and Yvor Winter's insistence on rhyming form is clearly tied to Puritanism, so they take away with one hand what they offer with the other. Pound noticed great metrical and rhyming work among the troubadours, but they were also influenced by the sensuality of Arab civiliza-tion, particularly Sufi religious sensuality. The face of Pound's mother appears so seldom in the *Cantos* that we have the sense at last that its form was broken, or never there, it did not come.

Donald Hall's piece is also maddening and misleading in that it implies that for true poetry nothing is needed but regression— the crib is the best workshop—but we know that is not true. He doesn't say that directly—only in his tone.

The form pole pulls the poem back then toward infancy, the content pole pulls it forward into adulthood. Adulthood seems to be the recognition that there are others in the universe besides you, greater causes and greater beings. The poem surely needs character—the drive forward into experiences—probably embodying pain—that the infant never dreams of in his crib.

Despite the regressive longing that I sense in his prose, I think his essay is a needed step forward in figuring out new ways to think of free verse. We have the right to ask of any poem in free verse before us: does it have these three sensualities? If not, it can never make a good opposite charge for its own content.

(1974)

Russell Edson

PORTRAIT OF THE WRITER AS A FAT MAN:

Some Subjective Ideas or Notions on the Care & Feeding of Prose Poems

. . . At first the fat man, who has seen himself only as the expanded borders of one larger than most, yet containing a consciousness of average size, perhaps smaller by the squeeze of his flesh, seeks now an episodic prose work, the novel; that harmony of diverse materials, his life. His novel is to be about a writer writing a novel about a writer writing a novel about a writer writing a novel, and so forth; a novel within a novel within a novel; an image reflected between two mirrors back and forth in ever receding smaller mirrors. . . .

He is a very fat person, more, simply, than the bulk of flesh, he vaguely sees this, though classed with others of such heft; his soul is also fatted with the lack of ability.

Yes, he is a very fat person because there are thin people. It is relative. He supposes that there are fatter people than he. Of course there are; and probably fatter people than those who are fatter than he.

This is silly, I am simply a fat man whose eyes are of average size, from where I look out from my flesh like anyone else.

And so it is that he wants to write about a fat man such as himself, who now commits himself to composition, growing itchy in his bed, not only from his constant eating, much of which takes place in his bed for lack of love, but because of ideas, excellent fictives, which give rise to an increased heartbeat, and an optimism not fully justified by talent or metabolic levels. But of course this is no longer of moment. Talent is, as he would say, a dilettante measure in my new frame of mind. He casts it out as a silly ornament.

All is will and power, both growing from the other like a single club, with which I shall force a fiction—as though I scrubbed floors to send my son through college that he might get a high-paying job and buy me a castle to live in, where I spend my remaining days simpering and whimpering about how I went down on my knees with a scrub-pail to send my son through college. . . .

2

The fat man sat down to his typewriter almost as though he were sitting down to a dinner, his face set with that same seriousness that must attend all his sittings down to dinner, like a huge transport vessel taking on fuel; a gluttony that has grown far beyond simple self-indulgence.

3

The fat man sat before his typewriter and wrote, the fat man sat before his typewriter and wrote, the fat man sat before his typewriter and wrote: It was better to find a single defensible place, a philosophy, if not a material barrier, that by its very nature offered no challenge to anyone.

To live in the refuse of others is to live in the negative of their desire. Assuming all the while that existence itself is the highest premium. Therefore, that I go unchallenged is the platform upon which I build my durance.

The fat man wrote: Many species have outlived their tormentors simply by offering no challenge, but living where their tormentors would not, by eating what their tormentors felt not fit for those in the position of seemingly perfect choice.

The fat man wrote: The tormentor grows into dilcttantism. The tormentor finds existence more an art than a practical concern. Nature becomes a drawing room where the fine music of bees is heard among the flowers, and the lisp of cool drink flows from glaciered mountains; and life with all its easy fruit becomes a boudoir of death. For nature is not constant, and turns like a restless sleeper in her bed; the earthquake, the flood. The clock of expectation cracks. The air is all in smoke, the hardy are run to gas, and the stink is everywhere. A stratum of complacency lays down its bones in the earth like a shredded lace.

The fat man wrote: There was a microbe that lived in the droppings of the great. The microbe had a much different set of values than the great, those who indulged themselves down the avenues of dependency, where only the rarest of flowers, mingled with the hissing of champagne, and a touch of indirect lighting in the warm summer evenings, gave moment to the endless ease. . . .

The fat man wrote: The young microbe worked the fields of refuse. . . .

The fat man wrote: Yet, the fat man may be the very one floundering in the easy avenue. . . .

4

Is the typewriter not like the console of some giant musical instrument designed to ruin one's head? wrote the fat man writing about a fat man.

. . . A sudden rush of dream figures pulls the head's womb inside out. . . . Belly of soft plumbing, unhappy fat man. . . .

The typewriter is the keyboard of an organ; the pipes run up through the world, contrived through trees and telephone poles. . . .

5

. . . It was as if to buy a farm you bought a cabbage. The fat man smiled and fell out of his head. The moon had risen. . . . What of that? . . . The pulse of days, moon-thud, sun-thud, regularity, even if one's own has gone. One becomes used to living in areas of time. Islands of memory surrounded by nothing.

The Twentieth Century, a country someplace in the universe; my species suffocating itself to death with its groin. Piling its redundancy beyond love or renewal; stool and child dropped with equal concern. . . . We were our own excrement.

Our young meant no more to us than mosquitoes. We burnt them, we starved them. We let the universe know that we meant nothing to ourselves. We hated God for igniting us with neuronic tissue. We created God as He had us. Why not, He didn't stop us? If we were made in His image, so was He also imprisoned in ours. . . .

6

The human intelligence sees itself as the only thing different from all things else in the universe; an isolated witness to a seemingly endless cosmological process, ever burgeoning as galaxies and morning glories. Human intelligence recognizing its frail root and utter dependency on the physical universe. . . . That out of the vast mindlessness was it born. . . . Must look upon its situation as absurd. Intelligence is in the care of mindlessness. . . .

7

The fat man comes to this: That the artifice of the novel is impossible for him; he has not enough faith to build a cathedral. He must work toward bits and pieces formed from memory. . . .

And yet, experience remains hidden and less important than the inscape it has formed. To find a prose free of the self-consciousness of poetry; a prose more compact than the storyteller's; a prose removed from the formalities of *literature*. . . .

8

. . . A prose that is a cast-iron aeroplane that can actually fly, mainly because its pilot doesn't seem to care if it does or not. Nevertheless, this heavier-than-air prose monstrosity, this cast-iron toy will be seen to be floating over the trees.

It's all done from the cockpit. The joy stick is made of flesh. The pilot sits on an old kitchen chair before a table covered with oilcloth. The coffee cups and spoons seem to be the controls.

But the pilot is asleep. You are right, this aeroplane seems to fly because its pilot dreams. . . .

We are not interested in the usual literary definitions, for we have neither the scholarship nor the ear. We want to write free of debt or obligation to literary form or idea; free even from ourselves, free from our own expectations. . . . There is more truth in the act of writing than in what is written. . . .

9

. . . Growing your own writing without going to the Iowa Writers Workshop, and without sending your work to known poets—your own garden, your own meditation—isolation!—Painful, necessary! . . . Finally the golden bubble of delight, one is saved by one's own imagination.

One comes to the writing table with one's own hidden life, the secret of the fat man; not dragging Pound's *Cantos*. . . .

The trouble with most who would write poetry is that they are unwilling to throw their lives away. . . . They are unwilling. . . .

How I hate little constipated lines that are afraid to be anything but correct, without an ounce of humor, that gaiety that death teaches!

What we want is a poetry of miracles—minus the "I" of ecstasy! A poem that as many people who read it each reads a different poem. A poetry freed from its time. A poetry that engages the Creation, which we believe is still in process, and that it is entirely an imaginative construction, which our creative acts partake of, and are necessary to. We are all helping to imagine the Universe.

Which means a poetry not caught and strangled on particular personalities. A poetry that can see itself beyond its obvious means.

And we wish above all to be thought of as "beneath contempt" by the pompous, those who have stood their shadows over the more talented.

How I despise the celebrity poet!

10

. . . The self-serious poet with his terrible sense of mission, whose poems are gradually decaying into sermons of righteous anger; no longer able to tell the difference between the external abstraction and the inner desperation; the inner life is no longer lived or explored, but converted into public anger.

Beware of serious people, for their reality is flat; and they have come to think of themselves as merely flat paste-ons. Their rage at the flatness of their lives knows no end; and they keep all their little imitators scared to death. . . .

And they are meddlers, they try to create others in their own image because theirs is failing. . . .

11

Poems of celebration in praise of the given reality are written by prayer writers and decorators. They, of course, have heaven in mind. In their bones they think they are securing a place next to God.

This kind of poet neglects content for form; always seeking the *way* to write; thus, in extremity, form becomes content. The ersatz sensibility that crushes vitality; the how-to poets with their endless discussion of breath and line; the polishing of the jewel until it turns to dust.

Of course this kind of poem must try to express itself as celebration and ecstasy, which is the empty mirror of soliloquy, the "I" poem, where the poet can't get past himself.

This is boring because it is not creative, it is middle-class mercantile morality. It is for those who in the name of craft, their hope of heaven, refuse to write poetry. Because at the heart of the "I" poem is little imagination and a total lack of humor; only the sensitive, self-serious soliloquist, who seems so dated and tiny in the box of mirrors he has built up around himself.

May I suggest the *Sleepers Joining Hands* section from the book of the same title, by Robert Bly, to show what an "I" poem can be, and at the same time what poetry can be. This is the kind of poetry that moves beyond its means, beyond its author, into possession and fascination. In the truest sense this is *wonderful* writing. . . .

12

Being a fat man one must depend on external structures for support, walls, doorways, furniture; but this does not necessarily mean that one needs external support for one's vision. A fat man may have to make his mind do what his body cannot, more perhaps than others with more physical function. In the limitation is found both the bridge and the barrier, which is as necessary as friction to walking. I don't wish here to create a perfect box. But I do wish to suggest that beyond the sense that all is lost is yet the real hope, the excitement of knowing that there is always a little more; and that *little more* is the joyous place from where one writes.

This is the sense of nothingness, that life is always poised on the edge of decay, that seemingly solid structures long to become dust, that time adores the future more than the present, and only man holds the past with any tenderness. The sense that all is passing away, even as I write this, that in a way the *new* means death; this sense creates the Angel of Joy, which is for me the true Muse. The fat man who has nothing to lose is allowed to be silly, the Angel of Joy prescribes it. . . .

13

. . . A poetry freed from the definition of poetry, and a prose free of the necessities of fiction; a personal form disciplined not by other literature but by unhappiness; thus a way to be happy. Writing is the joy when all other joys have failed. Else, but for the unsavory careerists, why write? It is good fun to ruin the surface of a piece of paper; to, as it were, run amuck. One hurts no one, and paper is cheap enough.

The idle man finds symbolic work. And more; the fat man is only capable of symbolic work. You do agree, I hope? Men are happy when they are working. Even idle men are made happy by thinking of work, even if only thinking of others at work. It is always a pleasure to see the naughty little hands of man engaged in something other than scratching.

Thus the work is found. The writer comes to blank paper. The difficulty is *what to write about?* Believe it or not, subject matter is the first concern of the beginning writer, and will remain the concern of the *real* writer.

Subject matter? Well, of course it's the psychic material that longs to be substance. It is not simply a hook on which to hang form.

In other words, speaking of writing, the way a thing is written is far less important than what the thing is about. This may sound very unliterary, but, after all, the object of creative writing is not literature; at least it shouldn't be, for that is a worldly measure that has so little to do with the work at hand.

We say the *how* comes into being by virtue of the *what*. Surely, if the subject matter is fully imagined, its physicalness fully grasped, then the subject matter will predict its form. Nothing can exist without a shape. But form does not exist without substance. The *how* is merely, or should be, the shape of the *what*. If it is not, the writing is boring. BORING!

If a writer cannot collect his psyche into a physical reality, he ought to think seriously of trying something other than writing.

14

. . . Then the prose poem: Superficially a prose poem should look somewhat like a page from a child's primer, indented paragraph beginnings, justified margins. In other words the prose poem should not announce that it is a special prose; if it is, the reader will know it. The idea is to get away from obvious ornament, and the obligations implied therein. Let those who play tennis play their tennis.

A good prose poem is a statement that seeks sanity whilst its author teeters on the edge of the abyss. The language will be simple, the images so direct, that oftentimes the reader will be torn with recognitions inside himself long before he is conscious of what is happening to him.

Regular poetry, even when it is quite empty of content, the deep psychic material, can manage with its ornaments of song and shape to be dimensional; which is to say, the ability to define space, which is very necessary to all the arts. Such a regular poem may seem the near "perfect object," albeit a beautiful box with nothing in it. Which is good enough; anything brought out of the abyss is to be honored. But *is* it good enough?! Isn't static predictability just rather boring?

As to the dimensional quality necessary to art, we mean depth, volume, in a word, shape; substance with a texture of parts that define space and durance. In the prose poem this sense of dimension is given by humor. The prose poem that does not have some sense of the funny is flat and uninformed, and has no more life than a shopping list. I don't mean the banal, high-schoolish snickering that one sees so often in so-called prose poems, but the humor of the deep, uncomfortable metaphor.

One does not necessarily have to be fat to write prose poems. Some of the best prose poems have been written by Robert Bly and David Ignatow, and they are not fat.

15

To come back to the prose poem. What makes us so fond of it is its clumsiness, its lack of expectation or ambition. Any way of writing that isolates its writer from worldly acceptance offers the greatest creative efficiency. Isolation from other writers, and isolation from easy publishing. This gives one that terrible privacy, so hard to bear, but necessary to get past the idea one has of oneself in relation to the world. I'm not talking about breaking oneself as a monk or a nun might, causing all desire and creativity to become the thick inky darkness that freezes function, but that the writer ought to look to himself, to his own means, that he may get past those means.

It is the paradox, that it is through ourselves we get to that place that is not ourselves; that is, in fact, all of us.

The fear of being alone is sometimes expressed in the elitist nonsense that the poet is some kind of special person owing something to the "inarticulate masses" (who in heaven ever coined that?), which is the same old messianic crap, that same old paranoia wrapped in the same old sentimental rags!

Oh where has the ideal of the ivory tower gone?

16

The prose poem is an approach, but certainly not a form; it is art, but more general than most of the other arts. This may sound odd because we know prose poems as things written on paper. But it is only incidental that they are written out; the spirit or approach which is represented in the prose poem is not specifically literary. My personal convenience is best served by writing only because writing is the fastest way. This kind of creation needs to be done as rapidly as possible. Any hesitation causes it to lose its believability, its special reality; because the writing of a prose poem is more of an experience than a labor toward a product. If the finished prose poem is considered a piece of literature, this is quite incidental to the writing. This kind of creating should have as much ambition as a dream, which I assume most of us look upon, meaning our nightly dreams, as throwaway creations, not things to be collected in a book of poems.

Abundance is also important. The re-working of something that might be saved is no good; better to go on and make something else, and then something else. Prose poems cannot be perfected, they are not literary constructions, unless anything written is to be so considered; prose poems have no place to go. Abundance and spontaneity; spontaneous abundance in imitation of the joy and energy of general creation and substance.

(1975)

Miroslav Holub

POETRY AND SCIENCE:
The Science of Poetry/The Poetry of Science

The Greek poet Constantine Cavafy is best known for his poem "Waiting for the Barbarians." The poem concludes:

> What does this sudden uneasiness mean,
> and this confusion? (How grave the faces have become!)
> Why are the streets and squares rapidly emptying,
> and why is everyone going back home so lost in thought?
>
> > Because it is night and the barbarians have not come.
> > And some men have arrived from the frontiers
> > and they say that there are no barbarians any longer.
>
> And now, what will become of us without barbarians?
> These people were a kind of solution.[1]

Listening to so many literary orators, senators and praetors, I have the recurring feeling that they really do believe in barbarians, in law-making barbarians, in barbarians bored by eloquence, even in barbarians threatening the sublime cultural edifices; barbarians who would be whole-hearted opponents of the artist's creative complex, of the preservation of the only and truly human nature protected by the arts and humanities; barbarians who would be at the same time a kind of solution of the inborn problems of aging societies and cultures; who would at least provide an easy, silent target for traditional humanitarian emotions, passions and conservational tendencies.

The barbarians are of course the scientists.

The romantic disjunction of head and heart is, after two hundred years, still not cured in an individual artist's mentality. The artist's primal and direct communication with the nature of Man and Things is still seen as an alternative and more genuine path of human creativity, opposing the analytical, cold and cynical scientific approach.

Science is spectrum analysis: Art is photosynthesis, as Karl Kraus has put it. Or, according to the Polish satirist Stanislaw Jerzy Lec, the hay smells different to the lovers than to the horses.

Let's take a look at the realm of the horses. Has it still the same constitution and structure as it had during Enlightenment and the romantic reaction to Enlightenment? Is the scientific paradigm, that is the apparatus of perception and the framework into which all observations are fitted,[2] unchanged throughout the last couple of centuries? Or are we confronted with another paradigm than were the Encyclopedists, the Rousseauians and the Herderians?

If there is something like a "Science," that is a complex of activities creating methods for acquiring applicable information on the world, then it is not a perennial rock increasing by simple accretion, but a slow, frequently unnoticed transition from the First to the Second and Third Science.[3,4]

In the First Science, introduced by the ancient Greeks, the method consisted of forming axioms from which some theorems could be deduced by the application of logical systems which would today be regarded as "philosophical" rather than "scientific." In the Renaissance, the First Science was gradually replaced by the Second. This was based on systematized observation with the naked eye or with tools developed at that time. It invented the interrogation of nature through experiments, which in turn were based on assumptions derived from direct observations, on entities conveyed by observation, on entities very similar or identical to the data of everyday sensual experience. The paradigm of the Second Science resulted in an enormous wealth of classifications, descriptions and notions of objects and elementary forces. The Second Science is metaphorically represented by the reality of scientific libraries bulging with wisdom, asserting to contain the World per se and the World for Man, by the tons of Handbücher and Systemata Naturae, and by the reality of scientific laboratories where uninvolved observers ask their questions and manipulate disparate objects, dissect them and rearrange them in chains of facts and abstractions.

The Second Science has enriched the vocabulary by an enormous wealth of terms and denotations attributed to natural objects and technological processes. At least in this respect it had a marked positive effect on the literary mind which followed the Second Science in the demythicization-by-denomination process, abandoning the broad notions of just trees, just flowers or just crafts and going for concrete, specific terms. At least in the descriptive approach to objects and forces the literary mind (and culture in general) made use of the Second Science paradigm.

Nevertheless, the devitalised library and the cool, white, unimaginative laboratory thought of as being Science itself still represent the scientific counterpoint to the deep, warm and increasingly sophisticated introspectiveness of the individual artistic mind.

Many times we find artists believing, at least in their privacy, that they are something fundamentally opposed to this science, to inimical science which is designed to endanger their minds, their aims and their ways of life, as well as the homeostasis of the planet. They still believe in "the Vulture whose wings are dull realities," as did Edgar A. Poe in "the crude composition of my earliest boyhood" in 1829. They content themselves on the one hand with a subnormal understanding of the present sciences in particular, and with a pretended general understanding of "Science" on the other, albeit they mix up science, technology and the application of both—which is rather the consequence of the given social structure than the responsibility of sciences. Some like to understand what they believe in. Others like to believe in what they understand, says Lec. This private artistic attitude amounts to a total misunderstanding, to a kind of artistic dogmatism and, at the same time, to artistic messianism. In Lec's terms—"Every wasp that fights the fan thinks it is Don Quixote."

"Humankind cannot bear too much reality," said T. S. Eliot.

It is astonishing how little change has occurred in the realm of lovers—in the mood and ideology of the traditional culture during the last eighty years. Almost the same controversy on culture, education and science developed in 1882 between T. H. Huxley and Matthew Arnold and in 1959 between C. P. Snow and F. R. Leavis. In both cases the issue was the impact of science, technology and industry on human life and on human values. But it was really Arnold who clearly understood what the Encyclopedists, the French Revolution and Hegel told the world, namely that Reason, Idea or Creative Imagination had become decisive in human destiny. For Arnold, culture was "the best that had been thought and said in the world."[5] Consequently, the contraposition of culture and science, in Snow's terms of traditional culture and scientific culture, appears to be an artificial one. The 1959 controversy is not a confrontation of two cultures, but only of two autoreflections of the artistic and scientific establishments—of the artistic sensibility, and the paradigm and material consequences of the Second Science.

However, in this century, the paradigm of the Second Science has been broken up and a new paradigm is emerging, that of Goodall's Third Science. The first step was the new development of physics where the material world was found to consist of entities basically different from anything we can experience by our senses. "The world of billiard ball atoms existing at definite times in simple three-dimensional space dissolved into the esoteric notions of quantum mechanics and relativity, which to the unsophisticated seem most 'unnatural.'"[4] The world of living things, consisting so far of sets of organisms endowed with names, was dissolved into a flow of development, of ontogeny and phylogeny, governed by somewhat "unhuman" forces of natural selection, at the same time introducing "the revolutionary idea that chance and indeterminancy are among the fundamental characteristics of reality."[5]

Interest has moved towards the study of general properties of systems, of information and organization. By this tendency science has enclosed many areas so far unexplored and so far regarded as being out of the scope of the hard-centered scientific approach.

But, most important, the involvement of the observer in the observed holds true in general (although this notion is still under dispute among physicists). The famous Heisenberg sentence maintains: "Even in science the object of research is no longer nature itself, but man's investigation of nature."[6]

The root of the matter is not in the matter itself, as I put it in a poem.

The situation is beautifully defined by J. Robert Oppenheimer: "We have a certain choice as to which traits of the atomic systems we wish to study and measure and which we let go; but we have not the option of doing them all. This situation, which we all recognize, sustained in [Niels] Bohr his long-held view of the human condition: that there are mutually exclusive ways of using our words, our minds, our souls, any of which is open to us, but which cannot be combined: ways as different, for example, as preparing to act and entering into a retrospective search for the reasons of action. This discovery has not, I think, penetrated into general cultural life. I wish it had; it is a good example of something that would be relevant, if only it could be understood . . . ."[7]

Last but not least, the present scientific paradigm and the organization of modern science provide a precise and lasting world memory and link distant causes with distant effects. They offer an operational framework of memory which was missing in the life of societies and in the culture.

No one of good will can fail to perceive current scientific events and their eminent role in our intellectual life. Science today "is the way of thinking much more than it is a body of knowledge" and ". . . if science is a topic of general interest and concern—if both delights and social consequences are discussed regularly and competently in schools, the press, and at the dinner table—we have greatly improved our prospects for learning how the world really is and improving both it and us," says Carl Sagan with a grain of idealism.[8] And Lewis Thomas, who is definitely less exuberant, states: "We need science, more and better science, not for its technology, not for leisure, not even for health and longevity, but for the hope of wisdom which our kind of culture must acquire for its survival."[9]

In my essay "Science in the Unity of Culture," l referred to science as an ally of the intellect of the ordinary citizen; an ally helping him to make order out of disorganization, out of chaos, regardless of what forms these take. From the citizen's viewpoint, what we may loosely call the "intellectual function" of science and art, overlap to form a unity, with each conditioning and complementing the other.[10] This, of course, does not imply that the citizen lives all the time in the atmosphere of scientific and artistic tides, it implies only that they are within his reach when he has a chance to gasp the breath of culture.

In particular scientific disciplines which have sometimes very little in common, the barbarians may well have created disparate images of a colorless world, cold and mute, alien to any sensual evidence. But at the same time they have subjected mankind to the pressure or freedom of basic and definitive technological progress, they have provided the human mind not only with new and innovative ideas, but also with new means of apperception, insight and expression. They have also produced the worldwide system of communications and the worldwide feeling of human simultaneity, as well as producing isolated, particular scientific universes with little possibility of intercommunication and translation into a universal scientific language. The universal paradigms are present rather by implication than in an explicit form.

It was William Butler Yeats who observed in "The Return of Ulysses": "The more a poet rids his verses of heterogeneous knowledge and irrelevant analysis, and purifies his mind with elaborate art, the more does the little ritual of his verse resemble the great ritual of Nature, and become mysterious and inscrutable."[11]

So, it is not only in the science-art relationship that we suffer or believe we suffer from the lack of a common language. It is also in the art-common sense relationship. It is also within the arts themselves. Bronowski states that there is a general lack of a broad and general language in our culture.[12] But it may be suggested that this lack is merely accidental, momentary and superficial. We may lack a common language and common sensibility, but we should be increasingly aware that we do share a common silence.

At first glimpse one might suspect that literature would be closer to the sciences than other art forms, because sciences also use words and depend on syntax for expressing their findings and formulating ideas. They have created specialized vocabularies of their own, mainly for purposes of higher precision and to approach the ultimate aim of highly formalized monolytic expression, if not a new syntax. Such a syntax has already been created by mathematicians and theoretical physicists. Writers use the same tools as scientists (except for mathematicians). They perform on the same stage,[4] but move in the opposite direction. The sciences and poetry do not share words, they polarize them.

The assumption that a poet using scientific words, scientific vocabulary, could produce writing which would be closer to science and its spirit, without being a scientist himself is—to paraphrase Waddington—like rendering Shakespeare in the language and philosophical framework of an evening newspaper. Even a poet-scientist finds it impossible to approach the essence of his science in his poetry. Actually, modern painting has in some ways come closer to the new scientific notions and paradigms, precisely because a painter's vocabulary, colors, shapes and dimensions are not congruent to the scientist's vocabulary. Their vocabularies are not mutually exclusive, but complementary.

Many present scientific disciplines are represented by their wording, or are embodied in the words, or are even seen as the thing said. Poetry is not the thing said, but a way of saying it (A. E. Housman).

For the sciences, words are an auxiliary tool. In the development of modern poetry words themselves turn into objects, sometimes "objets trouvés." For William Carlos Williams "The poem is made of things—on a field." Thus the poem dwells in a new space and a new time and is due in Williams' example to a "strange arithmetic or chemistry of art: '—to dissect away/ the block and leave/ a separate metal:/ hydrogen/ the flame, helium the/ pregnant ash. . . .'"[13] To paraphrase Heisenberg, the object of poetic research is no longer nature itself, but man's use of words. Hence poetry moves ahead, paralleling the scientific paradigm, into areas less comprehensible for a reader accustomed to forming coherent mental pictures from the sequence of phrases, that is to say—accustomed to the commonplace or scientific use of words.

In the use of words, poetry is the reverse of the sciences. Sciences bar all secondary factors associated with writing or speaking; they are based on a single logical meaning of the sentence or of the word. In poetry, very definite thoughts occur, but they are

not and cannot be expressed by words stripped of secondary factors (graphic, phonetic) and especially by words chosen so as to
bar all possibilities except one. On the contrary, poetry tries for as
many possible meanings and interactions between words and
thoughts as it can. This is not only for its inner freedom, but also
for the sake of communication with readers, for their own freedom. The poet uses "these words because the interests whose
movement is the growth of the poem combine to bring them, just
in this form, into consciousness as a means of ordering, control-
ling and consolidating the uttered experience of which they are
themselves a main part."[14] The experience, or more broadly put,
the tide of impulses "sweeping through the mind, is the source
and the sanction of the words."[14] For the reader, the words of the
poem are meant to reproduce similar, analogous or parallel plays
of feelings, thoughts and interests, putting him for a while into a
similar, analogous or related inner situation, leading to his particular response. Why this should happen, says Richards, is the mystery of communication.[14] Who knows how often it happens per
book, per reading or per lifetime. Definitely not as frequently as
we pretend.

One of the functions of words in a poem is to make pseu-
dostatements in Richards' terms. The sole function of words in
the scientific paper is to make statements which are not an end in
themselves, but the matter of verification for future experimenta-
tion or for a present or presented theory. The "truth" of poetic
statements is acceptable or verifiable by some attitude, within the
framework of the mood, style and reference of the poem. By reference I mean the relationship to a system of routine statements,
to common sense and to the literary traditions and contexts. "The
poetic approach evidently limits the framework of possible consequences into which the pseudostatement is taken. For the scientific approach this framework is unlimited. Any and every consequence is relevant."[14]

Interestingly, at least in my mind, which may be affected by
my profession, some essential scientific notions, postulates, laws,
some basic stones of the scientific syntax cannot be modified,
cannot be transformed into pseudo-statements even when used in
a poem. The poem too has to keep some bones of the scientific
skeleton of the world. The point is illustrated in my prose poem
"Žito the Magician":

> To amuse His Royal Majesty he will change water into wine.
> Frogs into footmen. Beetles into bailiffs. And make a Minister out

of a rat. He bows, and daisies grow from his finger-tips. And a talking bird sits on his shoulder.

There.

Think up something else, demands His Royal Majesty. Think up a black star. So he thinks up a black star. Think up dry water. So he thinks up dry water. Think up a river bound with straw-bands. So he does.

There.

Then along comes a student and asks: Think up sine alpha greater than one.

And Žito grows pale and sad: Terribly sorry. Sine is between plus one and minus one. Nothing you can do about that.

And he leaves the great royal empire, quietly weaves his way through the throng of courtiers, to his home in a nutshell.[15]

So, in the use of words and statements, poetry and science move in different and almost opposite directions. But they do not aim, in my mind, for opposite ends.

The aim of a scientific communication is to convey unequivocal information about one facet of a particular aspect of reality to the reader, and to the collective, anonymous thesaurus of scientific data. The aim of poetic communication is to introduce a related feeling or grasp of the one aspect of the human condition to the reader, or to the collective mind of cultural consciousness. As person-to-person messages, both kinds of communication involve a definite time of the full intellectual, or intellectual-emotional presence. In addition, both are concerned with the establishment of a lasting memory, of intellectual or intellectual-emotional debris in the individual mind and in the collective mind of culture. And both the scientific and poetic communications are a function of condensation of meanings, of the net weight of meaning per word, of inner and immanent intensity. Opposed to other written communications, they are—at their best—concentrates, time-saving devices. I have been repeatedly intrigued by hearing from scientific colleagues that they do read poetry; because it is short, instantaneous and rewarding on the spot, just as a good scientific paper should be.

And the notion of the specific high inner intensity shared by the scientific and poetic communication leads me to suggest that there is another common trait: the goal or gravitational force of sudden revelation, discovery or statement with a predictive value. Here we are actually referring more to the very scientific action than to the communication, and at the same time to the act of writing rather than to the completed poem. But we must not forget that even the present form of scientific papers is based on a proven narrative structure of introduction, technical elaboration and almost instantaneous presentation of the findings where the graphic, numerical or condensed textual statements sometimes attain the value of a revealing metaphor.

In some sciences, which are still fully dependent on the traditional syntax, a conscious application of some sophisticated literary forms may occasionally occur. So a form of a platonic dialogue between Prof. Soma (the name standing for the advocates of a somatic mutation theory) and Prof. Line (for germinal line theory) has been chosen by F. C. Osher and W. C. Neal for an impressive confrontation of the theories of generation of diversity (GOD) in immunological recognition. The article was published among "normal" scientific communications in *Cellular Immunology* (17:552, 1975). I'd even suggest that in these sciences the esthetic value of the literary communication still counts, and may become a noticeable quality. George Orwell may have been right when he remarked: "Above the level of a railway guide, no book is quite free from aesthetic considerations."

Comparing good scientific stuff with boring repetitive articles, as well as comparing accomplished poems with boring non-communicative stanza after stanza, it can be stated that the common denominator of quality, of goodness, is in both cases the notion of a little discovery, a discovery which is going to stay and attract our attention also in the future, in other situations and in different contexts. And the longing for making the little discovery and prediction is to my feeling the primary motivation of both the scientific and poetic action. William Carlos Williams: "Invent (if you can) discover or/ nothing is clear—will surmount/ the drumming in your head. . . ."

If the result is good, and this may happen at times, the great feeling is conveyed even to the reader of the scientific report. William Carlos Williams has remarked in a poem: "We/ have/ microscopic anatomy/ of the whale./ This is/ reassuring." I don't think that this poem is so ironic. For Williams has written too: "So much depends/ upon/ a red wheel/ barrow . . ." and this is taken seriously by everybody.

Or in an example from a recent scientific event: S. T. Peale, P. M. Cassen and R. T. Reynolds published in *Science* (March 2,

1979) a paper indicating that Jupiter's gravity, tugging the near side of Jupiter's satellite Io harder than the far side, would cause the interior of Io to yield and create friction and heating, the accumulated heat being sufficient to melt the core, so that widespread volcanism can be expected. They said: "Voyager images of Io may reveal evidence for a planetary structure dramatically different from any previously observed." Three days thereafter Voyager I reached Jupiter and transmitted pictures of Io's yellow, orange and white surface shaped by recent volcanic activity and later, clouds rising from a giant volcano. The human satisfaction one obtains from this episode equals the satisfaction from a great poem; the poetic quality is in the elegance of the prediction and in the coincidence of timing of the publication and the Voyager I success. No poetic qualities could be found in the paper itself.

On the contrary, an idea which appears extremely attractive in its human message, in its face value and in its wording, happens to be very dangerous and misleading in the scientific context. A recent example occurs to me. Somebody investigated the reason for frequent miscarriages in an area where men used to drag heavily loaded ships by ropes. The author examined the miscarried fetuses and found that they have been preponderantly of male sex, tend to turn away from the placenta, hold the umbilical cords in their hands and over their shoulder, as if they were ropes. This is definitely a very poetic idea. Confronted by the valid genetic notions on the inheritance of adaptive qualities, the idea is a disaster and the observation may be rather an example of wishful thinking and jumping to conclusions than of a scientific hard or soft fact. Human approaches do not count in science. The moral and esthetic values emerge at the very beginning and at the very end of the scientific activity, not in its mechanism.

What then is the difference or the likeness of the human experience in the very act of science-making and poetry-making? Are there common roots in the so-called creative impulse and are there common enjoyments in these two activities which we have described as basically different in the uses of words and handling of meanings?

Let us follow the single steps schematically:

1. Decision to act. In the lab, there is hardly ever the chance to start something new, to ask a purely personal, independent question. What one starts with is a heavy burden of accumulated literature which is supposed to be known. The statement of the question is determined by the literature, by the hard facts and by the gaps. However, the question still may be personal, since it

depends also on one's own interests, instincts for what may be important, the history of the work done (the profile of the lab) and the self-evaluation (what can I do with my skills, what can I afford with the given intellectual capacities and with the given tools). After many twists and revisions suddenly the point appears: this hasn't been done yet, this is technically feasible, this is going to work, and this may lead to some yes or no answers. The emergence of the theme has definitely an emotional quality and brings some sort of a permanent enthusiasm, which one experiences anytime one gets to the bench and to the work.

Now the poem: I cannot give here, of course, a generally valid psychological pattern. I have to refer to my own experience and rely on the vivisection of my own writing. The statement, or better, feeling, of the theme is primarily here; the confrontation with the work done by the subject and by the others is secondary. The theme appears to me as a general metaphor, as a shift from the obvious to the parareal. Its emergence implies the instincts for self-evaluation and personal style. What is strongly felt is again that . . . yes, this is going to work, this may work, if . . . this may lead to a poem. The emergence of the theme is at times the function of a definite emotional state which appears to be both the trigger and the driving and unifying force. At any rate, the emergence of the theme is connected with the feeling of elation, relief, and with the same sort of permanent enthusiasm which keeps one at work, even if it is not done at once.

The basic difference of the emergence of the scientific theme and the poem-theme is the notion and necessity of purification, definition and linearity of the former, and the notion of necessity of the openness, ramification-potential and multilevel-interaction of the latter. The scientific theme implies as much light as possible. If they are not here, they must be created, opened, found in the course of the poem. The basic likeness of both activities is the agreeable experience of the self, of the interior functioning, or even well-functioning machine. If this sounds heretical for poetry, I would refer to W. C. Williams: The poem is a machine made of words.

2. Doing it. In the lab, doing it is so complicated that it can be described in the simplest terms. In one of the few poems where I really could render something from the laboratory experience, I said:

> You ask the secret.
> It has just one name:
> again . . .

"Doing it," working in the lab, requires lots of self-restriction and discipline, of mastering momentary impulses for variations and deviations of the work, of tolerance for pitfalls and uncertainties, for the provisorial and not-yet-accomplished, for boring repetitions of the same step, for a pedantic order of actions and thoughts. It is at times a lonely, stubborn and defensive endeavor: there are always, as S. J. Lec says, some Eskimos around, who would advise the inhabitants of the Congo what to do during the hot summer. To this end, let me quote my poem "The Truth":

> He left, infallible, the door itself
>> was bruised as he
>> hit the mark,
> We two sat awhile
>> the figures in the protocols
>> staring at us like
>> green huge-headed beetles
>> out of the crevices of evening.
> The books stretched
>> their spines,
> the balance weighed just for the fun of it
>> and the glass beads in the necklace
>> of the god of sleep whispered together
>> in the scales.
> 'Have you ever been right?' one of us asked.
> 'I haven't.'
> Then we counted on.
> It was late
> And outside the smoky town, frosty and purple
> climbed to the stars.[15]

Now, "doing the poem" involves psychological mechanisms which I am tempted to describe in almost analogous terms. Metaphorically I would say, it means to run the lab in the mind, with discipline, with the uttermost sense of order and style, allowing for new incoming associations and notions only if they keep to the preconceived framework of possible consequences. W. C. Williams went as far as . . . "This combination of order with discovery, with exploration and revelation, the vigor of sensual stimulation, is of the essence of art."[13] The whole process is happening in one spot and in one time, or at least in one unique inner atmosphere which may occur at different times. It feels rather as if "it is being done" or "it is doing it" than "I am doing it."

The pitfalls and errors in the lab work can be repaired and abolished by repetitions. The pitfalls and errors in the poem lead more frequently to wreckage and abandonment. However, both activities involve the basic risk of possible definitive losing, up to the moment when one suddenly discovers that it works, in spite of all that.

3. "Finding it," the moment of success, or at least what one takes to be the proof of fulfillment, the experience of the little discovery, which is virtually identical when looking into the microscope and seeing the expected (or at times the unexpected, but meaningful) and when looking at the nascent organism of the poem. The emotional, esthetic and existential value is the same. It is one of the few real joys in life.

A strong feeling of reality. So strong that I've never dared describe it. Maybe also because I do not have enough personal experience with this moment. Nor in the lab. Nor in poetry.

But in any case, I feel compelled by all that I know, to answer the above stated question positively. Yes, there is the common root of so-called creativity, there is the same experience of fulfillment and inner reward. Therefore I could never quite understand people asking, can you do both these things that are so basically different. They are technically different, technically at opposite poles of the application of language, but emanate from the same deep level of the human urge, and the application of all available forces.

So far, I've tried to describe science-making and poem-making as if one would be alone with the theme, alone with the work, alone with the result. In reality, one is at almost all times deeply immersed in the collective process of life and survival, caring and worrying, winning and losing. There is no such thing as a "scientist" and there is no such thing as a "poet." One can pretend it, one may play the role, but the essence of "being it" is realized only in the rare moments described.

I can't be in other people's skin and I can't judge; but as for me, I would say that I have spent 95% of my time and energy in fighting my way through the wild vegetation of circumstances, looking for the tiny spots, for the little clearing where I eventually could really work, write or do research, albeit the second happens to be my profession.

Why then should it make so much difference, being the poet and being the scientist, when 95% of our time we are really secretaries, telephonists, passers-by, carpenters, plumbers, privileged and underprivileged citizens, waiting patrons, applicants, household maids, clerks, commuters, offenders, listeners, drivers, runners, patients, losers, subjects and shadows?

There is a tremendous amount of amateurism in everyday life and in professional life. The tension between the rocks of unprofessional tasks and burdens and between the grains of professionalism is the most frequent tension in our experience. Our hard-centered scientific approach, as well as our soft-centered artistic approach, appear to be of little use in solving both the profane and the deepest troubles of our lives in moments of urgent need, alarm, crisis and desolation.

We pretend to live inside a world-fruit of our creativity and culture. But in fact our work happens to be a tiny, subtle, at times permeating, but most of the time confined domain in a world and in an age dominated by the giants of management and advertising, by untamed autonomous suprastructures which look down at us as if at an easily manageable microbial culture.

And this is the last aspect of reality where there is a total amalgamation of science and poetry: some sort of actual helplessness. And this is exactly what we quoted from Oppenheimer: ". . . mutually exclusive ways of using our words . . . minds . . . souls . . . ways as preparing to act and entering into retrospective search for the reasons for action. . . ."

(1979)

NOTES

1. E. Keeley, P. Sherrard, *Six Poets of Modern Greece* (London, 1960).

2. T. C. Kuhn, *The Structure of Scientific Revolutions* (Chicago, 1962).

3. M. C. Goodall, *Science and the Politician* (Cambridge, Mass., 1965).

4. C. H. Waddington, *Behind Appearance* (Cambridge, Mass., 1970).

5. L. Trilling, *Beyond Culture: Essays on Literature and Learning* (London, 1958).

6. W. Heisenberg, *The Physicist's Conception of Nature* (London, 1958).

7. Robert Oppenheimer, *Some Reflections on Science and Culture* (Chapel Hill, 1960).

8. Carl Sagan, *Broca's Brain: Reflections on the Romance of Science* (New York, 1979).

9. Lewis Thomas, *The Medusa and the Snail: More Notes of a Biology Watcher* (New York, 1979).

10. M. Holub, "Science in the Unity of Culture," *Impact of Science on Society* 20:151 (1970).

11. W. B. Yeats, *Ideas of Good and Evil* (London, 1903).

12. J. Bronowski, *The Common Sense of Science* (Melbourne, 1951).

13. J. Hillis Miller, *Poets of Reality: Six Twentieth-Century Poets* (Cambridge, Mass., 1965).

14. I. A. Richards, *Poetries and Sciences* (New York, 1970).

15. M. Holub, *Selected Poems*, trans. I. Milner & G. Theiner (Harmondsworth, 1967).

Dennis Schmitz

GORKY STREET: SYNTAX AND CONTEXT

"Writing was in its origin the voice of an absent person," Freud says somewhere—where I can't recall—it's one of my notebook jottings. I don't remember even when I put down the note. I'm taking up Freud's voice by quoting—do I have the tonal flexibility? Whose voice was his voice? Is "voice" actually "voiceover," a device of documentary? Isn't that the kind of recording Freud is implying? "As soon as/ I speak, I/ speaks," Robert Creeley says in his poem "The Pattern." "It/ wants to/ be free but/ impassive lies/ in the direction/ of its/ words. . . ."

Voice is a way of saying things; it is not a container, nor the thing contained, but the way *contained* is poured out. What I'm talking about is not diction or tone; what I want to talk about when I say "voice" is a complex of compositional usages which would include the syntactical strategies particular to an individual poet. I'm assuming that in its development a poem wants to clarify, that later drafts individualize, that the writer gets to his or her end, finds the poem, in the process of generating sentences, following his or her own rhetorical cues, a process of attribution unique to that writer. A mature writer has a "voice," a "child" has another's manner, or merely makes comment sentences—the way W. H. Auden remarks that an adult has a face, but a child makes faces.

A mature writer, of course, writes in response, as writing is a sort of conversation with what one is considering. It is an organic process, accumulating in response—the way nature is said to work in making an organism part of an environment, testing for the specifics so that in a sense the worked-out organs, receptors or what have you, are part of the thing they are responding to. Words tend toward language; language moves and analogically arranges what it handles, conveying as it relates properties.

Insofar as I write poetry, I am a poet of fragments, of beginnings. This is to apologize for a process probably not much different from anyone else's practice. I start with words, working toward sentences; if I have sentences too early in the process, I know that I am using someone else's words. I began by loving the cumulative sentence, though I didn't know it at the time. I continue to work into poems the same way. It's the only way I know to talk, which is to say, the only way I know to find context.

Recently I read *Galton's Walk*, a study of heuristics by Duke University psychologist Herbert Crovitz. The title derives from an essay called "Psychometric Experiments," in which Francis Galton, the Victorian scientist and theorist of eugenics, suggested a model for gaining access to the contents of memory based on his experiment of associating event-images with places in a repeated walk back and forth along Pall Mall. Crovitz used this suggestion to speculate about how consciousness is organized, and he proposes the use of algorithms or method models in creative problem-solving, implying that the algorithms are merely concrete examples of what the mind already does in an unself-conscious and inefficient manner.

Early in the book, Crovitz gives the example of the mnemonist Vygotsky, quoting Russian research psychologist A. R. Luria on Vygotsky's testing at Moscow University. Vygotsky was formerly a reporter; he annoyed his editor by never taking notes but always remembering facts nonetheless. Vygotsky used a process similar to the one Galton chanced to discover, "Transforming material to be remembered into images, and attaching the images to locations on an accessible map . . . " which allowed "the recall of a great deal of information, in any sequence required—for sequence had become transformed into locations on the mental map of the street." On Vygotsky's Gorky Street algorithm, one may "memorize" a shopping list by associating images of the items on the list with locations of the oculist, the florist, the jail, newsstand and so forth. The Gorky Street map was Vygotsky's frame as several experiments continued, tying stimuli to responses, always in the same way. The methodical assignment of visual images: Vygotsky might note "caviar" on the shopping list for the "plumber" location by "picturing a plumber removing caviar from a fish by suction using a small plumber's helper." Vivid enough? Surrealistic? Popularizers of mnemonics have recommended similar systems.

In talking about "voice," aren't we talking about thought processes; in talking about thought processes aren't we talking about ways to acquire language? Like the Gorky Street model of Vygotsky or the relational algorithms that Crovitz later proposes to interrupt and direct the recurrence of content in the levels of consciousness, doesn't a poet have a syntactic-rhythmic model for sorting the contents of memory and the input of the physical world to make a poem in that poet's voice? William Stafford has his way of working—he's talked about it many times—sometimes, as with all poets, he seems to be writing the same poem over and over, and each stanza has the same development mode as the other. That's because the syntactic model is always the same. Mark Strand is another example. One of the delights of Sandra McPherson's poems is how she finds the way to the sentence.

W. D. Snodgrass, in discussing his poem "Old Apple Trees" for the anthology *Singular Voices,* analyzes the first lines of Whitman's "Out of the Cradle Endlessly Rocking" to show how Whitman "uses a sort of theme-and-variations device in building the rhythmic structure of a poem. Often, in his first line, he states a rhythm, repeating it with slight variation for the second half. The poem, then, is built upon this twice-stated rhythm, playing with it, lengthening, stress-loading, altering, sophisticating it. The resultant structure of rhythms is that poem's music, intimately involved with its structures of imagery and rhetoric." The third edition of *Leaves of Grass* has the poem beginning "Out of the rock'd cradle . . ."; seven years later, Whitman wrote, then rejected, the line as we know it, and published it four years later that way.

I didn't hear Robert Creeley's method until I heard *Creeley* about twenty-five years ago. Robert Hass, in his essay on *The Collected Poems of Robert Creeley, 1945-1975,* suggests Creeley read William Carlos Williams the way we read Creeley, if we know what he's about. The syncopation of rhythm that comes when you end-stop each line against whatever the development of the sentence is *is* the development of the sentence, the unit of meaning. The hesitation of articulation is the perception.

Every writer has his or her own system or Gorky Street, a syntactic frame, for having access to levels of consciousness. His or her task is to generate a set of possibles and recognize (discriminate) within the set. The contents of memory are turned over, considered or ordered, by visualization—showing oneself the possible orders, by sequencing or addition (making sentences), and by valuation or verification, which is a concomitant process.

I can work out procedures of syntactic combining, but at what point are word combinations invested with meaning, at what point is poetic choice exercised so that the text simultaneously has poetic meaning—that is the insight and the music derived from the insight's form, producing not only understanding and passion as a hearer's reaction, but seeming to have feeling inherent in the text itself? Word by word is a problematic process sometimes; by not writing for the sake of an ending, one becomes a composer of musical passages, a dead-ended Bach, a poet of ellipses. How to get farther on Gorky Street, to establish sequence?

II

Later in *Galton's Walk* Crovitz seems to be saying "trust the process," or perhaps "concentrate only on the process," when he cites some of the problem-solving models of Karl Dunker. He notes that the "switching of relational-filters is hard for problem-solvers to do naturally." Relational-filters are like the glass of the glass-barrier-between-the-chicken-and-the-corn experiment, he says. In the poet's case, a relational-filter would be the habit of appraisal which prevents the next step in sequencing, the next rhetorical move which results from developing a term, another attribution. In problem-solving, the wit (which really means the radical innocence to see afresh, the credulity) to recognize the solution in a list of possibles advances the process beyond what Crovitz calls "functional fixedness."

Dunker proposes a series of problems to be solved using a model consisting of a sequence of elementary sentences which exhaust the possible relations of term to term, forming a set, a relational-algorithm. For example, Dunker posits an inoperable stomach tumor and rays which destroy organic tissue at a certain intensity—how do you determine a procedure which can use the rays to destroy the tumor but not harm the surrounding tissue? Dunker gives two sets. Here is a selection from the "Take-Two-Rays List of Possibilities":

> Take a ray about a ray.
> Take a ray across a ray.
> Take a ray after a ray.
> Take a ray against a ray.
> Take a ray among a ray . . . & so forth.

The other set, "The Body-Ray List of Possibilities," is similarly designed. There are solutions in each set. Either "The ray across a ray" (the rays intersect at the tumor; neither ray is strong enough to harm surrounding tissue, but together they can destroy the tumor) works, or "Take a body around a ray" works (the body is rotated with the tumor at the center of rotation getting the cumulative effects of the ray).

The Dunker sets oddly resemble early draft workings of lines for a poem (a Hugo Ball Dadaist construct?), or the sentence kernels of a sentence combining exercise from generative rhetoric. "Concentrate only on the process" is often a writer's advice to himself or herself when the poem is blocked. You believe in your usual manner enough to carry on the process of attribution—a trip around Gorky Street.

III

Memory algorithms and relational algorithms are ways of talking about stages in composition in which a poet listens for and develops the sentence patterning of the words that associate meaning. Algorithms assume initial reference; in writing, you begin with nothing but edge into the familiar as words accumulate and patterning begins to carry narrative progression. The metrical format of the sonnet suggests a common algorithm, but all of the blanks have to be filled. The heroic couplet suggests the way Pope's head worked. But these are generic patterns until they carry the rhetorical signatures of the poets at work. Of course, you have to have words before you can use the ways to organize them. Crovitz says that when you have theories or models, you have answers and then must find the questions.

Crovitz says that "consciousness has the features of a plenum; that it may be entirely full of its contents . . ." therefore "all movement in consciousness may be cyclic." Where you are in the cycle is somehow determined by how you enter it. Things change in juxtaposition to one another—the familiar reveals new mystery as its setting modifies it. In a way, the practice of art is the practice of "found" art, the discarded things taking implication only because of countering what they were, taking wholeness in relation to what they're with. In turn, they give wholeness to their settings by giving a principle of organization.

Picasso knew how to enter the cycle; the contents of his dustbin became sculptures. "Baboon and Young" (1953) is in bronze; the original was plaster with metal, ceramic and two toy cars, one atop the other, for the baboon's head. The figure's eyes are the windshield halves of the upper car; the joint between bumpers of the inverted lower car and the upper car is the mouth of the baboon. The constructions and collages Picasso did in the first decade of the century (coinciding with his early cubist work) used materials that had meaning in the original forms of the things, like the newspaper cutouts, but the things changed in context. Do throwaways take another life because they are thrown away from what they were in a context of human use to become human art? Look at the language of the poems in John Ashbery's early book *The Tennis Court Oath*, for example.

I've suggested that sometimes the working method stimulates narrative progression—the poet finds the next step of the action by unrelenting use of the formal device (voice as instrument). I'm talking about following the sentence, then the paragraph-stanza, into a context of meaning. The process of writing is a way of extending the senses; the report which you give to other people is an organization of details which convey an impression. I've talked about sorting the details—how do you see wholes in the details? How to manage what the world presents, or rather, how to slow yourself enough not to interfere?

You see by showing. My assumption is that all writing is descriptive and that the development of expression is a version of the kindergarten "show-and-tell." Another assumption is that you can't say anything without first saying something. Keep saying until you recognize where you are—writing is finding the pattern, not making the pattern.

How do you see patterns, see wholes, except by matching congruities? If you assume that the shape of a poem depends on a dominant notion or scene, it's necessary to use subordination to discover the pattern of details. You use subordination in shaping sentences of meaning as well as in shaping the larger text. Context needs an interaction of foreground and background, and the purpose of background is "resonance." Poetry happens word by word, as music happens note by note, but making music is not merely "reading" music notation with the instrument. "It is a most helpful discipline to be able to play all the notes with equal value," says violinist Yehudi Menuhin, "but beyond that stage of attainment, you have to shape the phrase. You have to know: where the high point is, and where the phrase begins to wane: which notes represent the continuity, and which are only embell-ishments. . . ."

You see by showing. A good writer indicates what's most important to look at. A good writer blocks off ways not to look. A good writer shows how subordinated details modify what's im-portant to look at. Context. If you've made only comment sen-tences, you probably haven't heard your voice, haven't really fol-lowed Gorky Street.

Another analogy, to movie-making, might help explain that the process I'm outlining is not merely observation. Before D. W. Griffith, in earliest film-making, a stationary camera, relentlessly grinding, recorded what was before it. Imagine the limitations. Griffith started to combine shots—the tracking shot to produce illusion of movement, the pan shot to indicate stationary context, the shooting perspectives which indicate emphasis in a frame like close-up, medium shot and long shot—these declare the principle of organization, giving us impression, telling us how we should feel about things in their emotional context.

Griffith also did cross-cutting to show us that time and distance, events happening in different but related places, could become emotional wholes. Then, look at the composition of the frames; look at some of the stills from *The Birth of a Nation* and see how an event happens because the people in the event attend to it. At last, you have not merely filming but film-making. The mature writer works with subordination of scenes, focus, technical devices of sound and patterning to control the speaker's voice in a poem—all part of one's rhetorical self-cueing that is the process of composition from the juxtaposing of words to the symmetry in which musical phrasing and the apprehension of the matter of the poem become the same thing.

Let us understand that what I've meant all along by "seeing" is not what you do with physical eyes. And when you think about it, what you do with your physical eyes is as selective as the process you go through when you converse. You do indeed have an attitude of listening, cocking the head to some people, moving your hands with others, participating all the time in constructing discursive sequence, breaking the whole into units, taking meanings you have not prepared. The other person gives, and sometimes your anticipation jumps ahead in the sequence. If you are comfortable, there is a whole-body response and counterresponse.

The "seeing" process is so selective and other-coordinated a process that you do not even see when you see. In writing, visualization replaces seeing, and memory becomes the organ of visualization—it has a pupil to admit light; it responds to its own tonal patterns. In a way, there are response and sequencing, which are the ways one creates context. The thing is there, but you seem to take both ends of the "conversation" of visualization. I have suggested how memory is received. How does memory select? Why will memory not look at certain things? As a writer, how do you repress associations—cut off view lines—in order to get appropriate constructs?

Seeing is showing, showing to yourself first of all. Sequencing, the making of sentences, is the organization of detail, attributing to subjects or their modifiers qualities which bring meaning into focus at the same time that it shows subordinate relationships. The creation of a literal world out of which the figurative emanates, two simultaneous worlds, the cliché of science fiction, is the job of the writer. But a thing has to be itself before it can be anything else: the basis of metaphor is the matching of seeming incongruities in a figure-ground relationship, and the ground is the literal, a context.

(1988)

Sandra McPherson

THE TWO-TONE LINE,
BLUES IDEOLOGY,
AND THE SCRAP QUILT

This meditation began from a desire to know why I am so attracted to Swedish poet Harry Martinson's line: "In summer there is no cow on the ice." Why is it a more chilling line than, say, "In winter there is a cow on the ice"? Why erase a cow yet give us a cow? Why use an ice scene in negative to describe summer?

I wanted to know why I liked these lines about a woman shopping:

> She would buy the bulbs and the yellow bird;
> she would free the cage and step inside.
>
> (Laura Jensen)

Why I so enjoyed Percy Mayfield singing, in bass-baritone voice, "My heart rejoices in the sadness."

> My heart will make light of the sunshine.
> My heart will frown when skies are blue.
> My heart rejoices in the sadness
> Of the love that was left by you.

Neruda in "Toward an Impure Poetry" wants poems "smelling of lilies and urine." Why is that so attractive?

And why this: "a creamy basil mayonnaise a shade lighter than the Coast Range in August" (Robert Hass). And from "Seascape" Elizabeth Bishop's description of the mangroves' "bright green leaves edged neatly with bird-droppings/ like illumination in silver."

And why my pre-school daughter's "You're brushing your hair like a dead bird."

I have called these, out of an interest in pattern-naming, "two-tone lines." Of Jensen's couplet, the first line is one-tone and the second line is two-tone.

Why do these two-tone patterns delight as well when they are employed by blues musicians and by quilt-makers?

Galway Kinnell shows a tree struggling through juxtapositions within itself. He calls this normal:

Its grain cherishes the predicament of spruce, which has a trunk
   that rises and boughs that droop.
Its destiny is to disappear.
This could be accomplished when a beachcomber extracts its heat
   and resolves the rest into smoke and ashes; or in the normal
   way, through a combination of irritation and evanescence.
                                        ("Driftwood from a Ship")

"Normal," the Reverend Robert Small said of an African-American quilt with its "center" in one corner, "That's normal." The
normal in Kinnell's driftwood poem is not just irritation or
evanescence, or solely rising or solely drooping. Nor is the normal perfect balance and symmetry or even unification.

Adrienne Rich too accepts this multi-tonal melange as it is
lived: she describes her kitchen table occupied by odd neighbors—objects that in the traditional thought of the old IQ test do
not go together.

   . . . a dry moth's
   perfectly mosaiced wings, pamphlets on rape,
   forced sterilization, snapshots in color
   of an Alabama woman still quilting in her nineties . . .
                                        ("Culture & Anarchy")

In quilting terms, we could call this PIECED vision, the inclusion
of all the inconsistencies, the scraps, all you're left with. A sal-
vage operation, it is more inclusive than a simplification, a uni-
formity of fabric or pattern, would be.

I am wondering if two-tonedness (or multi-tonedness) is perhaps its own aesthetic, as when African-American quilt designers
reinterpret standard Euro-American motifs by aspiring to "a concept more important than order" (John Vlach, *The Afro-American
Tradition in Decorative Arts*). In such an aesthetic one design
may be made to confront another. A pattern established in one
square is varied, flexibly patterned, not repeated. Quilter Lucinda
Toomer explains some of her aesthetic satisfaction in doing this:
"I like to make them and put different pieces in there to make it
show up, what it is . . . if you just know what to make of it and
make a change of it, there's something good in it."

I also like this description by a scholar of African-American
quilts: "Lines, designs, and colors do not match up, but vary with
a persistence that goes beyond a possible lack of cloth in one
color or pattern" (Maude Wahlman, *Traditions in Cloth*). Quilter
Plummer T Pettway explains that many different patterns and

shapes make the best quilts: "You can't match them. No. It take all kind of pieces to piece a quilt . . . . You have to think about the next color." Placing her colors at uneven intervals, Plummer T creates patterns that appear to be constantly shifting. This process is like passages in Elizabeth Bishop's poems—she thinks about the next color, shifts her stance or assertion.

Mississippi quilter Pearlie Posey, when just a few years short of 100, stated her aesthetic choice: "I just like mine mixed up . . . ." And it does not mean at all an uncaring haphazardness. "When you cutting them little bitty pieces you got to study how to put them together, and you want it to hit just right," says Pecolia Warner. This is a woman who used nearly a hundred different hues in her finest quilts. Imagine if we used a hundred different tones in a poem!

Cavafy seems to have done so in "Myris: Alexandria, A.D. 340." This is an elegy but one never knows when a new tone will be introduced. The speaker is a man. All the italics are my own.

> When I heard the *terrible* news, that Myris was dead,
> I went to his house, although I *avoid*
> going to the houses of Christians,
> especially during times of *mourning* or *festivity*.
>
> I stood in the corridor. I didn't want
> to go further inside because I saw
> that the relatives of the deceased looked at me
> with evident *surprise* and *displeasure*.
>
> They had him in a large room
> and from the corner where I stood
> I caught a glimpse of it: all *precious* carpets,
> and vessels of silver and gold.
>
> I stood and *wept* in a corner of the corridor.
> And I thought how our gatherings and excursions
> *wouldn't be worthwhile* now without Myris:
> and I thought how I'd no longer see him
> at our *wonderfully indecent night-long sessions*
> *enjoying* himself, *laughing*, and reciting verses
> with his perfect feel for Greek rhythm;
> and I thought how I'd *lost* forever
> his beauty, lost forever
> the young man I'd worshipped so *passionately*.
>
> Some old women close to me were talking *quietly*
> about the last day he lived:

the name of Christ constantly on his lips,
his hand holding a cross.
Then four Christian priests
came into the room, and said prayers
fervently, and orisons to Jesus,
or to Mary (*I'm not very familiar* with their religion).

We'd known of course that Myris *was a Christian.*
We'd known it from the start, when he first
joined us the year before last.
But he lived exactly as we did:
more given to pleasure than all of us,
he scattered his money *lavishly* on his *amusements.*
Not caring a damn what people thought,
he threw himself eagerly into nighttime scuffles
when we happened to clash
with some rival group in the street.
He never spoke about his religion.
And once we even told him
that we'd take him with us to the Serapion.
But—I remember now—
he didn't even seem to like this joke of ours.
And *yes,* now I recall two other incidents.
When we made libations to Poseidon,
he drew himself back from our circle and looked elsewhere.
And when one of us in his *fervor* said:
"May all of us be *favored* and protected
by the great, the *sublime* Apollo"—Myris whispered
(the others didn't hear) "*not* counting me."

The Christian priests were praying *loudly*
for the young man's soul.
I noticed with how much *diligence,*
how much intense *concern*
for the *forms* of their religion, they were preparing
everything for the Christian funeral.
And *suddenly* an *odd sensation*
came over me. *Indefinably* I felt
as if Myris were *going from me*:
I felt that he, a Christian, was united
with his own people and that I was becoming
a stranger, a total stranger. I even felt
a *doubt* assailing me: that I'd been *deceived* by my passion
and had *always been a stranger* to him.
I rushed out of their *horrible* house,
rushed away before my memory of Myris
was captured, was *perverted* by their Christianity.
                                      (translators, Keeley and Sherrard)

The poem seems to be an elegy happening on the spot as the mourner gives himself leeway to change his mind and his feelings.

Blues too permits itself to change its mind—or express seemingly opposite opinions—in a very tight space. Here's Honeyboy Edwards in "Apron Strings":

> Mother-in-law don't treat your daughter mean.
> Mother-in-law don't treat your daughter mean again.
> You know she ain't good lord she's full of sin.
>   (stanza five)

He doesn't use an "even though" or a "but" to connect these seemingly contrary sentiments.

Hip Linkchain, in a stanza of his original song "You Must Be Shampoo, Baby, You Keep Bubblin' All the Time," sings,

> Gonna wake up early one morning,
> fix you breakfast while you in bed.
> Gonna put some shampoo on your foot,
> let you slide till you dead.

This kind of "logic" appeals to me immensely. In the Honeyboy Edwards example you might anticipate the final line and it seems as if it's going to be too predictable; what the lyricist gives you is completely the reverse: the askew—the truth of Edwards' and Linkchain's closing statements ("You know she ain't good lord she's full of sin" and "Gonna put some shampoo on your foot, let you slide till you dead") has not been destroyed by the claims of the first two lines in each case. It is as if we had two Christian lines finished off by, say, a Buddhist line. One feels—not a cancellation but a "whole-er" vision.

Blues copes with Pearlie Posey's "mixed-uppedness" in its very definition. Robert Curtis Smith calls it "a feeling that it's hard to do anything about: it's hard to know which way to go, what to do, the blues." And Roosevelt Sykes says, "Blues is a person who went in trouble and felt depressed, something worrying him, been mistreated . . . . And there's a happy feeling of the blues. Play the blues with a good feeling, it makes you feel good. Blues is an emotion, you see, of many different feelings. So it's called 'individual trouble.' So you can't know how a man feel. Every individual has an own feeling. He tries to bring it out in his songs, some happy or some blue."

Certainly Laura Jensen shares the blues ideology—which allows only for what David Evans calls "temporary successes"—when she writes, "She will free the cage and step inside."

Recently I found that my undergraduates' favorite assignment, based on the Cavafy poem, was what I called a Tonal Insecurity Poem. It allowed them to be as insecure as they naturally were and they felt at ease making certain art out of insecurity. They did not attempt some final resolution of the issue they wrote about.

Some poets evolve characteristic ways of two-toning: there's Elizabeth Bishop's Or-style: at the end of "Large Bad Picture" she says, about the ships in the painting, "Apparently they have reached their destination./ It would be hard to say what brought them there,/ commerce or contemplation." Two tonally distant alternatives.

"The Bight" ends: "All the untidy activity continues,/ awful but cheerful."

In "Faustina, or Rock Roses" Bishop describes the servant's "sinister kind face"—she suggests the two qualities can occupy the same place or position at the same point in time or space. Later she concludes: "There is no way of telling./ The eyes say only either."

In "Crusoe in England" she writes about "the volcano/ I'd christened *Mont d'Espoir/* or *Mount Despair/* (I'd time enough to play with names) . . . ." Here is the blues ideology—like blues it's seriously entertaining; Hope in French nearly being Despair in English is more than a word game.

"Under Our Window: Ouro Preto" opens up at the end to this:

> Oil has seeped into
> the margins of the ditch of standing water
> and flashes or looks upward brokenly,
> like bits of mirror—no, more blue than that:
> like tatters of the *Morpho* butterfly.

Her method here is truly scrap-piecing. No one scrap alone is sufficient to keep her warm. Or to keep the vision warm, in the sense of lifelike. Why wasn't she content with "flashes"? It has a flashy tone; "looks" is more of a humble gaze, tones the line down, is informal or inconspicuous. Why not then just be content with "looks"? It doesn't allow the flash—of insight perhaps, or the sense of possible sudden intelligence. Or other interpretations one could add.

Then in the next line she goes on in her self-correcting way, which is really an acceptance of various tones all applicable—

"That's normal"—even if contradictory, to the same object. One does not cancel the other.

In "Poem," Bishop's piecing is done for the expressed inclusion of several tones:

> Our visions coincided—'visions' is
> too serious a word—our looks, two looks.

In "The Moose":

> A moose has come out of
> the impenetrable wood
> and stands there, looms, rather
>
> . . . .
>
> Towering, antlerless,
> high as a church,
> homely as a house
> (or, safe as houses).

In addition to the literature many poets know and think themselves a part of, I have been using examples and analogies from arts which have not relied on academic training; the tonally rich line clearly is not a strained or artsy construction or the literati's game. It may actually represent a belief in scraps, like the quilter's. Or be a necessary singing comprised of many different feelings. Not a majority of any one feeling, just what you're left with.

Multiplicity solves the problem of "good behavior" for many a poet:

> I stood and wept in a corner of the corridor.
> And I thought how our gatherings and excursions
> wouldn't be worthwhile now without Myris;
> and I thought how I'd no longer see him
> at our wonderfully indecent night-long sessions . . . .

These lines of Cavafy's reject too much refinement. As William Stafford says, "If we purify the pond, the lilies die." For every Ten Commandments there are thousands of testimonials as to why the artist can't be perfect. But more fascinating perhaps than perfection is a poetic which preserves what textile scholar Georges Meurant calls "all its stages of development at once."

I am not talking about classic irony, where you say one thing and mean another. In these examples the artists mean what they say. And they say discrepancy, when unavoidable, is singable, sewable, writable. Fully complex, the two-, three-, or four-tone line (see Bill Knott's *Outremer*), is something larger than "tension," richer than "bittersweet," more variegated than Yin and Yang, and less the scholar's darling than "ambiguity."

When David Evans says, "The pianist must play the major and minor notes simultaneously or in rapid succession to achieve the effect of blue notes," we writers can see that writing this way induces an emotion that no other way of writing can achieve, what Leonard Michaels calls "a kind of truth that isn't available to us otherwise."

In accepting the concurrence and interaction of unlike truths, one may feel a relief like that in Adrienne Rich's "Integrity":

> Anger and tenderness: my selves.
> And now I can believe they breathe in me
> as angels, not polarities.

And in a later poem she grows to understand that

> Trapped in one idea, you can't have your feelings,
> feelings are always about more than one thing.

Later, in the same sequence, she modifies those lines:

> Trapped in one idea, you can't have feelings.
> Without feelings perhaps you can feel like a god.

It would seem that a two-tone aesthetic should preclude a poem's evoking only an emotion of the writer's own "holiness," righteous melancholy, and so forth. It would seem as if not only an acceptance of the ungodlike state, whatever that is, but a pleasure in exploring it is necessary for multi-toned vision. Call it mixed-uppedness, individual trouble, or confident uncertainty.

I've been looking for a happy definition of "ungodlike." First I found an entry to the concept in a catalog for an Oakland African-American quilt show: "Wanda Jones . . . says that when she was learning to quilt and would make a mistake, her mother would say: 'It's nothing about making it a little different. It's still the same pattern. You just added something of your own to it.'" Ungodlikeness may be our cherished predicament, like the grain of Galway Kinnell's spruce.

Then I ran across a testimonial by Bay Area quilter Arbie Williams: ". . . if you do it backwards, well sometime it fit in better than the way you had your ideals to go."

And then we encounter gods other than Greco-Roman,

Nordic, or Judeo-Christian. Multi-toned gods. With Robert Plant Armstrong we travel to the scene of a chicken being sacrificed to "a simple mound of earth . . . a mere bit of mud . . . at a crossroads outside a Yoruba village." The mound is a "shrine to Eshu, the Yoruba god of indeterminacy," asymmetry, the isolated phenomenon, odd numbers. Here is a god a poet might do well to believe in. Be like. Perhaps.

(1991)

SELECTED BIBLIOGRAPHY

Armstrong, Robert Plant. *The Power of Presence*. Philadelphia: Univ. of Pennsylvania Press, 1981.

Evans, David. *Big Road Blues*. Berkeley: Univ. of California Press, 1982.

Leon, Eli. *Who'd a Thought It: Improvisation in African-American Quiltmaking*. San Francisco: San Francisco Craft and Folk Art Museum, 1987.

Meurant, Georges. *Shoowa Design: African Textiles from the Kingdom of Kuba*. London: Thames and Hudson, 1986.

Traditions in Cloth: Afro-American Quilts / West African Textiles (Exhibit Catalogue). Los Angeles: California Afro-American Museum, 1986.

Vlach, John Michael. *The Afro-American Tradition in Decorative Arts*. Cleveland: The Cleveland Museum of Art, 1978.

Wahlman, Maude Southwell and Ella King Torrey. *Ten Afro-American Quilters* (Exhibition Catalogue). Oxford, Mississippi: The Center for the Study of Southern Culture, 1983.

2 The Poetic Line: A Symposium

Sandra McPherson

THE WORKING LINE

Having written in it for years, I began to speculate on why and how we use the line thanks to an article by Hayden Carruth in a *Hudson Review*. Taking a poem each by Charles Simic and John Haines, Carruth prints them as prose paragraphs characterized by "complacent suggestiveness, passiveness, inertness" of language that no typographical arrangement and punctuation can vivify, he claims. "The language, taken altogether, is so slack, so devoid of formal tension and impetus, that the poems cease to function. What purpose do these lines serve, beyond making us read with unnatural emphasis and in a joggy cadence? . . . when the line has ceased to function it is because the language has become too dull to sustain the measure . . . loss of formative energy . . ." and so on. Yet, when a poet begins to write something down, he has an innate sense of whether to write it down in long lines or short, in stanzas of two or twelve lines. Where does his feel for pattern come from? And what does the line do?

I

A first thought is that the line is a unit *to work in*. It is a compositional aid. A module of interest, surprise, or direction, which offers itself as distinct from what precedes and follows. Frequency of images may be built into it. The line as shelf that holds a certain number of books. Thus, a poem, after it is completed, may be collapsed back into a paragraph not to its discredit if the lines, as Dolmetsch says of musical bars, "are a sort of scaffold to be kicked away when no longer needed" (from Pound's "Vers Libre and Arnold Dolmetsch").

Then there is the illusion or illustration of *space,* the between-the-lines, the air around the slim or stocky poem-shape, the way that a picture has "area." What about this poem of Roethke's:

THE MOMENT

We passed the ice of pain,
And came to a dark ravine,
And there we sang with the sea:
The wide, the bleak abyss
Shifted with our slow kiss.

Space struggled with time;
The gong of midnight struck
The naked absolute.
Sound, silence sang as one.

All flowed: without, within;
Body met body, we
Created what's to be.

What else to say?
We end in joy.

Five, four, three, two. We almost assume an unwritten last stanza of one line, one breath, the content of which expresses oneness. Why do we respond to a shape? Does the space a poem takes transmit a mood, a density, intensity, a reach? Do groups of three lines suggest a triangle, whatever that suggests? Do seven-line stanzas seem solid, complete? Couplets, tense? What happens when we tamper with a poem's structure? Here's Sylvia Plath's "Sheep in Fog" as printed in *Ariel*:

The hills step off into whiteness.
People or stars
Regard me sadly, I disappoint them.

The train leaves a line of breath.
O slow
Horse the colour of rust,
Hooves, dolorous bells—

All morning the
Morning has been blackening,

A flower left out.
My bones hold a stillness, the far
Fields melt my heart.

They threaten
To let me through to a heaven
Starless and fatherless, a dark water.

Here it is in a sort of blank verse:

The hills step off into whiteness. People or stars
Regard me sadly, I disappoint them. The train
Leaves a line of breath. O slow horse the colour of rust,
Hooves, dolorous bells—all morning the morning
Has been blackening, a flower left out. My bones
Hold a stillness, the far fields melt my heart.
They threaten to let me through to a heaven
Starless and fatherless, a dark water.

The effect of the transposing, it seems to me, is a loss of suspense.
For a reverse example, this is section two (*Child*) from Seferis's
"Stratis the Sailor Describes a Man," Rex Warner's translation:

When I started to grow up, I was tortured by the trees.
Why do you smile? Were you thinking of spring, which is cruel to
    children?
I was very fond of the green leaves;
I think I learnt a few things at school because the blotting paper
    on my desk was green too.
It was the roots of the trees that tortured me, when in the winter
    warmth they came to twine about my body.
These were the only dreams I had in childhood.
In this way I became acquainted with my body.

Put in "Sheep in Fog" form it might read like this:

When I started to grow up,
I was tortured
By the trees.

Why do you smile?
Were you thinking of spring,
Which is cruel to children?

I was very fond
Of the green leaves;
I think I learnt a few things at school

Because the blotting paper
On my desk was green too.
It was the roots

Of the trees
That tortured me,
When in the winter warmth

They came to twine about my body.
These were the only
Dreams I had in childhood.

In this way
I became acquainted
With my body.

Maybe some of the narrative quality is lost because of the pauses
our minds insert at the end of each line. But otherwise there may
be no difference between these two passages: another mystery.

What does the line do? Hart Crane in prose would need a
machete: the reader would have to discipline his comprehension
to adjust to the dense language. Linebreak as machete. But for
most writers this would not be true. Without rhyme or strict meter
the line can still help distribute the cadences and aid our response
to the speed of a poem. Since variation in line length often gives
pleasure, the line elicits a physical response, an inner dancing.

In the long journey out of the self,
There are many detours, washed-out interrupted raw places
Where the shale slides dangerously
And the back wheels hang almost over the edge
At the sudden veering, the moment of turning.
Better to hug close, wary of rubble and falling stones.
The arroyo cracking the road, the wind-bitten buttes, the canyons,
Creeks swollen in midsummer from the flash-flood roaring into
          the narrow valley.
Reeds beaten flat by wind and rain,
Grey from the long winter, burnt at the base in late summer.
—Or the path narrowing,
Winding upward toward the stream with its sharp stones,
The upland of alder and birchtrees,

> Through the swamp alive with quicksand,
> The way blocked at last by a fallen fir-tree,
> The thickets darkening,
> The ravines ugly.
>
> (Roethke, "Journey to the Interior")

Even when not read aloud a verse has an unheard music. It is perhaps a conductor we watch.

Then finally, is the line a sort of scale?—saying weigh these words; this verse is just as heavy as this verse; I'm coming down equally hard with my pencil here, here, and here.

We write in lines because we plant a vegetable garden in rows, because we have ribs, because . . .

II

> there was once a woman who admired a dog
> the dog was handsome
> she liked his face
>
> that night the dog turned into a man
> he became her husband
>
> never tell anyone I used to be a dog
> never mention it at all
> he said to his wife
>
> for a long time they lived together
> she never thought of him as a dog
> she never spoke of it
>
> but one day she saw some dogs in the village
> they were all chasing a bitch
> everywhere here and there
>
> so she asked her husband if he would like to be one of them
> and instantly he said yes and turned back into a dog
> and away he ran with the others

Now let's consider the case of prose turned into a poem. The above is an adaptation by William Brandon (in *The Magic World*) of a Malecite Indian tale recorded by Frank G. Speck and published in *Journal of American Folk-Lore* in 1917. It's such a taut, spare story, condensed as poetry is—isn't it even more impressive presented in lines? It seems to me that lineation nearly always contributes to the tension of a work, if only because it is doled out to the reader one line at a time.

Dress, undress. The following prose could be a passage in a story or a paragraph of Loren Eiseley or Edwin Menninger's *Fantastic Trees*:

> But let me describe to you a killed chestnut tree. Leaves, fruit, even the bark have long fallen to the dark alien disease, and at last the tree itself lies down in a twisted, rising-and-falling shape, and it never rots. The smooth wood, pale and intense, undulates in a kind of serpentine passivity among waves of witch hazel and dogwood that wash along it summer after summer after summer. And so the killed chestnut has become something everlasting in the woods, like Yggdrasill.

It happens to be fifteen lines (in tercets) I admire from Hayden Carruth's "My Father's Face." So what have we proved? It is no disgrace to write beautiful language, whatever its form. Some narrations, observations, descriptions, or meditations work equally well as prose or poetry, especially when their language cannot be improved upon. And lengths of lines?—perhaps they are what is left of the instinct in us to be songwriters. "When the line has ceased to function" it may be because its job of pulling the poem out of the writer is over: the poem is written down.

P.S. When I wrote, "Does the space a poem takes transmit a mood, a density, intensity, a reach? Do groups of three lines suggest a triangle, whatever that suggests? Do seven-line stanzas seem solid, complete?" etc., I had not read what I ran across last night in Nadezhda Mandelstam's Hope Against Hope: *"Osip Mandelstam was always concerned about the number of lines and verses in a poem, or the number of chapters in a piece of prose. He was angry when I said I was surprised he thought this important. My lack of understanding struck him as nihilism and ignorance. It was not for nothing, he said, that some numbers—three and seven, for example—had magic significance for people; numbers were also a part of our culture, a gift which had been handed down to us.*

"In Voronezh M. began to compose poems of seven, nine, and eleven lines. Seven- and nine-line stanzas also began to appear as parts of longer poems. He had a feeling that some new form was coming to him: 'Just think what they mean, these fourteen-line groups. And there must be some significance in these seven- and nine-line stanzas. They keep cropping up all the time.' There was no mysticism about this, it was seen simply as an index of harmony."

(1973)

James Wright

A RESPONSE TO
"THE WORKING LINE"

Mr. Carruth argued that great poetry is a mystery, which we had better accept as such, while we labor for an intelligent minor verse. We labor thus because we want to live in our lifetime. We love the masters like Shakespeare, because they are so deep in our lives, and we too have our brief right to live. Shakespeare told us, about as plainly as anything can be told, that he wanted to be left alone.

Unless I completely misunderstand Mr. Carruth, the great poet—who may be some biological accident so nutty that not even Buckminster Fuller or W. C. Fields can understand how to imagine it—is best left alone and then discovered in a kind of late loneliness.

Then Mr. Carruth turned to Pound.

It may be that he thinks Pound was a great poet. I don't. His two good poems, in my opinion, derive themselves endlessly from Waller.

I love Waller. If I had begun this series of discussions, I would have proposed Herrick. But Pound's master Waller will do.

For the poets of my generation in America, Pound did.

The trouble with the new generation, many of whom love Pound, is that they have not yet found a succinct minor poet like Pound who has ideas about the art of verse.

We found them in his early letters (and manifestoes—his friends Joyce, Eliot, Yeats never made manifestoes—Pound made manifesto after manifesto—the great poets write their books in secret, we discover their books openly).

In one of his few helpful moments, Pound observed that the poet who wishes to write free verse should beware of writing bad prose hacked into arbitrary line lengths. It would be hard to overestimate the value of this observation, because it made possible a language Pound called the musical phrase. Pound helped many minor writers replace their outworn rhetoric with a rhetoric more suited to their own occasions: their talents and their serious hopes, as distinguished from their twitching daydreams, their lives.

Our lives, I should say, because Sean O'Casey turned out to be serious with his dead drunk joke. The whole world is in cold fact in a terrible state of chassis.

Any reader who requires me to document the cold fact at this time is lonely beyond my reach. But our own moment in the life of poetry, so rich and wicked in its solitary fertility, has brought forth a problem so difficult that not even the great Pound could have anticipated it. Our magazines abound with fine writings, and what they tell us for our lives is that there must surely be maybe five hundred thousand horse's asses in These States who have learned through television to write bad prose. Caught by the fever and fret of fame, as our beloved vice president might say, every God-damned fool in America quivers with the puce longing to win life by printing at us that he is sensitive. He and Viva know that rhyme and rhythm are out. Twitch is in.

Poetry is the enemy of twitch. Every poetry has a theory, whether the bad poets know it or not. The theory of our current free verse involves a complete rejection of the past. We have, in a lonely time, a limp surrender of intelligence to the rhetoricians of the government. I don't give a damn for their Democrats or their Republicans, and I could not care less for the Black Mountain versus the New York School. A rejection of the past is a rejection of intelligence. We have, for the moment, a confused embrace of the present for the sake of a hallucinatory future. The endless bad poems of our time distribute themselves automatically between masturbation and the exquisite phoniness of middle-class revolution.

What makes our bad poetry so bad, so ironically bad, has nothing to do with its sweet technique, which is sweet enough. By this time, God help us, everybody in college knows how to write like Pound, Olsen (sic), and like the minors (God save the mark). I urge your good friends to realize that what makes the new poetry so bad is its failure to realize that there is no sound poetry without intelligence. There is no poetry without its own criticism. You can take your minor elegance and throb around in it. I have nothing against the minor elegance, because I have nothing against the failure to think. But if the young friends who live and write after the generation of Pound are going to matter in the United States, they are going to have to develop a criticism of their own.

Personally, I find Pound aesthetically offensive, but he did at least offer some actual ideas by which a serious poetry could be written. He was not enough for the minor poets of my own time. Perhaps he helped his friends. What the new poets have got to do is stop imitating the students of Pound, and develop a criticism of your own. Friends, there may well be a great poet among you. If there is, he will die, and you will die, unless he learns his craft, as Dante did from *Can Grande* and Shakespeare did from the great craftsmen of his own muddled and lonely time.

Line! Line! Friends, let us all stop twitching and pay attention once more to the letters of John Keats.

Ezra Pound, for Christ's sake. Ezra Pound is dead, and unless the young replace him with their own intelligence, they too will be dead forever. There is no poetry without criticism. The language dies without intelligence, and I suppose this is why our beautiful writers the fictionists E. L. Doctorow, Hannah Green, and Cynthia Ozick are so much truer and finer and more abiding than Pound, and my versifying contemporaries, and the young. Unless they want merely to twitch.

(1973)

John Haines

FURTHER REFLECTIONS ON LINE AND THE POETIC VOICE

When I first began writing verses I was apt to let my lines run on to the end of the thought, as in a sentence. This made lines very long at times. Later, as a result of reading and influence, I learned to break the lines in some pattern, visual or other, and to make some effective use of the phrase as the language is spoken, or as I speak it myself. And all this has been very largely a matter of instinct. To write in more traditional measures, according to a determined number of stresses, though I found early that I could write that way, did not interest me. Verse was to be free, but not too free, and somewhere in the process I could find my own order and certainty. But it's worth noting that W. C. Williams wrote me once twenty years ago that "instinct is not enough for the master of his craft, free verse is not enough." And we know how much energy he devoted to finding a "measure" he could pass on.

I don't know where my sense of the line comes from, but it isn't fixed, it changes. Many lines in *Winter News* have a kind of bitten-off quality:

> On the road of the self-
> contained traveler I stood
> like one to whom the great
> announcements are made.

If I look at this critically today, the line breaks can strike me as arbitrary. Why didn't I write them out more naturally, according to the phrasing?

> On the road of the self-contained traveler
> I stood like one
> to whom the great announcements are made.

But somehow the short lines are better. The hard-bitten compression suits the material, the substance; it suited my life. And once written, the poem intends to stay fiercely in its form; it resists change. I don't understand this, it's mysterious like everything else that is important in poetry.

The decision to break lines at this or that point, to arrange them in whatever form or pattern, comes from the direction of the energy or impulse of the poet. This energy, this emotional charge, is going to change, to swerve, to rise and fall, to hurry and then relax from time to time, from poem to poem, or from moment to moment. Changes of line have a lot to do with changes in the poet's life; it's an internal affair as well as an outward, or technical, decision to write this way or that. And if you find yourself becoming restricted by your own style, then you must change it. But first you must change your life.

More recently it appears I'm allowing my lines to run on more easily and naturally according to their phrases and pauses; my impulses aren't the same today, at this hour:

> My chair by the handmade window,
> the stilled heart come home
> through smoke and falling leaves

For what it's worth, I find three stresses in each of those lines. And so much for the biography.

A verse line written to strict measure, or number, as I think the ancients used to have it, made good sense when a certain number of accents or syllables were built into it as a matter of custom, or there was supposed to be a certain frequency of sound at the end of the line in response to the art of song. But as Simpson seems to be saying, there aren't any rules these days. We might be better off if we had them, but we're stuck with the impulse, with intuition. Or is this what we've always been left with? Short lines, long lines, so many syllables, feet to a line, lines to a stanza, trimeter, quatrain? Call it free or accentual, the choice is the poet's and if she or he hasn't sound instinct, so much the worse.

A poem is a composition of words in space and in time. It is the structuring of thought and emotion. Ideally a line of poetry carries its justification as sound; we read it, hear it in a certain way. So much depends upon a red wheel barrow glazed with rain water beside the white chickens. Would that sentence, that bit of descriptive comment attract universal attention embedded in a paragraph? Not likely. As Joseph Conrad said: "A work that aspires . . . to the condition of art, must seek to carry its justification in every line." Lack of a firm sense of the line is a handicap. Is this why the prose poem is so much in evidence these days? There you don't have to justify your lines, just make the paragraph and let it go.

What this may come down to is a strong sense of voice. It is the voice of the poet, no two alike, that determines the line, the rhythm, structure, everything. Once heard, the voice creates the environment of thought and feeling which we come to accept and believe in as an unmistakable mark of the poet's work. The voice refined becomes the poet's style. Unfortunately, the voice is one thing that can't be taught or learned in any school or class, nor can it be counterfeited. It is discovered in the act of living and working, and nourished until it becomes as much a part of the person as an arm or a leg. When a poet writes badly, it may be because he has become false to his voice, loses his sense of it temporarily, and writes in another not his own. This is what literary influence does to a young writer. But influence from another writer or another literature can also help a poet identify and establish his own voice. Witness Dante's influence on Eliot, for example. Possession of the voice is an integral part of the gift of poetry.

Jim Wright is right. The young poets of this time need a criticism and they haven't yet produced one. Something may be brewing. The criticism, if it comes, ought to include an attempt to deal with what I sense as a major problem in our poetry, and that is the extent to which poetry is becoming merely a verbal event, separated from the reality of the life around us. And I think Wright is just in his remark about the rejection of the past. We don't live merely in the present. There is a past, and there is and will be a future. Out of nothing comes nothing. Maybe we need faith more than anything else.

Beyond all this fiddling, I think Carruth had something of value buried in his remarks. Most contemporary verse in English lacks memory value, musicality, it isn't repeatable. It relies on the image and on statement, and not much else. This is not just a matter of memorable sound, nor of rhythm, of course, but of sustained impulse, of emotion and intensity, and of substance. It has something to do with the connection, or the lack of it, of the poet with his time and his people. And it has also something to do with the relevance of the activity of poetry itself in our time. Stevens gave some thought to this once:

> If people are going to become dependent on poetry for any of the fundamental satisfactions, poetry must have an increasing intellectual scope and power. This is a time for the highest poetry. We never understood the world less than we do now nor, as we understand it, liked it less. We never wanted to understand it more or needed to like it more. These are the intense compulsions that

challenge the poet as the appreciatory creator of values and beliefs. . . .

I have not touched on form which, though significant, is not vital today as substance is. When one is an inherent part of the other, form too is vital.[*]

(1973)

---

[*]Wallace Stevens, "Statement on problems facing the young writer in America." April 16, 1946. *Letters of Wallace Stevens*. The entire statement is of great interest.

Donald Hall

THE LINE

The Line most obviously bodies forth the dance—the pause, balance, and sudden motion—that is Goatfoot. At line-end—by altering pitch or lengthening the hold of a vowel or of a consonant—the Line is Milktongue. By giving us units which we hold against each other, different and the same—and by isolating the syllable which rhymes, different and the same—the Line is Twinbird.

By invoking Goatfoot, Milktongue, and Twinbird, the Line is wholly serious, because it allows us to use parts of the mind usually asleep. When we take a lined poem and put it into paragraphs, we remove imagination and energy, we create banality. John Haines used this example; I use it again. It is no insult to William Carlos Williams, or to his poem, to say that the prose sentence, "So much depends upon a red wheelbarrow, glazed with rain water, beside the white chickens," is boring. The Line brings forth the etymological wit (depends/upon; wheel/barrow). The Line brings forth the assonance only half-heard in the prose: "Glazed/ rain"; "beside/ white"). And in fact the Line (in this poem and not in every poem) is an *intellectual* force, insisting on particularity by the value it gives to isolated words of sense.

When a critic takes a lined poem and prints it as prose, in order to show that the poem is inferior, he tells us nothing about the poem. (This series of notes began in response to a reviewer, in the *Hudson Review*, who tried to denigrate poems by Charles Simic and John Haines by printing them as prose.) Such a critic reveals that he is ignorant or disingenuous. Back in the silly wars about free verse, toward the end of the First World War, American critics who wished to prove that free verse was only prose took poems by Ezra Pound (or Amy Lowell) and printed them as prose. "See," they said triumphantly, like the man in the *Hudson Review*, "It's only prose." They only proved that they had no sense of the Line.

A sense of the Line disappeared from common knowledge some time ago. In 1765, an Englishman named John Rice proposed breaking Milton's lines according to sense, and not according to the pentameter, presumably changing:

Of man's first disobedience, and the fruit
Of that forbidden tree, whose mortal taste

Brought death into the world, and all our woe,
With loss of Eden, till one greater man
Restore us, and regain the blissful seat,
Sing heavenly muse . . .

to:

Of man's first disobedience,
And the fruit
Of that forbidden tree,
Whose mortal taste
Brought death into the world,
And all our woe,
With loss of Eden,
Till one greater man
Restore us,
And regain the blissful seat,
Sing heavenly muse . . .

This rewriting of Milton resembles bad free verse, which is usually bad rhythmically *because* the poet has no sense of the line as a melodic unit. The lines are short and coincidentally semantic and phonic. But Milton—need I say—is not damaged by this crude rearrangement. Damage only occurs to the critic (John Rice) who thinks that line structure does not matter, or to the reviewer who thinks that the poem must prove itself apart from its lineation— which is to think that line structure does not matter.

A hundred years earlier, John Rice's ear would have been more reliable. With the increase of literacy, and the vast increase in printed books of prose, people began to read poetry without pausing at the ends of lines. The Line I suppose was originally mnemonic. As far as I can tell, actors indicated line-structure by pause and pitch at least through Shakespeare's time, probably until the closing of the theatres. Complaints from old fashioned playgoers—that upstart actors like David Garrick no longer paused where the poet indicated that they should pause—occur in the 18th century. It is possible to connect literacy, capitalism, and puritanism with this insult to Goatfoot.

Of course the Line has continued to exist, even among certain actors, and among all good poets. *You cannot read Keats or Hardy or Pound as if they were prose without losing a connection to the unconscious mind, a connection made by sound.* Maybe the reason people *want* to speak poetry as prose, and therefore to belittle the Line, is that they are frightened of the psychic interior to which the Line, inhabiting mouth and muscle, may lead them. Such a reason would explain the way many professors of English read poetry aloud.

To speak with such seriousness of the Line is not to deny the frequency in poetry of other, perhaps vaguer things: metaphor, image, thought, and whatever people mean by "tension" or "density." But Williams writes without metaphor on occasion, Creeley writes sometimes without images, and Mother Goose writes poems with little thought. Mother Goose, who is all mouth and muscle, is a better poet than W. H. Auden.

(1974)

Shirley Kaufman

SOME THOUGHTS ABOUT LINES

In Jerusalem today I read about Micha Ulman's conceptual art, the Israeli exhibit at Sao Paulo's biennale. He dug holes in Jewish and Arab villages and then filled them in with earth from the other village. "An Exchange of Earth," he called it, photographing the holes as diamonds, people watching them.

An exchange of what? Last year a friend told me, "Poetry is my life." He'd been making a mess of both. I wanted to say, "But is your life poetry?"

Fill up your poems with life. Which village do you want? It's the same dirt.

Thinking of this while tractors move and drills cut into the rock across the road. Loud. The road I'm living on is called *Neve Sha'anan,* place of tranquillity.

Why do we have to keep shifting earth? And what will we dig up next? Whatever violates the mind. Whole populations exchanged. Filling the holes.

Poetry works against this. Poetry doesn't *give* us form to break against. Holes to fill. Or lines to walk out on. It tries to find what's really there or really not there. And live with it.

Well, lines. We write in the rhythm of our breath, our pulse. Simpson calls it *im*pulse. The pulse inside. It's something physical. And yet. And yet. Who stops to think *how* he breathes? Or where the next breath's coming from? After the first gasp, entering the light, we go on breathing. And yet. There's more to life than breathing.

Williams: It isn't what he *says* that counts as a work of art, it's what he *makes* . . .

Renoir, almost blind at the end, with brushes strapped to his crippled wrists, still painting, but only the smallest section at a time, his vision slivering. "Turn the head of the bird," he said, touching the paint to canvas, before he died.

Each line the view from these walled-in eyes of a small thing. But turn it, line after line. (Breath after breath.) It flickers. More than the act of turning it, each separate part, more than its sum. The whole head of the bird.

(1973)

William Matthews

A NOTE ON PROSE, VERSE AND THE LINE

"Lack of a firm sense of the line is a handicap," writes John Haines ("Further Reflections on Line and the Poetic Voice"), and asks, "Is this why the prose poem is so much in evidence these days? There you don't have to justify your lines, just make the paragraph and let it go."

Haines uses "justify" not in its typesetter's meaning, but in its religious meaning; writers of prose poems are like the lilies of the field.

I imagine one is drawn to write prose poems not by sloth, more purely practiced in hammocks, but by an urge to participate in a different kind of psychic energy than verse usually embodies.

Here are excerpts from etymologies of "prose" and "verse" in Webster's Third New International Dictionary. Prose is "fr. L *prosa,* fem. of *prosus* straightforward, direct." Verse is "fr. L *versus* row, line, verse; akin to L *vertere* to turn."

So the line in prose is like a fishing line, cast out as far as it will go, straightforward. And the line in verse goes out from the margin, turns back, goes out again, etc. Thus poetry is often linked to dance. The serpentine line of verse goes more down the page than across it.

I think of the long lines tending toward prose in Blake's prophetic books, Whitman, visionary passages from Ginsberg and Roethke. Such poems are questing, tentative, discursive—fr. L *discursus* ("past part. of *discurrere* to run about")—rather than direct. But in them the line takes on some of the characteristics we stereotypically associate with prose.

Short-lined, rhyming, metrically regular poems would presumably accommodate a different kind of psychic energy.

But counter-examples abound. I don't intend to propose laws, rather to notice tendencies. And to suggest that such tendencies, familiar to poets from memories—conscious and unconscious—of reading poems, are among the many factors influencing their decisions about lines.

(1974)

Charles Simic

SOME THOUGHTS ABOUT THE LINE

In my book of genesis, poetry is the orphan of silence. Maternal silence. That in everyone which belongs to the universe. The mother's voice calls its name over the roofs of the world. Whoever hears it, turns toward his ancestral home.

A moment of recognition. Timeless present which has no language. Whoever senses himself existing has no need to say much. Perhaps lyric poetry is nothing but the memory of that instant of consciousness. Clearly, at that point, something comes into being. Using that intelligence one begins the search for words that would equal the memory. A labor no less difficult, no less phantasmagoric than alchemy. But then, of course, the condition of the lyric is the belief in the impossible.

From that point on, I'm guided by a need for simplicity. A belief that the matter may be resolved by an utterance which is essential and archetypal. Simplicity is really another way of naming that attention that reveals what is close at hand. The obvious but overlooked and the miraculous being one and the same thing. "Under one's nose" as the idiom would have it. And so, sooner or later, I'm given a word or a phrase I can live with.

To see the word for what it is, one needs the line, and later the larger field of the stanza or whatever you care to call it. For me the sense of the line is the most instinctive aspect of the entire process of writing. The content imposes a time scale: I have to say x in x amount of time. The other considerations are dramatic and visual. I want the line to stop in such a way that its break and the accompanying pause may bring out the image and the resonance of the words to the fullest.

As one plays with words, as one makes them interact, the connotative aspect of each word becomes apparent. Incompleteness which demands fulfillment. Metaphorical possibilities which enlist time and space as forces, which create expectations. The organizational principle is the intonation, the living voice. The damn thing has to speak to someone.

To be truthful, it took me years to realize even this much. It's difficult to speak of it with precision, since one is describing an intricate psychic activity which has to do with the nature of time, both as its timeless instant and as its temporal extension. The causality, whatever of it is visible, is only a part of the story. What one meets more often are the innumerable paradoxes—the astonishment of finding oneself living in two worlds at once.

In the end, I'm always at the beginning. Silence—an endless mythical condition. I think of explorers setting over an unknown ocean, the distant light they see at the horizon in a direction where there's no known land. I love beginnings. I honor that lit window which is there and not there.

(1974)

3 The Image: A Symposium

Charles Simic

IMAGES AND "IMAGES"

> *"Madame X is installing a piano in the Alps."*
> Rimbaud

> *"The more impossible the problem, the more poetical the possibilities. An ideal situation."*
> Carl Rakosi

Image: to make visible . . . What?

To re-enact the act of attention.
The duration of the act itself as the frame (the field) of the image.
The intensity of the act as the source of "Illumination."

In Imagism, the faith that this complex event can be transcribed to the page without appreciable loss.

Something as simple and as difficult as a pebble in a stream. The instant when it ceases to be anonymous and becomes an "object of love." A longing to catch *that* in its difference and kind . . . A glimpse of the world untainted by subjectivity.

In such a "frame" analogies would be an interference, a distortion.

One wants the object looked *at,* not *through.*
A pebble stripped of its figurative and symbolic dimensions.
An homage to the pleasures of clear sight.

Nevertheless—the "image." The hunch that there's more here than meets the eye. The nagging sense that the object is "concealed" by its appearance. The possibility that I am participating in a meaning to which this act is only a clue. In short, is one an impartial witness, or is the object a mirror in which one occasionally catches sight of oneself imagining that impartiality?

To be conscious is to experience a distancing. One is neither World, nor Language, nor Self. One *is,* and one *is not.* It seems incredible that any of these could be accurately rendered by merely listing the attributes. "Listing" implies order, linearity, time. . . The experience is that of everything occurring simultaneously.

This is not something of which one can form an image by imagist means. However, since one needs to talk even about the incommunicable, one says, it is *like* . . . With that little word, of course, one has already changed the manner in which one proposes to represent the world.

If the source of light for the imagist image is the act of attention, in the universe of radical metaphor, the cause is the faith in the ultimate resemblance (identity) of everything existing and everything imagined.

The "image" is the glimpse of the "Demon of Analogy" at work. He works in the dark, as the alchemists knew.

To assert that A is B involves a risk—especially, if one admits the extent to which the act is involuntary. One cannot anticipate figures of speech. They occur—out of a semantic need. The true risk, however, is in the critique the "image" performs on Language as the shrine of all the habitual ways of representing reality.

This is its famous "Logic." The "image" never generalizes. In each entity, it detects a unique (local) logic. (A pebble does not think as a man or a stream does. It "thinks" as a pebble.) Michaux and Edson are masters of such dialectic.

It all depends on how seriously one takes the consequences of one's poetics.

The secret ambition of "image"—making is gnosis—an irreverence which is the result of the most exalted seriousness. One transgresses as one recognizes the rules by which one lives.

The "image" might come to one in a strange and mysterious

way, but it's no longer possible to offer it to the world in that spirit. To know history, even literary history, is to lose innocence and begin to ponder what the "images" are saying.

"Resemble assemble reply," says Gertrude Stein. Today to make an "image" is to make a theatre. On its stage, the old goat-faced Socrates, the philosophic clown, is taking a bow.

Thus, it's not so much *what* the "image" says, but *how* it works that is interesting. Its geometry, astronomy, zoology, psychology, etc. . . .

Poets can be classified by how much faith they have in truth via "images." It's for the sake of Truth that one makes one's grandmother ride a giraffe—or one does not.

Besides, any day now, "images" will attack poets and demand that they fulfill their promises.

I am not the first one to have said this.

(1980)

Donald Hall

NOTES ON THE IMAGE:
Body and Soul

1. As W. J. T. Mitchell puts it, "To speak of 'imagery' in temporal arts like . . . literature . . . is to commit a breach in decorum, or, to put it more positively, to make a metaphor." The poem's only genuine image is the squiggles of ink on paper which make letters and punctuation marks.

2. Sometimes people speak of the image as if it meant something else, and as if they knew what it meant. Here is a definition from a popular textbook: "Images are groups of words that give an impression to the senses. Most images are visual, but we can also make images of taste, touch, hearing, and smell . . . ." A sensible definition, no doubt—but it has little to do with what we mean when we use the word "image" in connection with a poem. When we speak of images in poetry, we speak of four or five different things, some of which have nothing to do with making "an impression to the senses."

3. Literary terms, by appointment in Samarra, eventually contain not only what they started with but the opposite of what they started with. "Spirit and image" meant "soul and body." But image has come also to mean precisely not-body, not-X because an imitation or a copy of X. From a copy or representation of a thing, the word can then move to mean the essence of a thing, therefore "image" comes to mean "spirit" which began by being its opposite.

As with literary terms so with literary movements. The manifestoes of the Imagist Movement praised the particular over the abstract, the local over the infinite; and we were enjoined not to speak of "dim lands of peace." When Pound reported in a metaphor taken from electricity that the image is language "charged with meaning," we no longer heard about description and detail; we heard about quality and value, about intensity and intelligence. Here was Imagism's appointment in Samarra: the movement which started as an assault on the symbol ended by requiring that symbolism house itself in the particular without an explanatory genitival conjunction linking it to an abstraction.

Two lines of Pound's are sometimes cited as the image's apogee: "The apparition of these faces in the crowd;/ Petals on a wet, black bough." Like most of us, I enjoy this morsel; but it is not only "an impression to the senses." The word "apparition" introduces magic—how infinite, how *fin de siècle*—which by its connotation governs what follows. Pound the magician poet, as gifted as Ovid's deities, metamorphoses faces into petals; because the word "apparition" is poetic, the word "petals" takes on the association of beautiful flowers; and the word "bough" completes a natural scene. Thus the faces are by association pretty as they stand out against the dull crowd: bright petals torn by storm, blown by wind, stuck by rain to dark limbs. It is all accomplished by assertion.

4. We make poetry of our conflicts, our warring opposites, although we do not always pretend to; and we may not even know we do. When William Carlos Williams wrote "no ideas but in things," I suppose that he was aware of the paradox: the statement disexemplifies itself, an idea made of no things at all. And his famous image poem depends upon something besides an image: "so much depends/ upon," claims W. C. W., with an imageless urgency that illuminates the picture of a red wheelbarrow shiny with raindrops next to some white chickens.

5. Or take Ted Hughes, from a poem in *Moortown*: "The wind is oceanic in the elms . . . ." Is this an image? The wind which is invisible to the eyes becomes tangible and visible with the cooperation of the elms; the elms by responding make the wind visible—more, they make it audible: this image of course is a metaphor (airy wind compared to watery ocean) and the comparison takes place to the senses not visually but audibly. For the image to raise itself to sense-perception, the metaphor had to operate first.

"The wind is oceanic in the elms" . . . Beyond the audible comparison there is comparison of size. The wind is as vast as the ocean. And this is not a piece of sense data but an idea, a conceptual metaphor. But if it is imaginable we imagine it in terms of extent; I believe that "extent" is an abstraction of a visual experience.

6. ". . . Dim lands of peace" *does* seem like rotten language; we prefer this syntactical arrangement when it attaches particulars: "the camera of my eye." But this image is not visual or sensuous but conceptual, for an eye regarded as a camera looks no different from an eye regarded as an eye; the metaphor suggests not a datum of sense but an idea of function or utility. . . .

But if we despise "lands of peace," do we also despise "sea of trouble"? The man suggested that he might "take arms against a sea," which is surely an image, fantastic as Cuchulain—which becomes less image and more metaphor when we add the genitive.

7. Lautréamont's is probably the most famous surreal image: the chance meeting on a dissecting table of a sewing machine and an umbrella. Of course one can see it if one tries; it is not especially interesting to try: we don't imagine it, we illustrate it.

Surrealism is typically visual, perhaps excessively visual. If its pictures are literary, its narratives are pictorial. Many surrealist poems could be descriptions of a series of paintings. And the name of each of them is The Strange Encounter. It is always the umbrella and the sewing machine, even when the umbrella wears shark's teeth and the sewing machine has goat's ankles.

8. There is also the metaphor that is perfunctory as metaphor, and vivid as image. "That time of year thou mayst in me behold . . ." Obvious not because of overuse but because of natural symbolism, night as death and autumn as age . . . but: "When yellow leaves or none or few do hang . . ." becomes more interesting not because of the image of turned foliage but because of the rhythm of its syntax, hurtling and hesitant by turns. Then: "Bare ruin'd choirs, where late the sweet birds sang. . ." The audacity is imagistic and metaphoric together; a comparison compared over again, a likeness distanced by a further likeness.

9. There are comparisons without images—"as futile as an old regret"—and of course there are images without metaphors: cold hands, sour cabbage, huge spider . . .

On occasion we may use image as an honorific gesture like "nice" from which we would wish to withhold the cold shower of definition. Is it possible that when we enhance "image"—calling it charged, calling it deep; when we refuse to call it "an image" unless it is unreal—that we are saying something like "I only respect an image when it becomes a symbol"?

Anyone who considers the ambiguity of "image" a modern degeneration should consult the OED. If I suggested using "image" to mean a sense datum, often but not always part of metaphor or component of symbol, I would accomplish nothing, because metaphor and symbol, words which we use as if they describe things that happen in language, are as imperfectly defined as image is.

(1981)

Robert Bly

RECOGNIZING THE IMAGE
AS A FORM
OF INTELLIGENCE

1

Before I set down some thoughts about the image, I'd like to set down some thoughts about its place among other powers that make up a good poem. I have asked myself what the powers are that make a poem forceful, and I have settled on six of these powers, elements, or energy-sources. Sometimes they change in my mind, but I'll set down the six I see now, and go over them briefly.

In the first niche we could set the image. I'll give two examples: "The blind man on the bridge is as gray as some abandoned Empire's boundary stone." "The landscape, like a line in the psalm book, is seriousness and weight and eternity." In the image the human sees his relationship to some object or a landscape. The human intelligence joins itself to something not entirely human. The image always holds to the senses, to one of them at least, smell, taste, touch, hearing, seeing of color or shape or motion. Statements such as "The good of one is the good of all" abandon the senses almost successfully. The image by contrast keeps a way open to the old marshes, and the primitive hunter. The image moistens the poem, and darkens it, with certain energies that do not flow from a source in our personal life. Without the image the poem becomes dry, or stuck in one world. The two images above are Rilke's, who seems to me the greatest contemporary master of the image.

However, we notice that even a brilliant image is lost if surrounded by stiff, petrified, archaic words. Writing poetry, we have to learn to leave archaic words behind, leave them, as Machado says, to the poets in whose age the words were not archaic. Walt Whitman in the Nineteenth Century and William Carlos Williams in the Twentieth, especially, made American poets alert to the language we speak, and, in general, most working poets today in the United States understand the spoken quality well. Kenneth Rexroth, Robert Creeley, Louis Simpson, Denise Levertov, Russell Edson, Gary Snyder—and we all know many more—are masters of it. The music of pitches enlivens spoken language; how to indicate on the written page where the pitches should fall is a problem not solved yet. Perhaps this difficulty is connected with the overly simplified syntax we have been using. But a lot has been done. So the sense of a speaking voice I'd put as the second power.

However, even if the image is marvellous, and clothed besides in lively spoken language, both will be lost if the tone of the language is fluffy, charming, and inconsequential. Something like psychic weight I would call the third power. During my twenties I had the experience many writers that age have: the writer reads over his or her poems; they seem well-written, and yet they lack a certain psychic weight. I think this weight, which comes later in development, is connected to grief, turning your face to your own life, absorbing the failures your parents and your country have suffered, handling what alchemy calls lead. Most Edward Arlington Robinson poems have psychic weight, all of Cesar Vallejo, Lowell's *Lord Weary's Castle,* James Wright's best poems, Anna Akhmatova's best poems, poems by many other poets we all know.

My sense is that it requires five to ten years of work for a young poet to develop the image, perhaps five more for spoken language, another five or ten to achieve psychic weight. I don't think the order is important. Some may work on them simultaneously; it would still take twenty years. I was forty-five or so before I felt all three of these energies in my own poems, firmly. Spoken language was the most difficult for me, and it wasn't until *This Body is Made of Camphor and Gopher Wood,* after ten years' work with the prose poem, that I felt my own pitches enter.

Let's suppose then that after twenty or twenty-five years of work, the poet has brought in these three powers: the image, carrying both the dark and light worlds, the music of pitches that comes with spoken language, and an adult grief that makes the poem feel heavy in the hand.

For myself, at this point I realized I was about half way to the poem, as it was understood in ancient times. For example, when I looked back at my work after finishing *This Body is Made of Camphor and Gopher Wood* I was surprised to realize how little emphasis I had put on sound.

As the fourth power, then, I'll name sound, particularly resonating interior sounds. Some poets learn to make a sound-structure, with internal resonances, sounds calling to other sounds. I don't believe poets can achieve this without studying, as the old Sanscrit poets did, sound itself, and studying it apart from rhythm or cadence or meter. Memorization of many poems is essential to touch this power. As we know, the Druid poetry schools required the memorization of several thousand lines of Celtic poetry before instruction was given. In Wallace Stevens we can hear sounds calling to sounds:

> Supple and turbulent, a ring of men
> Shall chant in orgy on a summer morn.

In Yeats:

> I will arise, and go now, and go to Innisfree.

The sounds make a structure of beams, and even if all the words were taken away, the beams would still, so to speak, be there. Russians say Pasternak's and Akhmatova's poems have this sort of inner structure. Among American poets living now, we feel some of this knowledge in Robert Francis and John Logan, but most American poets are not doing it at all.

Memorization of poems once more is the way, and the only way, I think, for the next power to become conscious. We are still talking about sound, and I want to talk next about sound as related to the drum beat. Robert Hass has written about that in his *Antaeus* article "Listening and Making," and written marvellously. He wants to make sure we understand that he is not talking about meter. "I have already remarked that meter is not the basis of rhythmic form." Donald Hall also wrote brilliantly about this power in *Field*. There he calls it Goat-Foot. If there is no drum beat in the line, the goat's foot has not come down. Yeats says:

> I asked if I should pray,
> But the Brahmin said:

The goat's foot comes down on "But." Blake says:

> The little boy lost in the lonely fen,
> Led by the wand'ring light.

The goat's foot comes down on "lost" and again on "led." All prose poems exist without the Goat's Foot, most Whitmanic poetry makes no place for it, and it is missing in almost all recent iambic poetry. In other words, the drum beat is very hard to find in poetry by living Americans. I find very little of it in my own poems.

I have one more power left to talk about, also rare in our recent poetry, I mean the power of the story. In our poetry, why are there so few personalities besides our own? The story depends on many personalities, not exactly "personas," either. Chaucer loves this power, so do Blake and Yeats. Edgar Lee Masters did too, and loved it so much that in *Spoon River Anthology* he leaps to this stage, without having done much work on sound or image first. The narrative poem carries some story power. Among living American poets Ed Dorn does this well, so do Russell Edson and William Stafford, but the master is Thomas McGrath in his *Letter to an Imaginary Friend.* No one pays any attention to it I think because we simply don't respect the power of the story, though Homer, *Beowulf,* Aeschylus, Rumi, Dante and Goethe make it clear how important it is.

With this said, we can return to a concentration on the image, but I wanted, by setting these thoughts down, to make clear that no matter how much I respect the image, I don't consider it to be the only important element in a poem, nor the most important. It is one of six or seven.

2

Poets my age and younger have probably placed too much emphasis on the image in recent years, too much, that is, in relation to the other powers. My own overemphasis on image has been partly at fault for that, but one could also say that other critics who should have balanced or corrected the overemphasis on image did not appear. I am glad of the new criticism appearing, by Robert Hass, Charles Molesworth, Frederick Turner, all practicing poets. The image brings so much moistness to a poem that it cannot, I think, be overpraised, but when a poet works on it solely or mainly he or she may, without intending it, let other beings in the poem starve. It's possible that Williams starved the resonating sound and drum areas of his poetry by working so doggedly on colloquial or spoken language.

The image belongs with the simile, the metaphor, and the analogy. Shelley said, "Metaphorical language marks the before unapprehended relations of things." Owen Barfield remarks in his marvellous book called *Poetic Diction* (which is about many other things as well) that he would like to alter only one detail in Shelley's sentence. He would change "before unapprehended relationships" to "forgotten relationships." He says that ancient man stood in the center of a wheel of rays coming to him from objects. As an example of a "forgotten relationship" we could mention the relationship between the woman's body and a tree. The Jungians have uncovered that recently, by reproducing old plates showing a woman taking a baby from a tree trunk. We all know other examples. Many relationships then have been forgotten—by us. They can be recovered. "For though they were never yet apprehended they were at one time seen," Barfield says. "And imagination can see them again." When a poet creates a true image, he is gaining knowledge; he is bringing up into consciousness a connection that has been forgotten, perhaps for centuries.

I think Barfield's understanding of the image is tremendous. The power of the image is the power of seeing resemblances. That discipline is essential to the growth of intelligence, to everyone's intelligence, but especially to a poet's intelligence. Emerson, who was Thoreau's master, said, talking of true analogies: "It is easily seen that there is nothing lucky or capricious in these analogies, but that they are constant, and pervade nature. These are not the dreams of a few poets, here and there, but man is an analogist, and studies relations in all objects. He is placed in the center of beings, and a ray of relation passes from every other being to him." The question we have to ask of an image, then, when we write it is: Does this image retrieve a forgotten relationship, or is it merely a silly juxtaposition, which is amusing and no more?

3

I'd like to go on, and discuss one more idea Barfield lays out. He maintains that every true image—every image that moves us—or moves the memory—contains a concealed analogical sequence. "Analogy" holds the word "logic" in it. He believes that the imagination calls on intuitive logic to help it create the true image, or to see the old forgotten relationship. He gives these lines as examples of images of that sort:

> My soul is an enchanted boat,
> Which, like a sleeping swan, doth float
> Upon the silver waves of thy sweet singing.

I'll try to work out the analogy implied. This is a possibility:

> My soul is to your singing
> as a boat is to water.

That's all right, but maybe a little bare.

> My soul is to your sounds
> as a sleeping swan is to water.

That sequence is better, because it includes the idea of enchantment, which has a secret resonance with "sleeping swan."

Barfield's idea then is that an image involves the logical intelligence; one has to be intelligent to create an image, and intelligent to understand it.

I'll set down one more image Barfield quotes, more mysterious this time:

> What is your substance, whereof are you made,
> That millions of strange shadows on you tend?

We can feel enormous energy enter the poem with the word "millions." The energy is thought-energy that Shakespeare gave to the creation of the image. Barfield remarks that "sometimes in retracing the path back to the hidden analogy, a great deal of abstraction is necessary before we can arrive at the ratio." The ratio is his word for the sequence of analogies which we unravel slowly but which the imagination saw in a flash as it was writing the poem. What is the hidden ratio that underlies Shakespeare's image? We could try this:

> Your inner personality is to ordinary personality as a great magnet is to a stone.

That's possible, but it doesn't feel quite right. Let's try this:

> Your substance is to the mysterious interior being as a great medium is to ghosts longing to speak.

That's better. Barfield suggests the ratio is this:

> My experience of you is to the rest of my experience as the sun is to the earth.

I like this delving. Delving like this makes clear that the true image has thought in it; complicated analogical, even logical, perceptions fuse with imagination to make a strong image.

That statement is true in eternity, and such a grasp of image is important now, in order to balance the disparagement of image that one sees here and there. Ira Sadoff, for example, in *APR* (Nov-Dec 1980) says: "While the deep image poem acted as an important corrective to the time-honored Anglo-Saxon tradition on the ascendancy of the head over the body, too often it also refused what can only be called intelligence, the possibility of reflection upon experience, the ability to make sense of our histories, our limits as well as our possibilities." He follows this observation with an image poem made up in three minutes, as if it were easy, as if any high school student could write as well as Trakl.

I know that Ira here is warning against the way the fun of creating images can lead to, and has led to, silliness, and I agree with him on that; but in his sentence he refuses to distinguish between the true image and the silly juxtaposition. His essay suggests that he has a grudge against the image; and it sets forth the doctrine that the word "intelligence" is to be reserved for the discursive poem. Such overstatements should not be let go without comment.

I like intelligence when it appears debating both sides of a question in the discursive poem, and I also like intelligence as it appears in an image. My respect for the image has deepened, rather than diminished, in the last ten years.

4

Having spoken about the discipline of creating images as an exercise of intelligence essential to the poet's mind, and called attention to Owen Barfield's ideas on that, I'll end this piece with an idea of my own about the image.

I've mentioned that the image joins the light and dark worlds. It is a house with a room for each. An image may join the world of the dead with the world of the living; it makes a house with a room for each. Trakl wrote:

> The oaks turn green
> in such a ghostly way over the forgotten footsteps of the dead.

It may connect what we know with what we don't. I wrote these two lines:

> So much lies just beyond the reach of our eyes . . .
> what slips in under the door at night, and lies exhausted on the
> floor in the morning.

It may join what is invisible with what is visible. Neruda said of death:

> It is like a shoe with no foot in it,
> like a suit with no man in it . . .

Nevertheless its steps can be heard,
and its clothing makes a hushed sound, like a tree.

Bert Meyers in his poem about his days as a frame-maker, polishing wood, said:

At dusk I drive home
the proud cattle of my hands.

These are not real cattle, but he is proud of his hands as the dairy farmer is of his superb Holsteins, that walk home, as Bert correctly sees, in some mood that looks like pride. So the unconscious contributed its body experience, and, momentarily, turned his small hands into immensely large cows.

Each of the images I've set down above merges two colors of consciousness, but the objects generally stand for something within human experience, or within human consciousness.

It's possible there is another sort of image, which the ancients knew about. It is less like a container and more like an arm. It reaches out of human consciousness to touch something else. We find it in Blake's "Tiger," and other poems of his. I noticed when putting together *News of the Universe* that Goethe, Novalis and Hölderlin open their poems to this sort of image, in a way rare in the English language poets of the time.

Apparently the power of a myth depends on at least one of these "arm" images. Such an image, once found, persists for centuries, and people never exhaust its possibilities. Yeats has a good example of it in his poem in which Mary speaks:

The terror of all terrors that I bore
The Heavens in my womb.

Here we feel the non-human universe has entered the human through some sort of channel given by the image. There is terror in it. The imagination has placed the Milky Way inside the womb. We don't feel it as an analogy.

Another example is the astonishing detail mentioned in the tale of Persephone's descent into Hades. She disappeared from the meadow, and when they found the hole into the earth, her footprints were gone, obliterated under the tracks of pigs. A herd of pigs had gone down with her. There is great power in that, and it is somehow related to the pigs Christ drove over the cliff.

Images of the "arm" sort carry us into the area in which matter responds to the human unconscious. No one knows much about that; we hear it touched on in events that happen "syncronistically": after longing for a book for a week you walk into a stranger's house and see it lying on the table. It appears also in the frightening experiences the subatomic physicists have had in the "Copenhagen experiment."

Both sorts of image present intellectual evidence against what I called in *News of the Universe* the "Old Position," the notion that human reason is alone in its intelligence, isolated, and unchangeably remote from the natural world. We do feel a gap between ourselves and nature. We can remain in the gap, and let the two worlds fall apart farther and remain separate. Or a human being can reach out with his left hand to the world of human intelligence and with the right hand to the natural world, and touch both at the same time. Barfield says that the power that makes us able to touch both is called "imagination." It has the word "image" in it. I recently came across an image the ancient Norwegians created for Thor: lightning over a ripe barley field. There it is again: the ancient Gothic imagination was unwilling to accept the severe categorizations of outer and inner, divine and human, intelligence and matter, that Aristotle and Descartes acquiesce in. This true union, this oneness of worlds, is what Wallace Stevens means by the word "Harmonium." I'll end this piece with four divine lines by Wallace Stevens, when he is stating his belief that human beings will once more understand this union.

> And in their chant shall enter, voice by voice,
> The windy lake wherein their lord delights,
> The trees, like serafin, and echoing hills,
> That choir among themselves long afterward.

(1981)

Russell Edson

IMAGE AND LANGUAGE

The image comes all at once. Language is the enemy of the image, because language likes to describe and tell stories. Language would like to reduce the image to mere description.

Yes, poems are made of language, but the image is essentially nonverbal; and since it is, the poor image has more in common with dreams than it has with language.

The art of the poem is the making into language what *cannot* be made into language.

Still, the image must stand away from the language that carries it. The image belongs more to its own physical universe than to the idea that the poem has of it.

The psychological object should have about it the sense of something not fully discovered. If the language of the poem succeeds in completely translating the image, the image has failed. There must remain always something hidden from language; an intuitive presence stronger than the language that carries it. Then the image has dimension and reality.

It is best to let the image be what it means to be, and not force it into literary ideas and ambitions. For the freed image tells more of this world by showing us another.

As long as the language of the poem is rational enough not to muddle the image, and doesn't attempt to go beyond the image, anything is possible.

The madder the image the better, the stranger the image the more wonderful. And if clams come to play accordions, rejoice in their music . . .

(1981)

Marvin Bell

NOUN/OBJECT/IMAGE

We are greedy. We want the image to be more than the object, despite how hard it is merely to see an object and render it accurately. We are self-centered. We want the image to be partly subjective. We are proud. We want the image to carry our "vision." We are vain and competitive. We want the image to be *our* kind of image, *our* signature, *our* brick wall.

But photographers can do the object, and painters redo it, better than we. What can we do with it that they cannot?

We can put the object into motion, a motion even more continuous than that in film, where the screen must stay put. We can give the image a non-imagistic context. Hence, the object alone will suffice if deftly placed, and will be treated thereafter as if it itself presents inside and outside, self and other, here and there. Of course we can also make of the image a place. We can locate there. And we can use the image to objectify our emotions, even sometimes to express them.

Most of the talk about imagery sounds like broadcasts of Army football games of the forties. Mr. Inside and Mr. Outside (Doc Blanchard and Glenn Davis), working together, couldn't be beat. And it's true that a star or two will compensate for one's deficiencies elsewhere. In our country, a so-so mind with a talent for vivid imagery will be praised, while a brilliant mind and ear lacking it will generally be ignored. We are not just tv watchers. We have become tv readers.

Pound's definition of the image—"an intellectual and emotional complex in an instant of time" (from *Poetry,* March 1913)—is often reduced in conversation about the image. For all his learning, Pound's heart remained in popular song—Provençal lyrics. He would never have made poetry by squeezing it just from his brain, as have his more esoteric followers.

Pound's image has two parts, and produces an equation between feeling and object. Stieglitz was making such an equation when he photographed clouds and called them "equivalents." The clouds were equivalent to his emotions. No emotions, no images.

Imagism, remember, in reaction to the second-best poetry of its time, published a complete set of principles for tight, dramatic writing. Its advice to show, not tell, was only a part of its program. When it turned into what E.P. called "Amygism" (for Amy Lowell)—poems by poets who imitated the method but lacked emotional depth—Pound got out.

Now the image doesn't work the way we say it does. Take probably the two best-known examples of Imagism. First, Pound's "In a Station of the Metro." Pound finds it necessary to use half the poem to explain what's coming: "The apparition of these faces in the crowd." Only then can he lay before us an image: "Petals on a wet, black bough." The poem accomplishes an image, but not without explanation.

Second, Williams' "The Red Wheelbarrow." "so much depends," he writes, "upon// a red wheel/barrow," and says nothing about what depends on it. The poem argues for Imagism, but its method is rhetorical: the effect of the poem *depends* on the rhetorical beginning of its only sentence and on those expectations which it may thereby establish and frustrate. From the frustration itself arises the point to be made. In other words, though one could argue the propriety and advantages of a red wheelbarrow, it could have been something else.

Are the greatest accomplishments of American poetry those of imagery? I myself think not. Thinking about American poetry (and also about the poetry of young Americans and even about what might be called "Workshop Poetry," good or bad), it occurs to me that it tends to be heavy on rhetoric but light on imagery. Indeed, the colloquialization of rhetoric may be an American accomplishment. The British are better in court but their poetic rhetoric wears leaden boots. The French do more acrobatics but say less. Our idiomatic lingo is heavily rhetorical and metaphorical.

Our practice of Imagism (I would argue that we have been practicing at it ever since the Movement) much of the time has been mindless—the one great flaw in American poetry by which our practice is shown to be limited by an absence of sufficiently considered theory.

Now to your questions. Of course my ideas about imagery have in some ways changed and in some ways remained constant just as I have changed and remained constant. I don't usually think about imagery apart from other concerns. I am fairly certain that a preoccupation with images is characteristic of our technological society and will remain so. I am fairly sure that images in poems have less effect and less value than is claimed by those who are dependent upon them. I know that imagery can be a breeding ground for the fraudulent visionary, the mystifier. I suspect imagery has kept many unthinking poets writing and publishing, but there's always something. Those among us who love Imagism too much are held by its dead hand. So are those of us who hate it. To be free, one must proceed as if writing is an adventure into the unknown. From where one begins, one may see or imagine many images. And later there may be many surprises, some of which may be images. The "so much" that "depends" on each object/image is the object/image itself. In a field, and in a *Field,* we too are among those objects. The notion that man's brain is superior to a tree will lead to the premature end of civilization. But so will the notion that a tree is superior to a brain. At least the tree, as far as we can tell, is too smart to think so.

Now if we get into the poetry of William Carlos Williams, the most misunderstood, mislabelled and poorly-imitated poet of our time (still!), we shall never see the end of our discussion. For Williams is a poet of syntax and idea far more than he is a poet of things or images. His "thing" poems are mere exercises. His great works are not at all dependent on images. Rather, like most great poems, they are each centered in one image—that one from which the poem derives or toward which it proceeds. The image of the *poem* is vastly more important than the image of the *line.*

My book titles are images, but not always things. Is this possible? The titles are *Things We Dreamt We Died For*; *A Probable Volume of Dreams*; *The Escape into You*; *Residue of Song*; *Stars Which See, Stars Which Do Not See*; and *These Green-Going-to-Yellow.* Each of them stops short of presenting a single object to which a reader might attach his or her understanding of the whole phrase. In each case the image is, to my mind, bigger than that. To my mind, an object which has been turned on its head or covered with a shroud is still just an object. In such cases, one tends to turn it right-side-up or uncover it in one's mind, thus enjoying the pleasures of the riddle. But for me, writing is not a riddle, anymore than the unexplored Polar Cap was a riddle for Byrd. Call it a riddle if one likes, it was a great space.

In my generation, the best image-makers include Mark Strand, Charles Simic, Louise Glück and Charles Wright. In the generation ahead of mine, one would have to name Galway Kinnell and the late James Wright. In the poetry of James Wright, we can trace the development of what is best in American poetic imagery. In mid-career, by way of Spanish and German poets (notably, Trakl), he develops the crisp, startling, "deep" imagery of *The Branch Will Not Break.* Imagery is not enough, so he puts back more rhetoric in *Shall We Gather at the River.* In the end, in *To a Blossoming Pear Tree*, he writes a plain, colloquial, narrative line, made glorious, heightened and also relieved by gorgeous images—many of them emotional correlatives, not to what has already been expressed outright, or will be, but to other, deeper responses. In such work, Wright refines one of the most powerful uses of the image (to tell us something more, from underneath) and also implies by his continuing need for rhetoric the limits of the image (for the "deep" image, once allowed to dominate the surface of the poem, becomes only the surface).

Images are not the essence of poetry, even for those who make them well. They are only one among many symptoms of a poet's quality of mind and force of imagination. Still, I too am knocked out by them. Who would not wish to have written these lines by Roethke: "Is that dance slowing in the mind of man/ That made him think the universe could hum?" I myself think this an image. I also think an image is contained in these lines: "The rain/ is too heavy a whistle for the certainty of charity." Those are my own lines, and they have haunted me for years.

The image is bigger than the object. But the noun is larger still. The secrets of the mind take the form of nouns. Those images in dreams which are taken to signify: they are merely the surface of things.

(1981)

4 Poetry and Values

Günter Eich

SOME REMARKS ON "LITERATURE AND REALITY"

All the views that have been presented here[*] assume that we know what reality is. I have to say for myself that I do not know. That we have all come here to Vézelay, this room, this green tablecloth, all this seems very strange to me and hardly real.

We know there are colors we do not see, sounds we do not hear. Our senses are uncertain, and I must assume my brain is too. I suspect our discomfort with reality lies in what we call time. I find it absurd that the moment I am saying this already belongs to the past. I am incapable of accepting reality as it presents itself to us as reality.

On the other hand, I do not wish to play the fool who does not know he has bumped into a table. I am prepared to orient myself in this room. But I have the same sort of difficulties that a deaf and dumb blind man has.

Well, all right. My existence is an attempt of this kind: to accept reality sight unseen. Writing is also possible in these terms, but I am trying to write something that aims in another direction—I mean the poem.

---

[*]At a conference in Vézeley, France.

I write poems to orient myself in reality. I view them as trigonometric points or buoys that mark the course in an unknown area. Only through writing do things take on reality for me. Reality is my goal, not my presupposition. First I must establish it.

I am a writer. Writing is not only a profession but also a decision to see the world as language. Real language is a falling together of the word and the object. Our task is to translate from the language that is around us but not "given." We are translating without the original text. The most successful translation is the one that gets closest to the original and reaches the highest degree of reality.

I must admit that I have not come very far along in this translating. I still am not beyond the "thing-word" or noun. I am like a child that says "tree," "moon," "mountain" and thus orients himself.

Therefore, I have little hope of ever being able to write a novel. The novel has to do with the verb, which in German is rightly called the "activity word." But I have not penetrated the territory of the verb. I shall still need several decades for the "thing-word" or noun.

Let us use the word "definition" for these trigonometric signs. Such definitions are not only useful for the writing but it is absolutely necessary that he set them up. In each good line of poetry I hear the cane of the blindman striking: I am on secure ground now.

I am not saying that the correctness of definitions depends on the length or brevity of texts. A novel of four hundred pages is likely to contain as many "definitions" as a poem of four lines. I would consider such a novel a poem.

Correctness of definition and literary quality are identical for me. Language begins where the translation approaches the original. What comes before this may be psychologically, sociologically, politically or any-cally interesting, and I shall gladly be entertained by it, admire it and rejoice in it, but it is not *necessary*. The poem alone is *necessary* for me.

(1956)
translated by Stuart Friebert

Jean Follain

MEANINGS OF POETRY

a talk given at the Maison de la Culture at Thonon, 1967

At the invitation of the Tel Quel group, my friend Francis Ponge gave a fine, long talk about poetry, and, using a perfectly concrete example, attempted to explain the meaning of poetry.

He said this: "You are on the main street of a big city. Newspapers hot from the presses have just arrived on the stands. An important piece of news has broken: let's say, as was the case not long ago, the assassination of a great head of State. You rush up to buy some daily paper, caught up as you are in the news and a powerful desire to know more about it. If at the same moment you take hold of the paper you don't smell (as powerfully as you felt the desire to get hold of the newspaper), if you aren't conscious at the same time of the smell of fresh printer's ink and also that, above you, of the leaves, then you don't feel the thing we call poetry." Thus Francis Ponge substantially spoke.

This being granted, the variety of forms written poetry takes is a fortunate thing. Traditional forms may be as valid as those freely composed. I do not like the expression "free verse" which may be equivocal. A poem, even if it does not conform to traditional poetry, is composed according to rules and forms which allow it to exist.

Without being overly systematic, it can be said that two forms of poetry exist, two extremes, that is, all intermediate forms can be found between them. This would mean, on one hand, the poetry of effusion, and on the other, the poetry of concentration. The latter tends to a great economy of means. It expresses itself through a concentrated use of words. The poetry of effusion will more readily tend to use a fast flow of words, it will attain certain bright flashes and reflections, certain touches of expression that would not have come to light without its prolixity.

The poem can be generated by a vocable in common use and suddenly perceived gorged with all its meaning, surrounded by a sort of magnetic aura. It can also be generated by the sight of a simple object, never before seen in such a way, bearer of all its significative values and touching off the poem. The object thus seen appears in its complicity with the rest of the universe and situated in that universe.

Much is said about the use of images in poetry. It is certain that in the broad sense of the term, all poetry contains images. In the narrower sense, many poems contain similes and metaphors. Numerous poets today and in the past have given us admirable examples. As far as I am concerned, I have come to the point of writing almost none at all. Perhaps because simile and metaphor imply comparison, and I can compare no one thing to any other in this multifarious universe nonetheless full of mysterious affinities between all things. I have sometimes felt, charmed by other poets' metaphors and similes, that I wanted to write my own, did and found them satisfactory, then disowned them all the next day upon realizing they are simply not me. But from time to time I may save one of them.

This brings me to speak about the maturation of a poem. It is certainly possible for a poem to come out exactly right on the first draft. For me, at least, that remains the exception. When a poem I have conceived and written does not manage to hold together, to find home, to exist, I file it away only to return to it after several months, even years. Then, sometimes thanks to a single word removed or added, the poem begins to hold together. That is precisely why Max Jacob wrote me one day, during his first stay at Saint-Benôit-sur-Loire: "Poetry needs to age like wine in a cellar."

There are curious connections between the poet's art and that of the painter. I may say to myself, looking at a text: I need some red there, or some gray or other; but of course I don't get my red by putting some red thing in my text, but, for example, by adding a pronoun or some syllable of a word which, for me, is a stroke of red.

I do not think we should, as we have had too great a tendency to, make poetry too sacred, try too hard to establish its relation to mysticism. Certainly, there are a few examples of great mystics who were also great poets. Witness St. John of the Cross. On the other hand, a woman whose mystical experience was extraordinary, St. Therese of the Child of Jesus of Lisieux, wrote poems that were sincere and deeply felt but flat, showing no gift for poetry.

Alongside mystical knowledge, it is possible that a certain poetic knowledge exists, enabling us more than anything else to grasp certain of the world's givens and coordinates. This is what Bergson grasped fully, especially when he asserted that poets explain Time better than philosophers.

As Mallarmé said to Degas, poetry is not made of ideas, but of words; in any case, poetry is made, he stated, to "Give the tribe's words back their full and the purest meaning, their true weight and all their freshness." Meaning the poet must, unless consciously rejuvenating one, disdain clichés, evidence that a vocable is wearing out. "You settle for little or nothing," said Francis Ponge, "if to express grandeur you simply use the word grandeur."

As for myself, I would rather see muted brilliance than too much brilliance in poetry. Jean Cocteau expressed the same thing by saying he liked the wrong side of certain bright colored silk ties, full of attenuated brilliance and subtle iridescence, better than the right side of the same ties.

The poet must not succumb to what Jean Paulhan has called literary terror. This would make him shy away from certain simplicities of style and artificially refine his writing. I point out in passing that Maurice Garçon, in his reply given at Paulan's Académie Française inauguration, made a great mistake in suggesting Paulhan promoted this terror, while in fact he denounced it.

What is essential in poetry is an absence of vagueness as well as of stiffness in writing. Lines of Racine's impeccably obey the strictest rules, and take no liberties, yet there is a certain deliberate awkwardness in the play of syllables that contributes to their great poetic worth.

It appears that poetry eminently linked to the beauty of the universe is assured of perennial existence. Poetry tries desperately to free this beauty and all the ineffable, even the tragic, it keeps in the context of the World.

Poetry also tries to rediscover a certain innocence of the world which is not illusion but profound truth, and which subsists though and in the face of everything, and despite all of history's diabolical tricks.

(1967)
translated by Mary Feeney

Gary Snyder

POETRY, COMMUNITY & CLIMAX

I

I wrote a small piece ten years ago called "Poetry and the Primitive." It was subtitled "Notes on Poetry as an Ecological Survival Technique." In a brisk and simple way, I was trying to indicate what modern people might want to learn and use from the way poetry/song works in a strong, self-contained preliterate society. I have also spoken of poetry's function as an occasional voice for the nonhuman rising within the human realm, and the value of that. Survival.

But it's clear now, 1979, that survival is not exactly the problem. Not for human beings, who will survive come hell or high water—and both may—to find themselves sole operators of the equipment on a planet where vertebrate evolution has come to an end. Clouds of waterfowl, herds of bison, great whales in the ocean, will be—almost are—myths from the dreamtime, as is, already, "the primitive" in any virgin sense of the term. Biological diversity, and the integrity of organic evolution on this planet, is where I take my stand: not a large pretentious stand, but a straightforward feet-on-the-ground stand, like my grandmother nursing her snapdragons and trying at grafting apples. It's also inevitably the stand of the poet, child of the Muse, singer of saneness, and weaver of rich fabric to delight the mind with possibilities opening both inward and outward.

There is a huge investment in this nation: bridges, railway tracks, freeways, downtown office buildings, airports, aircraft carriers, miles of subdivisions, docks, ore-carriers, factories. All that belongs to somebody, and they don't want to see it become useless, unprofitable, obsolete. In strict terms of cash flow and energy flow it still works, but the hidden costs are enormous and those who pay that cost are not the owners. I'm speaking of course not only of human alienation but air and water, stands of trees, and all the larger, more specialized, rarer birds and animals of the world who pay the cost of "America" with their bodies—as mentioned above. To keep this investment working, the several thousand individuals who own it have about convinced the rest of us that we are equal owners with them of it; using language like "don't turn out the lights," "let's not go back to the Stone Age," and "you've worked hard for what you got, don't lose it now." Their investment requires continual growth, or it falters. A "steady state economy" and "small is beautiful" are terrifying concepts for them because without growth, the gross inequalities in the distribution of wealth in this land would become starkly clear. From this it's evident that the future of capitalism and perhaps all industrial society is intimately staked on the question of nuclear energy—no other way to keep up growth. This leads to the disastrous fast breeder reactor (which is not dead yet by a long shot), and the fast breeder leads to a police state. But food shortages may bring it down even before energy shortages—the loss of soils and the growing inefficiencies of chemical fertilizers.

I repeat this well-known information to remind us, then, that monoculture—heavy industry, television, automobile culture—is not an ongoing accident; it is deliberately fostered. Any remnant city neighborhood of good cheer and old friendships, or farming community that "wants to stay the way it is" are threats to the investment. Without knowing it, little old ladies in tennis shoes who work to save whooping cranes are enemies of the state, along with other more flamboyant figures. I guess there are revolutionaries who still hope for their own kind of monocultural industrial utopia, however. And there are some for whom alienation is a way of life, an end in itself. It's helpful to remember that what we'd hope for on the planet is creativity and sanity, conviviality, the real work of our hands and minds: those apples and snapdragons. Existential *angst* won't go away nohow, if that's how you get your energy.

Although it's clear that we cannot again have seamless primitive cultures, or the purity of the archaic, we can have neighborhood and community. Communities strong in their sense of place, proud and aware of local and special qualities, creating to some extent their own cultural forms, not humble or subservient in the face of some "high cultural" over-funded art form or set of values, are in fact what one healthy side of the original American vision was about. They are also, now, critical to "ecological survival." No amount of well-meaning environmental legislation will halt the biological holocaust without people who live where they are and work with their neighbors, taking responsibility for their place, and *seeing to it:* to be inhabitants, and to not retreat. We feel this to be starting in America: a mosaic of city neighborhoods, small towns, and rural places where people are digging in and saying "if not now, when? if not here, where?" This trend

includes many sorts of persons, some of whom are simply looking out for themselves and finding a better place to live. The
process becomes educational, and even revolutionary, when one
becomes aware of the responsibility that goes with "rootedness"
and the way the cards are stacked against it; we live in a system
that rewards those who leap for the quick profit and penalizes
those who would do things carefully with an eye to quality.
Decentralization could start with food production. Old/new-style
biologically sophisticated farming doesn't imply total local
self-sufficiency, but at least the capacity to provide food and fiber
needs within a framework of two or three hundred miles. Then
come new definitions of territory and region, and fresh ways to
see local government limits—watershed politics, bioregion consciousness. Sense of community begins to include woodpeckers
and cottontails. Decentralization includes the decentralization of
"culture," of poetry.

II

Now to speak of twenty-five years of poetry readings in the
U.S. When I was working on the docks in San Francisco and occasionally taking night courses in conversational Japanese around
'52 or '53, writing poems and sending them off to magazines,
Kenyon Review, and *Hudson Review* and *Partisan,* and getting
them back, we had no sense of a community of poets and even less
of an audience. Kenneth Rexroth held open house in his apartment
on Friday evenings, and four or five or sometimes ten people
might drop by; some out of an old Italian anarchist group, some
from the filmmakers' and artists' circles of the Bay Area. In 1954 I
knew virtually every poet, filmmaker, and artist in the region. I
hardly know who works in Berkeley anymore, let alone the rest.

In 1955, because Allen Ginsberg and Philip Whalen, Michael
McClure, Philip Lamantia and several others, and myself, found
ourselves with large numbers of unpublished poems on our hands,
it occurred to us to give a poetry reading. It was like holding a
sale. In those days all we ever thought of doing with poetry was to
get it published; we didn't know who saw it, and didn't think to
offer it up publicly. But we went ahead and organized a poetry
reading. We did have a model or two; Dylan Thomas had passed
through a year before; Ted Roethke had come down from Seattle
and read; the San Francisco Poetry Center had organized a few
readings in five or six years. Still, poetry readings were definitely
not a part of the cultural and social landscape. That reading held

in November, 1955, in a space borrowed from an art gallery, was a curious kind of turning point in American poetry. It succeeded beyond our wildest thoughts. In fact, we weren't even thinking of success; we were just trying to invite some friends and potential friends, and we borrowed a mailing list from the art gallery and sent out maybe two hundred postcards. Poetry suddenly seemed useful in 1955 San Francisco. From that day to this, there has never been a week without a reading in the Bay Area—actually more like three a night, counting all the coffee shops, plus schools, the art museum, the aquarium, and the zoo. Those early readings led to publication for some. *Howl* became the second book in Ferlinghetti's Pocket Poets series, and Ginsberg's extensive early readings all over the United States began to draw audiences of a size not seen before. Kerouac's novels were published, and the "beat generation" was launched. Allen was to a great extent responsible for generating the excitement, but a number of other poets (myself not among them because I had gone to Japan) traveled widely over the United States landing like crows first in coffee houses and later becoming gradually accepted more and more into the network of universities.

One thing that was clearly an error in the mentality of the early fifties literary world was the idea that poetry cannot have an audience, and indeed that it was a little shameful if a poem was too popular. There are people who still believe that, incidentally. There was also the defeatist attitude that "we live in a philistine culture" and "no one is interested in art anyway, so we'll just write to each other." My generation found that boldly, to put it bluntly, having something to say helped with audiences. It also should be apparent that one is not *owed* an audience by the culture; but one can indeed go out and try to build an audience. Building that audience is done in part by going on the road and using your voice and your body to put the poems out there; and to speak to the people's condition, as the Quakers would say, to speak to the conditions of your own times, and not worry about posterity. If you speak to the condition of your times with some accuracy and intention, then it may speak to the future, too. If it doesn't, fine, we live in the present. So poetry readings as a new cultural form enhanced and strengthened poetry itself, and the role of the poet. They also taught us that poetry really is an oral art. It would be fascinating to undertake an examination of how poetry of the last twenty years has been shaped by the feedback that comes with reading in front of people. Poems go through revisions, adaptations and enhancements following on the sense of how audiences have been hearing you. So there is a communal aspect to the evolution of the art. Does this mean that poets, knowing that they were writing for an audience, might have catered to that possibility? Sure. But it also means that audiences have come up to the possibility of hearing better over the years. My experience is that the latter tends to be the case and that audiences have grown in maturity and the poetry with them. With a skilled audience, such as you often find in New York or San Francisco (and recently in Midwestern cities like Minneapolis), the poet knows that he/she can try for more, and really push it to the difficult, the complex, the outrageous, and see where the mind of the people will go.

This practice of poetry reading has had an effect on the poets who were quite content to regard poetry as a written art that sits on a printed page and belongs in libraries, too. They have been forced to actually learn how to read poetry aloud better out of sheer competition if nothing else. There are economic rewards involved.

Poetry belongs to everybody, but there are always a few skilled raconteurs or creators or singers, and we live in a time in which the individual actor or creator is particularly valued. The art wouldn't die out if we lost track of the name of the fellow who made it up, though, and the fact that we don't know the names of the men or women who made the songs in the past doesn't really matter.

All of this goes one more step, then, to a conscious concern and interest on the part of some poets in the actual performance skills of preliterate people. My own studies in anthropology, linguistics, and oral literature brought me to the realization that the performance, in a group context, is the pinnacle of poetic activity and precision, and we have yet to develop the possibilities of that circle with music, dance, and drama in their original archaic poetic relationship. The Ainu singers of Hokkaido chant their long epic stories to a beat. The güslars of southern Yugoslavia use a little dulcimer-like stringed instrument. No wonder we say "lyric poetry"—they used to sing with a lyre. Most of the songs that you hear on the country and western hit parade are in good old English ballad meter, showing that the ballad is the backbone of English-language poetics and will be for a long time to come. Other examples, simple examples: Robert Bly knows almost all his poems by heart and Roethke knew his. Reciting from memory (which I can't do) liberates your hands and mind for the performance—liberates your eyes. Noh drama, with its aristocratic spareness and simplicity, could be another model. Percussive, almost nonmelodic music is very strong; a bare stage is all you need.

In this era of light shows, huge movie screens, and quadraphonic sound systems, it is striking that an audience will still come to hear a plain, ordinary, unaugmented human being using nothing but voice and language. That tells us that people do appreciate the compression, the elegance, and the myriad imageries that come out of this art of distilling language and giving it measure which is called poetry.

III

The next step then is to ask what has a more public poetry done for the possibility of community? The modern poetry audience has a certain kind of network associated with it. Everywhere I go I meet people I know—from one corner of the United States to the other I never give a reading anymore but at least one person comes out of the audience, an old friend. A dozen other people that I haven't met before step up to tell me about how they are riding their horses or growing sunflowers somewhere, or are in the middle of making a zendo inside an old building downtown. It's a fine exchange of news and information, and also the reaffirmation of a certain set of interests to which I (among others) speak. The community that is called together by such events is not just literary. It's interesting to see, then, that the universities have served as community halls, public space, that draw out people from beyond the immediate academic world. In other times and places such public spaces have been riverbeds—which is no-man's land—where the gypsies and the traveling drama companies are allowed to put up their tents, or where the homeless samurai are allowed to act out their final duels with each other and nobody cares—it might be riverbeds, it might be the streets, or temples and churches—or in the tantric tradition of late medieval north India, some groups met in cemeteries.

What is this network of interests and old friends I speak of? None other than that branch of the stalwart counterculture that has consistently found value and inspiration in poetry, and intellectual excitement in watching the unfolding of twentieth-century poetics. Also certain sets of values have been—in recent decades—more clearly stated in poetry than any other medium. (Other post-World War II cultural branches are primarily affiliated to music; some to more specific and intellectually formulated political or religious ideologies; a few go directly to crafts, or to gardening.) Anyway: the people who found each other via poetry readings in the late fifties and sixties produced another generation of poets who were committed to an oral poetics and a nonelite vision of communicating to larger and more diverse audiences. There are roughly three shoots from that root. I'll call them the dealers, the home-growers, and the ethnobotanists.

The "dealers" came in part with the growth of a certain academic and social acceptance of new poets and their readings, which led to the poetry policies of the NEA; the founding of the little magazines and small presses support organizations, the poets-in-the-schools programs, and on the academic side, several MFA-in-writing programs at several universities; workshops in poetry. At this point, via the poets-in-the-schools programs in particular, twentieth-century poetry began to find its way into ordinary American communities. The programs employed people who had gotten their MFA or a little book published (through a small press, with federal aid often)—and put them into high schools or grade schools, doing creative work, creative word playfulness, image playfulness; generating imagination and spontaneity among school children whose usual teachers couldn't. I consider this quite valid as a mode of poetic imagination and practice, in its broadest sense, filtering down through the population. The school districts themselves, after some resistance, began to accept the possibilities of poets and other artists doing local residencies. For every horror story of a brought-in poet reading a poem to the sixth grade with the word "penis" in it, there are countless unadvertised little openings of voice and eye as children got that quick view of playfulness, of the flexibility and power of their own mind and mother tongue. I've watched this at work in my own school district, which is rural and short on money, but has backed the artists in schools as far as it could. In fact this school district (and many others) has chosen to keep arts programs going even after state or federal funding is withdrawn. One local poet found that what the children needed first was an introduction to the basic sense of story and of lore. He became the master of lore, myth, and word-hoard for the whole district. By much research and imagination, he provided, following the calendar and seasons, the true information—as story—about what Easter, May Day, Christmas, Hanukkah, Halloween, and Lammas are about. Neither the parents nor the school teachers in most cases could provide this fundamental lore of their own culture to the children. The poet was Steve Sanfield, doing the work of mythographer to the community in the ancient way.

The "home-growers" (and the above folks often overlap with this) are those poets who themselves live in a place with some intention of staying there—and begin to find their poetry playing a useful role in the daily life of the neighborhood. Poetry as a tool, a net or trap to catch and present; a sharp edge; a medicine, or the little awl that unties knots. Who are these poets? I haven't heard of most of them, neither have you; perhaps we never will. The mandarins of empire-culture arts organizations in the U.S. might worry about little-known poets working in the schools, because they are afraid of a decline in "standards of quality." I think I am second to none in my devotion to Quality; I throw myself at the lotus feet of Quality and shiver at the least tremor of her crescent moon eyebrow. What they really fear is losing control over the setting of standards. But there is room for many singers, and not everyone need aspire to national level publication, national reputation. The United States is, bioregionally speaking, too large to ever be a comprehensible social entity except as maintained at great expense and effort via the media and bureaucracy. The price people pay for living in the production called American society is that they are condemned to continually watch television and read newspapers to know "what's happening," and thus they have no time to play with their own children or get to know the neighbors or birds or plants or seasons. What a dreadful cost! This explains why I do not even try to keep up with what's going on in nationwide poetry publishing. We are talking about real culture now, the culture that things *grow* in, and not the laboratory strains of seeds that lead to national reputation. Poetry is written and read for real people: it should be part of the gatherings where we make decisions about what to do about uncontrolled growth, or local power plants, and who's going to be observer at the next county supervisors' meeting. A little bit of music is played by the guitarists and five-string banjo players, and some poems come down from five or six people who are really good—speaking to what is happening *here*. They shine a little ray of myth on things; memory turning to legend.

It's also useful to raise a sum of money for a local need with a benefit poetry reading, and it's good to know this can be done successfully maybe twice a year. It works, a paying audience comes, because it's known that it will be a strong event. Sooner or later, if a poet keeps on living in one place, he is going to have to admit to everyone in town and on the backroads that he writes poetry. To then appear locally is to put your own work to the real test—the lady who delivers the mail might be there, and the head sawyer of the local mill. What a delight to mix all levels of poems together, and to see the pleasure in the eyes of the audience when a local tree, a local river or mountain comes swirling forth as part of proto-epic or myth. (Michael McClure once said his two favorite provincial literary periodicals were *Kuksu,* "Journal of Backcountry Writing," and *The New York Review of Books.* Two poetry reading invitations that I count as great honors were to the Library of Congress, and the North San Juan Fire Hall.) It is a commitment to place, and to your neighbors, that—with no loss of quality—accomplishes the decentralization of poetry. The decentralization of "culture" is as important to our long-range ecological and social health as the decentralization of agriculture, production, energy, and government.

By the "ethnobotanist" shoot from that sixties root I mean the roving specialists and thinkers in poetics, politics, anthropology, and biology who are pursuing the study of what it would mean to be citizens of natural nations; to be part of stable communities; participants in a sane society. We do this with the point in mind that the goal of structural political change is not a crazy society, but a sane one. These are in a sense studies in postrevolutionary possibilities, and in the possibilities of making small gains now; "forming the new society within the shell of the old." Such are (and though I list them here it doesn't mean they necessarily agree with all or anything I say) Bob Callahan and associates at Turtle Island Foundation; Peter Berg and the Planet Drum group; Joe Meeker, Vine Deloria, Jr., and others working on the "new natural philosophy"; the Farallones Institute; Jerome Rothenberg and the *New Wilderness Newsletter;* Dennis Tedlock and *Alcheringa* magazine; Stewart Brand's *Coevolution Quarterly;* the long list of useful publications from Richard Grossinger and Lindy Hough; the Lindisfarne Association; New Alchemy; and in another more technical dimension, Stanley Diamond's work and his journal *Dialectical Anthropology. Organic Gardening* and other Rodale Press publications, with their consistent emphasis on *health* as the basic measure, might also belong on this list. There are others; I'm not even mentioning poetry magazines in this context. As a sort of ethnobotanist myself, I make the following offering:

IV

Poetry as song is there from birth to death. There are songs to ease birth, good luck songs to untie knots to get babies born bet-

ter; there are lullabies that you sing to put the babies to sleep—
Lilith Abye—("get away negative mother image!"); there are
songs that children sing on the playground that are beginning
poetries—

> baby baby suck your toe
> all the way to Mexico

> kindergarten baby
> wash your face in gravy

(I get these from my kids) or

> Going down the highway, 1954,
> Batman let a big one, blew me out the door—
> wheels wouldn't take it,
> engine fell apart,
> all because of Batman's supersonic fart.

(If you start poetry teaching on the grade school level, use
rhyme, they love it. Go with the flow, don't go against it. Children
love word play, music of language; it really sobered me up to realize that not only is rhyme going to be with us but it's a good thing.)
And as we get older, about eleven or twelve years, we go into the
work force and start picking strawberries or drying apples; and
work songs come out of that. Individually consciously created
poetry begins when you start making up love songs to a sweetie,
which are called courting songs. Then some individuals are sent
out in adolescence to see if they can get a power vision song all by
themselves. They go out and come back with a song which is their
own, which gives them a name, and power; some begin to feel like
a "singer." There are those who use songs for hunting, and those
who use a song for keeping themselves awake at night when they
are riding around slow in circles taking care of the cows; people
who use songs when they haul up the nets on the beach. And when
we get together we have drinking songs and all kinds of communal
pleasure gathering group music. There are war songs, and particular specialized powerful healing songs that are brought back by
those individuals (shamans) who make a special point of going
back into solitude for more songs: which will enable them to heal.
There are also some who master and transmit the complex of
songs and chants that contain creation-myth lore and whatever
ancient or cosmic gossip that a whole People sees itself through. In
the Occident we have such a line, starting with Homer and going

through Virgil, Dante, Milton, Blake, Goethe, and Joyce. They
were workers who took on the ambitious chore of trying to absorb
all the myth/history lore of their times, and of their own past traditions, and put it into order as a new piece of writing and let it be a
map or model of world and mind for everyone to steer by.

It's also clear that in all the households of nonliterate ordinary farming and working people for the past fifty thousand years
the context of poetry and literature has been around the fire at
night—with the children and grandparents curled up together and
somebody singing or telling. Poetry is thus an intimate part of the
power and health of sane people. What then? What of the danger
of becoming provincial, encapsulated, self-righteous, divisive—
all those things that we can recognize as being sources of mis-
chief and difficulty in the past?

That specialized variety of poetry which is the most sophisticated, and is the type which most modern poetry would aspire to
be, is the "healing songs" type. This is the kind of healing that
makes whole, heals by making whole, that kind of doctoring. The
poet as healer is asserting several layers of larger realms of
wholeness. The first larger realm is identity with the natural
world, demonstrating that the social system, a little human
enclave, does not stand by itself apart from the plants and the animals and winds and rains and rivers that surround it. Here the
poet is a voice for the nonhuman, for the natural world, actually a
vehicle for another voice, to send it into the human world, saying
there is a larger sphere out there; that the humans are indeed children of, sons and daughters of, and eternally in relationship with,
the earth. Human beings buffer themselves against seeing the natural world directly. Language, custom, ego, and personal advan-
tage strategies all work against clear seeing. So the first wholeness is wholeness with nature.

The poet as myth-handler-healer is also speaking as a voice
for another place, the deep unconscious, and working toward inte-
gration of interior unknown realms of mind with present moment
immediate self-interest consciousness. The outer world of nature
and the inner world of the unconscious are brought to a single
focus occasionally by the work of the dramatist-ritualist
artist-poet. That's another layer. Great tales and myths can give
one tiny isolated society the breadth of mind and heart to be *not*
provincial and to know itself as a piece of the cosmos.

The next layer, when it works, is harder: that's the layer that
asserts a level of humanity with other people outside your own
group. It's harder actually because we are in clear economic

dependence and interrelationship with our immediate environment; if you are gathering milkweed, fishing, picking berries, raising apples, and tending a garden it shouldn't be too difficult to realize that you have some relationship with nature. It's less obvious what to do with the folks that live on the other side of the mountain range, speaking another language; they're beyond the pass, and you can faintly feel them as potential competitors. We must go beyond just feeling at one with nature, and feel at one with each other, with ourselves. That s where all natures intersect. Too much to ask for? Only specialists, mystics, either through training or good luck, arrive at that. Yet it's the good luck of poetry that it sometimes presents us with the accomplished fact of a moment of true nature, of total thusness:

> Peach blossoms are by nature pink
> Pear blossoms are by nature white.

This level of healing is a kind of poetic work that is forever "just begun." When we bring together our awareness of the worldwide network of folktale and myth imagery that has been the "classical tradition"—the lore-bearer—of everyone for ten thousand and more years, and the new (but always there) knowledge of the worldwide interdependence of natural systems, we have the biopoetic beginning of a new level of world poetry and myth. That's the beginning for this age, the age of knowing the planet as one ecosystem, our own little watershed, a community of people and beings, a place to sing and meditate, a place to pick berries, a place to be picked in.

The communities of creatures in forests, ponds, oceans, or grasslands seem to tend toward a condition called climax, "virgin forest"—many species, old bones, lots of rotten leaves, complex energy pathways, woodpeckers living in snags, and conies harvesting tiny piles of grass. This condition has considerable stability and holds much energy in its web—energy that in simpler systems (a field of weeds just after a bulldozer) is lost back into the sky or down the drain. All of evolution may have been as much shaped by this pull toward climax as it has by simple competition between individuals or species. If human beings have any place in this scheme it might well have to do with their most striking characteristic—a large brain, and language. And a consciousness of a peculiarly self-conscious order. Our human awareness and eager poking, probing, and studying is our beginning contribution to planet-system energy-conserving; another level of climax!

In a climax situation a high percentage of the energy is derived not from grazing off the annual production of biomass, but from recycling dead biomass, the duff on the forest floor, the trees that have fallen, the bodies of dead animals. Recycled. Detritus cycle energy is liberated by fungi and lots of insects. I would then suggest: as climax forest is to biome, and fungus is to the recycling of energy, so "enlightened mind" is to daily ego mind, and art to the recycling of neglected inner potential. When we deepen or enrich ourselves, looking within, understanding ourselves, we come closer to being like a climax system. Turning away from grazing on the "immediate biomass" of perception, sensation, and thrill; and re-viewing memory, internalized perception, blocks of inner energies, dreams, the leaf-fall of day-to-day consciousness, liberates the energy of our own sense-detritus. Art is an assimilator of unfelt experience, perception, sensation, and memory for the whole society. When all that compost of feeling and thinking comes back to us then, it comes not as a flower, but—to complete the metaphor—as a mushroom: the fruiting body of the buried threads of mycelia that run widely through the soil, and are intricately married to the root hairs of all the trees. "Fruiting"—at that point—is the completion of the work of the poet, and the point where the artist or mystic reenters the cycle: gives what she or he has done as nourishment, and as spore or seed spreads the "thought of enlightenment," reaching into personal depths for nutrients hidden there, back to the community. The community and its poetry are not two.

(1979)

Larry Levis

SOME NOTES ON THE GAZER WITHIN

I.

When I began thinking about this a few months ago, I decided that what I would not talk about was craft. As Mark Strand states in a recent article in *Antaeus*: ". . . these days with the proliferation of workshops, craft is what is being taught." Well, talking is teaching: when Sandra McPherson or Donald Justice or Robert Hass writes about craft, such talk fascinates me, and craft becomes, rightly, that most private of dialogues between the poet and his language. But Strand is right, too. Often my workshop at Missouri (especially the graduate workshop) is involved with prescribing remedies for poems—remedies which have to do with the necessary, technical, and not at all visionary work of repairing one line, or weighing, as if in the palm of a hand, a caesura. Of course, I talk most about poems that are *most* finished. Then the multitude of formal decisions that are made are worth troubling over, worth talking about. But I am, then, talking about technique: when a poem is very poor, silence falls quickly, and there is little to say about that poem. There may be a great deal to say, however, about poetry itself, about the imagination, about vision. And I risk foolishness by talking about such subjects. I know, really, that if I don't talk about it, someone else will. And I may not agree with what he or she has to say. So I must either talk about the imagination, or be silent.

Of course, there is that as an alternate, and even absolute, stance; there is silence. Why say anything about the imagination at all? And if it is possible, after enough experience, for a poet to make generally correct formal decisions in the moment of writing a poem, why talk about poetics, about craft or technique? After all, the influence of a theorist like Pound has been deeply assimilated. Now, when most poets write, they do not have to admonish themselves: "Don't be viewy." They already know that they won't be, and for this they can thank Pound for having entered, inextricably, into their own poetry and into their very culture. Besides, couldn't there be something damaging to the poet, and something even unlucky, in trying to understand the principles of what must be, at some moments, a mysterious and

133

sullen art? A poet as gifted as Margaret Atwood thinks so, or thought so in *FIELD* #4: "I don't want to know how I write poetry. Poetry is dangerous: talking too much about it, like naming your gods, brings bad luck . . . you may improve your so-called technique, but only at the expense of your so-called soul." As a notion about poetry and about the psyche, this states powerfully enough the fear that the soul can be lost simply by talking too much about poetry. I could expect, then, that Keats and Eliot and García Lorca were damaged by writing about such ideas as "negative capability" and the "objective correlative" and "duende." And this is a possibility. But unless I am very superstitious about the early deaths of Keats and García Lorca, I could just as well believe that such ideas, in prose, helped the poets concerned, and helped their poetries, even when they broke the rules they made. It occurs to me also that one of the ways in which Pound entered our culture was by the public stridencies of his own criticism, his prose. That is, our century and our poetry didn't simply happen. Pound happened *to* us.

*

What interests me here is a deeper poetics, one that tries to grasp what happens at the moment of writing itself—not a discussion that indulges in prolonging what Marvin Bell has called the pointless "dualisms" of form vs. content; nor a poetics that praises one kind of poem as *organic* while denouncing another as artificial. Ultimately, the trouble with such classroom determinations is that they do reduce poetry to technique, to something stripped of vision, something which gives the illusion of being soluble through *either/or* choices; they make poetry harmless. And in doing so, they lie. We all know that poetry had better come, if not "as naturally as Leaves to the Tree," then at least with something more alive and luminous than a servile, cynic's technique. We know that a poem made to order from theory is slave labor, just as we also know that a poem, any poem, is artificial in one huge respect—if only because, as Eliot's character so famously complained: "I gotta use words when I talk to you."

II.

But if this circumstance is true, where do poems come from? It seems to me that any poetry, any realized "making," comes almost directly from some kind of actual center, some location of energy. This morning, reading at random in *Pavannes & Divagations*, I found this in "Madox Ford at Rapallo," an interview:

> Pound: What authors should a young Italian writer read if he wants to write novels?
> Ford: (Spitting vigorously) Better to think about finding himself a subject.

Ford's exasperated (or mock exasperated) reply is simple and direct enough. But I would go further and stress, beyond the unwitting Ford, this: to find a subject is also, simultaneously and reflexively, the act and art by which anyone finds himself, or herself. A poet finds what he or she is by touching what is out there, finding the *real*. Yet the mistake I see made so often by beginning poets is that they want "to look into [their] hearts, and write!" But at nineteen a poet usually doesn't have much experience to depend on. When such poets write "from the heart" they often doom themselves to trite poems, to greeting cards full of clichés, or to poems that are truly and entirely subjective; i.e., entirely incomprehensible. The best beginning poets I know are also the most literary: what they demonstrate is a love for poetry rather than a love for *themselves*. Let me exaggerate and be at once overly literal and the mind's peasant for a moment: to look into my heart is to look into a muscle. To really look inquiringly inward as Sidney advises or as the most well-intentioned guru advises is to encounter, at least on some very honest days, my own space; it is to discover how empty I am, how much an onlooker and a gazer I have to be in order to write poems. And, if I am lucky, it is to find out how I can be filled enough by what is not me to use it, to have a subject, and, consequently, to find myself as a poet. I like to oversimplify Husserl by saying: *Consciousness is always consciousness of something*. I am no phenomenologist, and I know that such a "something" is different from the simple materiality of the world that I mean. But here I have misunderstood Husserl just enough for him to be meaningful, meaningful to *me*. His remark becomes, in its way, as possible for me as George Oppen's lines: "Two./ He finds himself by two." And of course "he" does, or I do; and how else could it, and "I," have taken place at all: for example, that miracle of dawn or twilight along the road and me there, looking out of my skull, a witness to it? And this must occur many times, with regularity, or else the world would be nonsense, a mute noise.

III. Landscapes

What is "out there" is a world, a landscape. I don't know what could be more unfashionable just now than the whole "idea" of landscape, but at times, for me, the world *is* a landscape, and I think of my own poems as if *they* were landscapes, or as if I could refer to them by virtue of their places. A recent poem, for example, is spoken by a ghost on the banks of the Missouri River; another has as its focus a cemetery in Granada, in Spain; still another poem remembers an orchard and then remembers consequently a small, decaying, California seaside resort with its stucco motel, once a coral red, fading to an almost thoughtful shade of pink. A poem I worked on last night is introduced by a few moths outside an asylum in a small town in Missouri, and earlier I was thinking of a line about a steel mill in Syracuse, New York, a place in which I once worked, and which was, I suppose, ugly and dangerous; its appalling, final meaning must be that republic of iron filings in the lungs of the men who have to work there. I did not, of course, praise the place in my poems. But it was human, a human landscape. I confess that the gazer inside me had a grave affection for the fire glaring in the furnaces from evening until midnight.

In fact, the landscapes I choose for my poems, often, have nothing to do with the landscape that surrounds me: when I look out my window I see my neighborhood, and I know that beyond it is a small, midwestern university town. I find that I have very little desire to write anything about it, though its intimacy occurs, surely and obliquely, in my recent poems. But I wonder if my own neighborhood, some tract housing with lawns and trees, makes me uncomfortable as a poet. Do I merely choose asylums, steel mills and cemeteries in García Lorca's birthplace out of personal morbid fascination and depravity? Maybe . . . but such an aesthetics would be at once sentimental and cynical, and my poems are still not much like *Baretta*. It could be that I choose painful subjects because such sterility, human sterility and loneliness, is part of so many modern landscapes. By this I mean the shopping mall, the suburbs, the business loops, the freeways and boutiques with cute names. They are all part of a modern reality that I would prefer to forget, or ignore. To most people I suppose such landscapes are slight, and unmenacing. To me they are the death of landscapes, and the eye's starvation. Therefore, the asylum, the steel mill, the cemetery, the ghost on the riverbank, the dying resort beside the unfading Pacific are locations, for me, of a human fertility within time.

But if any poet has tried, recently, to confront almost exclusively these most sterile landscapes, it is Louis Simpson in his two most recent volumes; his *Searching for the Ox* comes closest, I suppose, to that place where most of American living gets done, the suburb. And yet, the domestic crises detailed so beautifully, and documented with real grace in such poems as "The Stevenson Poster" and "The Foggy Lane" are poems of *wealthy* suburbs, and such wealth may be as necessary to Simpson's purposes as it is to John Cheever's. Yet even amidst such a setting, Simpson needs, if not Chekhov, at least the ghost of Chekhov's irony, and Chekhov's distance from his setting. All this affords Simpson's poetry its romance, and such a romance is just what the suburb needs; it needs to be soiled by the human. This is, by the way, an explanation and an admiration of Simpson, not a criticism. Who doesn't need Chekhov by now, and need him badly? To confront this reality without a context, without the possibility of a romance, is, as Stevens phrases it, "to confront fact in its total bleakness." This is so, essentially, because a wilderness of tract homes is a world without imagination, and a world without imagination is a lie. Such a world tries to assure its inhabitants that there is no death, no passion, no vision. This is, I think, what prompted Zbigniew Herbert to say, jokingly one day as we were driving through South Pasadena and talking about architecture, that the only "solution" to Los Angeles was to burn it. There is an early, and brilliant, and even vicious poem by William Stafford which is eloquent about this world without imagination. After telling his readers, "We moved into a housing tract," Stafford, with all the proper rancor and customary modesty, closes his poem in an address to Bing Crosby, whose ranch he visits, accidentally, it seems, on his way west: "Every dodging animal carries my hope in Nevada./ It has been a long day, Bing./ Wherever I go is your ranch." Who would have expected Stafford to strike such a Marcusian chord, and to sound it so clearly?

In his essay "The Noble Rider and the Sound of Words" Wallace Stevens states that his phrase "the pressure of reality" means ". . . the pressure of an external event or events on the consciousness to the exclusion of any power of contemplation." And though Stevens goes on to state that this is what the poet evades and escapes through the balance of his imagination, which takes *in* reality, Stafford's poem remains firmly affixed by the pressure Stevens has described. Somehow, in its design, Bing's ranch is outside history, outside time; there are no deaths in the barracks of the suburbs, only disappearances. Outside time, the pressure of reality continues undiminished.

Such pressures and such landscapes have proliferated and become obstinate in recent years. Sometimes I believe that the one vast and wedded consciousness that was required to win World War II, built, almost simultaneously, the tract home, the atomic bomb, and the Dixie Cup. I am not, of course, saying much here that is genuine sociological news. But my interest is personal: I don't believe I can bear witness to such landscapes for long without feeling merely exhausted, drained, and spiritually beaten. In these places *I* must do all the looking, all the gazing. Because no one has ever died *into* such landscapes, it may be that no one can live in them, either; I don't know. I do know that as I watch my eyes pay enormous taxes while the gazer inside me dies for a few moments.

This death has something to do with time. Tract housing, most suburbs, malls and shopping centers on the perimeter of any city or town seem to wish, in their designs, to be beyond time, outside time. To stare for three hours at a K-Mart is to feel myself rapidly again, not K-Mart. And this is not an experience of my own mortality, either. It is only a way of feeling how that mortality can be insulted. And though I am not about to try to stare down any buildings, I do think of those who must work there, and of the alienation, even from themselves, that laboring in such places will make them feel.

Yet the authentic experience of any worthwhile landscape must be an experience of my own humanity. When I pass fields or pass the deserted streets of a small town in the midwest at supper time, or pass avenues of closed warehouses I am not alone, I think. Someone or something has lived here; some delicate linkage is preserved between past and present. I am filled by, *looked at* by, the landscape itself; the experience is not that of a mirror's, but a true exchange, until even something as negligible as some newspapers lifting in the wind on a street, at night and before a rain, are somehow soiled by an ineradicable humanity, and by the presence of the dead, of the about to be born.

IV.

And yet Williams is right: anything *is* a proper subject for a poem. To deny this is to deny a central tendency in American poetry today. But this is not what I am doing, of course. The essential problem is always the poet's, not the theory's. I agree with James Wright that Williams was able to do what he did do because of the truculence of his vision, because of his character. Williams could use anything in the world as a subject precisely because the poet's imagination had contended so arduously with the pressures of reality (*The Desert Music* reaches the same conclusion as Stevens reaches regarding this) that Williams began to break down and demolish the bedrock of dualisms that had kept Williams himself and the world the world. Consequently, the usable world, the broken bits of a green bottle lying between the walls of a hospital on cinders, held under the magnification of the poet's lyric, became an impersonal lyric, a lyric which the poet had evacuated. The poem was Williams', of course; that is, he wrote it. But really, insofar as it was a moment, merely, of perception, it was everyone's moment. And that is its problem, its availability. One student, writing about the poem on an examination, said it proved that one could find beauty anywhere. Does it do that, and if so, should it? I believe, as Susan Sontag states, that good modern art looks back with a stare; it doesn't tell me what to feel or provide me with easy clues. But can a poem really stare back? Can words *be* things? Can they *not* mean? To what extent is my student's interpretation verifiable? Doesn't Williams tell us that the cinders are a place "where nothing will grow"? Is this poem both impersonal and corny? There is a way in which it may have taken all the lovely, later work of Williams, and the work of many of the best poets of our time, to recuperate the poet. This has been, I believe, one of the tasks of contemporary poetry—to recover the poet and the idea of the poet for our time. Such has been the constant example provided by such poets as James Wright, Anne Sexton, Philip Levine, Adrienne Rich, John Ashbery, Sylvia Plath, Mark Strand, and Margaret Atwood,—to name only a very few who occur to me at the moment—poets who created the role and reality of the poet during the 1960s and 1970s. Yet it would be false to assume that this poetry has been concentrated wholly upon the Self, or exclusively upon the Self. In many ways it may have sought only to rescue poetry from some extremes, some abysses, of modernist impersonality. There may be a way in which the more contemporary poet has been engaged upon a recovery of an *idea* of a poet—so that his or her choice of subject reveals him or her *as poet*.

And certainly the pressure of reality exists externally for newer artists just as terribly as it did for earlier ones—or almost as terribly. I think against myself now and then, and think now of

T. S. Eliot watching for German aircraft from the roof of Faber &
Faber during the bombing of London, or of Pablo Neruda, who
wrote of such pressures and of the power they had of embarrassing any motive for metaphor, or simile: "The blood of the chil-
dren/ flowed out onto the street/ like . . . like the blood of children." Neruda in mid-stride suddenly realized that to make poetry
out of this circumstance is to endanger his own humanity, but he
is too honest, and too terrible, to back down. As Stevens also
noted, in his *Adagia*: "As the world grows more terrible, its poetry grows more terrible."

And yet the poets who have written of such a "terrible"
world have done so, it seems to me, out of a memory of it, or at
least at some distance from it. Or they have invented a subject
through which such a world can be documented, felt, and re-expe-
rienced. Or they have introduced a new method or style into their
poetry; a Japanese friend informs me that after Hiroshima *haiku*
and *tanka* forms fell into disuse, and Surrealism became the rul-
ing aesthetic. Do such devices, such methods, bring the poet closer to the world or hold attention at a workable distance, or both?
And what does anyone write *about* in such a world? That is, how
do poets achieve that final invention, themselves?

V. Poetry and Animal Indifference

I'll only presume to answer, to attempt an answer, from my
own experience, and from my own reading of others' experiences.
My most frequent problem as a poet is to have no subject, to have
"nothing at heart," an ailment that Stevens once denied as misery.
The corollary to such misery is an extreme and moody self-consciousness, which of course prevents me from finding anything to
write about. Once, after not writing anything worth typing up for
a few weeks, I complained to a friend, a remarkable poet who is
gifted with an unfailing intuition. His advice was simple; he said
to try writing "about yourself at an earlier age, or an animal." I
wondered, then, why he mentioned an animal. Now I think I know
why. Animals are objects of contemplation, but they are also,
unlike us, without speech, without language, except in their own
instinctual systems. When animals occur in poems, then, I believe
they are often emblems for the muteness of the poet, for what he
or she cannot express, for what is deepest and sometimes most
antisocial in the poet's nature. The other thing that occurs infalli-
bly when the poet places the animal in the world, or in the world
of the poem, is the recovery of the landscape. It is no longer a

world without imagination, or the world of tract housing beyond time. In animal poems the fox may live in the yellowing wood behind the service station; the hawk may be above the billboard. But if they are there, so is time there.

*

So many poets have written, recently, about animals, that I don't feel now like making out a long and tedious list of them. What interests me is what the choice of such muteness suggests or openly testifies about poetry, and about the role of the poet. Seemingly, the poem sustains a paradox: the poet is *speaker*, of course, and yet the poet, evading the pressure of reality by a contemplation of the animal, also desires to express a mute condition. The poet wants to speak of, or to, or through, what is essentially so other that it cannot speak. The muteness or silence of the animal equals that of the poet. Perhaps there is some secret similarity between humans and animals, some desire to close the gap between species. Keats remarks, in passing, on this.

> I go among the Fields and catch a glimpse of a Stoat or a field-mouse peeping out of the withered grass—the creature hath a purpose and its eyes are bright with it. I go amongst the buildings of a city and I see a Man hurrying along—to what? the Creature hath a purpose and his eyes are bright with it.

In his poem, "Horse in a Cage," Stanley Plumly notes how his father approaches a horse: "my father, this stranger, wanted to ride./ Perhaps he wanted only to talk." These instances, in which the poets note animals and humans sharing characteristics, are rare, however. And perhaps D. H. Lawrence's short poem about the youth and the horse attains the apotheosis of such contact—when the boy and the horse are "so silent they are in another world." They are rare not because animals are not often given human characteristics, but because in these examples the role of the poet is extremely modest; the poet is never quite there, never blocking the poem. It is what Keats might have called, on a charitable day, "disinterestedness."

*

In many poems, of course, the animal is not natural, because in a poem the beast may be wholly imagined, and therefore altered from the prison of nature, and paroled, briefly, by the poem itself, and by the poet. And sometimes a poet chooses an animal because the poet is mute, and also because, as in the poem below, the poet is prophet.

THEY FEED THEY LION

Out of burlap sacks, out of bearing butter,
Out of black bean and wet slate bread,
Out of the acids of rage, the candor of tar,
Out of creosote, gasoline, drive shafts, wooden dollies,
They Lion grow.
                    Out of the gray hills
Of industrial barns, out of rain, out of bus ride,
West Virginia to Kiss My Ass, out of buried aunties,
Mothers hardening like pounded stumps, out of stumps,
Out of the bones' need to sharpen and the muscles' to stretch,
They Lion grow.
                    Earth is eating trees, fence posts,
Gutter cars, earth is calling in her little ones,
"Come home, Come home!" From pig balls,
From the ferocity of pig driven to holiness,
From the furred ear and the full jowl come
The repose of the hung belly, from the purpose
They Lion grow.
                    From the sweet glues of the trotters
Come the sweet kinks of the first, from the full flower
Of the hams the thorax of caves,
From "Bow Down" come "Rise Up,"
Come they Lion from the reeds of shovels,
The grained arm that pulls the hands,
They Lion grow.
                    From my five arms and all my hands,
From all my white sins forgiven, they feed,
From my car passing under the stars,
They Lion, from my children inherit,
From the oak turned to a wall, they Lion,
From they sack and they belly opened
And all that was hidden burning on the oil-stained earth
They feed they Lion and he comes.

Philip Levine's poem creates an entirely imagined beast, an un-real lion from the too real landscape. Against this place, the poet invents a voice which the Lion cannot, in its utter otherness, even recognize. As an imaginative act, this cat derives what power it has from the fact that it is unseen, and existant in an apocalyptic future. But it is a future produced by the dialectic of the present:

the mute law of the Lion. The poet's tone is not really rancorous; it is not even avenging. Such preciously ethical positions have withered here into prophecy.

And such prophecy (or what Ginsberg once called "spoken lonesomeness") is Levine's American inheritance. In earlier poems he confesses that his "page is blanker than the raining skies," and that since he no longer speaks, he "goes silent among men." But such muteness was not the death of the poet at all, it was only preparatory and purifying. It was only the necessary immersion into voicelessness, the prophet's apprenticeship. So the poet who is "silent in America," who has "nothing" to say, becomes the most formidable architect of himself and his place and his community, though it is a community of the lost. The contemplation of such a Lion must have been, for this poet, an inward, anxious, and prolonged gazing. And an outward witnessing. To invent such a beast is to recover, simultaneously, its landscape, to appropriate all memories of such places, to find oneself.

*

Why do I admire this terrible Lion? Because, though it may stare back with a blank look, it will not lie; it will not be "reasonable." It is this *lack* of response, this honesty and taciturn otherness that fascinates me. Whitman noted this, but contrasted it almost satirically to human society, so that his leaf beginning "I think I could turn and live with the animals" remains a lyric complaint *about* human society, and only ostensibly about animals. But poem animals, like the Lion above, are something more contemporary, and something much different. They are entities without any specifiably inherited significances:

> Bull or world that doesn't,
> that doesn't bellow. Silence.
> This hour's so huge. A horn or a sumptuous sky;
> black bull that endures the stroking, the silk, the hand.

Beyond all the clichés about the bull, there is the bull Vicente Aleixandre includes here, an animal of possibilities which makes the hour "huge" rather than banishes time. It exists before it means, or can mean, anything. That *fact*, the mute bull, is the subject of the poem. In some ways, that fact *is* the poem.

Ted Hughes suggests this even more clearly. For him, poems "have their own life, like animals, by which I mean that they seem quite separate from any person, even from their author, and noth-

ing can be added to them or taken away without maiming . . .
killing them." Hughes is fascinated by the indifference of the animals he chooses, and by their power, which is like the poet's.

THRUSHES

Terrifying are the attent sleek thrushes on the lawn,
More coiled steel than living—a poised
Dark deadly eye, those delicate legs
Twiggered to stirrings beyond sense—with a start, a bounce, a
    stab
Overtake the instant and drag out some writhing thing.
No indolent procrastinations and no yawning stares,
No sighs or head-scratchings. Nothing but bounce and stab
And a ravening second.

Is it their single-mind-sized skulls, or a trained
Body, or genius, or a nestful of brats
Gives their days this bullet and automatic
Purpose? Mozart's brain had it, and the shark's mouth
That hungers down the blood-smell even to a leak of its own
Side and devouring of itself: efficiency which
Strikes too streamlined for any doubt to pluck at it
Or obstruction deflect.

With a man it is otherwise. Heroisms on horseback,
Outstripping his desk-diary at a broad desk,
Carving at a tiny ivory ornament
For years: his act worships itself—while for him,
Though he bends to be blent in the prayer, how loud and above
    what
Furious spaces of fire do the distracting devils
Orgy and hosannah, under what wilderness
Of black silent waters weep.

Hughes praises the "efficiency" and even the "genius" of the
birds' instincts and contrasts this, in the poem, to the doubtings
and "head-scratchings" of ordinary humans. And yet this instinct
is related to art and sometimes manifested in it: "Mozart's brain
had it." This may be the only poem in any language in which
Mozart shares something with the self-devouring shark, and in
which neither composer nor shark is afflicted with anything as
naive as ethics. Both are totemic and equated, really, with the
inhuman, the *other* which Hughes envies, and in whose presence
Hughes is terrified. The only general solace offered to "a man" in

the poem is that "his act worships itself." And the acts, carving, writing, or the contextually moral "heroisms on horseback," are only a dismaying mimicry of both instinct and heaven's or hell's "Furious spaces of fire." The only way in which Hughes can come close to the innocence, indifference and terrible perfection of his bestiary is by a persona, by disguising himself as an animal, and finding himself and his landscape shamanistically.

*

Increasingly, it becomes evident to me that poets are not fascinated by what is, in animals, like humans. And certainly no modern poet would be found sentimentally detailing such phenomena. No. Poets thirst after what is pure and other and inhuman in the animal, in the poem animal, anyway. D. H. Lawrence's snake, for example, retreating from its drink of water at Lawrence's trough is "thankless." The eyes of Elizabeth Bishop's fish in her famous poem "shifted a little, but not/ to return my stare." And Cesare Pavese, in "Atavism," writes of an inertly self-conscious adolescent who gazes after a horse trotting by and admires, of all things, its nakedness: "It seemed forever—/ the horse moving naked and shameless in the sun/ right down the middle of the street." These animals are thankless, or shameless, or unaware, and they are praised for that. But this is very different from the ultimately ironic envy of Keats: "O for a life of Sensations over Thoughts!" Rather, in each example, the poet makes enviable that animal which is not him or not her. The animal stands for, if anything, its poem. Of course these are poems *about* animals as well, but somehow each animal is translated into something neither adequately a symbol, nor, any longer, an undisturbed animal. Each beast, in fact, seems a criticism of what Hughes called the "general lifelessness" which surrounds all poems.

It is no wonder that such animals are often a source of fear; they may be too "alive." Robert Lowell's skunks, at the close of his famous poem, seem to represent a pure and disinterested instinct, which is incapable, unlike Lowell, of fear. And the bees in many of Sylvia Plath's poems are animals that inhabit an impermeable, somehow distant world. Otherness is what Plath avidly pursued, and she could, in some of her later moments of writing, feel that she could pick up her genius as if it were an instrument of some kind—as if it, too, were other, and in a late poem she could call words "indefatigable hooftaps."

*

But what happens if a poet should attain a kind of oneness with his animal, become it, however briefly, in a poem? This is what goes on in Galway Kinnell's poem, "The Bear." Strangely, the poet at the end of this poem is impoverished by his own revelation: "what, anyway,/ was that sticky infusion, that rank odor of blood, that poetry, by which I lived?" As the poet Marcia Southwick has noted, if the animal means poetry, then by killing it the poet has effectually ended his poem, or the life of his poem. And she is right: it is all past tense; the poet's ability coincides and evaporates with his vision because he invades the animal. The experience, repetitive and regressive, which Kinnell dreams inside the bear offers the poet a spiritual access which is both liberating and appalling. What the poet learns is that the body of the bear is the body of the poem, of "poetry." Everything is made of words after all, and asleep, beyond anyone's will, words dream, as Gaston Bachelard says they do, just as intensely as the hunter in this fabulous poem. By restoring and broadening the senses this poetry does accomplish one thing—it ignores and bypasses, like the praised and envied animals of Hughes, what Kinnell would call the "closed ego of modern man." The poet in "The Bear" is really hunting a larger, buried self, a mute self. Therefore, when the poet and hunter journeys this outrageously, when he pursues the poem, the animal, this ruthlessly, it is as if the "unconscious"—accustomed to being lured out quietly and obliquely in poems, or present as personae, is suddenly and simply there: body alone inside a bear's body, both gestative and dead.

VI. The Moment of Writing

But can a poet take on, if not the body of his or her animal, then at least its spirit? Can a poet imitate in mind the grace of an animal's body? James Dickey desires this:

> It seems to me that most animals have this superb economy of motion. The instinctual notion of how much energy to expend, the ability to do a thing thoughtlessly and do it right, is a quality I esteem enormously. I want to get a feeling of instinctualness into my poetry. How to do this linguistically is a difficult thing. That it can or should be done might be an illusion. But it fascinates me to try.

A "feeling of instinctualness" must be close to the kind of thing Hughes admires. And I remember Philip Levine once saying that a poem began, for him, with an almost "visceral" sensation, as if the poem, in its otherness, or what Levine called "the animals I am not," originated at once in body and mind and wanted to reject neither.

To acquire the "instinctual" in the qualified sense of its usefulness above is also, I believe, to perform at least one ancient and liberating act: it is to go beyond whatever shallowness inheres in the daily ego, to concentrate upon something wholly other, and to contemplate it—the Muse taking the shape, momentarily, of deer, mole, spider, whale, or fish. As the poet attends to these shapes, he or she goes, as Gary Snyder says, "beyond society." For some time now I have been puzzled by another notion of Snyder's in *Earth House Hold*: "Outwardly, the equivalent of the unconscious is wilderness: both these terms meet, one step further on, as *one*." I suppose, therefore, that the real wilderness is, like the unconscious, what is unknown; and it is also, increasingly, what is meant by the term "nature." Traditionally "wilderness" has had connotations of the unlimited, the unmastered, an inexhaustible source—and even now it remains the favored preserve of what, in nature, may be wholly *other*. So a poet, no matter what his or her subject may be, and no matter what the landscape, goes "beyond society." And so this is what happens at the moment of writing: the wave takes the shape of the fire. What is "out there" moves inside. The poet becomes threshold.

VII. Gazing Within

To write poems that come back out again, into society, to write poems that matter to me, I must become, paradoxically at the moment of writing, as other as a poet as any animal is in a poem. Then true craft, which is largely the ear's training, can occur. Before this, my ear can hear nothing—or it plays back whatever rag of a tune it caught that day since its true desire and purpose is to thwart the world and hear nonsense, which it will do in the end. Unless this absorption into the other occurs, I am condemned to be immured within the daily ego, the ego that lives in the suburbs.

This was my problem when I began a long poem, "Linnets," in 1973. Basically, I had nothing to say—so I had to find a way to say that with finality, with a stare, with style. At least, this is what I thought, anyway. So I chose the least likely incident possible for a poem: my brother shooting a small bird with a shotgun in his adolescence, in my childhood. I thought that by choosing such a subject I would learn how to write about nothing at all, which seemed to be my lot. But then, as I mentioned earlier, I become exceedingly self-conscious when I am not writing. It is this that prevented me from seeing what I could write about, what subjects there really were, and how I could be moved by them, feel them. The more I thought about the absurd subject of my poem, the more possibilities it began to offer. To begin with, there was the bird itself, and the *story*. The more I thought about it, the more I forgot myself, the more I became immersed in the other. Luckily, I had problems right away, problems of form. I had to tell a story and establish it as a frame and do this quickly: it all took some thinking which may have saved me, suddenly, from myself. (Coleridge, in a journal entry on the boat to Malta, notes some sailors teasing a bird on deck, a pelican, and scolds them in his handwriting. Then he remarks that it's not their fault: it's lack of thought that leads to lack of feeling. *Not* the other way around.) After deliberating, I fashioned the story into prose, where it belonged as a narrative, and cast it as a parable of sorts, or fable. But a fable with no values. Any ready-made significance would have made my poem pretentious, and silly. I quote below the second section of the poem, the fable of some kind of wild justice done to my brother.

> But in the high court of linnets he does not get off so easily. He is judged and sentenced to pull me on a rough cart through town. He is further punished since each feather of the dead bird falls around me, not him, and each falls as a separate linnet, and each feather lost from one of these becomes a linnet. While he is condemned to feel nothing ever settle on his shoulders, which are hunched over and still, linnets gather around me. In their singing, they cleanse my ears of all language but that of linnets. My gaze takes on the terrible gaze of song birds. And I find that I too am condemned, and must stitch together, out of glue, loose feathers, droppings, weeds and garbage I find along the street, the original linnet, or, if I fail, be condemned to be pulled in a cart by my brother forever. We are tired of each other, tired of being brothers like this. The backside of his head, close cropped, is what I notice when I look up from work. To fashion the eyes, the gaze, the tongue and trance of a linnet is impossible. The eyelids are impossibly delicate and thin. I am dragged through the striped zoo of the town. One day I throw down the first stillborn linnet, then another, then more. Then one of them begins singing.

One major lesson I had to learn was to become empty and dumb and trusting enough to write every day. For this I needed, at

times, blind patience, not theories about art. I worked more or
less steadily on the poem from March of 1973 to June of that year.
I was, throughout, relatively untroubled about what the poem
might mean to anyone, or what it should mean. One thing led to
another, bird to bestiary:

4.

Whales dry up on beaches by themselves.
The large bones in their heads, their silence,
is a way of turning inward.

Elephants die in exile.
Their tusks begin curling, begin growing
into their skulls.

My father once stopped a stray dog
with a 12 gauge, a blast in the spine.
But you see them on the roads, trotting through rain.

Cattle are slaughtered routinely.
But pigs are intelligent and vicious to the end.
Their squeals burn circles.

Mice are running over the freezing snow.
Wolverines will destroy kitchens for pleasure.
Wolverines are so terrible you must give in.

The waist of a weasel is also lovely. It slips away.

The skies under the turtle's shell are birdless.

Certainly, the poem meant nothing very clear to me: it only satis-
fied me, and in many ways I stopped caring about what it meant at
all. I only tried, as Forster said, to "connect. Only connect." It felt
better to connect than to know anything in advance, and besides,
what did I care if it made sense? The only friend I showed the
poem to in rough stages, David St. John, was too kind to do much
but praise it. What I wanted was to write it; to feel myself become
suddenly steeper and more daring every day I worked on it. I say
"steeper" because that was how I felt or how it felt. I confess I
don't remember much of those moments of writing the poem—
which is to say I don't remember much of those months, or the
days of those months. I remember my desk, how the light would
fall on it, the colors in the room. It seemed to me that I could feel

the almost palpable solitudes inside the grain of wood in the desk,
or inside the ink in the fountain pen. Aside from that I was anyone
forgetting himself inside a task: the only other thing I tried to do
in the poem concerned craft. I tried to break a rule in each section—do something I'd never done before. And that was enormously pleasant. I'd begun to love going to this poem each day, as
a child loves going to a secret place, inhabited by a secret love,
speaking to that intimate No One. And after all, isn't the her-
mitage of the poem like that place? The words appear: the wave
takes the shape of the fire: the trees turn green again for some reason. When I remember writing "Linnets" I see myself staring out
at those trees, late at night, when they are illumined by street-
lamps. I watch myself bend to the poem again. I am at peace.

10. At the High Meadow

In March the arthritic horses
stand in the same place
all day.
A piebald mare flicks her ears back.

Ants have already taken over
the eyes of the house finch
on the sill.

So you think someone
is coming,
someone already passing the burned mill,
someone with news of a city
built on snow.

But over the bare table
in the morning
a glass of water goes blind
from staring upward.

For you
it's not so easy.
You begin the long witnessing:
Table. Glass of water. Lone crow
circling.

You witness the rain for weeks
and there are only the two of you.
You divide yourself in two and witness yourself,
and it makes no difference.

> You think of God dying of anthrax
> in a little shed, of a matinee
> in which three people sit
> with their hands folded and a fourth
> coughs. You come down the mountain.

Gazing within, and trying to assess what all this represents, I find I've been speaking, all along, about nature, about the attempt of the imagination to inhabit nature and by that act preserve itself for as long as it possibly can against "the pressure of reality." And by "nature" I mean any wilderness, inner or outer. The moment of writing is not an escape, however; it is only an insistence, through the imagination, upon human ecstasy, and a reminder that such ecstasy remains as much a birthright in this world as misery remains a condition of it.

(1978)

David Young

THE BITE OF
THE MUSKRAT:
Judging Contemporary Poetry

It is never easy to make sound judgments about the art of one's own era. The typical sources of difficulty are well known. When we add to them the variety and energy of contemporary American poetry, the problem is greatly compounded. How do we sort out good from bad, phony from authentic, original from derivative?

Why not leave it to the work of time? That is, of course, one solution. A hundred years, even fifty, will show us which poems and poets were best. And the impulse to turn away from judgment is surely connected with the laudable fact that American poetry has taught itself to accept wider horizons. It has shaken off the schizophrenia of the Fifties *(either* Wilbur *or* Ginsberg), and opened itself to many new and invigorating influences, putting Auden to one side and ending his temporary domination. One result has been an air of generosity and community among poets in the last decade that does them credit.

But the healthy variety I spoke of is best served in its own time by sound judgment and sensible standards. The new tolerance needs a counterbalancing force, and we cannot expect the poets to provide it. They have agreed, in effect, to disagree. Each is bound to believe in his or her own work, preferring it to that of others and fashioning friendships and allegiances accordingly. That is to be expected. It is the editors and critics who ought to counteract the circles of friendship and promotion formed by workshops, common influences, and mutual admiration. Yet to glance through most magazines and anthologies, or to search for sound criticism, is to realize that editorial discrimination scarcely exists, and that what little criticism there is is marked by ineptitude and irresponsibility. The magazines either resort to backscratching and bias, or, when they aspire to some catholicity, combine prestige with unreadability because their editorial policies lack real conviction, consisting merely of old-fashioned tastes which try to coexist uneasily with a feeble response to "trends."

The situation is curiously similar with criticism. At one extreme are the poets, hustling their friends or indulging themselves in commentary that is stimulating but so opinionated or eccentric as to be sharply limited in value. At the other are the few professional critics who deal with contemporary poetry and who undertake discussions that are generally plodding, banal, and out of touch with the life of the language and possibilities of the imagination. It is a paradox worth pondering that America contains more people who have devoted their lives to studying, teaching, and writing about literature than any other era one can think of; at the same time probably no era has been so lacking in sensible and discriminating criticism of its own literature. Part of the blame must lie in the area of education, where teachers of literature—especially in the graduate schools—devote their lives to literature only as a phenomenon of the past. They are afraid to engage their minds and imaginations with it as a living entity, and they tend to constrain their students to the same lifeless patterns.

My purpose here is not to write a jeremiad on education or literary editing, however. Nor can I claim, having briefly diagnosed an illness, to undertake an instant cure. I do think, though, that an effort to try to describe, clearly and carefully and a little bit at a time, the basis of excellence in contemporary poetry, is worthwhile.

I propose to begin that task here by juxtaposing two poems, one by William Stafford and one by James Dickey. One may well be a source for the other; Dickey quoted the Stafford poem admiringly in a review at one time, and later, it seems safe to venture, was inspired by it in a poem of his own. But the point here is not to indulge in source-hunting or to suggest that the relation of one poem to the other by influence is an adequate basis for judgment. It is too easy, as Roethke's fine essay "How to Write Like Somebody Else," points out, to dismiss something as derivative. Indeed, the term needs careful definition. In this case, I am going to assume that it makes no difference which poem came first or whether there is any question of borrowing. My interest in bringing the two poems together lies in their different treatments of similar subjects, and in the fact that one poem can be identified as good and the other as inadequate by means of study and discussion that have no reference to other poems, personalities, or questions of literary reputation. If this is true, then the problem of identifying excellence is not so severe as it might seem, for my approach suggests that careful reading, along with a trust in one's own responses and an honesty about those responses are reliable, if not infallible, guides to making sound judgments about contemporary poetry.

Here are the poems:

CEREMONY

On the third finger of my left hand
under the bank of the Ninnescah
a muskrat whirled and bit to the bone.
The mangled hand made the water red.

That was something the ocean would remember:
I saw me in the current, flowing through the land,
rolling, touching roots, the world incarnadined,
and the river richer by a kind of marriage.

While in the woods an owl started quavering
with drops like tears I raised my arm.
Under the bank a muskrat was trembling
with meaning my hand would wear forever.

In that river my blood flowed on.

> William Stafford, *West of Your City* (1960)

THE POISONED MAN

When the rattlesnake bit, I lay
In a dream of the country, and dreamed
Day after day of the river,

Where I sat with a jackknife and quickly
Opened my sole to the water.
Blood shed for the sake of one's life

Takes on the hid shape of the channel,
Disappearing under logs and through boulders.
The freezing river poured on

And, as it took hold of my blood,
Leapt up round the rocks and boiled over.
I felt that my heart's blood could flow

Unendingly out of the mountain,
Splitting bedrock apart upon redness,
And the current of life at my instep

Give deathlessly as a spring.
Some leaves fell from trees and whirled under.
I saw my struck bloodstream assume,

Inside the cold path of the river,
The inmost routes of a serpent
Through grass, through branches and leaves.

When I rose, the live oaks were ashen
And the wild grass was dead without flame.
Through the blasted cornfield I hobbled,

My foot tied up in my shirt,
And met my old wife in the garden,
Where she reached for a withering apple.

I lay in the country and dreamed
Of the substance and course of the river
While the different colors of fever

Like quilt patches flickered upon me.
At last I arose, with the poison
Gone out of the seam of the scar,

And brought my wife eastward and weeping,
Through the copper fields springing alive
With the promise of harvest for no one.

James Dickey, *Helmets* (1964)

Even typing the two poems, as I drafted this essay, showed me a difference. The Stafford poem was a pleasure to put on paper because of the sense of rightness and balance that pervades it; its length is perfect because it says what it has to say and clears out. The Dickey poem, on the other hand, seemed to drag on; I kept glancing ahead to see how far I had to go. I think the secret truth about poems like "The Poisoned Man" is that we accord them respect when we run across them in places like *The New Yorker* (where it first appeared) while we cannot in fact accord them interest or admiration. Maybe if magazine editors and anthologists had to type or set for the printer the poems they sometimes select by happy skimming or by automatic response to reputation, we could begin to move toward a higher standard.

Anyone who teaches poetry might like to undertake the experiment of asking a class to discuss and evaluate these poems. From such a discussion would emerge, I predict, the valuable lesson (not often found in textbooks of New Critical, or any other, persuasion) that the presence of characteristic literary devices—symbolism, mythic references, use of a persona—is no guarantee that literature has been achieved: on the contrary, in Dickey's

poem the heavy use of such devices (the garden and apple allu-
sions, the too-familiar wasteland pattern) becomes rhetorical in
the bad sense, signalling the absence of the kind of authentic
grounding in experience and consciousness the shorter poem has.
One has to tread carefully here; students might leap to the easy
conclusion that because they are inclined to believe that Stafford
really was bitten by a muskrat (despite the strategic choice of finger) and to doubt seriously whether Dickey's poisoned man and
rattlesnake have any existence outside their poem, excellence has
somehow to do with realism versus fantasy. But it's scarcely that
simple. Indeed, it's just possible that Dickey was bitten and did-
n't know how to treat the experience except by a lot of "literary"
falsification, while Stafford, unscathed, had the skill and imagination to make a fiction plausible. Similarly, we cannot say that
one poem succeeds because the poet seems to speak directly, in
his own voice and from his own experience, while the other fails
by erecting a persona, the poisoned man, to tell us the story. It is
rather a question of authenticity of voice; the voice in Stafford's
poem, whether his own or an invention for the needs of the poem,
is believable and natural, while the voice in Dickey's poem
seems forced, speaking not out of urgency or insight but in
response to demands of the author for a certain "poetic"
ambiance and sequence. Students who thought from these examples that a persona tended to falsify a poem as a general rule,
could be disabused by studying a poem that used persona successfully—one of Jarrell's or Roethke's—in conjunction with
one of those "confessional" poems in which the poet succeeds
only in convincing us that his or her life is capable of boring us to
tears.

The mention of confessional poetry points toward another
crucial difference between these poems: the humility from which
the Stafford poem springs as opposed to the essential egomania of
the Dickey poem. It's interesting, I think, that the speaker in the
Stafford poem is wry about his effect on his environment as he
bleeds into the river. "The world incarnadined" and the responsive calling of the owl show us how easily the personal converts
to the universal, but we sense the speaker's awareness that this is
illusory. In fact, the "kind of marriage" in the sharing of meaning
between hand, muskrat, and river moves away from the distinctly
personal. The "my" at the end of the poem has lost its possessive
ring, and the final image glimpses that loss of self associated with
visionary experience and with much great poetry. The movement
of "The Poisoned Man" is quite the opposite. The speaker's
"dream" becomes the reality of the poem, allowing him to see his

experience as crucial to, and more important than, the world it is part of; his universe is homocentric, his poisoning is the poisoning of everything, he is Adam and the wounded fisher-king of the wasteland. Dickey does hedge at times. Picking up, perhaps, on Stafford's "I saw me in the current," his speaker "dreams," only "feels" that his heart's blood has great power, and is generally feverish. But there seems to be little irony at work in the poem. We are asked to take the enormity of the man's interaction with his environment seriously, and the ending is grandiose and apocalyptically downbeat. It is partly a question of tone: Stafford's is complex but controlled, while Dickey's skids around yet is relatively single-minded.

One might go on to further speculation about the two poets from this difference. Stafford's poems are characteristically self-effacing, and to good effect again and again, while Dickey pursues what we might call the poetry of the swollen ego pretty relentlessly. What interests me about this particular difference between the poems, however, is not what it may illustrate about the poets, but its possibility as a way of discriminating among all sorts of poems, and perhaps as an indication of the fundamental weakness of what is called "confessional" poetry. Let me suggest that there are two basic directions in which the current of a poem may flow: toward the ego and its concerns, or away from the individual self and toward the existence of things beyond it, be they other people, animals, plants, stones or water. In the first case the ego ingests and incorporates the world, colonizing, as it were, rattlesnakes and rivers; the world becomes the self. In the second, the opposite happens; the outward flow, the "negative capability" that obliterates self-concern, allows the self to become the world. It's easy to see how the two experiences can appear to be identical: world equals self on the one hand, self equals world on the other. Isn't that saying the same thing? But the difference is surely crucial. One kind of poem is selfish, receding into a childish and fearful ignorance. The other is selfless, moving toward maturity, acceptance, understanding. If this difference is valid, then it helps to explain the unease one feels with poetry in which the concerns and demands of the self are exalted, even idealized. It looks like poetry, but it is an inversion, even a parody, of the real thing. The difference is greatly apparent between poets like Anne Sexton and Gary Snyder. Evidently, it is also present, in a subtler form, between poets like Stafford and Dickey. I invite the reader to test it on other examples.

In addition to these fundamental differences, a discussion of "Ceremony" and "The Poisoned Man" could explore a number of details. The two poems provide an object lesson in meter versus true rhythm. Dickey characteristically relies on his rocking-horse anapests, occasionally lapsing into prose, as in the sixth line, where "blood" and "shed" deserve equal emphasis but where our ears, constrained by the first five lines, give "blood" short shrift in order to be able to continue at the gallop. The eighth line carries a similar stumble. The Stafford poem ties itself to no "system" except an average of four stresses to the line, but its range includes the deliberate flatness of the fourth line, where "mangled hand" and "water red" have a slowing and numbing quality, the easy colloquial movement of the fifth, where Stafford characteristically converts cliché to his own superb use, and the graceful symmetry of the eighth, where the alliteration points up the balance.

Then too, there is the question of diction. Dickey's seems to me to suffer from a kind of verbal hypertension. This tactic consists of introducing plenty of strong verbs, whether they belong or not, plus adjectives and adverbs, often verb-derived, to whip up a spurious sense of energy and stretched perspectives. Thus, when the blood hits the "freezing" river in "The Poisoned Man" it *leaps* up and *boils* over, while the speaker feels that his blood could "flow// Unendingly" and "deathlessly," splitting bedrock in the process. It is all very dramatic, and Stafford's quiet "made the water red" and "flowing . . . rolling . . . touching roots" may seem tame by comparison. But each word in "Ceremony" is judiciously chosen and subtly deployed, in a way that will bear scrutiny far more effectively than the diction of "The Poisoned Man."

A comparative study of form in the two poems offers another instructive contrast. Both the lines and the quatrains in "Ceremony" are genuine units, dividing the experience of the poem into meaningful segments of insight, reinforcing the movement of meaning from chance accident to the sense of ceremony that is somehow concentrated in the final, isolated line. Dickey's triplets, on the other hand, while they provide a look of order and control, seem, especially by comparison to Stafford's, perfunctory and even arbitrary.

The value of the class discussion I have imagined might well be the teacher's as much as anyone's. For Dickey's poem is precisely the sort that takes teachers in. They realize that they can "teach" it by pointing out its "devices," which frees them from the task of evaluating it. They have learned to identify literature by plugging in certain categories. Cut loose from certifiable classics, they tend to lack real discrimination. Students are often wiser in these matters—having fewer preconceptions—than their teachers.

They'll be quick to sense, I predict, that Dickey's poem is pretentious, manufactured, and lacking in interest. If asked to consider it next to the Stafford poem, having something fresh and genuinely resonant to compare with, they'll arrive at a sound judgment with ease and rapidity.

Is there a principle or two to be derived from this double example? Some readers will think I am writing to pillory Dickey and praise Stafford, but that is not the case. Dickey has written better poems than "The Poisoned Man," Stafford has fallen short of "Ceremony." It may be true that the examples I have chosen show some of Dickey's characteristic weaknesses and highlight Stafford's strengths, but that line of investigation would require a much more detailed discussion of both poets. My purpose has been to use these examples to look for some kind of rule or standard, derived from their juxtaposition and the lesson of the clear difference between their levels of achievement, that a reader might take along to other poets and quite different poems.

Perhaps it is simply the lesson that Poetry is not poetry. Put it another way: a poem may be loaded with techniques and conventions we have been taught to think of respectfully as belonging with great poems, and all for nothing. If the result is boring, we ought to be willing to say so. I am not talking about snap judgments. If we find our minds wandering, our glance drawn to the window as we read, we ought to ask why. The answer may be that we have hold of a poet whose world is not easy to enter or comprehend—a Stevens, a Montale, a Pound—and who will reward patience. But it may also be that we know quite well what the poet is doing and we are not truly involved or interested. He or she is going through the motions, and so are we. I used to be upset with myself when I could not get interested in contemporary poems I had seen vigorously praised, or volumes that had won large national awards. Not any more. Boring is boring. Pretentious is pretentious. A reader can perform the test of time by means of patience, honesty, and discrimination.

Put it yet another way: good poetry just can't be manufactured. My feeling about Stafford's poem is that its best moments surprised him, while I also feel sure that Dickey had the *idea* for his poem and wrote it out accordingly, mixing in myth and meter as if writing a poem were like following a recipe. Whether my sense of the matter exactly corresponds to the creative process in both cases doesn't really matter; it's the fact that the poems manage to convey those separate impressions that makes one succeed and the other fail. And the failure of Dickey's is especially ironic in light of its pretense to the visionary. Epigrams and satires and propaganda poems may perhaps be written to order, but there is just no way, American know-how and technological confidence notwithstanding, to manufacture the visionary. "The Poisoned Man," with its bloated cargo of visionary apparatus, sinks down to depths that illumination can never penetrate; "Ceremony," lightweight and unassuming, soars up into daylight. It has the kind of vision and perspective we hope for from poetry and seldom get.

I offer, then, four precepts. 1. The reader's *experience* of the poem, the degree of interest and the depth of involvement, is still the best guide to the identification of true excellence. 2. A good poem is not a bundle of devices that add up to literature, but an unerring trajectory into insight, where excellence has no inherent relation to length, use of "technique," complexity of situation, or literary reputation. 3. The creative process can't be an assembly line, especially where the lyric and the visionary are involved; a good poem transcends its author's intention and understanding, while a bad poem is under its overconfident author's control, alas, at every point. 4. Poetry which indulges the self in its greed and obsessiveness is inimical to the true spirit of poetry, which seeks self-transcendence.

These notions are so simple that I would be embarrassed to present them if I did not see them violated daily by publishers, editors, critics, and teachers. I know too that some readers will wish I had chosen a less obvious example, as for example, two poems by the same poet. That, I would agree, ought to be the next step, and it would perhaps prove to be a more crucial one. But let those who think the Stafford-Dickey example too basic or obvious glance through the leading magazines that feature poetry or inspect one of the familiar anthologies; or let them talk to the average college English teacher.

Literary theorists may shake their heads too, at the vagueness of my precepts, their failure to cover every case, their risky suppositions about inspiration. Of course they are inadequate. But let this demonstration of a few basic principles be a beginning, a first exploration. I will abandon my formulations in favor of rules enunciated by the theorists when I know those theorists can deal adequately with the task of discriminating successfully among contemporary poems. As for my readers, they will have to determine whether my pronouncements, extrapolated and used in practice, have any validity. If they help at all to distinguish between the bite of the muskrat and the bite of the rattlesnake, I'll be pleased.

(1972)

Alberta Turner

NOT YOUR FLAT TIRE, MY FLAT TIRE:

Transcending the Self in Contemporary Poetry

"Look in thy heart and write," said Sir Philip Sidney, and today's poets would add, "There is no other place to look and no one else to write about and no one else to listen." Locked in the fiction of time and space, the poet knows that the *I* he puts on paper is only his *eye*, that the self he reveals in any sentence that begins with *I* is as whole as and no more whole than, as true as and no more true than, the deliberately fictional *I*'s of Shakespeare's Hamlet or Milton's Satan or Joyce's Molly Bloom, that the self is part of the world the self looks at, and that any representation of it by itself is bound to be shaped or distorted by its own refractional peculiarities. Yet knowing this, and knowing that nothing a poet can say about himself can be equally or identically true for any other self, the poets of the sixties and seventies continue to delve in increasingly intimate detail into their own lives in order to communicate with selves which do not and never will know them as neighbors or care about their hospital bills, their children's colds, or that flat tire on the lonely road just beyond Bellows Falls, Vermont

The reason is not, I believe, that contemporary poets are talking merely to themselves and don't care if the reader overhears. Nor do I think they merely "confess" themselves in the spirit of the gossip column, assuming that because one is a poet (like a movie star or a president) every reader is interested in the smell of one's dirty socks. The poets, I believe, are working on the same assumption that has always underlain both the making of fictional characters and the telling of autobiography—that the universally common experiences created by human psychology, physiology, and history insure that any cluster of specific, concrete details of any single human being's experience *can be made* to evoke similar responses from all human beings. I stress the words *can be made* because though the tape-recording of a poet's whole life would include all these common experiences and reactions to experience, no group of persons merely hearing it would be able to perceive and evaluate all its data by merely hearing it, or, if they could, would perceive and evaluate it the same way. The poet selects and points to its patterns so that they will be noticed. If he is not skillful, his selection and pointing may garble the patterns by conflicting, oversimplifying, twisting, or merely not making the necessary connections, thus distorting one self's perception even of its own perceptions so that other selves cannot recognize mutual perceptions in it. It is this problem of presenting the data of one unique self so that other unique selves will recognize it as their own that poses the chief artistic challenge to contemporary poets who probe their own selves for the sake of transcending the individual in order to reveal the universal self.

Older writers and literatures handled the problem by such devices as myth, allegory, personification of inanimate objects, the voice of divine inspiration, persona, narrator, and of course most often, by direct author-to-reader exposition of the universal meaning of the author's experience. All of these devices select out of the poet's experience a specific part which he wants to share with the reader in a particular way, and they effectively prevent the reader from finding and putting together material which the poet thinks is none of his business. Contemporary poets still use these devices, and with equal success (Eliot's Prufrock persona, Berryman's Henry and Mr. Bones, Merwin's mythical seeker who carries the egg of genius, Wilbur's dialogue, "The Aspen and the Stream").

But what of the poet who has given us what seems to be a random catalog from his desk top, a literal tape-recording from his breakfast quarrel with his wife, or his last medical report? He uses first person; he often omits or disguises all categories of metaphor; and he is careful to avoid overt interpretation. By omitting conventional clues as to what universals he perceives in the experience, he hopes the reader will perceive these for himself; but in so doing he runs the risk of interesting his reader only as any bit of gossip about a total stranger would interest him. He runs the risk of hearing those words most unpleasing to a poet's ear: "So what?"

I should like to illustrate what I mean by this risk by briefly analysing several contemporary poems which take the risk, but succeed in transcending individual eccentricity to create a universal experience, and several which take the risk, yet fail.

Gary Snyder's "By the Tama River at the North End of the Plain in April"[1] takes that risk:

> Round smooth stones
>   up here in the weeds
>   the air a grey wet,

Across the Tama river
 a screen drum turns sorting gravel:
   dumping loads in
 dump trucks one by one.

Deep in the hills
   the water might be clean

Grilling raw squid over smoky twigs
 a round screen perched on broken bricks

Masa bending on the rocks
Staring close to the water,
Nanao and Nagasawa
 with their lifted cups of shochu,

Friends and poets
Eating, drinking in the rain,
 and these round river stones.

The poem is a literal and quick sketch of a picnic, yet a picnic that could not be duplicated anywhere: the combination of Masa, Nanao, and Nagasawa, the Tama river, rain, grilling squid, sorting gravel, Masa bending over the water, and the round stones. Yet even this unique picnic could have been described by dozens of other details equally unique. What makes it into a universal other than itself is the position of the round, smooth stones in the sequence. Roundness, smoothness, and stoneness suggest a sort of geological perfection achievable only by greater-than-human effort and greater-than-human time. Rain, river, hills do the necessary work for this kind of perfection. The human efforts seem inconsequential in comparison: sorting of truckloads of gravel, grilling bits of food over smoky twigs, broken bricks. But there is a connection made between the two: the friends and poets are gathered in the rain, on the smooth stones; one looks into the water, one reflects on the surface of the water, all perform the one essential act for life—eating and drinking. They are like the round, smooth stones in that they too are acting their part in the geological process. That process is not bleak but good, comforting as well as inevitable. A picnic has been turned into a perception of natural process by means of selection and sequence of the details of unique personal experience. Strategically, the round, smooth stones have been put in the first and last lines.

  Denise Levertov uses the same method with equal success in "The Curve:"[2]

Along the tracks
counting
always the right foot awarded
                the tie to step on
the left stumbling all the time in cinders

towards where
            an old caboose
samples of paint were once tried out on
is weathering in a saltmarsh
                to tints Giotto dreamed.

'Shall we
ever reach it?' 'Look—
the tracks take a curve.
We may
            come round to it
if we keep going.'

The incident, again, is unique to the poet and is described literally: the track, the feet limping on the ties, the old caboose as the conscious goal, the apparent indirection of the curve which "may/ come round to it/ if we keep going." The last stanza, reinforced by the title, makes this particular curve of track into universal dependence on faith, hope, persistence, and reason, to achieve desired ends by means not immediately perceived as fruitful. A poem like this could conceivably happen by accident or without the poet's knowing it, but the severe editing of random details which is necessary to curve this curve to its particular conclusion is quite evident here. If the poet had instead asked, "I wonder if this curve doesn't bring us out at that old caboose that someone tried samples of paint on," we should lose the quality of faith and hope and persistence necessary to quest. If the caboose were mentioned as something the railroad stored tools in, we should lose the implication of aesthetic search.

In a considerably more complex poem Robert Lowell uses the same method of selection and sequence to make an unsatisfactory short vacation in a Maine fishing village into an expression of the universal and multiple frustrations found in one kind of human relationship:

WATER

It was a Maine lobster town—
each morning boatloads of hands

pushed off for granite
quarries on the islands,

and left dozens of bleak
white frame houses stuck
like oyster shells
on a hill of rock,

and below us, the sea lapped
the raw little match-stick
mazes of a weir,
where the fish for bait were trapped.

Remember? We sat on a slab of rock.
From this distance in time,
it seems the color
of iris, rotting and turning purpler,

but it was only
the usual gray rock
turning the usual green
when drenched by the sea.

The sea drenched the rock
at our feet all day,
and kept tearing away
flake after flake.

One night you dreamed
you were a mermaid clinging to a wharf-pile,
and trying to pull
off the barnacles with your hands.

We wished our two souls
might return like gulls
to the rock. In the end,
the water was too cold for us.[3]

There is nothing in the poem or its title that could not occur in a letter, a conversational anecdote, or a diary. It might at one level be the answer to a casual, make-conversation question like "Where did you go for your vacation and how did you like it?" But the poem is not about a seascape, but about the relationship between two people. Their coldness toward each other has made them see the bleakness in the scene. In stanzas one and two, *boat-loads of hands* pushing off for *granite quarries*, leaving *bleak*

houses, *stuck* like *oyster shells on rock* is the selective seeing of a
self aware of bleakness, rockness, and the frustration of being
stuck, the mechanical impersonality of being not a person but a
hand. Every effort of such people will seem to such a viewer as
self-defeating, feeble: their weirs *matchstick*, their houses *oyster
shells*. The poet's self remembers the rock as the color of *rot*, as
eroding by *flakes* under the impact of the sea. His lover's dream is
a dream of frustrated freedom: the mermaid doesn't tear off the
barnacles, but only tries. The wish to return like gulls, who could
master this element, is understood as an impossible wish. The end
is only another in this series of frustrations. Since persons in a different frame of mind might just as well see the rock as firm, the
weirs as ingenious, the houses as conspicuously well cared for,
and the water as cold enough for cod, the reader must need con-
clude that the selection and sequence of the quite real details
which comprise the poem are calculated to make the *water* of the
title and the last line mean not only a wet saline solution but the
whole frustrating rigor of the relationship. Yet not only of this single relationship. House, rock, water, dreamed impotence, wish to
be another being, the daily vehicle to the daily chore are frustrations we all share: We all have felt constriction and loathed it; we
all have seen things flake, felt cold, and known relationships for
which the words *cold, flake, stick* and, yes, *bleak* are the appropriate metaphorical equivalents. Lowell's self has become *our*selves.

But not even Lowell is always successful in using this
method. In "Symptoms" he uses the same kind of personal experience without making it into anything more:

SYMPTOMS

A dog seems to lap water from the pipes,
a wheeze of dogsmell and dogcompanionship—
life-enhancing water brims my bath—
(the bag of waters or the lake of the grave. . . . ?)
from the palms of my feet to my wet neck—
I have no mother to lift me in her arms.
I feel my old infection, it comes once yearly:
lowered good humor, then an ominous
rise of irritable enthusiasm. . . .
Three dolphins bear our little toilet-stand,
the grin of the eyes rebukes the scowl of the lips,
they are crazy with the thirst. I soak,
examining and then examining
what I really have against myself.[4]

As in "Water," Lowell has described a biographical incident, this time a bath he took in a bathroom whose water pipes gurgled and whose toilet stand was supported by three dolphins molded in the usual way, with their eyes slanted up and mouths drawn down. As in "Water" he has selected and sequenced the details to recreate his mood at the time. It's a mood which progresses from comfort to desolation to a resolve to face and try to explain that desolation sensibly and so overcome it. The gurgle in the water-pipes reminds him of the comforting companionship of a dog; the full tub seems lifegiving, like the amniotic fluid in a womb; then the mood changes in mid-line to the fear of drowning. The uterine bath will not be succeeded by a mother's arms, as at birth. As his emotion veers, his intellect recognizes the onset of his recurrent mental illness. The dolphins embody his own emotional contradiction. They both grin and scowl. They crave and are unsatisfied, as he is. In the midst of all that watery comfort he (like them) is basically thirsty. The reason, he decides, must be that he hates himself, and he lies there in physical comfort, trying to figure out the reasons for his mental distress. All of this must be very interesting to his psychiatrist—he has very accurately recorded the symptoms of his mental illness, but he has not universalized it to include me. In spite of the fact that I too tackle many of my problems while soaking in the bathtub, I feel that Lowell has only succeeded in putting me into his *bathtub*, not into his tortured self. It is not enough to say that he is depressed, to recognize his symptoms and resolve to face them squarely. To universalize the poem he has to make me more than an onlooker, an understander. He has to make gurgle, wetness, dolphins depress me and resolve me to confront and analyse my own fears. I think he could have done that if he had used more descriptive details and less interpretation. If he had said "water brims" instead of "life-enhancing water brims," if he had gone on to describe the bathtub ring or the streaks of rust down the dolphins' faces or a water stain on the floor instead of explaining his recurrent symptoms as "lowered good humor, then an ominous/ rise of irritable enthusiasm," in other words, if he had continued to recreate the experience by means of its concrete details as he did in "Water," we too might begin to understand what anyone in such an illness might really have against himself, because we could recognize similar symptoms and a similar search in ourselves.

Sometimes a poet transcends and universalizes autobiographical details only to discover that he has merely reproduced a cliché. He has failed, not to universalize what he perceived about himself, but failed to perceive deeply enough in the first place. For example, Anne Sexton's "I Remember":[5]

> By the first of August
> the invisible beetles began
> to snore and the grass was
> as tough as hemp and was
> no color—no more than
> the sand was a color and
> we had worn our bare feet
> bare since the twentieth
> of June and there were times
> we forgot to wind up your
> alarm clock and some nights
> we took our gin warm and neat
> from old jelly glasses while
> the sun blew out of sight
> like a red picture hat and
> one day I tied my hair back
> with a ribbon and you said
> that I looked almost like
> a puritan lady and what
> I remember best is that
> the door to your room was
> the door to mine.

In this poem she remembers a typical experience—a good love affair—and recreates its feeling of bliss by recalling its strictly individual details of season, place, and a couple of more quirky oddities, such as gin in jelly glasses and her lover's comment on her hair ribbon. This combination of details is unique to this one experience, yet they are so typical that no reader would have trouble in substituting similar ones from soap opera for the same effect. The last two lines reaffirm and climax the good feeling that the affair has left with the poet and lets the reader share the feeling because the bedroom is a common symbol of privacy, and the larger meaning of *door* as any kind of opening is equally universal. What weakens the poem is that what has been universalized is not the full complexity of such an experience, but only the most familiar part, that most often celebrated in poetry. The poem mentions the bliss of privacy, but does not really explore that privacy and so cannot point to any of the important universal perceptions of privacy which grow from a unique and full experience of it.

A poem which exaggerates and thus clarifies the reason why so much confessional poetry fails to universalize is Ron Padgett's "When I Think More of My Own Future Than Of Myself."[6]

> Coming out of the bathroom
> That one has to go down the stairs one half flight
> Out a door into an elevated courtyard
> Along a little balcony to get to
> I often have the thought
> "How sad it is that I must die"
>
> I do not think this thought proceeds
> From emerging from the bathroom
> Though emerging from the bathroom
> Can change one's thoughts
> —Just as, since my college studies,
> When the thought was made available to me,
> I have never been able to make any sort of really reasonable
>   connection
> Between Love and Death

Granted that this poem may be conscious parody, it is still a very bad poem. This bathroom is absurdly hard to get to. Padgett emphasizes its oddity. His reaction is personally idiosyncratic: most people don't think ruefully of death on emerging from the bathroom. The oddness of the thought suggests to him another bit of experience just as personal and odd: his college studies have made it impossible for him to figure out a logical connection between love and death—this even though college studies would have presumably familiarized him with the stories of Tristan and Isolde, Admetus and Alcestis, and Romeo and Juliet.

If the poem's main purpose is implied by the title, the speaker is saying that trying to explain ourselves to ourselves, especially to project our futures, is a futile and silly act. But to make me feel the futility and silliness of it he would need to develop the actual experience further. He has merely said that emerging from the bathroom gave him the thought. He evoked the thought from the sensations presented to his eyes, skin, and viscera even less than Lowell did, and he gives us no sensations connected with his college studies at all. The result is that he seems to be saying, "What a wonderful, strange, complex being am I!" The reader will not be interested unless as a result of the poem he can say those words about himself too.

My examination of these poems which use the technique of selecting and sequencing literal autobiographical detail for the purpose of universalizing it presents no new insights into the poetic process. Basically poets have always looked into themselves and transformed what they saw into what they hoped was universally true and universally appealing. But the selection of the autobiographical material to *seem* as if it had not been edited, the sequencing of it to *seem* accidental, the hiding of artifice so that the reader feels that he has stumbled on a bit of diary or overheard a bit of conversation or listened in on a mind talking to itself or peered through a borrowed eyesocket without the owner knowing it—this is a technique especially dear to the contemporary poet. If he fails to universalize his unique experience, he says, in effect, "Look how interesting I am." But if he succeeds, the *reader* says, "Look how interesting I am." And the poem which makes a reader say *that* is a poem he'll keep.

(1975)

NOTES

1. *Regarding Wave* (New Directions, 1970), p. 7.
2. *Relearning the Alphabet* (New Directions, 1970), p. 65.
3. *For the Union Dead* (Noonday, 1964), p. 3.
4. *The Dolphin* (Farrar, Straus and Giroux, 1973), p. 18.
5. *All My Pretty Ones* (Houghton Mifflin, 1962), p. 11.
6. *The Young American Poets*, ed. Paul Carroll (Follett, 1968), p. 327.

David Walker

STONE SOUP:

Contemporary Poetry and the Obsessive Image

It seems a central metaphor of our poetry. Even a glance at half a dozen recent volumes yields enough stones to fill a geologist's knapsack. Moreover, the stone in contemporary poetry is characteristic. It is not Sisyphus' boulder or Yeats' stone "in the midst of all" or Williams' rock split by saxifrage. Rather, it appears in contemporary poems in ways like these:

> The soup bubbling on the back of the stove
> The stone staring into the sun
> > Philip Levine, "How Much Can It Hurt"

> The stones are given out
> one to a customer. I keep mine
> separate. With such a companion
> why should I want anyone else?
> > Richard Shelton, "The Mute"

> And so I run
> into the mute acres of stones
> > Larry Levis, "The Long Distance Runner"

> before me stones begin to go out like candles
> guiding me
> > W. S. Merwin, "The Search"

> Bah, say the stones,
> we are old.
> > Danny Rendleman, "One Chair for Chess"

With notable exceptions, when the image of a stone appears in the work of these poets and many others, it generally serves to suggest a fairly narrow range of landscape and associative process. This is probably much more the result of some facet of contemporary consciousness than a question of poetic influence; I should make it clear that I admire the work of these poets and the others I shall discuss. But by examining the pervasiveness of a single image—its characteristic use and misuse—in a few poems, I hope to add something to the discussion of how contemporary poetry can be read and judged more sensitively.

Stones appear again and again in Robert Bly's 1962 book *Silence in the Snowy Fields* and can be closely tied to his insistent attention to what the new American poetry needed to be. His knowledge of the imaginative achievements of the Spanish surrealists, the psychic energies of Blake, and the generosity and openness of Whitman led him to stress a poetry shaped not by technique but by vision, discovered through attention to the subconscious sources of darkness and dream. Such poems leap into imaginative knowledge, transcending the limitations of our rational, daylight selves, and the "corridors to the unconscious" which they open up depend upon the associations they establish between images. Consider Bly's "Poem Against the Rich":

> Each day I live, each day the sea of light
> Rises, I seem to see
> The tear inside the stone
> As if my eyes were gazing beneath the earth.
> The rich man in his red hat
> Cannot hear
> The weeping in the pueblos of the lily,
> Or the dark tears in the shacks of the corn.
> Each day the sea of light rises
> I hear the sad rustle of the darkened armies,
> Where each man weeps, and the plaintive
> Orisons of the stones.
> The stones bow as the saddened armies pass.

The poem's weaknesses can be summarized quickly. Its language is undistinguished; both the slackness it allows itself ("sad rustle," "plaintive orisons," "saddened armies") and the obtrusive echo of Dylan Thomas ("the round/ Zion of the water bead/ And the synagogue of the ear of corn") make much of its impassioned statement sound like mere rhetoric. And its argument is too insistent, as if the speaker were trying by repetition ("the tear inside the stone," "the weeping in the pueblos," "the dark tears in the shacks," "each man weeps") to get us to believe it—which is particularly troublesome if we are inclined to feel that the posture of the rich man/poor man dichotomy is essentially false. But what seems to me important is the directness with which the poem marks out the territory of inward vision. Its effectiveness depends on the tension between the usual closed surface of objects and the assertion of the power of the spirit to apprehend and enter them.

And this context makes the closing image of the poem particularly apt: solid, inorganic, impassive, the stone points up the quality of the speaker's vision (and, consequently, the paucity of the rich man's) far more effectively than, say, a bird or a tree would. Whatever the shortcomings of the poem, it seems clear that the image is integrally related to the impulse behind it, the attempt to find an entrance to the mysterious life.

Bly's ideas have, of course, been enormously influential, and his interest in and promotion of such poets as Neruda and Tranströmer give continuing currency to what has been one of the most fruitful and invigorating strains in contemporary literature. But it has proved easier to learn the forms and textures of the "deep image" and the new surrealism than to understand and explore the spiritual vision that sustains the best poems of their kind. Many recent poems appropriate the terms of the relationship between the self and the object that Bly suggests, without entering the kind of sympathetic consciousness that would lift their fantasy into art. Galway Kinnell, in his *Ohio Review* (Fall 1972) interview, says much the same thing:

> If the things and creatures that live on earth don't possess mystery, then there isn't any. To touch this mystery requires, I think, love of the things and creatures that surround us, becoming one with them, so that they enter us, as Rilke says. They are transformed within us and our own inner life finds expression through them. . . . If a poem remains at the level of surrealism, possibly it means that no integration takes place, that the inner world and the outer world do not come together.

If Kinnell's assumption—that the primary impetus of much contemporary poetry is toward the kind of visionary wholeness he describes—is correct, then we ought to be able to use this principle and its implications to discriminate among poems, and to support our judgments.

Here is a poem from Gregory Orr's first volume:

THE STONE THAT IS FEAR

The stone sat at a desk lit by a single candle.
The walls of its room, like the inner walls of its body,
were covered with mirrors.
The stone was writing. It looked up occasionally,
staring at the thousand reflected candle flames
that seemed to be points of light perforating a dark sky.

It glanced at its watch that ran on blood.
It returned to its writing.

Burning the Empty Nests (1973)

There are some interesting details in this poem—primarily its spatial sense and the implications of the title—and yet it does not seem to me very successful as a whole. It moves in too many directions at once without following through on any of them. The "watch that ran on blood," for instance, comes as a complete surprise; it seems totally unrelated to the cool, glittering, singularly bloodless world established in the previous lines. Nor is the final line effective; it cuts the mooring of time and space, leaving the poem adrift in vagueness, rather than anchoring its suspense, as I suspect it was intended to do. The poem's principal shortcoming is its failure to explore its central image with any real interest, with the consequence that the image does not seem intrinsic to the rest of the poem. Would the effect be radically different if we substituted for the word *stone* the word *shoe*, or *wind*, or even *poet*? Perhaps Orr has introduced the surrealist vein a little too easily. The stone appears to be used to inject into the poem more of the kind of mythic consciousness that hovers around the mirrors, the candle, the watch that runs on blood. But at least in my reading experience, this simply doesn't work. The personification seems too simply a way of investing the poem with mystery or surprise, and it backfires: instead of any image I can take very seriously, I see a cartoon figure uncomfortably close to the Taylor Wine grape, impossible to reconcile with the lyric beauty and mystery the rest of the poem seems to be moving toward. And the resulting uncertainty of tone prohibits any very clear or satisfying imaginative effect.

THE STONE

The stone lives on.
The followers of the man with the glass face
walk around it
with their glass legs
and glass arms.

The stone lives on.
It lives on air.
It lives on your looking.
It lives inside and outside

itself and is never clear
which is which.

That is why
the followers of the man with the glass face
walk around it proposing
the possibilities
of emptiness.

The stone lives on,
commending itself to the hardness of air,
to the long meadows of your looking.

Darker (1970)

Mark Strand's poem seems to me more completely realized than Orr's, but less successful than his best. There is no inconsistency of tone here; the problem is that the imaginative design or impulse isn't active enough. Strand has written other poems ("Coming to This," "Black Maps") in which nothing actually happens, yet which are marvelously activated by their verbal tension, by the energy of elaboration, of constantly evolving paradox. "The Stone" tries to sustain itself on tone alone, and loses itself in the emptiness it describes. And once again this can be tied to the failure to use the central image adequately. The followers of the man with the glass face seem largely diversionary; the poem really wants to focus on the stone, and the second stanza is clearly the central one. Of course this is a poem about endurance, *about* nothing happening, as the repetitions and the circular structure make clear. But the combination of a deliberately indifferent and featureless subject with Strand's characteristically spare, flat language (even more transparent here than usual: the pun at the beginning of the second stanza is the only wordplay, and is too fragile to support much inspection) simply doesn't produce enough imaginative energy. Giving himself too much up to the image, not maintaining enough distance, Strand allows his poem to slip into a stonelike, resolute blankness, and thus to evade contact with the visionary lucidity that impels and deepens his best poems.

Finally, Charles Simic's "Stone":

Go inside a stone
That would be my way.
Let somebody else become a dove
Or gnash with a tiger's tooth.
I am happy to be a stone.

From the outside the stone is a riddle:
No one knows how to answer it.
Yet within, it must be cool and quiet
Even though a cow steps on it full weight,
Even though a child throws it in a river;
The stone sinks, slow, unperturbed
To the river bottom
Where the fishes come to knock on it
And listen.

I have seen sparks fly out
When two stones are rubbed,
So perhaps it is not dark inside after all;
Perhaps there is a moon shining
From somewhere, as though behind a hill—
Just enough light to make out
The strange writings, the star-charts
On the inner walls.

Somewhere Among Us a Stone is Taking Notes (1969)

This poem is extraordinarily successful in its treatment of the relationship between self and object, primarily because it establishes convincing imaginative sympathy without then losing self-consciousness. The quality of Simic's observation has terrific authority; his language matches the spareness, the evocativeness of a Lorca or a Vallejo while remaining absolutely his own. Not content to build the whole poem on a single effect, he mirrors the jumpy electricity of the imagination, constantly darting into and then away from the stone, surprising us with every move. In the line about the cow, for example, the stone suddenly shifts from subject to object, bearing the cow's placid, deliberate, and somehow very comic weight, which we sense—ingeniously—from the inside; in the next line, we are unexpectedly in flight. And through all this shifting focus runs the thread of the second line, the musing, inventive self-consciousness that keeps reminding us in complex ways that the stone both is and is not a metaphor for the self. Yet the poem is utterly unpretentious. The speaker evades both complacency (the problem of Strand's poem) and self-delight (the weakness of Orr's); we are allowed to share his keen pleasure of invention without thinking him egocentric. Effortlessly establishing a world where someone can become a stone, a dove, a tiger's tooth, the voice nonetheless remains human, tentative, fallible. With wry humility, he recognizes the fiction of his observation yet at the same time—and this is the magic of the poem—makes us believe it. Linking description of great clarity and intensity with the insight and freedom of surrealism, Simic uses his central image to achieve what seems to me authentic and exhilarating vision.

What generalizations can be drawn from this discussion? Certainly not that there are too many poems about stones. I could as easily have used vegetables, or moles, or snow, or breath as my example; the obsessive image is a cornerstone of contemporary poetry, and continues to inspire such good poems as Strand's "The Sleep," Orr's "The Man in the Suit of Mirrors," Margaret Atwood's "Songs of the Transformed," Sandra McPherson's "Seaweeds." Surely what distinguishes the best poems of all those that are focused around a single "deep" or "subjective" image is the way in which they *use* the image to attain significance and interest. The deep image can be a suggestive and exciting device, but it doesn't constitute a very satisfying poem in itself. This seems obvious enough, but there are dozens of poems which seem to be written in the belief that by mentioning the word *stone* one can plug the poem into a current of hermetic insight and gnomic utterance previously established by other poets like Bly and Simic. Such an assumption, it seems to me, automatically robs the poem of originality. The most valuable poems of this kind appear to work in the opposite direction, to begin with attention to the object itself without regard to other poems written about it, in the hope that—in Kinnell's terms—the inner world and the outer world will come together and transform each other. Poems whose imaginative center is the relationship between the self and the world, the psychic ties which bind them, have to maintain a precarious balance. When they are controlled too much either by the mind or by the object, they risk on the one hand solipsistic distortion, and mindless passivity on the other. Only those poems which manage this tightrope, satisfying the demands of both inner and outer worlds, create the simultaneous surprise and instinctive rightness we associate with genuine vision.

It should be clear that I am not talking about sincerity (a term which has probably lost whatever usefulness it might once have had in these matters), but about imaginative integrity. And this principle ought to apply equally well to other contemporary poems, whatever their dominant manner. Poems which seem to exist primarily by virtue of the cleverness of their rhetoric or imagery limit themselves to a relatively superficial interest; conversely, poems which restrict themselves too much to the inner world provoke the windy excesses of confessionalism. Perhaps this distinction will help provide a standard by which contemporary poetry can be measured and evaluated, and which in turn will encourage the kind of imaginative energy we look for in the best poems of our time.

(1975)

David Young

LANGUAGE: THE POET
AS MASTER AND SERVANT

My subject is the special qualities of language that I think characterize the best modern poetry, and since what I have to say will inevitably be an expression of personal taste and bias, I may as well begin with personal anecdote. The time is 1954 and I am a college freshman, a newly fledged reader and writer of poetry. I have the habit of browsing in the library stacks, looking for volumes of American poetry that interest me; one day I pull out a volume by a poet named Wallace Stevens, *The Auroras of Autumn*, published four years earlier. I have no idea who the poet is, no inkling that I have inadvertently entered the late phase of a great and difficult poet who to this day tends to elude his commentators. What I do know immediately is that I am in the presence of language that is used in exciting and brilliant combinations. Poems have titles like "Large Red Man Reading," "The Owl in the Sarcophagus," "Saint John and the Back-Ache." Opening at random, I find passages like the following:

> The crows are flying above the foyer of summer.
> The winds batter it. The water curls. The leaves
> Return to their original illusions.
>
> The sun stands like a Spaniard as he departs,
> Stepping from the foyer of summer into that
> Of the past, the rodomontadean emptiness.
>
> *Mother was afraid I should freeze in the Parisian hotels.*
> *She had heard of the fate of an Argentine writer. At night,*
> *He would go to bed, cover himself with blankets—*
>
> *Protruding from the pile of wool, a hand,*
> *In a black glove, holds a novel by Camus. She begged*
> *That I stay away.* These are the words of José . . .
>
> from "The Novel"

Though the poem is beyond me, the effect of the language is immediately intoxicating and I recognize that I have encountered a poet whose words and ways will be important to me for the rest of my life. I carry the book around for weeks, taking small, delighted sips.

Jump ahead a few years now. It is the fall of 1957, I am a senior and I now know my way around the library and the work of modern poets with some confidence. One day, in the English Department office, I notice a new book on the shelves where the textbooks are kept. It's called *Fifteen Modern American Poets*, edited by George P. Elliott, and contains many names that are new to me. I happen to open it to the work of a poet named Roethke. I have by this time learned to be wary of flashy effects; my teacher Reed Whittemore has written wittily and instructively about "goody-droppers," poets who create dazzling surfaces but don't finally have much beer under all that foam. On that basis I have begun to qualify my admiration for Dylan Thomas and the early Robert Lowell. But Roethke has an unmistakable ring of authenticity, and the beginning of a poem called "Give Way, Ye Gates," jumps right off the page at me:

> Believe me, knot of gristle, I bleed like a tree;
> I dream of nothing but boards;
> I could love a duck.
> Such music in a skin!
> A bird sings in the bush of your bones.
> Tufty, the water's loose.
> Bring me a finger. This dirt's lonesome for grass.
> Are the rats dancing? The cats are.
> And you, cat after great milk and vasty fishes,
> A moon loosened from a stag's eye,
> Twiced me nicely, —
> In the green of my sleep,
> In the green.

Again, the meaning mystifies me. Roethke seems to be defying the rules of clarity, and aside from an obvious preoccupation with sexuality, the poem seems to have no discernible subject. But I am ready to trust the poet because of the brilliance with which he is using language. It's like that moment in *King Lear* when Kent says he wants to serve Lear; he admits he doesn't know who Lear is, but says "you have that in your countenance I would fain call master." "What's that?" Lear asks, and Kent answers: "Authority." Later I was to see Roethke's explanations, that he wanted poetry "to extend consciousness as far, as deeply, as particularly as it can," and that he sought to write poems "which try in their rhythms to catch the very movement of the mind itself." Those statements would help me to explain my excitement, but I did not need them before I could begin to feel it, any more than I had with Stevens.

Enough about me as ephebe in the Fifties. I have introduced these bits of personal history only to suggest a way of thinking and talking about the bewildering variety of contemporary poetry that surrounds us; the energy and mastery of language to which we respond even before we discern "subject" or "meaning" may also provide a source of discrimination and evaluation. I advance this standard a little defiantly, not because I think I have discovered or rediscovered an infallible touchstone (it did not take me as quickly into all the poets I have come to revere, e.g. Williams), but because it seems to be at odds with the way so many people, critics and reviewers especially, find poetry worthy of praise or blame. If it has any worth, its use, which I will sketch out with some negative and positive examples, may help readers to trust their own responses more fully. It may even persuade some critics (I am having a fit of optimism) to modify their categories of importance and enlarge their sense of the distinctive features that language as poetry ought to have.

Let me try to define my subject a little more fully; am I addressing myself to sound? rhythm? diction (what Hugh Kenner calls "the family alliances of words")? Alas, I cannot be quite that precise. I am addressing myself to the totality of effects whereby the poet, any poet, makes language special and unique, sets it off from its mundane and prosaic uses. In any given poet the components of this total will differ radically enough that no formula can be applied in advance. We will recognize the achievement, I've suggested, in part by the immediacy of our response, by results. Later, using patience and hindsight, we may put together a description of the particulars. Thus in the case of Stevens we would want to talk about the ingenious control of diction that accommodates words like "foyer" and "rodomontadean" to words like "crows" and "winds" and "sun." That would have to include a glance at the effect of proper names— "Spaniard," "Parisian," "Argentine," "Camus," "José"—in the passage I quoted. The movement of the poem, by which I mean its rhythms from phrase to phrase and line to line, as well as its remarkable ability to do jump-shifts that appear to change the subject drastically when in fact there is genuine continuity, is another factor. And the sound itself is masterful. The line "The sun stands like a Spaniard . . ." wins us with its image but also with its sound relationships, especially "stands" and "Spaniard." The overall effect is a sense that there is nothing this poet cannot do with language. Since we are as often as not at the mercy of language, fighting for good words, good sense and eloquence, Stevens' easy command of it breeds

the excitement and wonder I spoke of earlier. A similar exercise
with Roethke would make us particularly attentive again to patterns of sound, to the effects and kinships of his short, bullet-like
sentences, to the crafty mixture of interrogation, exclamation,
assertion and command he employs, and ultimately to those dec-
larations of purpose I cited earlier about extension of consciousness and the rhythms of the mind. Any fine poet's mix is
distinctive, so that my subject resists generalization and must, as
I've suggested, be explored through examples.

Choosing these examples, especially the negative ones, is
bound to mislead, as though I am going out of my way to attack
some of my contemporaries; but I have in fact selected arbitrarily
from poems and poets that happened to come to my attention
within a period of two months. What follows is not a series of pet
peeves and predilections, but my reaction, as in the anecdotes
about my salad days, to my current browsing among books and
periodicals.

Let me begin, then, with a poet, A. R. Ammons, and a critic,
Harold Bloom. Bloom's essay, in a recent issue of *Salmagundi*, is
called "A. R. Ammons: The Breaking of the Vessels," and it
bemused me precisely because of the discrepancy between my
own reactions to Ammons' work and those of Bloom. I should add
that this was not my first encounter with either figure. Ammons is
a much-praised and laurelled poet, and Bloom is one of our best-
known literary critics, who certainly deserves respect and praise
for his willingness to consider poetry as a phenomenon of the present as well as the past. But I admit to not having had as much
success with the work of either man as their reputations would
seem to warrant, so I was glad to have an opportunity for another
look at both. Bloom begins his essay with the serious claim that
"No contemporary poet, in America, is likelier to become a classic than A. R. Ammons," and is soon quoting directly from
Ammons' recent *Sphere: The Form of a Motion*:

> . . . the gods have come and gone
> (or we have made them come and go) so long among us that
> they have communicated something of the sky to us making us
> feel that at the division of the roads our true way, too,
> is to the sky where with unborn gods we may know no
> further death and need no further visitations: what may have
> changed is that in the future we can have the force to keep
> the changes secular: the one: many problem, set theory, and
> symbolic signifier, the pyramid, the pantheon (of gods and
> men), the pecking order, baboon troup, old man of the tribe,

> the hierarchy of family, hamlet, military, church, corporation,
> civil service, of wealth, talent—everywhere the scramble for
> place, power, privilege, safety, honor, the representative
> notch above the undistinguished numbers: second is as good
> as last: pyramidal hierarchies and solitary persons; the
> hierarchies having to do with knowledge and law . . .

Bloom goes on quoting for six more lines, but I'll stop there. Now, what does Bloom have to say about this passage? He calls it "extravagantly pell-mell" and finds it characteristic of a struggle that recurs in Ammons' poetry between a union of mind and nature and a belief that nature can never be adequate to the mind. The first view has, he says, a transcendental strain, "but the second is almost unmatched in our century in its exaltation and high sorrow." Presumably "exaltation and high sorrow" characterize the passage in question.

It amazes me, frankly, that that passage seems to strike Bloom as fine poetry. I cannot see why he does not find the language and movement of it inadequate: wordy, uninteresting, flaccid. It might do as prose, if you liked that sort of philosophizing, but I cannot see anything distinctive about its diction or any significant justification for its lack of economy and intensity. To me, "extravagantly pell-mell" is a polite way of saying "Ammons won't shut up," and Bloom's characterization of Ammons as a "fierce Emersonian" may serve to remind us that Emerson was a master of prose, not poetry.

But one example may be unfair. Let us move on. Bloom next quotes several passages in which Ammons talks about, and with, the wind:

> I went to the summit and stood in the high nakedness:
> the wind tore about this
> way and that in confusion and its speech could not
> get through to me nor could I address it:

*

> Actually the wind said I'm
>   if anything beneficial
>   resolving extremes
> filling up lows with highs
> No I said you don't have
> to explain
> it's just the way things are

*

<pre>
            unlike the wind
        that dies and
     never dies I said
     I must go on
                consigned to
        form that will not
     let me loose
            except to death
                        till some
        syllable's rain
     anoints my tongue
        and makes it sing
                to strangers
</pre>

The first of these is from *Sphere*, the second and third from earlier work, *The Wide Land* and *Joshua Tree*. I have shortened what Bloom quotes in the first two instances, but not, I think, distortively. Now, it's interesting that Ammons talks about the wind a lot in his poetry, but the recurrent problem I see in all three passages is precisely that he does talk about it, rather than render it for us convincingly. And when the wind itself talks, in the second quote, it sounds more like Ammons. In each passage there is diction that I think a good poet would flinch at— "high nakedness," "resolving extremes," "consigned to form"—because it is prosaic and explanatory. The movement of the second passage seems reasonably effective, while the first and third are clumsy and facile, respectively. None of the passages uses language in a way that produces excitement or interest in me or makes me want to read more.

But none of this seems to concern Bloom. Around the quotation of these lines he is busy talking about "the extraordinary poignance of prophetic self-presentation," about Ammons being "punished into song." He says that we can say "that the wind, throughout his poetry, serves as Virgil to Ammons' Dante," that "the wind subsumes those aspects of the Emersonian-Whitmanian tradition that have found and touched Ammons." Ammons, he goes on, "always affectionate towards the wind, confronts it more directly than any poet since Shelley." Well, who cares? If these connections and cross-references are to be of use, they must surely be based on a distinctive, masterful poetry. Throughout the essay, Bloom never really deals with this issue: he seems to assume that Ammons' greatness, if we have any doubts about it, will be demonstrated by the passages cited for discussion. And that, as I've suggested, is just what doesn't happen in my case. The poetry sounds mostly graceless and garrulous to me, and no amount of impressive analogy from the Lurianic Kabbalah or talk of "the High Romantic quest for oblivion" will make that problem go away. The trouble with Bloom's criticism, I suspect, is that it is interested in ideas, as they appear in analogous patterns in Romantic and modern poets, while poetry, as poets have been trying to make clear for some time now, is not written with ideas but with words. At the level of language, where good poetry is to be distinguished from bad, Bloom seems to lack the necessary attention and discrimination.

I should add that of course Ammons is not responsible for the claims a critic makes on his behalf. He may very well be embarrassed by the kind of attention that Bloom and others have lavished on him. But I can't help thinking how much more useful it might have been to him as a working poet if critics, sympathetic or unsympathetic, had addressed themselves to the inadequacies of texture, movement, and diction in his work instead of making him grist for their theoretical mills.

Let me move on to another poet, this time without a critic in tow. My second choice is Diane Wakoski. A poem of hers called "Harry Moon from My Child's Anthology of Verse" came to my attention just the other day because one of the editors of a magazine called *Grove* asked me if I had liked "the Wakoski poem." I realized I had not read it through, which is what often happens with me and a Wakoski poem. I sat down to have another try. It's a fairly long poem, approaching two hundred lines. I'll quote a few representative passages to give an idea of its subject and manner:

> People want to create themselves
> as characters,
> as the principal actors in their own . . .
>
>   no, I will not say
> "drama"
>   Wisdom, no, that is not the word either.
>   age? maturity? vision? sensibility?
>   something begins to give the unspoken,
>   the unnamed more credibility;
>   silence becomes the only rejoinder.
>
>   *
>
> Saturn.
> The planet of silence.

Its rings of broken rock. Rocky silence
Circle me.
Marry my lips to each other.
I was once the moon,
a small body causing the tides.   Names
are
accidental.

                              *

In my mind, I knew
that I savoured
in my own mind
the *idea* of walking on the beach,
barefoot in the rain,
but actually I was sitting by the fire,
savouring in my mind
a girl riding naked on her zebra,
in the rain,
wearing only her diamonds.

The passage I quoted first is the beginning of the poem, and that
is where I must have stopped the first time around, because it
seems to me exceptionally undistinguished as poetic language. It
lacks economy, energy, wit, particularity, grace of movement, or
interest as sound. The other two passages are on the whole more
interesting, but not by much. They are not only characterized in
themselves by a kind of repetitive insistence, but they take their
place in a poem that circles back round again and again to the
same words, phrases, ideas. The image of riding naked on the
zebra, for example, shows up four times. Walking barefoot in the
rain comes up seven times. It is not as though the poem modifies
the meanings of the images in a way that makes their recurrence
striking or welcome. It is rather as though the poet hoped that the
constant recirculation of the images would make them powerful
or believable. And indeed the general repetitiveness and rambling
effect of the poem suggest a belief that colorless language moving
along without strong or intense rhythms will transcend itself if it
is insisted upon at sufficient length. I don't find that to be true; I
am less convinced by the time I get to the end.

      Wakoski fans will not agree with me, and they must surely
exist, for she is well known, frequently anthologized, reviewed
with respect, and has read her poetry about as widely as any
American poet I know of. That last point is worth acknowledging;
a poem like this will do better out loud, not because of rich and

subtle sound effects—there aren't any—but because we are less bothered by the garrulous and repetitive when we hear it than when we see it. If the poet speaks the words of the poem, we are saved the efforts of scanning the page word by word, and can tune in or out as we like. And I think we are often tempted by things that make poetry easier for us, such as a dwelling on the obvious, because poetry is hard work; we have to muster our best and most concentrated attention for reading or hearing it when it is good.

Is there anything else that accounts for Wakoski's reputation, that causes readers to overlook the prosaic and meandering features of her work? I think there is; it lies this time not in the kind of intellectual games Bloom can play with Ammons, but in her sincerity. She is a vigorous, likable person; if her poetry lacks concentration and energy, she does not, and there is something very attractive to our culture about her self-promotion and her willingness to spread her feelings out as openly as she does in her poetry—to ride naked, as it were, on her zebra. But the point I am pressing is that personal sincerity, as in her case, and playing around with ideas, in the case of Ammons, are no substitute for the heightened and magical command of language that characterizes good poetry. Neither, for that matter, are moral earnestness, political commitment, theological concern, or frankness about one's sex life. Any of these elements may serve to enhance a poem, but that is not the same as saying that they can be equivalent to the sound, movement, energy and economy that language ought to have in poetry.

Ammons and Wakoski were brought together here, as I've suggested, more or less by chance, and few commentators would think to lump them together. But they share, it seems to me, a fatal discursiveness, a strange conviction that any word or thought that issues from the poet's pen or mouth must by nature be poetry if it is sincere or thoughtful. If I've seemed to grumble, it's because poets who know how hard-won the real stuff is resent easy approximations. If I had to find a phrase to characterize the work of these two writers, I would call them "verse essayists," in order to distinguish their use of language from the language of lyric poetry. And if my subject here was the verse essay I would embark on a discussion of its variants and practitioners. It seems to exist in at least three categories: the Whitman sort, which Ammons and Wakoski roughly share; the Pound sort, rather spuriously based on *The Cantos*; and the Auden variety, chatty and tasteful and clever, based on the poet's late work. Perhaps the verse essay is a respectable and legitimate genre, but I wish it wouldn't be confused with lyric poetry; if you order bourbon and get ginger-ale because someone thinks they are roughly the same thing, you have a right to protest. There are writers who mix the two (essay and lyric) effectively, who manage to combine the discursive and prosaic elements of the verse essay with the exhilarations of poetic language, e.g. John Ashbery, but this is not the place to discuss highballs or analyze brands of ginger-ale. Take what I've just said as a cautious little digression.

I turn now to my positive examples. If my comments thus far have suggested that there are poets who, despite the praise they have received, lack the mastery of language that would affect some hypothetical undergraduate as Stevens and Roethke affected me, I want to go on to argue that there are indeed poets and poems these days that reflect such mastery and should produce such excitement. Again, I will simply draw on my recent reading for these examples, without implying that they are the sole instances I could come up with and without insisting that my criterion for discriminating them from poets like Ammons and Wakoski is the only one that should be used.

My first example is Charles Wright. I had known and liked this poet's work previously, but it was his new book, *Bloodlines*, which I read quite recently, that gave me, from the start, a sense that I was in the presence of a poet whose care for words and mastery of the possibilities of language were of a very high order. I am going to take the first poem in that collection, where I had my first strong reaction, and where most readers might have theirs. Quoting the poem in its entirety may seem unfair to Ammons and Wakoski, whom I dealt with in excerpts, until you recall that my point about them was partly that they went on at a length I did not care to follow because their language lacked essential interest. With Wright's poem, "Virgo Descending," there was no question of my not finishing the poem:

> Through the viridian (and black of the burnt match),
> Through ox-blood and ochre, the ham-colored clay,
> Through plate after plate, down
> Where the worm and the mole will not go,
> Through ore-seam and fire-seam,
> My grandmother, senile and 89, crimpbacked, stands
> Like a door ajar on her soft bed,
> The open beams and bare studs of the hall
> Pink as an infant's skin in the floating dark,
> Shavings and curls swing down like snowflakes across her face.
>
> My aunt and I walk past. As always, my father
> Is planning rooms, dragging his lame leg,

Stroke-straightened and foreign, behind him,
An aberrant 2-by-4 he can't fit snug.
I lay my head on my aunt's shoulder, feeling
At home, and walk on.
Through arches and door jambs, the spidery wires
And coiled cables, the blueprint takes shape:
My mother's room to the left, the door closed;
My father's room to the left, the door closed—

Ahead, my brother's room, unfinished;
Behind my sister's room, also unfinished.
Buttresses, winches, block-and-tackle: the scale of everything
Is enormous. We keep on walking. And pass
My aunt's room, almost complete, the curtains up,
The lamp and the medicine arranged
In their proper places, in arm's reach of where the bed will go . . .
The next one is mine, now more than half done,
Cloyed by the scent of jasmine,
White-gummed and anxious, their mouths sucking the air dry.

Home is what you lie in, or hang above, the house
Your father made, or keeps on making,
The dirt you moisten, the sap you push up and nourish.
I enter the living room, it, too, unfinished, its far wall
Not there, opening on to a radiance
I can't begin to imagine, a light
My father walks from, approaching me,
Dragging his right leg, rolling his plans into a perfect curl.
That light, he mutters, that damned light.
We can't keep it out. It keeps on filling your room.

There is much to praise here—the skillful mixing of life and death, waking and sleeping, familiar and strange, as well as the narrative power and the sense of exact detail—but what I am going to emphasize is the fact that language in this poem becomes a separate and magical reality; it may resemble language as we ordinarily know and use it, but it transcends that use in its power to express what we had thought inexpressible. We experience descent and dream and death, terror and wonder and acceptance, we go where the worm and the mole cannot go, because the language takes us there, makes it real. To say that this is because of the sound of the poem, or its movement, or its imagery, or its juxtapositions of sense-textures, is impossible, because it is of course all of these, working in a powerful combination unique to this poem. But an example or two will illuminate the combination. Take the pair of lines in the first stanza:

> My grandmother, senile and 89, crimpbacked, stands
> Like a door ajar on her soft bed.

Anyone who writes poetry can tell you that it is very difficult to write a line as long as that first one, with that many pauses in it, and get it to hold together and seem inevitable. There are three "ands" in the line ("grandmother," "and," "stands"), at the beginning, middle, and end. There are three long i vowels, one hidden in the number "89." There is an attentive exploitation of the power of consonants to invoke physical experience, most clearly exemplified in the word "crimpbacked." To use that particular word, a relatively rare one, with that exactness and in that precisely contrived context, is evidence of a care for language and a love of the individuality of words that ought to characterize the work of a good poet. I included the line that follows for contrast; it is short and it looks easier. We might simply marvel at the comparison, "Like a door ajar on her soft bed." But that kind of simplicity is, if anything, harder to come by, and the rhythm and sound of the line, its balance and succinctness, have as much to do with its effectiveness as the simile itself. And of course the way the two lines go together, long and short, hectic and smooth, emphatic and relaxed, helps to remind us that mutual enhancement must occur not only among the words of a line but from line to line and throughout the poem.

I'll take my second example, or group of examples, from the last stanza. Notice how it begins: "Home is what you lie in, or hang above, the house/ Your father made, or keeps on making." It sounds a bit like Frost for a moment, but in this context there is a walloping difference. I cite it to illustrate the rhetorical range of the poem; when this poet sounds discursive, it is not because he doesn't know what else to do, or doesn't care, but because he wants to borrow from and echo discursive language (and that is often the case with Frost too, of course, though not perhaps as often as we'd like) for a special purpose. Look at the next line, as the "discursiveness" is displaced: "The dirt you moisten, the sap you push up and nourish. . . ." "Moisten . . . sap . . . push up . . . nourish"—surely the immediacy through careful choice of words and sounds is self-evident. Watch how the beautiful line-breaks, the turns of the verse, act out the meaning in the lines that follow:

> I enter the living room, it, too, unfinished, its far wall
> Not there, opening on to a radiance
> I can't begin to imagine, a light
> My father walks from, approaching me.

And then the last three lines, end-stopped for equally valid reasons, with the double consonant words—"Dragging," "rolling," "mutters," and "filling"—as just one instance of the powerful interweaving of individual words as patterns of vowel and consonant and meaning that characterizes this poem and the book in which it occurs. Wright's poem, for me at least, shines and pulses with its love of language and the evocation of language's special powers for poetry. Most important of all, perhaps, is that all of its effects flow toward its total meaning and purpose. None are used for their own sake, to dazzle or impress us; there is no "goody-dropping" here.

Since Wright's book has obviously made an enthusiast of me, I must resist a strong temptation to go on—about this poem and about the rest of the book. It would be relevant to my subject to say why I think "ham-colored clay" is so superb, but that would require another paragraph, as would a consideration of Wright's mastery of lists, here and elsewhere. But I must move on to other examples. I want to talk about two poets whose work I had not seen until this month, poets who are new and not well known. The point I want to make, of course, is that the kind of excellence I am calling for is not limited to master poets of the recent or distant past, or even relatively established poets of the present, like Charles Wright (*Bloodlines* is his third book). It will always turn up, I suspect, as long as we have language, poets who care deeply about it, and readers who can respond.

A first book by a poet named Reg Saner, *Climbing into the Roots*, reached my desk just two weeks before I began this essay. It came with credentials—the Walt Whitman Award for a first book of poetry—but credentials don't always tell you much. The test must finally lie in your own reactions. Reg Saner lives in Colorado and writes a lot about the mountains. What's important is not my recognition that he knows them, but his ability to make me know them, to take me there, finding language that is adequate to the experience of climbing in the Rockies. Here are the first two sections of his poem, "Camping the Divide: Indian Peaks, Colorado":

1

Refrigerator tropics. Trees thick
as rain. Even the light is sopping.
We climb following a bootlace
stream, creek and waterfall by turns
through forest so dense
the dead spruce can barely topple.

They squeak down, taking years
to hit. Hummocks muzzle windfallen pine
that dissolves in a lard of sponge
stumps and fern swale
deepening the bog-soft ground.
On a log wide as a barge or small
fat ship I straddle and watch the stream
pour by, falling alongside so fast
it's hard to believe we're not
headed to the Divide by water.

2

At timberline we begin hiking
the grand smash and hurl
over a crockery grind of shale—
working up a perfectly useless sweat,
hugging boxcar faults like lovers—
to squirm among
this difficult magnificence
where we are most our own.

Evocative, hard-won, carefully marshalled language. The poet must know the things he writes of, know their ways and their particular, beautiful names, and he must have considered deeply how to move us forward among this welter of detail. The overall effect, compounded of sound, movement, imagery and precise juxtaposition ("bootlace stream," "crockery grind of shale," "boxcar faults") is an exhilarating tension of the sublime and the ridiculous, of gravity and legerity. Since we have had Ammons on wind, I think we ought to look at the third section of this poem too:

3

Here in the havoc country
what's left of trees finishes in talons.
The split sky goes manic, booming
its laundry strangle up down and sideways
at once. Nubbled trunks of Engleman
and fir, wrist-thick, blown bald
as potato skin in front. A bossy
one-way wind unfurling this last, highest
lake. We watch its ice-water chop
jogging in place.

I don't suppose this would lead any critic to talk of "the extraordinary poignance of prophetic self-presentation," or say that the wind is Virgil to Saner's Dante, or claim that he confronts it more directly than any poet since Shelley. But surely the wind is here, present to us, in this passage in a way that was not the case with Ammons. And it's worth stressing that Saner is not simply evoking the mountains, rockslides, water and wind for the sake of impressing us with his descriptive abilities. You'll recall that Bloom spoke of the struggle in Ammons' work between a union of mind and nature and a disjunction of the two. Well, that struggle, or tension, is far more present and moving in Saner's poem than in the passages cited from Ammons. Here is its final section:

> Like the dead we see ourselves
> slipping off into the weather. Delicate
> flurries of white and whiskery ash
> stir from a few red lumps
> as the old wind rises again. We stretch
> in mummy bags to the chin, timing
> our talk to the tent's nylon whip and crackle.
> Near the bank where water tongues
> try the lips of stones
> a gone light winks and paddles,
> making wingbeats in our eyes.
> We follow it further off
> into a mindless applause that carries
> and fades—daylight broken into voices,
> our hike's big picture breaking
> down, its sky blown over the lake's lower
> edge and falling apart
> into the Valley of the North St. Vrain.
> Under us all night we hear dark stones
> talking over the way we came. And somewhere
> far back in our sleep
> feel a high river, going home.

Is that not plain enough, not discursive enough, for a critic who might want to plug in Whitman or Shelley? It is for me, in fact it's just right. I would grant that Saner is sometimes a little too self-conscious about what he's doing and how he is accomplishing it, but that's a pebble compared to the boulders that obstruct me in the over-insistent and shoddy language of my negative examples. I'm willing to stay with Saner's poem because I develop a kind of trust based on his care for and love of language, his willingness to muster all its resources for a serious purpose. I want a poet to love language more than message, more than himself/herself. Is that formula unfair?

My next example is a young poet, Greg Pape, whom I know only from a new collection of poets under forty, *The American Poetry Anthology*. Here again, I think I must quote in full a poem called "For Rosa Yen, Who Lived Here:"

I

Mice in the garbage
mockingbirds in the attic
your iron
gasping over pockets and collars
you dream back into
the hollows of the night. . .

An ocean rocks
under the shadow of a gull
your father stands in the cold water
at dawn
his face and dark hair
tossing in a cloud
his bare feet sucked down
by sand

II

Those mornings
you never saw him leave
you'd slip down from the bed
while your mother slept,
move quietly across the room
and open the tall door
to your own world . . .

Light in the cat's eye
started you singing;
you followed your breath
around the house
and no one saw the schools
of bright fish swim through your fingers
no one saw you walking in and out
of yourself while the sun built a bridge of light
over Culiácan and Kowloon.

III

All night trucks droned
under the bridge at Highway City

dragging their dirty skirts of wind,
blackening the oleanders,
bruising the sleep of workers;
men like your father
who came to this valley and were robbed
and hidden like seeds,
men with too many border crossings
stamped in their faces
whose palms were worn smooth
on the slow fruits of their lives.

All night I sat still
and dreamed you; little girl,
woman, sister to the walls.
I spoke your name
as a charm against nothing
and waited . . .

IV

At the first touch of sun
mist rushes from the grass
and darkness goes back
to its nest of hair
swirling in a toilet
to its bottle of rainwater and dead laughter
lying in the weeds outside.

In this room filling with light
I'm alone as you were
with your beautiful man
nailed to the wall.

I would scream peacocks, break a window,
go back to sleep if I could

but this is California
where no one sleeps
California where your father
pointed a long finger
at the lizard and the dog
and this is the white shack
leaning into the orchard
where you lived Rosa.

If you pinned me down I would say that I have a few reservations
about this poem, a few small questions about its movement, some

of its images, here and there a slight over-insistence, usually through a verb. But on the whole it is a poem of extraordinary delicacy and sympathy, a poem to trust and cherish. It has some relation to the Wakoski poem in its way of meditating on questions of selfhood in that ambivalent California landscape, but aside from questions of the relative value of her self-preoccupation and his ability to move out in a fluid gesture of imaginative projection, what strikes me about his poem is the sensitivity to the possibilities of language. Each detail is placed carefully and has its evocative effect, partly as image, partly as a woven texture of movement, sound, and the energy released by imaginative juxtaposition. For example, those trucks, "dragging their dirty skirts of wind,/ blackening the oleanders,/ bruising the sleep of workers." The images themselves are stirring, but partly because of the way they echo other images and not least from a crafty marshalling of vowel and consonant. The same must be said of the passage in which "darkness goes back/ to its nest of hair/ swirling in a toilet/ to its bottle of rainwater and dead laughter/ lying in the weeds outside." A poet who thought the effectiveness of such a passage came entirely from its subject matter or through its images (in the sense of what the words refer to) would not be able to write that way, would ignore the other elements, the aspects of language itself as palpable, physical reality, at his or her peril. If you asked me whether Greg Pape has a future as a poet, I should certainly say yes.

Let me close with a few caveats and qualifications. Using a few examples, negative and positive, inevitably makes my comments sound more prescriptive than they are meant to be. I have not, for example, been arguing for the ornate rather than the plain style in poetry, for lush effects over spareness. I mentioned a reverence for Williams; when I read him as an undergraduate I sensed his deep care for language, but did not know how to listen to it or appreciate its distinctiveness. And I might well have cited other poets here—Jarrell, Stafford, Simic, Strand—whose varieties of a plainer style are quite as immediate and enchanting as Roethke and Charles Wright. The idea that language in poetry must constitute a separate, vivid, and transcendent reality is not narrow; its possibilities are multitudinous.

I think it should also be clear that if I am a fan of Stevens, if I enjoy John Ashbery, I am not an unyielding foe of discursive and even philosophical language in poetry. My main notion has simply been this: if you read a poet and begin to feel that his or her language excites and stirs you, that the text and the texture are somehow rightly married, that the pressure of the imagination on language is giving rise to a new and unique reality, then you do right to read on, trusting your intuitive response. If you find such elements lacking, then you do well to ask why, letting nobody tell you that it is important by reasons of content, good intentions, or reputation. Accept no substitutes!

Finally, let me point out it is merely chance that kept any women poets out of my positive examples. I was tempted to cite Sandra McPherson or Laura Jensen, but they have both appeared frequently in *FIELD*, and admiring their uses of language might have seemed like a roundabout way of citing my editorial acumen. But I'll close with a short poem by Laura Jensen that appeared in our last issue, "The Cloud Parade":

> In deference to the cloud parade,
> the horse has shed its winter red,
> stamped its last horseshoe out of the shed,
> has moved away, leaving no forwarding
> address. The heavens turned furniture,
> attics and beds, men with moustaches
> heels over heads, they cover the sun
> to a gloomy shade,
> in deference to the cloud parade.
>
> Scarves! Echoes! Pavillions!
> The meat grain in bacon, the star-stun
> in roast, the bone down the well, the moon
> down the wane, the smoke from the fireplace,
> beautifully made,
> in deference to the cloud parade.

There, especially in the second stanza, is that miraculous quality that I have urged as the sign of true poetry. And what I have described as mastery is in fact a kind of happy servitude. Octavio Paz has said it: "Each time we are served by words, we mutilate them. But the poet is not served by words. He is their servant. In serving them, he returns them to the plenitude of their nature, makes them recover their being. Thanks to poetry, language reconquers its original state. First, its plastic and sonorous values, generally disdained by thought; next, the affective values; and, finally, the expressive ones" (*The Bow and the Lyre*).

(1976)

David Young

SECOND HONEYMOON:
Some Thoughts on Translation

Suppose we begin with Joseph Brodsky. This distinguished Russian poet, recently arrived in our midst, has twice aired his views on translation in *The New York Review of Books*. In a review of the Hayward and Kunitz translations of Akhmatova (August 9, 1973) he wrote:

> For most American poets, translating from Russian is nothing but an "ego trip." [There follows an attack on "free verse" and a suggestion that modern American poets don't possess enough technique to handle rhyme and meter.] . . . Translation is not original creation—that is what one must remember. In translation some loss is inevitable. But a great deal can be preserved too. One can preserve the meter, one can preserve the rhymes.

Akhmatova's forms, he argues, have a spiritual as well as a technical meaning; to change them is thus a kind of sacrilege. He has some kind words for Kunitz and Hayward, finally, but the above quotations characterize his general tone. On February 7, 1974, he returned to the attack, this time in a review of Mandelstam translations by, among others, Clarence Brown and W. S. Merwin. Again, the general outlines of his position are unmistakable:

> Meters in verse are kinds of spiritual magnitudes for which nothing can be substituted. They cannot even be replaced by each other, and especially not by free verse. . . . Form too is noble, for it is hallowed and illumined by time. It is the vessel in which meaning is cast; they need each other and sanctify each other reciprocally—it is an association of soul and body. Break the vessel and the liquid will run out. What was done to Mandelstam by Merwin, and to an even greater extent by Raffel, is the product of profound moral and cultural ignorance.

These statements are pretty silly, but I knew as I read them that scores of academics were nodding their heads in agreement. That is why I should like to make them my starting point. It is tempting to discuss Brodsky's literary manners, but I will only note in passing that he is no less presumptuous than the translators whose motives and skills he treats so severely. In his case the presumption lies in his assurance that he can gauge the effectiveness of Russian translations as poems in English. The ideal critic of translation would surely be master of both languages, and that Brodsky lacks these credentials is indicated by his insensitivity to the real excellence in the translations by Kunitz and Merwin, and by the fact that he himself needs translators to get his views before us (both reviews were translated from the Russian). When he uses phrases like "self-assured, insufferable stylistic provincialism," it is rather like spitting into the wind.

It is also interesting to speculate why *The New York Review of Books* should wish to promote such views, though I suspect the answer lies simply in their infatuation with names and their apparently passive editorial policies (one sometimes feels that if you are famous enough you can be boring at almost any length in their pages). But what interests me here is not such incidental issues; it is, rather, the theoretical position from which Brodsky argues. It is seldom so dogmatically stated, but it is widely held, and it lies behind the practice of more translators than Brodsky suspects. I am going to argue that it is precisely the attitude the translator must avoid; it is not the only risk translation runs, but it is a very large one, and I would dread reading translations by a Brodsky far more than those by Merwin or Kunitz or any number of contemporary poets who have given their time and imaginative energy to this peculiar art.

For it is an art. Translating lyric poetry, like writing it, is done against enormous odds. Its illusions and exhilarations are similar, and its rewards are singular and immeasurable. A lyric poet engaged in translation is intent on capturing in the language he cares most about a prize object that is supposed to be the private property of another language. "It will do you no harm, Latin," he says, "if I take this lyric of Catullus and try to bestow it as a gift on my own language, which suddenly seems to me impoverished without it; you will still have Catullus when I am through, quite undamaged, and something new, not otherwise possible, will have come into existence." Surely we can give a measure of sympathy to the smugglers at whom Brodsky shakes such a righteous fist.

I suggest an analogy between translation and what is more readily acknowledged as creative activity not so much to vindicate the translator (if you want a good vindication read George Steiner's preface to *The Penguin Book of Modern Verse Translation,* recently retitled *Poem Into Poem),* as to shed light on the process of translation at its best, and on the possible criteria that might be advanced for success or excellence. Listen for a moment to Günter Eich:

> I write poems to orient myself in reality. . . . Only through writ-
> ing do things take on reality for me. . . . Writing is not only a
> profession but a decision to see the world as language. Real lan-
> guage is a falling together of the word and the object. Our task is
> to translate from the language that is around us but not "given."
> We are translating without the original text. The most successful
> translation is the one that gets closest to the original and reaches
> the highest degree of reality.

Eich uses translation as a metaphor for poetry. In doing the
reverse, I'm suggesting that among the various motives that can
be advanced for translating poetry, the one that means the most to
me and seems most consistent with the activity as I know it, is the
one that Eich advances: the achievement of 'real' language, a
merging of the word and the object. The fact that the translator is
working with an original text, an already achieved poem where
word and object fuse, is scarcely the irony it might seem at first
glance, for the decision to see the world as language that Eich
speaks of means in his case one language, German, just as it does
in my case English. American English. And word-object marriage
licenses do not cross linguistic borders. The whole romance,
courtship, and marriage must occur again, almost as exciting for
being a recurrence and a renewal, a sort of second honeymoon. To
translate a poem is to undertake to prove that it is not *just* a language formation, but a reality, not a marriage license but a marriage. To translate, then, is to affirm and celebrate, even as one
winces at the risks.

   I'm quite aware that to say that translating poetry is a great
deal like creating it is not the same as saying that poets automatically make good translators. Creativity requires discipline, and
the problem is just what *kind* of discipline translation needs. I can
go a long way with Brodsky in indignation at sloppiness and irresponsibility among contemporary translators. In fact, I can provide an example from Mandelstam, a poet I revere every bit as
much as Brodsky does. Many readers will be familiar with the
"adaptation," published in *Poets on Street Corners,* by Robert
Lowell of one of Mandelstam's most famous lyrics:

> In the name of the higher tribes of the future,
> in the name of their foreboding nobility,
> I have had to give up my drinking cup at the family feast,
> my joy too, then my honor.

> This cutthroat wolf century has jumped on my shoulders,
> but I don't wear the hide of a wolf—

no, tuck me like a cap in the sleeve
of a sheepskin shipped to the steppes.

I do not want to eat the small dirt of the coward,
or wait for the bones to crack on the wheel
I want to run with the shiny blue foxes
moving like dancers in the night.

There the Siberian river is glass,
there the fir tree touches a star,
because I don't have the hide of a wolf
or slaver in the wolf-trap's steel jaw.

A moving poem, partly because Mandelstam is having to say,
"Arrest me, send me to Siberia. I cannot survive in your state," and
his "request" was granted. When the act of writing a poem can
cost the poet his life, the importance of poetry is unmistakable,
and the poet becomes a figure of courage and heroic resistance. I
was wary of this "adaptation," however, knowing Lowell's habits,
even before I read Vladimir Nabokov's discussion of it *(NYR,*
Dec. 4, 1969). Nabokov begins by providing a literal version:

For the sake of the resonant valor of ages to come,
for the sake of a high race of men,
I forfeited a bowl at my fathers' feast,
and merriment, and my honor.

On my shoulders there pounces the wolfhound age,
but no wolf by blood am I;
better, like a fur cap, thrust me into the sleeve,
of the warmly fur-coated Siberian steppes.

—so that I may not see the coward, the bit of soft muck,
the bloody bones on the wheel,
so that all night the blue-fox furs may blaze
for me in their pristine beauty.

Lead me into the night where the Enisey flows,
and the pine reaches up to the star,
because no wolf by blood am I,
and injustice has twisted my mouth.

Even without Nabokov's sardonic guidance, the reader can immediately perceive some of Lowell's strange transformations: a
wolfhound has become a wolf, being a wolf by blood has become
dressing up in a wolf-skin, the river has frozen, and the involun-

tary snarl of disgust at injustice has been magically transformed into a wolf-trap. But let me quote Nabokov on two central images:

> L. 8: actually "of the Siberian prairie's hot fur coat," *zharkoy shubi' sibirskih stepey*. The rich heavy pelisse, to which Russia's Wild East is likened by the poet (this being the very blazon of its faunal opulence) is demoted by the adaptor to a "sheepskin" which is "shipped to the steppes" with the poet in its sleeve. Besides being absurd in itself, this singular importation totally destroys the imagery of the composition. And a poet's imagery is a sacred, unassailable thing.

> Lines 11-12: the magnificent metaphor of l. 8 now culminates in a vision of the arctic starlight overhead, emblemized by the splendor of gray-blue furs, with a suggestion of astronomical heraldry (*cf.* Vulpecula, a constellation). Instead of that the adaptor has "I want to run with the shiny blue foxes moving like dancers in the night," which is not so much a pretty piece of pseudo-Russian fairytale as a foxtrot in Disneyland.

The points about imagery are extremely telling. The original poem is beautifully organized around the image, one might say the texture, of fur. Mandelstam is a deeply sensuous poet, passionately concerned with physical being and with the smallest details of sensation—in this case the warmth, softness, and possible protectiveness of fur. The poet is like a small animal, hunted as if he were a dangerous wolf by the century he has the misfortune to live in. His instinct is to go to ground—a kind of hibernation-death in Siberia—where nature can take him back with comforting transformations: the starlight as soft and beautiful as blue fox fur, the soft pine (not the accidentally punning and much stiffer tree of Lowell's version) brushing a star—the same kind of contact, the poet released from the snarl that has begun to twist his mouth and make him incapable of pronouncing the true words of the poem. Like a fur cap thrust into a fur coat, he'll be bundled into the good arctic earth that implies his extinction.

I am sorry Lowell didn't get that into the poem. Without it his "adaptation" is superficial and melodramatic, reaching for easy effects that Mandelstam would never have settled for. But the problem, surely, is one of content rather than form. I am never very easy with the form-content distinction, but if we use it to begin a consideration of Lowell's version, we can see that he has in fact followed the formal characteristics of Mandelstam's poem fairly faithfully. The Russian original has a rhyme scheme, and

Lowell's does not, but otherwise both poems are four quatrains, and their lines correspond closely in terms of syntax, length, and order. In this respect, then, Lowell has been surprisingly orthodox. He does not seem to have felt that he might make his English version more effective by experimenting a little with a different line length or stanza size, special rhythms, enjambment, or any of the techniques that can be used to give a poem effective movement and a life and character of its own. And this despite the fact that his faithfulness to Mandelstam's external form sometimes leads him into clumsy effects, such as the cumbersome line, "I do not want to eat the small dirt of the coward," which sounds to my ear like a lot of other translations I have read where sense (of a sort) crosses over but grace and precision stay behind. Lowell seems in fact to have used a formula, consciously or not, whereby he held to the form as far as possible (conceding on the difficult issue of replicating the rhyme scheme) and played fast and loose with the content. He is not, in other words, as different as we might have thought from that host of translators who have labored in the past to make translations that duplicate the formal characteristics of their originals, and produced monstrosities: bathtubs that talk, tricycles that swim, people with their heads on backward. These are the translators who, approaching a Rilke sonnet, seem bent, as Harold Rosenberg once said, on giving us a sonnet in which Rilke will come and go, if he is lucky enough to appear at all, when what the English language needs is not one more bloody sonnet, but Rilke, as vital and potent and moving as he is in German, where the fact that he was writing a sonnet was perhaps the most incidental aspect of his achievement.

Brodsky would of course disagree with that last statement. Yet if we return to our original analogy, where translation is matched with the creative process, we can find support for giving external form a low priority. For the freedom a poet feels when he is writing is a freedom about form—he may *choose* the formal characteristics into which he translates his feelings and experiences and ideas—at the same time that he feels an obligation to be as faithful as possible to the feelings themselves, to the experience on which he draws. He wants to capture something exactly, and he will use any formal and technical means available to him. If he is trying to characterize his sadness, for example, he will not say that he is happy for the sake of meter or rhyme scheme or any other "formal" consideration; he will sacrifice "form" for the demands of "content" every time, unless he has mistaken means for ends and believes that form and technique themselves constitute poetry, in which case he has problems too severe and pathetic for me to consider here. My business is to observe that the translator would do well to follow the lead of the poet, and to treat what he is translating with the respect that a poet has for his subject, *a respect that does not include preconceptions about form.* To be told that you must translate a sonnet from one language into a sonnet in your own language is like being told that you must choose the form of a poem before you know its subject—and that is turning the creative process around; as Robert Francis observed about writing sestinas, it is rather like stuffing a cat. And the results are likely to be feeble, mannered, mechanical, and dull. If translators were to give themselves the *same freedoms* that good poets have, *and* hold themselves to the *same disciplines*, we would have a great many fewer stuffed cats around posing as effective translations.

Perhaps it begins to be clear that besides finding myself diametrically opposed to Mr. Brodsky's ideas about priorities in translation, I think he is working from simplistic notions about poetic form. The artificial division between content and form tends to disappear when we can rid ourselves of unnecessarily narrow definitions of the latter, based on external and quantifiable features, the syllables and rhymes and feet and stanzas that you can name and count. Surely there is another aspect of form in poetry, less definable perhaps, but ultimately of greater importance. That is the poem's use of familiar configurations of experience in a way that emphasizes their form, the formal possibilities that inhere in them, their order and outline. I think that the animal-fur-burrow-warmth-arctic night-softness-wildness cluster of associations in the Mandelstam poem helps to provide what we might call its true coherence, its inner form, the shaping of experience that gives it its power to speak to our own imaginations.

But I will give a more familiar example. Yeats, as we all know, spent a great deal of his life pursuing the interests of spiritualism, which meant going to seances and trafficking with mediums. I remember noticing some time ago how he had put his intimate knowledge of seances to good use in what I think is one of his most interesting plays, *The Words Upon the Windowpane*, but it was only quite recently that I realized with a sort of start that he had used that knowledge all his life as a means of giving form to his poems. Again and again, Yeats's poems are built around the basic situation of a man summoning and conjuring—calling up the dead, the figures of imagination and the supernatural, in order to give them a message, ask them a question, or meditate on their nature and meaning. Here is a clear instance, it seems to me, of a poet drawing on experience to find a form, a ritual, an ordering device that would make poetry possible and give it true coherence. And if we are to speak intelligently about the *form* of poems like "In Memory of Major Robert Gregory," "The Tower," "All Souls' Night," and "A Dialogue of Self and Soul," then we must speak not only of their stanza forms, rhyme schemes, and sectional divisions, but of this kind of form as well. I don't know whether it is much discussed by the critics, but it is important to the translator because it is an aspect of the form of the poem that *is* translatable; that is, it does not inhere so much in the language as in the experience from which the poet has abstracted it in order to give it a verbal character of its own. If we remember that a translation of a poem must begin again, and that new words must be found, then we should admit that new words imply new sounds and new rhythms, and, quite possibly, new form. But the translator will presumably seek all those things in the interest of recreating the pre-verbal aspect of the poem—its configurations of experience at the threshold of their transformation into formal expressive language. That, I think, is just what Lowell failed to do with the Mandelstam poem; and like it or not, Brodsky's theory has too much in common with Lowell's practice. It also has too little imagination about the way that good poems get written and effective translations made.

Pages of illustration should of course follow. It would be necessary to show that there is no reason to claim that the translator *must* alter the "form" (in Brodsky's sense) of the original. And it would surely be useful to consider examples of Chinese translation, where the differences between the two languages are so pronounced and obvious that attempts to reproduce "form" faithfully are misguided in a way that should be unmistakable to anyone. I trust it is clear, even in the absence of examples, that I am not arguing for careless and irresponsible translation; the habits I recommend are far more demanding than attempts to reproduce rhyme and meter. I am simply arguing against an attitude toward translation so restrictive and pedantic as to close out altogether the possibility of great translations. The translators Brodsky castigates may indeed be inadequate (though as I say I find much to admire in the work of Merwin and Kunitz), but if they are it is not because Russian meters and rhymes and stanza forms are missing; it is because, in being creative, they have not been creative enough.

(1974)

Shirley Kaufman

HERE AND THERE:

The Use of Place
in Contemporary Poetry

I

There is an old Hasidic story that Gershom Scholem has retold:

> When the Baal Shem had a difficult task before him, he would go
> to a certain place in the woods, light a fire and meditate in
> prayer—and what he had set out to perform was done. When a
> generation later the "Maggid" of Meseritz was faced with the
> same task he would go to the same place in the woods and say:
> We can no longer light the fire, but we can still speak the
> prayers—and what he wanted done became reality. Again a gen-
> eration later Rabbi Moshe Leib of Sassov had to perform this
> task. And he too went into the woods and said: We can no longer
> light a fire, nor do we know the secret meditations belonging to
> the prayer, but we do know the place in the woods to which it all
> belongs—and that must be sufficient; and sufficient it was. But
> when another generation had passed and Rabbi Israel of Rishin
> was called upon to perform the task, he sat down on his golden
> chair in his castle and said: We cannot light the fire, we cannot
> speak the prayers, we do not know the place, but we can tell the
> story of how it was done.

Now, near the end of the twentieth century, we are even losing the
story. So perhaps we must find the place again and start over. The
Hebrew word for place, *makom*, is also one of the names of God.
According to the Midrash, He is the place of the world.

David Ignatow has a poem that begins like this:

> I have a place to come to.
> It's my place. I come to it
> morning, noon and night
> and it is there. I expect it
> to be there whether or not
> it expects me—my place
> where I start from and go
> towards so that I know
> where I am going and what
> I am going from.

Perhaps this small poem can help me to define what the Baal Shem meant by place. It is a location with a strong personal meaning. "My place." It is set in time, in history: which means that events *happen* there. "Morning, noon and night" could be past, present, and future or the progression from birth to death. But it is also outside of time, simply by being there. Permanence within impermanence, a constant in a universe of flux, a fixed point that gives meaning to our movement through time and space, from beginning to end, from here to there. Call it God, call it center of being, place of the world. Call it Ignatow's room in New York where he writes his poems.

Yet Ignatow only speaks of his place in the abstract. It has no landscape (or cityscape) and no history. He does not see it, or smell it, or connect with it through memory or experience. I have been wondering why the work of many poets who are *not* Americans seems to have a different relationship to place. As if their breath, their language, their vision come from somewhere very real that surrounds and enters them. Who they are is where they are. Few Americans write out of this kind of necessity, a physical and emotional involvement with the places they know and return to. American women even less. I want to understand this.

II

George Seferis and a number of other contemporary Greek poets are like the Baal Shem. Their place in the woods of the world is Greece, with all that implies: the fire, the fuel for the fire, the gathering of myth and history, meditations and stories. Seferis writes in his journal of the days between 1945 and 1951 when he returned from exile to his home and left it again:

> . . . I went out after noon; my first walk since I got sick. Anaphi-otika, the Acropolis, the trees on the Areopagus, the grove of Philippapus. Light strong and pure, revealing everything with such astonishing clarity that I had the *serious* feeling of a sudden hallucination in broad daylight. Returning, as I was looking at the north side of the Acropolis, rocks and marble together with the Byzantine chapel below—just as one discerns faces and shapes on an old wall—I *saw* the tall skeleton of a woman, bones snow-white, looking at me with a proud air like the ghost of a hero. She looked from a world that was no longer of today, but a future world where nothing of what I know, things or persons, had survived. I felt the same love that I have now for life with all its beauties and evils—exactly the same love for this snow-white

skeleton in the sun. These are strange things I've written and yet it *was* that way. I can't express it more precisely. I have the impression that I saw a moment of eternity.

An hallucination like the visions of the Hasidic rabbis. Out of a certain place. When Seferis returned to Athens after the Second World War, the months that followed were marked by civil war, Greeks fighting Greeks, political intrigue, government chaos, foreign intervention, and unmitigated suffering. All the agony of that time is in the journal. Together with the timeless. And drafts of poems.

On August 17, 1922, the Turks burned Smyrna to the ground and killed every Greek who had not fled. Seferis was born in the village of Skala outside of Smyrna in 1900, and although his family had left before that catastrophe, the destruction of Smyrna and its Greek community haunted him throughout his life. Twice in 1950, while he was working in the Greek embassy in Turkey, he returned to his first home. The pain of that encounter, as he records it in his journal, is almost too much to bear:

> I've memorized the map of Smyrna from an 1898 English guidebook. I'm trying to apply this to both the ruined and the new buildings before me. I lie on my side on the beach and spread it out; then I abandon myself to the sorcery of memory. I think it was Alexandria which was compared to a cloak. Smyrna too is a cloak spread out as far as the castle of Pagus. Except that the whole center has been burned; the outskirts remain, and a huge pit which they have tried to patch with trees, kiosks, and other things with the plasticity of cement, and side boulevards that lead you to the despair of the roads of Giorgio de Chirico.
>
> From our house I found myself suddenly at the Central School for Girls, one of the very few old buildings that have survived. As far as I can recall, in my day the two neighborhoods were some distance apart. You had to wind through alley after alley, see many windows and many faces, pass through so much life—in order to get from one to the other. Now, among these empty, intersecting streets, one stride seems enough; all the proportions have changed for me. You still pass by the burned debris (left by the fire of 1922) and piles of dirt which look like offal from the crude sprouting of reinforced concrete. And it seems only yesterday that the great ship was wrecked. I feel no hatred; what prevails within me is the opposite of hatred; an attempt to *comprehend* the mechanism of catastrophe.

Ruin and catastrophe. And the images from "so much life" passed through in those alleys of his childhood coming into the poetry. A place is not only a clearing in the woods, a dot on the map, a city, a village, a farm, a river, a neighborhood, a house. A place is what happens in it and the memories that flow from it. How far do the memories go?

III

What do I remember about Seattle where I grew up? Born to immigrant parents with a Polish-Russian-Austro-Hungarian Jewish background, I was educated in California and lived for twenty-seven years in San Francisco. A West Coast sensibility. I started another life in Jerusalem in 1973. Am I an American poet living in Israel? Or an Israeli poet writing in English?

When I was a child I remember spending our summers on Puget Sound or on the numberless small lakes around Seattle, and my father would take me out in a rowboat. Once I was standing on a dock where the water was slapping against the wood and the boats were tied up to pegs. My father was already seated in the leaky little boat, the tin can ready for my job which was to keep bailing out the water, the oars in their locks, as he worked at the knot around the peg. Just when I put my foot into the boat, he loosened the rope and pushed off. I swayed there for an instant, one foot in the boat, the other on the dock. "Jump in," he yelled as my legs were losing each other. I jumped, and fell into the water.

IV

Memory is always connected to a place. Kimon Friar has said that the closest links between modern and ancient Greece have little to do with refurbished myth. "The true perennial factor is Greece itself; that mountainous, harsh, limestone peninsula, with its scatter of islands, its violent storms, its white-washed chapels, its poverty, its superstitions." And, for Seferis, the landscape of Smyrna as well.

Seferis, writing about Cavafy, might be describing himself. He says, although "they talk about Cavafy's worship of Hellenism . . . [he] never loses touch with his own life; it burns him, and he knows it is exactly the same when he expresses it in the Alexandria of Lathyrus, the Antioch of Julian, or the area of Rue Lepsius. . . . What makes Cavafy interesting is this give and take of life he maintains with the world of the past."

"The world of the past" and "his own life." As Seferis in his poem "The King of Asine," exploring the ruined acropolis of

Asine to recover "only one word in the Iliad," finds a gold burial
mask and relates it to his present existence:

> Behind the large eyes the curved lips the curls
> carved in relief on the gold cover of our existence
> a dark spot that you see trembling like a fish
> in the dawn calm of the sea:
> a void everywhere with us.
> . . . .
> and the country like a large plane-leaf swept along by the torrent
>   of the sun
> with the ancient monuments and the contemporary sorrow.

The past is so palpable, the lost grandeur of ancient Greek civilization, the memory of his lost home at Smyrna, Seferis feels that
he touches with his own fingers the King of Asine's "touch upon
the stones." The "dark spot," the "void everywhere with us"
which he finds in the gold mask of Asine, seems like a mirror
image of the passage quoted earlier from his journal where he
perceives Smyrna as a cloak with the whole center burned, "a
huge pit."

Or in "Thrush." The voice of a friend who gives him some
"wood from a lemon-tree" is heard with the voices of the dead in
Hades, voices from the Odyssey, from Socrates. Oedipus stares at
him out of the sea where he looks at the wreck of a naval transport
sunk in World War II.

When Seferis uses myth, the objects and place where he is
dramatize his own state of consciousness. His personal identification cuts through time:

> sometimes, near the sea, in naked rooms
> with a single iron bed and nothing of my own
> watching the evening spider, I imagine
> that something is getting ready to come . . .

Poets all over the world raid Greek mythology, for it is the symbolic heritage of western culture, but when Seferis uses it the traditional figures are truly alive and part of his own landscape.
They belong to the Greek poet writing in his own time as they
belong to nobody else.

(When American poets work honestly with similar material,
their mythical figures are somewhat different. Gerald Stern, in his
wonderful poem "Too Much, Too Much," finds a dead spider in
the pages of the Philadelphia *Inquirer* and evokes Turk Mendel-

sohn and Samuel Rappaport. He has a brass table instead of an iron bed.)

Seferis spent his childhood in Smyrna, his university years in Paris, and his mature life in various diplomatic posts. This wandering gave him the greatest longing and nostalgia for his own land. The poetry is suffused with exile. There are a few amazing poets to whom place means nothing—and everything, who live in a continual place of exile, homeless and yet at home, absorbing the humanity of the whole world into their art. St. John Perse, whose great poem "Exile" was written on the shores of New Jersey, was one of them. I think also of Yvan Goll's "Lackawanna Elegy," or Vallejo, and especially of Czeslaw Milosz.

Seferis is unique in that he alternated exile ("the world's become/ a limitless hotel") with being uneasily "at home." Most of his poems struggle to define what it means to be Greek. He could lie in a room anywhere dreaming of Elpenor "with a cigarette butt between his lips," or Circe "gazing absently toward the gramophone." Elpenor, Circe, Seferis. They were in it together. Anywhere.

V

The wandering Greek. And the wandering Jew. Is that why the poems of Seferis have meant so much to me since I first read them in translation twenty years ago? The Greek summons Elpenor and Circe. What does it mean to be Greek? The Jew summons Abraham and Lot's wife. What does it mean to be Jewish? To return to the Jewish homeland? To be an Israeli?

> . . . wandering around among broken stones, three or six thousand years
> searching in collapsed buildings that might have been our homes
> trying to remember dates and heroic deeds:
> will we be able?
>
> having been bound and scattered,
> having struggled, as they said, with non-existent difficulties
> lost, then finding again a road full of blind regiments
> sinking in marshes and in the lake of Marathon,
> will we be able to die properly?

This fragment from Seferis' *Mythisforema* might have been written by an Israeli poet if we substitute sand and the Sinai desert for "marshes" and the "lake of Marathon." Just as Greek poets such

as Seferis, Odysseus Elytis, Yannis Ritsos return again and again
to their ancient history and literature to understand their relationship to the world, to give meaning to the suffering of their own
time, to renew the legends and make them fresh again, to forge a
link between the past and future—so, too, Israeli poets like Amir
Gilboa, Abba Kovner, and Yehuda Amichai use the stories from
their Hebrew Bible and Midrashic literature in contemporary
terms. Their landscape is the old-new land of Israel. And it is very
similar to Greece, with its sun-baked stones, olive, fig, and pome-
granate trees, ancient ruins, Mediterranean light.

The generation of Israeli poets who were born in Europe and
survived the holocaust, bringing with them the accumulated experience of the diaspora, like Seferis recalling Smyrna, like the
three I have mentioned above, have never lost their sense of exile.
Whatever simmers in the Jewish collective unconscious from the
time of the destruction of the Temple and the first Exile, distilled
through many exiles in many lands, becomes the actual exile in
their own lifetime. Even the younger writers, born in Israel, feel,
as Yoram Kaniuk said in a recent interview, that when they met
the refugees from Europe and the ghosts and echoes they brought
with them, "our personal biographies became interwoven with
theirs . . . myth and autobiography became indistinguishable."

When Gilboa tells the story of Abraham and Isaac on their
way to the famous sacrifice, they are not on the road to Mt. Mori-
ah but in the forests of Europe under the Nazis, and in a terrible
reversal of roles, it is Abraham who says: "It's I who am
butchered, my son,/ my blood is already on the leaves."

Kovner sees the ashes of his Vilna ghetto in the Sinai desert,
and when he stands at midnight under the fluorescent street lamps of
modern Jerusalem facing the Turkish walls of the old city, he asks:

> Mount Zion, does it really exist
> or is it like our love that glows from another light
> rising night
> after night.

Amichai regards Saul in his poem "King Saul and I" with the
same kind of intimacy Seferis feels for Odysseus. Amichai:

> He was my big brother
> I got his used clothes.

Compare this to Seferis in "Upon A Foreign Verse":

> I imagine he's coming to tell me how I too may build a wooden
> horse to capture my own Troy.

Amichai's images are drawn from the entire lexicon of Jewish
history together with the intensely experienced actuality of modern Israel—its loves, its wars, its terrorism, its absurdities. The
past is always contained in the present.

In a long sequence by Amichai titled "Travels of a Latter-Day
Benjamin of Tudela," there is one poem I'd like to quote in full:

> I am sitting here now with my father's eyes,
> and with my mother's greying hair,
> in a house that belonged to an Arab
> who bought it from an Englishman
> who took it from a German
> who hewed it from the stones
> of Jerusalem, my city.
> I look upon God's world of others
> who received it from others.
> I am composed of many times
> I am constructed of spare parts
> of decomposing materials
> of disintegrating words. And already
> in the middle of my life, I begin
> gradually to return them,
> for I want to be a decent and orderly person
> when I'm asked at the border, "Have you anything to declare?"
> so that there won't be too much pressure at the end
> so that I won't arrive sweaty and breathless and confused
> so that I shan't have anything left to declare.

When Amichai writes, "I am composed of many times," we know
he feels it in his blood. "My father's eyes" are those of his real
father, but they are also the eyes of THE FATHERS: Abraham,
Isaac and Jacob. Amichai has written hauntingly of them, buried
in their tombs in the Cave of Machpelah in Hebron, in another
poem written after the 1967 war. And of the other MOTHERS.
The burden of memory is too heavy to bear. There are too many
"spare parts/ of decomposing materials."

In the poems of Amichai and these other Israeli poets their
sense of history, their spiritual inheritance, their struggle for survival on every level, calls forth a nervous longing to make some
sense of it all. Like Seferis, their work is filled with the tension of
contradiction, the conflict of the past thousands of years with the

impossible present and the timelessness of their own imaginations. They are able to use their ancient national literature to
translate experience, to sift one layer of history through another
and, in the process, illuminate each layer. And to let their myths
use them. For them there is no conflict between the public and the
private. And strongly located in place (chaotic as it is) and ancestral tradition, their voices resonate far beyond any borders.

VI

There is an interesting relationship between the work of
Seferis and the Swedish poet Tomas Tranströmer in Tranströmer's
cycle of poems *Baltics*. The *persona* in many of Seferis' poems is
a sea-captain, the ghost of Odysseus, the mythical father. And it is
Tranströmer's sea-captain grandfather who begins his exploration
in *Baltics*. Seferis writes (in "Upon A Foreign Verse"): "how
strangely you gain strength conversing with the/ dead when the
living who remain are no longer/ enough." Here is what Seferis
tells us about Odysseus' father:

> . . . I still see his hands that knew how to judge
> the carving of the mermaid at the prow
> presenting me the waveless blue sea in the heart of winter.

And here is Tranströmer's grandfather:

> He took them out to the Baltics, through
> that wonderful labyrinth of islands and water.
> . . . .
> . . . His eyes reading straight
> into the invisible.

Like Seferis and the Israeli poets, Tranströmer also works
toward an understanding of the alienated present through history,
but it's family history, not the history of an ancient people. His
place is an island in the archipelago off the east coast of Sweden
where his family lived for many years and where he returns each
summer. In *Baltics*, as he wanders over the island confronting the
relics he finds there, the baptismal font "in the half dark corner of
the Gotland church," reliving the death of his mother after a long
illness, recalling his grandparents, experiencing a sense of the
Baltics as frontier and route for communication, he seems to be
passing through fear and hazard and sorrow to a place where he is
at home in the difficult world. The island provides him with the

necessary distance and isolation and restores a feeling of connection with the less temporal. "Only inside there is peace, in the water of the vessel no one sees,/ but on the outer walls the struggle rages."

Robert Hass, in an illuminating article on *Baltics* and Tranströmer, writes that his work has always seemed that of a deeply rooted man:

> Friends have told me about his Swedishness, in "Evening—Morning" for example, where the image of the dock and the half-suffocated summer gods seem inseparable from the paradisiacal long days of the short Swedish summer, and in "Sailor's Tale," how the *barvinterdager*, the dark winter days without snow in November and December are so central to the poem that it can almost not be felt without knowledge and experience.

Being completely local and rooted, yet despairing of where mankind is heading, when Tranströmer moves into himself in the fifth section of *Baltics*, the island, its wind, its sea, and its forest, surrounds and enters him:

> The wind that blew so carefully all day—
> all the blades of grass are counted on the furthest islets—
> has lain down in the middle of the island. The matchstick's flame
>   stands straight up.
> The sea painting and the forest painting darken together.
> Also the foliage of the five story trees is turning black.
> "Every summer is the last." These are empty words
> for the creatures at late summer midnight
> where the crickets sew on their machines as if possessed
> and the Baltic's near
> and the lonely water tap stands among the wild rose bushes
> like an equestrian statue. The water tastes of iron.

That taste, that image of the "possessed" crickets, the water tap as "an equestrian statue" caught in the wind and the light, the Baltic landscape—all these are strongly physical, as if the place and Tranströmer were one and the relationship were symbiotic. The bond is memory, both recent and mythic, extending through all time and space.

At the end of *Baltics* he arrives at the two-hundred-year-old fisherman's hut which is the family house:

> So much crouching wood. And on the roof the ancient tiles that
>   collapsed across and on top of each other
> (the original pattern erased by the earth's rotation through the
>   years)

it reminds me of something . . . I was there . . . wait: it's the old
    Jewish cemetery in Prague
where the dead live closer together than they did in life, the stones
    jammed in, jammed in.
So much encircled love! The tiles with the lichen's letters in an
    unknown language
are the stones in the archipelago people's ghetto cemetery, the
    stones erected and fallen down—

The ramshackle hut shines
with the light of all the people carried by the certain wave, the
    certain wind,
out there to their fates.

Finally the place—the certain wave, the certain wind, the certain
hut—joins him with "all the people."

VII

If poems come out of our whole being, out of much I have
not dealt with here—imagination, intelligence, sensory perception, the music in our heads, a personal form and structure—and
if we live in the world, why look for any specific place? The
answer comes from Seferis and Amichai and Tranströmer. And
the Baal Shem in the story with which I began. To be grounded.
To be "in touch." To gather what's needed for the fire and light it.
To know, as Ignatow's poem puts it: "where I am going and what/
I am going from."
    But how does one cope with America as a place? So huge. So
diverse. So brief a history. In his poem "About History,"
Tranströmer says, "Memory is slowly transmitted into your own
self." What happens when the memory is short?
    Americans came to the New World rejecting history, reject-
ing the old ways. They wanted to make something new.

We want a national literature commensurate with our mountains
and rivers . . . a national epic that shall correspond to the size
of the country . . . and to the unparalleled activity of our people. . . . In a word, we want a national literature altogether
shaggy and unshorn, that shall shake the earth, like a herd of buf-
faloes thundering over the prairies.

These words were written by Henry Wadsworth Longfellow 130
years ago, and he met his own challenge with *Hiawatha*.
Hiawatha!

It was Whitman, of course, who opened his form to fit the place, who heard America singing and wrote it down. Beyond the flawed moments of bombast, he was always "of Manhattan the son," although the only bookstore in New York that would sell *Leaves of Grass* when the first edition was printed in 1855 was a "phrenological depot" on Broadway, and a contemporary critic said he "combines the characteristics of a Concord philosopher with those of a New York fireman." Whitman saw himself as the poet of the People and set out to "define America, her athletic Democracy" in his poems. "The United States themselves are essentially the greatest poem," he said.

Calling Whitman "the first white aboriginal," with "the true rhythm of the American continent speaking out of him," D. H. Lawrence wrote:

> And lots of new little poets camping on Whitman's camping ground now. But none going really beyond. Because Whitman's camp is at the end of the road, and on the edge of a great precipice. Over the precipice, blue distances, and the blue hollow of the future. And there is no way down. It is a dead end.

Was it a dead end? "The Open Road goes to the used-car lot," Louis Simpson tells us.

American poets have been wandering down that road ever since. And it has led to a variety of strange places besides the used-car lot. Most, since the ambitious failures of Hart Crane or Sandburg, and leaving aside the expatriates Pound and Eliot, have limited themselves to a smaller territory than the whole of America, because the whole is unmanageable. One city, one state, one region is more like the size of Greece or Israel or Sweden, and possible to encompass. So Frost, born in San Francisco, returned to the animals, trees, barns, voices of his father's first home in New England. Williams, continuing Whitman's search for new forms and wanting to record the living language exactly as it was spoken, insisted even more on the local. The open road led to *Paterson* and the "radiant gist." From there Olson took it to Gloucester, writing in "Maximus to Gloucester, Letter 27 (Withheld)":

> An American
> is a complex of occasions,
> themselves a geometry
> of spatial nature.
>   I have this sense,
> that I am one

```
with my skin
   Plus this—plus this:
that forever the geography
which leans in
on me I compel
backwards I compel Gloucester
to yield, to
change
   Polis
is this
```

This poem seems to contradict the feeling I get from the European poets, the Greek, the Israeli—that they do not have to "com-
pel" their geography backwards in a conscious act. It simply and
naturally "leans in" on them, and compels *them.* Still Olson knew
his own center. Even with a risky over-muchness.

In some ways Paterson and Gloucester are only metaphors.
Yet out of a certain place—begin. To draw perimeters before you
erase them, to know the place of the first belonging, its local history (ALL history for Olson), its voices, the struggles of parents,
the stories of grandparents, a generation whose memory still links
us to a richer tradition we think might matter.

For Frost and Williams, even with a more limited historical
range, and for Olson who over-reached after an ancient past of the
human race, much as for the other poets I have been looking at,
the place chose them as much as they chose the place. How do we
find the "certain place" of the Baal Shem now, in a country with
endless mobility, poets moving wherever their jobs take them?
How do we make poetry out of Texas or Idaho if we've grown up
in New York? How deep can it go? "The poet becomes threshold,"
Larry Levis wrote in a recent article in *FIELD*, but how long does
it take for "what is out there" to "move inside" and be authentic?
And how do we shift from nostalgia to historical memory, or find
a tradition, the fuel to light the fire, in the vast, crazy woods of
America where the only images or symbols common to most people are bombers unloading over Vietnam or ads for Coca Cola and
Johnson's Wax? And where the generations have lost touch with
each other?

Americans wander from one place to another, but we are not
the exiles I was describing earlier. Our displacement or alienation
is not like the exile of Seferis and those European poets like
Milosz who carry their past wherever they go. Not even like the
exile of Amichai, Gilboa, and Kovner who are more "at home" in
Israel than they ever were in Germany, the Ukraine, or Vilna. The

wandering of the American poet does not usually make him long for the place where he was born. In fact, he's often glad to be out of it.

Still, something nags at us in our dreams. The search for roots became the contemporary cliché of the sixties and seventies, but it started much earlier and has been going on for a long time. Some wanted, like Olson, to repossess a tradition older than America, some to repossess the America of their childhood, and others, like Lowell in much of his work, to repossess an America constructed out of history and childhood together. A complicated search. James Wright kept returning to Ohio, to the Shreve High football stadium, to the "hobo jungle weeds/ Upstream from the sewer main" along the dying Ohio River to the great Depression and the WPA swimming pool, until he arrived at his late epiphany and transformation of sorrow and loneliness, "Beautiful Ohio":

> Those old Winnebago men
> Knew what they were singing.
> All summer long and all alone,
> I had found a way
> To sit on a railroad tie
> Above the sewer main.
> It spilled a shining waterfall out of a pipe
> Somebody had gouged through the slanted earth.
> Sixteen thousand and five hundred more or less people
> In Martins Ferry, my home, my native country
> Quickened the river
> With the speed of light.
> And the light caught there
> The solid speed of their lives
> In the instant of that waterfall.
> I know what we call it
> Most of the time.
> But I have my own song for it,
> And sometimes, even today,
> I call it beauty.

Tranströmer's "lonely water tap," a projection of his own loneliness, on his island, and Wright's "sewer main." This is not the only poem of Wright in which it appears. "All summer long and all alone." Both poets arrive at the same moving perception of Tranströmer's "encircled love." So that Tranströmer's ramshackle hut and Wright's waterfall both shine with an uncanny light. In another poem, "To the Creature of the Creation," Wright says, "The one tongue I can write in/ is my Ohioan."

I think if we put James Wright's Ohio poems together, or
Philip Levine's Detroit poems, we might get something like
Tranströmer's *Baltics*. A movement through the poet's own
childhood and adolescence, family, poverty and war, the immediate past—toward what may be ultimately the only question—
not what does it all mean, but what am I doing here? HERE. As
against THERE. HERE might be Reznikoff's Brooklyn ghetto
and Manhattan, Donald Junkins' Atlantic coast and Swan's
Island, Wendell Berry's Kentucky, or Gerald Stern's Pennsylvania
and New Jersey. Or even a place without family connections. The
Arizona desert as Richard Shelton knows it, Hugo's small dying
towns in Montana, John Haines in Alaska, or the phantasmagoria
of Avenue C in New York as Kinnell experienced it.

HERE and THERE. Ginsberg in a supermarket in California
or the Wichita vortex or the urban jungle of New York, Robert
Hass in northern California and in Buffalo, George Oppen in New
York, Maine, and the northern California coast—"that beach is
the edge of a nation . . . ," Gary Snyder in the Cascades, or Japan,
or the Sierras, and now the whole globe: Turtle Island. Few Americans end up where they started. We have to know many places.
As well as we can.

VIII

So I sit at my desk in Jerusalem, looking back at Seattle and
San Francisco, looking back at the women in the Bible who keep
getting into my poems, looking down through the excavated layers of the First and Second Temples, Roman forum, Moslem
mosques, Crusader citadel, Mameluke fountain, Turkish walls,
looking into the sad, outrageous history of my people, at the
ruins, the arches with nothing behind them, the broken stones, the
violent history of this country where I now live, looking out at the
guard in front of the mayor's house. He is bored and hot in the
bright glare of the afternoon sun. He walks up and down in the
shade of the jacaranda tree. Only a few steps in either direction to
where the light burns the sidewalk. My husband calls out the window to ask if he's thirsty and takes him a can of beer. The name of
the beer is Maccabbee. Our hero who started the Hasmonean
dynasty in 145 B.C.

Is this my history? Is this my place? The name of my street is
Rashba, an acronym for the Talmudic scholar *R*abbi Soloman
(*Sh*lomo) *b*en *A*braham Adret, who lived in Barcelona in the thir-
teenth century. The Jewish encyclopedia says "he distinguished

himself by his clear logical thinking and by his critical penetrating understanding." He issued a decree excommunicating anyone who wanted to study philosophy before he was twenty-five. And he attacked the mystical doctrine of some of his contemporaries. It doesn't seem like a good street for a poet to live on.

Sometimes I let this poem of Berryman unhinge me:

ROOTS

Young men (young women) ask about my 'roots,'—
as if I were a *plant*. Yeats said to me,
with some pretentiousness, I felt even then,
'London is useful, but I always go back

to Ireland, where my roots are.' Mr Eliot,
too, worried about his roots
whether beside the uncontrollable river
the Mississippi, or the Thames, or elsewhere.

I can't see it. Many are wanderers,
both Lawrence, Byron, & the better for it.
Many stay home forever. Hardy: fine.
Bother these bastards with their preconceptions.

The hell with it. Whether to go or stay
be Fate's, or mine, no matter.
Exile is in our time like blood. Depend on
interior journeys taken anywhere.

I'd rather live in Venice or Kyoto,
except for the languages, but
O really I don't care where I live or have lived.
Wherever I am, young Sir, my wits about me,

memory blazing, I'll cope & make do.

Does it negate everything I've been trying to put down here? Don't all of us depend on our interior journeys more than anything else? Exile is in our time like blood. But Berryman had a "memory blazing" and couldn't have written those voices of Henry and Mr. Bones without the sound of a place in his head. He protests too much. "Whether to go or stay" does matter. He did much more than "cope & make do." (Though finally he didn't.)

I wanted a good place to settle:
Cold Mountain would be safe.

Light wind in a hidden pine—
Listen close—the sound gets better.
Under it a gray-haired man
Mumbles along reading Huang and Lao.
For ten years I haven't gone back home
I've even forgotten the way by which I came.

That's Snyder's translation of one of the Cold Mountain poems. "I wanted a good place to settle" is the unspoken yearning of Berryman and most of us "exiles." State of mind *and* real place in the mountains of China, Han-Shan in the eighth century (give or take a hundred years) was talking about the place he arrived at. He didn't forget the way by which he came. The poems are full of it.

I cope and make do and read the Hasidic stories:

When the Baal Shem had a difficult task before him, he would go to a certain place in the woods, light a fire and meditate in prayer—and what he had set out to perform was done. . . .

(1980)

Larry Levis

EDEN AND
MY GENERATION

The following was delivered as a lecture at the Aspen Writers'
Conference in July 1980, at Aspen, Colorado.

I. The Connoisseurs of Loss

At least since the Bible and Milton, much of English poetry has
been preoccupied with the loss of Eden and the resulting knowledge which partially and paradoxically compensates for all solitary exile. But as myth became, in the artistic *and* general consciousness, more and more possible only in a radically *secular*
way, poetry began to locate Eden, not in public myth, but in the
privacy of personal experience, and to explore it in the lyric rather
than the epic mode. Eden became a real *place;* it could be named,
spoken of, lived in and remembered. The Romantic poets understood Eden, not as an elsewhere, but as a place inside the poet's
own life. Wordsworth's landscape becomes, in his recollection,
his private, unauthorized, unorthodox Eden. Yet Wordsworth's
decision to *make* such a landscape Edenic is a compromise in
which he stands, warily but finally, at the center.

In just this fashion, the named, autobiographical, particular
place, whether Paumanok or Paterson or Big Sur or Vermont,
became a way to locate the theme—became, as place, the new and
personally experienced Eden. The poetry of my own generation,
however, has been turning away or aside from such named, secular
but sanctified places. Instead, it generalizes self-consciously about
the Edenic theme of loss and exile. And with that change has come
a corresponding change in language. This resistance to a resolutely imagistic, autobiographical poetry, and a preference for a more
abstract, meditative mode of thinking testifies not merely to private loss, exile, and knowledge, but to a *collective and genera-
tional* loss, exile, and knowledge. The very language used has
become increasingly less innocent, or such innocence increasingly
less possible. In a way my generation has had to invent a way of
thinking and a language which could not only record its losses, but
could also question the motive behind every use of that language—
especially its own. This need, however, is not only some necessary
Oedipal and dialectal *agon* of one generation reproaching another.

It is simply that for my generation there was no access via experience to the Eden of its parents. For to replace Eden in their own expressionist language is simply to mimic Eden or mock it. To find it is to find the words it needs in one's own time.

II. Place

Donald Hall begins an interesting essay on the nature of place in poetry with the following remarks:

> For some poets, poetry derives from a place. Poem after poem reaches back and touches this place, and rehearses experiences connected with the place: Wordsworth's "Nature"; the Welsh farms of Dylan Thomas; T. S. Eliot's St. Louis and Dry Salvages; Wallace Stevens' Florida; Walt Whitman and Paumanok; architectural Italy for Ezra Pound; Gloucester for Charles Olson . . . But I am not thinking only of poetry which is geographic or descriptive. I am thinking of places which to the poets embody or recall a spiritual state (205-07).

But how do poems "embody or recall" these "spiritual" states? Hall's notions here have the flavor of truth, but perhaps it is wisest to realize these ideas specifically, as poems do. To begin with one personal example, the poet Gary Soto's San Joaquin Valley is the same geographical region I am from, and yet his experience of that place, both sacred and blasphemous, is that of a Mexican-American, and it is vastly different from my own experience of it as the son of a farmer, an "Anglo." In a way, we lived side by side, but in different worlds. Similarly, a few miles to the north in Fresno, David St. John was growing up, but into a place which even then considered itself a city. Against that more or less brutal and degenerating ambience, St. John refined his poetry, distilled it into a bitter elegance. And ninety miles south, in Bakersfield, where *every* variety of vine refuses, finally, to grow, Frank Bidart must have been working. Talking once about his poems, and speaking in defense of their lack of imagery, their brazen love of the abstract statement, I found myself saying that such an aesthetic as his could come only from Bakersfield, that the poems' lack of imagery resembled the impoverishment of their soil. I was naive, of course; it wasn't the poetry of Bakersfield; it was only the poetry of Bidart's *Golden State*. It is the geography of the psyche that matters, not the place.

And so a place in poetry, if it is good poetry, may be a spiritual state and not a geographic one. Compare, for example, T. S.

Eliot's Gloucester with Charles Olson's. Similarly, my San Joaquin Valley is like no one else's, even though the same vineyards and towns may appear there. And obviously, a reader can't learn as much, factually, about a place from a poet as he can from a decent journalist. The place of a *poem*—Levine's Detroit; James Wright's Ohio; Lowell's Boston; the various Northwests of Gary Snyder, Carolyn Kizer, Richard Hugo, William Stafford, David Wagoner; Elizabeth Bishop's Nova Scotia—these are places we can never get to, and not simply because those places, every place, are subject to change and decay, or subject to that peculiarly ominous breeze at the end of Hugo's "Death of Kapowsin Tavern": "wind black enough to blow it all away." Rather, the poet has sealed those places away into the privacies of his or her work forever, so that, as William Gass observed, Joyce's Dublin is vastly superior to the real one. In a way, we can never get to those places because they don't exist—not really, anyway. But once, I tried to find such a place. I walked for days through Boston, wondering, idly, how it got there, and why. I did remember one line from Stevens: "The wise man avenges by building his city in snow." But mostly it was the grave, ruefully humorous poetry of Lowell's *Life Studies* that kept ringing quietly in my mind: "Boston's hardly passionate Marlborough Street" (which is actually a phrase Lowell borrows from William James) or "the trees with Latin labels" on Boston Common (they do have labels!). But then, to mimic Lowell, I was so out of things. At eighteen, I was so Californian I thought even Detroit was an "Eastern" city, and to discover Boston through Lowell was like trying to discover Italy through Ezra Pound. I felt like a tourist with one of the most idiosyncratic and beautiful guidebooks ever written. But I did feel like a tourist. *Life Studies* gave me a way to *feel* a place which was not there anymore. It could never be there at all for me, really, for Lowell's Boston childhood and harrowing adult life consist primarily of what Bachelard would call "intimate" space—Lowell's poems usually occur in closed rooms, in privacies ("endurable and perfect") given up to him by his memory. It is not surprising that Lowell traces the inception of the first poem he wrote for *Life Studies* to the obsessive, recurring image of a "blue, china door-knob." And no doubt, by the time I arrived, someone else was living at 91 Revere Street. I don't know; I was too shy to go up and knock.

Place in poetry, then, or for that matter in much fiction, is often spiritual, and yet it is important to note that this spiritual location clarifies itself and becomes valuable only through one's absence from it. Eden becomes truly valuable only after a fall, after an exile that changes it, irrecoverably, from what it once was. When I returned to California in 1970 to teach, I returned to a withered Eden, and there was, all around me, even in the cool cynicism of stoned kids on Hollywood Boulevard, enough to confirm its demise. In one of his earlier poems, Robert Hass phrased that demise in strict couplets: "My God it is a test,/ This riding out the dying of the West." Fallen, I returned to my home, and, if I did not have any real vision then, I did have eyesight. I could *see* the place—that is one of the consequences of falling.

It is no wonder, then, that Donald Hall, in his essay, goes on to ask:

> What kind of place must it be? It must be a place where we felt free. It must be a place associated not with school or with conventional endeavor or with competition or with busyness. It must be a place, therefore, in which we can rehearse feelings (and a type of thinking) which belong in evolutionary terms to an earlier condition of humanity. And it is this earlier mind that we wish to stimulate, in poetry. Sometimes we speak as if we wish to return to it; actually, we want it to return to us, and to live with us forever. Therefore the place which is golden is a place where we have loafed and invited the soul, and where the ego—not yet born—has made no demands on the soul (207).

Perhaps all of this *is* true, even the earlier mind theory, if only in the substrata of the poet's memory. And yet the particular struggle, the *agon* and play which is a poem, usually records, laments, or testifies to our distance from this "golden place." That may be why, when Robert Hass writes a later and more analytical poem, "Meditation at Lagunitas," he begins by saying: "All the new thinking is about loss./ In this it resembles all the old thinking." It is almost as if, from "Tintern Abbey" to Lowell's "Grandparents," variations on the same theme were struck up, in different music, different chords. Even if we look at one of the most Edenic and pastoral of modern poems, Dylan Thomas' "Fern Hill," the poet's final agony is apparent when he concludes: "And wake to the farm forever fled from the childless land./ Oh as I was young and easy in the mercy of his means,/ Time held me green and dying/ Though I sang in my chains like the sea." It is only in his absence from such a farm that he can see its paradoxical meaning, that one is always in a state of becoming, and that one is always, also, becoming nothing. If we endure our Edens, Thomas says, and that is what we must do, all easy jubilation ends.

But suppose a poet does not leave his home, his place, does not fall from his Eden, but in fact seems to stay there, as James Wright seems to stay, through memory and imagination, in his native Ohio? But how can any Eden endure the Self? Much of the painful power and beauty in Wright's work comes from his witnessing the decay of his place:

> For a proud man,
> Lost between the turnpike near Cleveland
> And the chiropractors' signs looming among dead mulberry trees,
> There is no place left to go
> But home.

He has almost said, or he may as well have said: "There is no home left to go to." When we fall, we begin to know, we begin to see. To stay in that special, spiritual place is, simply, to watch its dismemberment through time. As we mature, or just grow older, we are given *sight,* or rather our memories give us a particularly subjective (hence objective and objectifying) ability to remember what once was in distinction to what is, at each moment, around us. Such imagery, such memory and witnessing, affords the Ohio of James Wright much of its power. Even the place names, "Wheeling Steel," "Benwood," "Marion," participate in a past, not a present. The same is true of Lowell's *Life Studies,* Levine's *1933,* Gerald Stern's *Lucky Life,* Snyder's *Myths & Texts,* Bishop's *Geography III,* Robert Penn Warren's *Or Else*—the possible list is endless. Even if a poet chooses not to name his place, as Stanley Kunitz chooses in his poem, "Father and Son," the remembered place, the pond, becomes a radiance.

For many, of course, my idea of the Edenic will seem difficult to accept, or it will appear archaic, or merely silly. As a concept, it aligns itself so clearly to the Bible and to Milton that it seems permanently to recall its sources, and to recall orthodox conceptions of sin, guilt, death, sex, or at least the knowledge of these. But I intend the term only in its loosest, and perhaps most relevant, sense: that is, I may not believe in the myth of The Fall, but it is still possible for me to feel *fallen.* Why? Because I can see, and perhaps because the myth and the feeling is explainable as Freud explains it, in *Civilization and its Discontents*:

> Originally the ego includes everything, later it detaches from itself the outside world. The ego-feeling we are aware of now is thus only a shrunken vestige of a more extensive feeling—a feeling which embraced the universe and expressed an inseparable

connection of the ego with the external world. If we may suppose that this primary ego-feeling has been preserved in the minds of many people—to a greater or lesser extent—it would co-exist like a sort of counterpart with the narrower and more sharply outlined ego-feeling of maturity, and the ideational content belonging to it would be precisely the notion of limitless extension and oneness with the universe—the same feeling as that described by my friend as "oceanic" (15).

Later elaborations of this, perhaps even Lacan's "stade du miroir" theory, attest to similar separations. In his essay on the growth of landscape painting, Rilke phrases the idea with a simpler grandeur: "For men only began to understand Nature when they no longer understood it; when they felt that it was the Other, indifferent towards men, without senses by which to apprehend us, then for the first time they stepped outside of Nature, alone, out of a lonely world."

Poetry, the poetry of the spiritual place, can remind us, then, of the Edenic, even of the "oceanic." What seems to be a curious phenomenon of nineteenth and twentieth century poetry in particular is that the Edenic or "oceanic" is often retrievable only through a poem with a highly *specified* place: "Tintern Abbey"; "Little Gidding"; "Brooklyn Bridge"; "Paterson"; "Paumanok"; "Gloucester"; "Dover Beach"; the New Englands of Dickinson and Frost; the South of Dickey, Penn Warren, Tate, Jarrell, Ransom; Jeffers' Big Sur; Bly's Minnesota. This involvement with Place, from Romantic and Modernist poets to the present, has come about in part I think because a poet wants to locate himself or herself somewhere, to be "a man (or a woman) speaking to men (or women)"; it is also a way of testifying to the demands and limitations of lyrical experience, to say: "I was the man, I suffered, I was there." The lyric wishes to be antidogmatic, nondidactic, *honest*. Williams articulated the idea this way: "It is in the wide range of the local only that the general can be trusted for its one unique quality, its universality." And "the local" is that vestige of the "oceanic" which Freud says we carry within ourselves, withered, out of childhood. And it *is there*, in the place recalled by the poet, the sacred home. It can't be otherwise, the poems seem to tell us—the holy place *is* a few miles above Tintern Abbey; or is just under a particular cedar growing in the place of a vanished New England farm town in Frost's "Directive"; or it is in the burned-out remains of Hugo's Kapowsin Tavern; or in Levine's unburned Detroit in 1952; or on a mountain top in the Cascades where Gary Snyder pauses, "between heaven and earth," before going down "to stand in lines in Seattle, looking for work." It will be there, or nowhere, the poems *deceive us* into believing. Actually, reading such poems, we discover, excavated by another's feeling, those places in ourselves.

*

However, I don't intend to suggest that poets write only about such places. They don't. And there are any number of strong poets whom I cannot associate with any particularized place, such as Creeley, Strand, Ashbery, Rich, and Merwin. And yet because of the predominance of place, especially in American poetry of recent decades, it is only to be expected that a turning away from a particular, named, autobiographical poetry of place might occur, and this is what I believe is happening in the work of some of the younger poets writing now. I should say that this poetry, abstract or meditative as it might be, is not new, however—see Rilke and Stevens. And I also want to say that even when this poetry is at its most meditative, the inhabiting or recalling of a spiritual place continues, and without serious impediments. But first I think it is important to speculate, at least for my own purposes here, on what sort of shift has occurred, and to ask why it has occurred. For to turn away from one's own autobiographical, personal memory of a particular place is to appear, often enough, to have accomplished a dismissal of one tradition: that of the alienated, isolated artist.

And yet most younger poets still testify precisely to this alienation and isolation, this falling from Eden. Only they have changed it. It is as if the whole tradition has become, by now, shared, held in common, a *given*—or as if the poems confer the same sort of loss upon all of us, not only upon the privately suffering poet. And yet for a while, in the late sixties and early seventies in this country, it seemed to me that almost every American poem was going to locate itself within a more or less definite place, was going to be spoken usually in the first person singular, and would involve, often, the same kind of testimony to the poet's isolations. The problem of that poetic stance was, unfortunately, its real power—its irresistibly attractive, usually imagistic surface. So many young poets, responding honestly to the work of Bly, Wright, Snyder, Plath, Stafford or Merwin, tended to write poems that looked stylistically imitative, even derivative, of those and of other poets. That imitative gesture began to feel faint, inauthentic, often simply insincere or naive. And finally, as if in despair of recreating the reality of prior visions, this poetry often took on a sarcastic or sardonic attitude toward experience (some of the dark humor of James Tate and Bill Knott might be read as a visionary reaction to older poets) and toward place itself, as in Cynthia MacDonald's funny satire of Bly's Midwest, in which an otherwise sensible young woman gives up her prior life, and, following Bly's advice, moves to South Dakota and spends the rest of her years working in a service station, far from anything except a randomly passing client. But many of the poems were not informed by any satirical purpose. They were *serious* and heartfelt. Even so, too many of the poems about Ohio or Illinois really began to merely anthologize a few clichés or commonplaces about the Midwest—clichés available to anyone who can read the cartoons in *The New Yorker,* or worse luck, *The Reader's Digest.* Often, the cartoons in *The New Yorker* at least were much more imaginative than some of the poems. The vast increase in small magazines, in the sheer number of them, seems in retrospect to have had nothing to do with authenticating American places: often the poets had no interest in becoming the mythographers of the place in which they happened to be, anyway, and so Gary Snyder's advice to this effect had little sway. What did this kind of poem typically look like? I will quote only one example, a poem called "Driving East"—I am withholding the name of the poet, however, because this is, for him, a very early poem, and because his later and more mature work seems to me very beautiful and haunting:

> For miles,
> the snow is on all sides of me,
> waiting.
> I feel like
> a lot of empty cattle yards,
> my hinges swing open to the wind.

Pretty, yes, but as a whole it is just too easy. Besides, hinges don't swing open to the wind; gates do. Too often the poet could look like a tourist dressed in some other poet's style, and style itself, as is usually the case in America, became too important. More seriously, place meant nothing very important to these poets, and nothing very spiritual, and such a poetry wasn't even "regional." The larger problem, obvious by now, was that there simply wasn't much experience or craft in poems such as "Toledo, Ohio, As Seen from the Balcony of the Holiday-Inn." What had been a truly visionary prospect in the poetry of James Wright or Philip

Levine became trivialized in the more immature imitations. But I am not maligning anyone, here, for being influenced. There probably isn't any other way to learn how to write poetry.

Still, so many of the poets of the sixties and seventies had no place to go—and no home worth returning to.

Again, in some unspecifiably social sense, it may be that places themselves became, throughout much of America, so homogenized that they became less and less available as spiritual locations, shabbier and sadder. A friend from Alabama once lamented to me that he had, as a young fiction writer, no South left to write about, that the topless bars and MacDonald's in Birmingham were like topless bars and MacDonald's everywhere. He could only imagine a South that had disappeared, and this was a literary South. But to create such an imagined place in spite of the reality around him would eventually make him participate in a merely literary regionalism. And the problem with a poem, or a story, that is strictly regional is its vulnerability (like those too numerous photographs of collapsed barns) to time. For example, it is still possible for me to admire Sandburg's "Chicago," but much of my admiration for it must be mixed with indistinct feelings of nostalgia, distrust, even embarrassment. Yes, I say, Chicago is strong, and its ugliness is a variety of the Beautiful, and yet it is impossible not to know that what Sandburg celebrates is as corny as it is destructive. The poem has matured into a period piece. With shrewder art, this is not the case. For example, old brick buildings in New York can seem charming to me, even powerfully evocative, but then I remember that they are so evocative in this very precise way because I am remembering Edward Hopper's *Early Sunday Morning*, which is not, by the way, regional at all, but great. In a way, I don't, or can't, because of Hopper, see the place at all. Thus, sometimes, the world can turn comically into, and mimic, the art we thought was *about it*. But where the title of *regionalist* is conferred, isn't there a sense, too, of the anachronistic about the region, if not the artist? The regional dissolves almost too obediently into the picturesque. So *Spoon River Anthology*, in which Masters is often brilliant, remains *regional*. It survives, but it survives, like any truly regionalist poem, like those curious museum towns in New England, like the Maine town in "Skunk Hour" which Lowell satirizes—what once was vital and real comes down to a matter of a few old buildings, kept chronically on display, and housing a boutique, a restaurant, or antique shops. In a way, the *patina* used by the regionalist resembles the renovations of the decorator: it obscures the place.

And yet, I am not advising anyone to move into the extreme alternative; besides, no one, knowing what he or she cannot possibly not know about American cities today, could justifiably celebrate Chicago as Sandburg once could celebrate it. But then, poets don't necessarily celebrate Chicago or Denver or Los Angeles, they celebrate loss, they celebrate Eden—the myth of the place in the psyche.

Now it would be easy, and too convenient, to divide older and younger poets into two groups: older poets who appear to have places, and homes, and younger poets who are writing a more abstract, contemplative, unlocalized poetry. Any distinction along these lines would be sophomoric and wrong, however. There are many younger poets who identify themselves with one or more places, and who do this, who claim a place, in methods that renew the tradition of older poets. Robert Hass, Dave Smith, Carolyn Forché, Greg Pape, David St. John and Stanley Plumly are all poets whose work displays a strong attachment to place. Yet they are never limited *by* place, and often write a poem which could happen anywhere.

And yet, so many younger poets today seem to have no home worth returning to, or worth specifying in the way that Hass specifies the Bay area of California, or Gary Soto specifies the San Joaquin Valley, or Smith specifies his particular region of the South. Jon Anderson, Thomas Lux, Laura Jensen, Michael Ryan, Tess Gallagher, Daniel Halpern, Marcia Southwick, and so many others appear to have experienced a kind of orphaning by and in America. It may be that this experience, this new homelessness, is what a number of these new poets have in common when they practice the "meditational" mode—for what they tend to hold in common is, at heart, a contradiction: an intimate, *shared* isolation. This isolation is a growth of all the older isolations, but the nature of it has been somewhat changed. Instead of the private loneliness of the first person point of view, there appears to be, even when unstated, a narrator who behaves as a "we" rather than an "I." Another distinction in this work is its reliance upon increasingly abstract statement and metaphors rather than upon image only. It is interesting to witness Robert Hass, a poet of place if there ever was one, in a sort of transition from one method to another. (I should note here that many other poets are involved in the same kind of shift, and that it is dramatically obvious in David St. John's *Hush* and *The Shore*.) For what occurs in Hass's poem "Meditation at Lagunitas" is memory, autobiography—but also the turning away of the poet from the place he confronts and from the poet he once was. It is as if the reader bears witness to a poet seeing through his own need for a place, for location. Truth is not at Lagunitas; it is within the meditation itself. And though this was always the case, Hass stresses it through the larger, abstract claims he makes in the poem.

MEDITATION AT LAGUNITAS

All the new thinking is about loss.
In this it resembles all the old thinking.
The idea, for example, that each particular erases
the luminous clarity of a general idea. That the clown-
faced woodpecker probing the dead sculpted trunk
of that black birch is, by his presence,
some tragic falling off from a first world
of undivided light. Or the other notion that,
because there is in this world no one thing
to which the bramble of *blackberry* corresponds,
a word is elegy to what it signifies.
We talked about it late last night and in the voice
of my friend, there was a thin wire of grief, a tone
almost querulous. After a while I understood that,
talking this way, everything dissolves: *justice,*
pine, hair, woman, you and *I*. There was a woman
I made love to and I remembered how, holding
her small shoulders in my hands sometimes,
I felt a violent wonder at her presence
like a thirst for salt, for my childhood river
with its island willows, silly music from the pleasure boat,
muddy places where we caught the little orange-silver fish
called *pumpkinseed*. It hardly had to do with her.
Longing, we say, because desire is full
of endless distances. I must have been the same to her.
But I remember so much, the way her hands dismantled bread,
the thing her father said that hurt her, what
she dreamed. There are moments when the body is as numinous
as words, days that are the good flesh continuing.
Such tenderness, those afternoons and evenings,
saying *blackberry, blackberry, blackberry.*

The focus of the poem throughout is either directly or tangentially upon the problem of language itself—its uses, its illusions. In this sense the poem's vision is only partly personal, for Hass' speculations come as much from philosophical considerations, from Lacan or Derrida, as from his own experience. In fact, I think Hass would stress, *does* stress in the poem, that thinking itself

amounts to experience, to a life, just as any other thing we do—
play, work, sex, talking—amounts to a life.

As *art* the poem is considerably calmer, seemingly more
detached and reasonable in its phrasings than much of the poetry
which flourished in the late sixties or early seventies. There is
nothing very surreal in Hass's methods, no concern over a deepening image, and in the poem's imagistic modesty there may be even
a buried admonition (if only to the poet himself) that the impulse
and gesture which can willfully create a wild imagery for its own
sake is perhaps not worth the trouble, is perhaps even aestheticaly
ly disingenuous or dishonest. The gain of such a calm is real: the
poet is free of what Stevens called "the pressure of reality," and he
is at least allowed a place for meditation. The poem resists mere
autobiography through a rapt, abstract energy or impulse. Hass
has no sooner introduced the woman into his poem than she is, at
least until his conclusion, dismissed. For a moment she even turns
into a *law:* "Longing, we say, because desire is full/ of endless
distances. I must have been the same to her." But Hass is so conscious of what he is doing! He is conscious enough, even, to distrust the very method of thinking which has afforded his poem,
and so, at poem's end, he returns to the truth of remembered, personal experience; then, characteristically, revealingly, he generalizes such experience: "Such tenderness, those afternoons and
evenings,/ saying *blackberry, blackberry, blackberry.*"

And yet how traditional Hass' poem is in its use of a spiritual place! Hass' river, the river of his childhood, provides the same
Eden any other poem might. It is much more modest, of course,
than Wordsworth's Wye, and it appears, as Hass mentions it so
casually, even minimal, a random memory, though it is not. What
is a little surprising, however, is the way in which Hass sup-
presses the name of that river, Feather or Sacramento, from his
poem. Why? It is obvious that the name of the river does not figure importantly in his purposes here, and yet the fact that it does
not is, to my way of thinking, full of implications. To name a
place, in memory, is to singularize the Self, to individuate the
Self, and to maintain belief in the power of the place *through* its
name. But the intimation of this poem as a whole suggests that the
New Intimacy of Hass or of other poets now working has gone or
is going beyond the need for specified locations, and that naming
itself, as a first human and poetic act, is what Hass is analyzing
here into a sensuous mystery. For the entire, final burden of the
poem depends on its success in reminding us that speech is pleasure, and that, paradoxically, the repetition of a word actually

empties that word of meaning, of association—which is Hass' earlier fear in the poem. A place, any place, therefore, could be said only to exist *after* language itself, and to be anterior to language, or created by it. Hass' poem intends, like so many poems since the Romantics, to create the same spiritual place, but Hass is more aware of his traditions, of exactly what he is doing, and it is this which allows him to suggest that we are baptized, not into a location, not into any body of water, but into names, into a river of names. "A word is elegy to what it signifies" because the word is a reality as much as its referent. The new thinking about loss resembles the old thinking about loss exactly through the use of language, through poetry. The more we try to return to the Edenic place, the more our methods, our words, lock us out and turn the pain of our collective separation and exile into poetry. This is not exactly a victory, the poem reminds us, because you can't make love to a poem, and, in "Meditation at Lagunitas," it is sex that recalls Eden more honestly, more innocently and inarticulately, than art does.

And ultimately, a conscious attending to a collective loss is a little different from an attention to a private or confessional loss, even though the same sympathies may occur, finally, as a product of the poem. This poetry, as Stanley Plumly so rightly observed, is often haunted by an Idea more than an Image, a Mind more than a Life. There is a steadiness of control about it, and a poet like Jon Anderson is fond of collapsing private griefs and the singularity and isolation of the poet by stressing, in his own rather austere loneliness and alienation ("My grief is that I bear no grief/ And so I bear myself"), how deeply such loss is intimately shared by others: "My friends and I have all come to the same things." In another poem, while passing houses at night, he says: "Each had a father./ He was telling a story so hopeless,/ So starless, we all belonged." Below the "I" in Anderson's work there is often the abstract argument of a "we"—friends and loved ones. This "we" never lets us forget our participation in the poem, our inclusion by *it*.[*]

These distinctions can be clarified or thrown into higher relief more or less simply, I think. When Robert Lowell writes, in "Memories of West Street and Lepke":

---

[*]Note: I notice that Ira Sadoff, in his article on meditative poetry (*APR*, September/October, 1980) uses the same examples of Hass and Anderson for his argument. I think it is curiously substantiating that both of us, two poets working unbeknownst to each other, should come up with the same examples.

> Only teaching on Tuesdays, book-worming
> in pajamas fresh from the washer each morning,
> I hog a whole house on Boston's
> "hardly passionate Marlborough Street,"

he is intimating, through the naming of a place, a private, autobiographical experience. Its virtues are very much like those of Realism in fiction. He is saying, like Huck Finn, *this is what happened to me*. His narration will be, therefore, modest, insular, unpretentious, without a sermon for the reader. The reader can respond to the honesty or sincerity of that first-person pronoun, that "I." If a poet says, on the other hand, "Much that is beautiful must be discarded/ So that we may resemble/ A taller impression of ourselves," our whole experience of the poem will be dramatically different, and we will be much more aware that the poet (John Ashbery), in his choice of method, is both criticizing the alternative and more personal mode at the same time he is admonishing his audience, through his collaborative theme, against the choice, suicide, which the character in his poem has made. In a larger, historical sense, I am aware that both of these methods, in varying degrees of popularity and use, have always been at large in poetry. And of course as *methods* both are very much in use now, and neither one is superior, as an aesthetic choice, to the other. But they are different. Why have so many younger poets now working adopted the latter, the second method? It is often suggested that the influence of Ashbery has had something central to do with this, but I have my doubts that this is entirely true. I think that all of us, finally, live and have to live within a much larger and more various culture than the culture of poetry, and it is impossible for me to forget that most younger poets came of age in the late sixties and early seventies, a time of real trouble in America. What I most remember, and what seems to me most valuable, even though it is now a subject of easy satire, is the sense of shared convictions and tenderness among my generation at that time. There was, for a while, a feeling of community, however frail or perishable, which mattered, and which is not apparent in the *chic* lame, New Left political rhetoric of the time—a frustrated rhetoric. So often what one felt as shared or communal could not quite be spoken or brought into speech, much less into poetry. Poets of an older generation, responding to that era and those pressures, wrote mostly out of singular agonies. If they were excessive at times in their use and dependence upon hyperbole and imagery, I think that the sheer ugliness of U.S. foreign policy might have had as much to do with that as the influence of Latin American translations. Often the insistence, in their work, on the beauty of the wild or surreal was a reflex of their anger. In retrospect, I think that what the poets of my generation experienced was not only a deep suspicion of any easy political rhetoric, but a suspicion of what began to seem to be poetical rhetoric as well, of a mannered imagistic poem which effectively kept the poet away from his or her experience. And if that generation felt an enormous disillusionment with the society itself, it felt, also and finally, an equally real disappointment with itself and with its inability to do the impossible task which it had promised itself to do, to reconstruct an Edenic place out of America. I have a clear memory of walking on a cold, winter day through the Haight-Ashbury district in 1970—a place that looked as if it was being evacuated before an approaching army. But there was no army coming. No one, anymore, was coming. There were only young men in pairs who would pass by on each side of me, asking if I wanted to buy acid or speed. The place looked, as someone said, like "a teen-age slum." And the subsequent phenomenon of hip boutiques in suburban shopping centers was not a solution to any problem; it was merely a betrayal of values, and a continuance (how could it be otherwise?) of capitalist culture. When Vietnam ended, my generation appeared, oddly enough, to be so much a part of the culture it had resisted. It was like America, or it was America. Without an enemy, it could not continue.

If the "we" of the younger poets is a plural pronoun, it is also obsessed with loss, but I think it is a loss more profound than the loss of political goals or partisan feelings. Part of what got lost is the possibility of wholly believing in the grand fiction of Romantic alienation and individuation. And yet the new poetry, the "meditative" poetry, appears to be an outgrowth of the more isolated imagistic thinking, and its subject, like that of its parents, is precisely that same testimony to alienation and loss. But it is a collective loss more than a private one. It would be comforting to think that even *collective,* as used here, might have some vestigial political significance, but the loss usually attested to has little to do with political solutions. In fact, the poems seem intensely wary of any political diction, seem to avoid it with great skill, for to locate one's loss in political terms is to locate it within time. But the loss and fall from the Edenic place is final, mythic, a thing that cannot be changed. To talk of it, to talk of some collective loss, means, quite possibly, to deflect one's attention from the subject which provokes the poem. In Marvin Bell's poem

"Stars Which See, Stars Which Do Not See" the *ut picture poesis*
of *La Grande Jatte* is both oblique and searingly personal.

> They sat by the water. The fine women
> had large breasts, tightly checked.
> At each point, at every moment,
> they seemed happy by the water.
> The women wore hats like umbrellas
> or carried umbrellas shaped like hats.
> The men wore no hats and the water,
> which wore no hats, had that well-known
> mirror finish which tempts sailors.
> Although the men and women seemed at rest
> they were looking toward the river
> and some way out into it but not beyond.
> The scene was one of hearts and flowers
> though this may be unfair. Nevertheless,
> it was probable that the Seine had hurt them,
> that they were "taken back" by its beauty
> to where a slight breeze broke the mirror
> and then its promise, but never the water.

Deflection? The name of a river. What matters is that the poem
withholds its private sufferer, its poet, so that the place can be
seen, and the common misery of the inhabitants can be seen: "it
was probable that the Seine had hurt them," because the place is
the location of their loss. The figures in the painting, the withheld
figures they stand for, can not quite understand the nature of their
loss, and so blame it on the Seine, deflect what they can no longer
articulate onto the river, the place itself which changes and does
not change, but does not undergo the final change of the
observers, those whose promise is broken by nothing outside
themselves as they are reminded of it by something as ordinary as
a "slight breeze."

What is it, then, that one loses? That everyone loses? Where
I grew up, the specific place meant everything. As a child in California, I still thought of myself, almost, as living in the Bear Flag
Republic, not in the United States. When I woke, the Sierras, I
knew, were on my right; the Pacific was a two hour drive to my
left, and everything between belonged to me, *was* me. I was
astonishingly sheltered. It was only gradually that I learned the
ways in which place meant everything, learned that it meant 200
acres of aging peach trees which we had to prop up, every summer, with sticks to keep the limbs from cracking under the weight
of slowly ripening fruit. It meant a three-room schoolhouse with

thirty students, and meant, also, the pig-headed, oppressive Catholic church which, as far as I could determine, wanted me to feel guilty for having been born at all. And it meant the gradual self-effacement and aging of my parents. Even in high school when I began to write, even when I hated the place most, and when I rejoiced when I read that Rimbaud (at fourteen!) called his home town of Charlesville a "shit-hole"—even when the desire to get away was strongest, I was dimly aware that my adolescent hatred of the place was transforming it, was slowly nurturing an Eden from which I was already exiling myself. After I had left for good, all I really needed to do was to describe the place exactly as it had been. That I could not do, for that was impossible. And that is where poetry might begin.

SOURCES

Freud, Sigmund, *Civilization and Its Discontents* (New York: W. W. Norton & Co., 1962).

Hall, Donald, *Goatfoot Milktongue Twinbird* (Ann Arbor: University of Michigan Press, 1978).

(1982)

C. D. Wright

A TAXABLE MATTER

We are driving around another beltway of light. There are no houses no trees; there is no body of water. Things are as they seem. A hand glows under the radio's green dial. Both of us are taken up for a time with our own itinerant thoughts—something to do with borrowed binoculars, the mineral rights to an unknown relative's land or the dog's welfare—poetry's dropcloths. Flares from refineries ignite our faces. For several hours we don't talk; then we do. Should we get off and look for a café where they serve charcoal and beer or should we go on; does the car need a ring job, and are the lives of poets worth living. We are at a point in space where the animate dark meets inanimate darkness. It is late; no one is waiting for us, the dog is in better hands than ours, we can say whatever we want. We can take the rest of the night.

In my book poetry is a necessity of life, what they used to call a taxable matter. I cannot objectively trace how I reached this exaggerated conclusion, but between us we can summon the grounds for our brand of tectonics in what would seem to many to be an age antithetical to the effort. Ultimately I don't believe any age is antithetical to the effort. I do believe years of reaction promote a thwarted artistic front. "Art is like ham," Diego Rivera said. I have often been reassured by this inexplicable claim. "Sometimes art (poetry) is like a beautiful sick dog that shits all over the house," Frank Stanford scribbled in a notebook. Not without sadness, I agree with this claim too. And if this hejira has become somewhat teleological, well, what is the long stretch of road for if not to sort out the reasons why we are here and why we do what we do from why we are not in the other lane, doing what others do.

You understand, we come from a country that has made a fetish if not a virtue out of proving it can live without art: high, low, old, new, fat, lean and particularly the rarely visible, nocturnal art of poetry. What America cannot sell it can barely stomach. Herein lies a major reason for its creation—to contribute toward the devaluation of the dollar. At the very least, the secular soul of the species is at stake. If this be smart-mouthing it is nonetheless truth-saying. We must do something with our time on this small aleatory sphere for motives other than money. Power is not an acceptable surrogate. Consider that the United States does not rank among the top five countries in literacy (Japan, Iceland, Sweden, East Germany and Finland); yet in advertising it outspends by more than five to one what Japan spends, the second biggest ad spender. We are talking about money spent, to be kind, on distortion. Poetry and advertising (the basest mode of which is propaganda) are in direct and total opposition. If you do not use language you are used by it. If you not recognize the terms *peacekeeper missile* and *preemptory strike* for oxymorons, your hole has already been dug. If you do not detect the blackest of ironies in the Army's made-up-on-Madison-Avenue, *Be All You Can Be,* never mind the perennial for no one will remember you.

Moreover, poetry is tribal not material. As such it lights the fire and keeps watch over the flame. Believe me, this is where you get warm again. And naked. This is where you can remember the good times along with the worst; where you are not allowed to forget the worst, else you cannot be healed. This is where your memory must be exacting—where you and your progeny are held accountable but also laudable. Even and especially in our day, in our land, poets are the griots of the tribe, the ones who see that the word does not break faith with the line of the body.

Moreover, it is poetry that remarks on the barely perceptible disappearances from our world such as that of the sleeping porch or the root cellar. And poetry that notes barely perceptible appearances. In the booklength poem, *Tjanting*, Ron Silliman jerks us into critical awareness by creating syntactical disturbances with cultural ephemera calling up everything in our "two-ply kingdom" from "baskets to hold wire garlic" to "a little swoop cesnas by." In the immediacy of *Tjanting* a woman with blue hair claims *Eraserhead* saved her life.

Finally it is left to poets to point out the shining particulars in our blunted lives like the strands of blue lights Cotter, Arkansas, draped every haunting Christmas from one empty storefront to the empty storefront across the street for eight unoccupied blocks. And it falls to poetry to keep the rain-pitted face of love from leaving us forever. I am even willing to argue passion is what separates us from other life forms—that is, beyond the power to reason is our ability to escape from the desert of pure reason by its own primary instrument, language. And if it be poetry that makes the words flesh, then it is no more escapable than our bodies. But it is at least that free.

While veering in the elusory direction of freedom, I would submit it is a function of poetry to locate those zones inside us that would be free and declare them so. Always there are restrictions: as traditional conventions of rhyme and meter are more or less disavowed, others such as enjambment and assonance remain constant for longer periods, and another, such as anaphora, is revived after long periods of disuse. We might see a formal limitation appropriated from another discipline for the course of one poem by one poet, i.e., the application of the fibonacci number system to passage lengths in Silliman's *Tjanting*, the application of time to line in Bernadette Mayer's *Midwinter Day*. Poetry without form is a fiction. But that there is a freedom in words is the larger fact, and in poetry, where the formal restrictions bear down heavily, it is important to remember the cage is never locked.

Pods of satellite dishes focus on an unstable sky. We begin to look for an exit. Maybe find a café where there are people. Or a bar. Some place where we can watch the fan work the smoke. We might even take a room. This is where imperfection gives way to perfection—where there no houses and no trees and no body of water. Have I said, poetry is the language of intensity. And that because we are going to die an expression of intensity is a necessity.

(1989)

5 Portraits and Self-Portraits

David Shapiro

URGENT MASKS:

An Introduction to John Ashbery's Poetry

Some movement is reversed and the urgent masks
Speed toward a totally unexpected end
Like clocks out of control. Is this the gesture
That was meant, long ago, the curving in

Of frustrated denials. . . .

("Song," *The Double Dream of Spring*)

. . . But there was no statement
At the beginning. There was only a breathless waste,
A dumb cry shaping everything in projected
After-effects orphaned by playing the part intended for them,
Though one must not forget that the nature of this
Emptiness, these previsions
Was that it could only happen here, on this page held
Too close to be legible, sprouting erasures, except that they
Ended everything in the transparent sphere of what was
Intended only a moment ago, spiralling further out, its
Gesture finally dissolving in the weather.

("Clepsydra," *Rivers and Mountains*)

John Ashbery once took a course of lectures in music by Henry Cowell at the New School. Cowell remarked that the intervals in music became wider as music grew more sophisticated. "For instance, if you compare 'The Volga Boatmen' and the 'Love Duet' from *Tristan und Isolde*, you see how vastly wide the intervals have become; and the ear seemingly becomes accustomed to unaccustomed intervals 'as time goes by.'" Chromaticism is also apparent in the tone clusters of Cowell himself, analogous to the striking juxtapositions of Ashbery, but one can deny expectations with a much wider palette of possibilities. One cannot really anticipate the next note in many serial pieces, and this suspense is a fine quality of Ashbery's own work, and a theme:

> These decibels
> Are a kind of flagellation, an entity of sound
> Into which being enters, and is apart.
> Their colors on a warm February day
> Make for masses of inertia, and hips
> Prod out of the violet-seeming into a new kind
> Of demand that stumps the absolute because not new
> In the sense of the next one in an infinite series
> But, as it were, pre-existing or pre-seeming in
> Such a way as to contrast funnily with the unexpectedness
> And somehow push us all into perdition.

("The Skaters," *Rivers and Mountains*)

When Ashbery interviewed Henri Michaux for *Art News*, the French fabricator of imaginary communities spoke of surrealism as *une grande permission*, in the sense of an army leave. Surrealism tends to be used and abused; for example, Robert Bly tends to exaggerate certain overblown qualities of Spanish surrealism. Ashbery's surrealism is subtler. Raymond Roussel's flat, bland, and objective style, typified by Michel Leiris as "French as one is taught to write it by manuals in lycées," a French that can comically be compared to Larousse, has been a minor if decided influence. Ashbery was a connoisseur of Roussel and began a doctoral dissertation on him, but decided not to go through with it, although characteristically he collected many minute particulars about the eccentric. One associates the modulated parodies of narration in *Rivers and Mountains* with the labyrinthine parentheses of Roussel's poems and novels. One must remark of this contagion of the parodistic tone, that it seems to lead structurally to a "chinese box" or play-within-a-play. Apart from this parenthetical mania, other idiosyncrasies of the author of *Locus Solus* did not impinge on the early work of Ashbery, who did not read him thoroughly until the 1950s, which he spent in France. Later Ashbery wittily employs another device of Roussel—specious simile, "the kind that tells one less than you would know if the thing were stated flatly." In place of the organic and necessary simile, Ashbery learned from the French master an extravagance of connection that leads one nowhere, as in Koch's "as useless as a ski in a barge," though this example is perhaps still too suggestive. "As useless as a ski" would be Ashbery's paradigmatic revision. Ashbery is also a master of the false summation, the illogical conclusion couched in the jargon of logic, reminding one of the false but rich scholarship of Borges:

> We hold these truths to be self-evident:
> That ostracism, both political and moral, has
> Its place in the twentieth-century scheme of things;
> That urban chaos is the problem we have been seeing into and
>   seeing into,
> For the factory, deadpanned by its very existence into a
> Descending code of values, has moved right across the road from
>   total financial upheaval
> And caught regression head on . . . .
> . . . .
> To sum up: We are fond of plotting itineraries
> And our pyramiding memories, alert as dandelion fuzz . . . .
>
>   ("Decoy," *The Double Dream of Spring*)

> The rise of capitalism parallels the advance of romanticism
> And the individual is dominant until the close of the nineteenth
>   century.
> In our own time, mass practices have sought to submerge the
>   personality
> By ignoring it, which has caused it to branch out in all directions.
>   . . .
> . . . .
> And yet it results in a downward motion, or rather a floating one.
>
>   ("Definition of Blue," *The Double Dream of Spring*)

Ashbery has properly been called a "business-like and rather peculiar" child of the muse of Rimbaud. Auden also places him, in the rather distant tones of the Introduction to *Some Trees*, within the tradition of Rimbaud's *dérèglement de tous les sens*. Contrary to expectation, Ashbery denies French poetry as a major influence. He does, however, acknowledge the influence of Pierre Reverdy, whom he read as a "simple poet" accessible to a student with limited French; he later translated some cubist concoctions. He admires "the completely relaxed, oxygen-like quality" of Reverdy, whose cadences he likens to "breathing in big gulps of fresh air."

Roussel, of course, is a very "prosy" poet and Ashbery too is interested in the poetic possibilities of conventional prose, the prose of newspaper articles. His recent poems in particular function by proceeding from cliché to cliché, in a "seamless web" of banality transformed, by dint of combination and deformation, into a Schwitters-like composition in which the refuse of a degraded quotidian is fused into a new freshness:

> It is never too late to mend. When one is in one's late thirties, ordinary things—like a pebble or a glass of water—take on an expressive sheen. One wants to know more about them, and one is in turn lived by them. Young people might not envy this kind of situation, perhaps rightly so, yet there is now interleaving the pages of suffering and indifference to suffering a prismatic space that cannot be seen, only felt as the result of an angularity that must have existed from earliest times and is only now succeeding in making its presence felt through the mists of helpless acceptance of everything else projected on our miserable, dank span of days . . . . The pain that drained the blood from your cheek when you were young and turned you into a whitened spectre before your time is converted back into a source of energy that peoples this world of perceived phenomena with wonder.

("The New Spirit," *Three Poems*, to be published by Viking)

The use of prose elements in poetry, as in Williams and Pound, is so diffused a technique that it rarely provokes sensations of novelty, but Ashbery's intense employment is an adventure, as interesting as the day Jasper Johns remembers dreaming of painting the American flag. The prosaic elements in the early Auden influenced Ashbery; the touching qualities of ordinary speech and journalism and old diaries in *The Orators* were precursors. Collage elements for Ashbery's poem "Europe" were taken from a book for girls written at the time of the First World War. The book, entitled *Girl of the Bi-Plane*, which he picked up by accident on the quais of Paris, is one reason for much of the placid plane imagery of "Europe." At the time, Ashbery was "collaging" a great deal as a symptom of an imagined "dead-end" period in his writing, and also due to the fact that living in France he felt cut off from American speech. He often received American magazines and manipulated their contents as a stimulus and pretext for further poetry. The grand collapses often noted in "Europe," its dashes and discontinuities called a "new poetic shorthand" by Koch, are one result of his *collagiste* direction. Though Ashbery's poetry has led most recently to a calm clearness, it began with the presentation of "objects" and "idioms" in explicitly dislocated form.

>   sweetheart . . .   the stamp
>   ballooning you
>   vision I thought you
>   forget, encouraging your vital organs
>   Telegraph. The rifle—a page folded over.
>
>   More upset, wholly meaningless, the willing sheath
>
>   ("Europe," *The Tennis Court Oath*)

His poetry had something of the "pathos of obscurity" as Lovejoy speaks of it, and the "pathos of incomprehensibility" was very much part of the mystique of such writing, though Ashbery always pointed toward principles of cohesion by discontinuity, if using the concealments of riddles and hints:

>   She was dying but had time for him—
>   brick. Men were carrying the very heavy things—
>   dark purple, like flowers.
>   Bowl lighted up the score just right
>
>   ("Europe")

Stein furnishes a specimen source for the opacities of this text. One must with Ashbery discriminate carefully between the non-grammatical, the non-sensical, the semantically inappropriate, and the tabooed. In the manner of a linguist obtaining the "feeling" of the limits of a grammar, Ashbery has developed the theme of "unacceptability," and related it with great wit to allied concepts of *absurdité*, *sottises*, *bétises*, and *l'absurde*.

There are a plethora of analogues in the associated arts. At the time Ashbery was writing as art editor for the International Edition of *The Herald Tribune*, de Kooning, Kline and Pollock with extreme dash and discontinuity were calling attention to the expunging of the copula and the coherent figure, and to the the-

matic of composition itself. Later the New Realists were to revive
Duchamp's abrupt presentation of everyday objects as an
introduction to what Ashbery called, in a comment on the New
Realists, "the colorful indifferent universe." The self-conscious
mid-progress shifts of narrations in Ashbery's *collagiste* poems
are distinctly and masterfully of the age in which Jackson Pollock
threw himself on the canvas, a proof and "permission," though
Ashbery unexpectedly characterizes himself as more aural than
visual, despite his participation in the art world.

The influence of psychoanalysis, permitting a more or less
watery relationship with the unconscious and everyday mind, and
corollary devices of "dipping into" an almost completely associational stream ("What else is there?") is another common heritage
of technique Ashbery shares with the abstract expressionists and
surrealists. The Arthur Craven translation, "Elephant Languor,"
was interesting to Ashbery largely because he felt it resembled
certain associational, disjunct narrations that he had already
achieved. Ashbery has called attention to more than one neglected
poet, and as a matter of fact has considered editing a kind of
anthology of Neglected Poets, one that could include Wheel-
wright, David Schubert, Samuel Greenberg, and F. T. Prince,
bizarre cousins or in-laws of Ashbery, all applying the same "syntax of dreams" for dramatistic purposes.

Ashbery's work, begun with kinds of *disjecta membra*, coa-
lesces at certain periods in big coherent works: "Europe," "The
Skaters," "The New Spirit," "The System." The development from
collage of seemingly despairing fragments to unbroken paragraphs of di Chirico-like prose (Ashbery admits to di Chirico's
prose, not painting, as an influence, of which more later) may be
likened to the development of one of Ashbery's favorite com-
posers—Busoni. "Busoni wrote a piano piece entitled 'The Turning Point,' and all his later music fittingly seems different from
music earlier than that piece." The disjointed and indecisive has
the look, at least, of a highly unified music. Ashbery's large com-
positions achieve this "look" of compositional unity while
remaining what Coleridge has called a "multeity." Composition in
these works is not random but more a matter of parsimoniously
distributing disparate images and tones and parodies than of uni-
fyings and harmonizings. Ginsberg found the tone of Pope in
"The Skaters," and the mock-heroic here does sometimes bear
resemblance to the highly polished surface of "The Rape of the
Lock." The highly polished surface in Ashbery, however, is less a
social hint than a memento mori of the veneer of a world of man-

ufactured objects and smooth, unbroken concrete. "The Skaters" may be thought of as a radiant porphyry of a variety of rhetoric, including imitations of Whitman, Baudelaire, science textbooks, William Hung's Tu Fu translations, Theodore Roethke, and John Ashbery. As he has described them, his intentions in respect to "The Skaters" were "to see how many opinions I had about everything." The most alarming feature of this style is the way it keeps upsetting our charming equilibrium and understanding of tone. After a quaint satire on the classic Oriental story of the failing student, Ashbery announces: "The tiresome old man is telling us his life-story." To some, his meditations upon or within meditations of self-laceration add more to the absurdity of the universe than interpret it, but these are finally friendly satires which point to the fact that unity, as we dream of it, is not realizable. One dreams of the perfect language within the fallen universe. Ashbery's deceptive drifts and accumulations of parody always erupt in the dramatic return which surprises and regulates, as in Proust. By his grand multeity in unity, his surprising simultaneity in unity, and a type of probabilistic unity, he achieves something of the misery and joy of a Jacques Callot baroque. He has always avoided the vanity that, as Señor Borges warned this writer once, derives from purely random techniques. But the spectre of indeterminacy and uncertainty shadows his structural convolutions and involutions, if only in the numerous, self-lacerating dwarfs that appear and disappear throughout his poems.

Ashbery called my attention recently to a discussion of reticence by the poet Margaret Atwood [see page 21]. "I don't want to know how I write poetry. Poetry is dangerous. I believe most poets will go to any lengths to conceal their own reluctant scanty insight both from others and from themselves. Paying attention to how you do it is like stopping in the middle of any other totally involving and pleasurable activity. . . to observe yourself suspended in the fatally suspended inner mirror." Ashbery has been most extreme in his reluctance to pad his poetry with what he calls the "stuff of explanation," just as he has been reluctant to be anything but a "practical" or "anecdotal" critic of the arts. He has, however, for one of his central topoi the one called for by F. S. C. Northrop in his discussion of the future of poetry—the breakdown of causality in the nineteenth century sense. His discontinuities tend to throw us most clearly in the middle of the century of the Uncertainty Principle; one in which Whitehead called for the expunging of copula for a clearer style. The montages of Pound's cinematic Oriental translations are part of this lucid tradition of juxtaposition. Most of the best passages of Ashbery's poetry, moreover, like Stevens', deal with the practitioner's point of view and *praktik,* however veiled. His poetry, though not vulgarly explanatory, is in the manner of the "action" painters a criticism of poetry itself as much as of life. A dice-playing God does indeed reign over the "sly Eros" of Ashbery's kingdom.

Ashbery's first book, *Some Trees,* is already filled with revitalizations of forms that had become connotatively encrusted. His sestina, "The Painter," an early example of such revitalization (1948), is influenced by Elizabeth Bishop. Her sestina in *North and South* employed certain common-end-words such as "coffee" and "balcony" that charmed Ashbery, and certainly the meticulously comical, soft-voiced rhetoric shows the rapport between them. Ashbery has elsewhere spoken of his love of Bishop's more recent "Over 2000 Illustrations and a Complete Concordance," a properly Pierre Meynardesque title which culminates in the—for Ashbery—inexhaustibly numinous line, "And looked and looked our infant sight away." The copula of "and" and its *mysterium* in repetition is part of the theme of Bishop's poem, and of Ashbery's poetry in general. The sestina form, therefore, with its arbitrary and sometimes comically stiff canon is a fitting "receptacle" for the play of discontinuity and copula. Ashbery's sestinas, as opposed to the more coherent ones of Auden and Pound, make much of a purposeful barrage of the unusual mid-progress shifts and blurred drama. Another example of disjointed and spiky writing within rigid form is the eclogue published in *Turandot*:

Cuddie:	I need not raise my hand
Colin:	She burns the flying peoples
Cuddie:	To hear its old advice
Colin:	And spear my heart's two beasts
Cuddie:	Or cover with its mauves
Colin:	And I depart unhurt

("Eclogue")

"This poem was written after a bleak period of unproductiveness in 1951, when I was in publishing. I was somewhat awakened by a concert of John Cage's music." This music, more than anything then happening in painting, shook him and seemed to give once more the permission to find a form in the fertile formlessness into which he had wandered. There is a kind of simultaneous irony or depth to Ashbery's work, as if a critic paused to announce that he was invalidating all his critical statements including the present one he was making, and yet continued. His simultaneity is also that of chamber music, in which the "narration" of four voices can seem, as in Haydn, to re-create the comic possibilities of a domestic quarrel over the dish-towel. His domesticity and Firbankian penchant for gossip can be seen further enlarged in his collaborative venture, *A Nest of Ninnies*, which received the comically negative critique of Auden that it was one of the few contemporary novels that lacked sex. His pantoum, in *Some Trees*, inspired by the one in Ravel's "Trio," is another example of a witty use of an arbitrary and musical form. Again, it is music, not the rhyming dictionary (though see his "Variations, Calypso and Fugue on a Theme of Ella Wheeler Wilcox" for some canny couplets), that inspires Ashbery's poetry. He is averse to "melodious poetry," though not to melody itself; he is most interested in sound as it joins and soon flies apart from the meaning of the words, a disjunction reminiscent of the practice of Webern of setting a poem with a meager amount of imitative music. Busoni's music appeals to Ashbery in the sense that the notes, in his judgment, seem to imply that they could be "any notes and they just happen to sound this way." They have a "built-in arbitrariness that is not aleatory." Opposed to the pedanticism of Reger and the syn thetic cubism of Schoenberg, the music of Busoni seems to Ashbery to enjoy the double status of generating a new grammar and then commenting on it.

Although Ashbery's own intellectual music is associated journalistically with O'Hara and Koch, and there were and are certain useful reasons to link them, the discrimination of their differences is equally useful. They were at first pragmatically and conspiratorially joined against poets of a different aesthetic (e.g. Wilbur). They also share a common *traditio* of French surrealism, a taste for Russian poets of revolution, and a somewhat similar procedure by montage, yet the characteristic Ashbery tone is not that of either, though we cannot be detained here by such considerations. Suffice it to say that Helen Vendler's characterization (in the *New York Times*) of the poets of the so-called New York School as "cheerful and Chaucerian" does not stand alongside the meditations of Ashbery, no matter how much he may be seen to lack the transcendental quality.

As for "the melancholy subject of Poetic Influence," Ashbery has indeed digested the influences of both Stevens and Whitman. He particularly loved the long poems of Stevens, on which he wrote a paper for F. O. Mathiessen at Harvard. His ubiquitous third-person narrator may very well have been derived from

Stevens as a way of "entering" the poem, as in "Esthétique du Mal." The dreamlike imagery of "He," however, does indeed derive from a veritable dream; some have been envious of Ashbery's dreams, and one is reminded of Eliot's dictum on Freud and the *Vita Nuova* that those who expect much from their dream-life will receive it. Much of the clumsy appropriateness of dreams is imitated in Ashbery's poems, though the flat lyrical catalogues of "Grand Abacus" derive from the long lines of Whitman, Ashbery being more spellbound by Whitman's technical virtuosity than by the spontaneous image of the bard mumbling in his beard. Ashbery's marvelous catalogues, like that of musical instruments in "The Skaters," also derive from Webern's "Cantata," where things "go bumping and rumbling for a time after you thought they were going to stop." One also associates certain elements of Ashbery's catalogue raisonné with prose, and Cage's noisiness:

> True, melodious tolling does go on in that awful pandemonium.
> Certain resonances are not utterly displeasing to the terrified eardrum.
> Some paroxysms are dinning of tambourine, others suggest piano room or organ loft
> For the most dissonant night charms us, even after death. This, after all, may be happiness: tuba notes awash on the great flood, ruptures of xylophone, violins, limpets, grace-notes, the musical instrument called serpent, viola da gambas, aeolian harps, clavicles, pinball machines, electric drills, que sais-je encore!

> ("The Skaters")

As Ashbery says, "Cage taught me the relevance of what's there, like the noise now of those planes overhead"; however, he would hardly imagine the sole strategy of his poetry to be the capture of a probabilistic everyday, no matter how prehensile the poet. His poetry sees the everyday in its relation to the supreme moment, the in-between moment, the pedestrian moments, "and one cannot really overlook any of them." Ashbery's divinely drab modulations and equitably and imperturbably distributed polarizations between these instants have led one critic to the delusion that this is "a poetry without anxiety," but it is actually more intense than decorative, and, while rococo in parts, it has much of the Laforguian quick shifts of pose. It is not merely a deliquescence into an *exercice de style* along the lines of Raymond Queneau. It is a less whimsical palette of possibilities.

Certain of the poems, "Clepsydra" for instance, combine along with a drabness a quasi-religious tone and some almost impenetrable details of landscape. Ashbery admits to having the Valéry-esque experience not of a vague rhythm but a vague vision previous to a poem. "Clepsydra" was favorably foreseen as a "big slab, with no stanza breaks and like a marble slab down which a little water trickles." The tone-feeling of the poems is not equally stony, as a lot of exalting of the prosaic goes on. He utilizes a repetition of "after all" as a replica of a hack journalistic digression in:

> It had reduced that other world,
> The round one of the telescope, to a kind of very fine powder or
>   dust
> So small that space could not remember it.
> Thereafter any signs of feeling were cut short by
> The comfort and security, a certain elegance even,
> Like the fittings of a ship, that are after all
> The most normal things in the world. Yes, perhaps, but the words
>   "after all" are important for understanding the almost
> Exaggerated strictness. . . .

He also refines a kind of legalistic diction, as in: "And it was in vain that tears blotted the contract now, because/ It had been freely drawn up and consented to as insurance. . . ." One thinks of the sweet transpositions of legal diction in Renaissance argumenta. Surely, here too is a poetry ready to be accused of yoking disparate tones and images with difficulty together, but the Johnsonian criticism tends to falter under the steady and sensible pressure of such thoughtful and feeling lines as Ashbery's, in which the strange connections and obscure jargons are, after all, quite beautiful.

Though classic parody has a target, these modulated parodies do not quite break their lance against ignorance or excess. They are targetless parodies which attempt to annihilate the idea of parody, since parody is, for Ashbery, almost an indecent idea. He is interested in flattening out all parodistic devices, using multiple and shifting targets of parody to blur the Bergsonian function of intimidating the inelastic target. Ashbery successfully reinstates the poetic qualities of all possible sources—journalism, degraded ditties, bad poetry, etc.—by implying that there is no such thing as *the poetic*. His poems are not ready-mades, as in the tradition of Duchamp, and he feels little kinship with Duchamp, "who was a supremely glamorous negation of everything." Ashbery negates

"so that we can go on to what is left." The urinal of Duchamp is a
witty negation of art, but Ashbery is trying to ennucleate that
negation among many (thus the fragments of ready-made poetry
within his poetry). He finds too many supreme culminations and
duplicate negations of everything Duchamp did in today's art and
literature. There are now certainly some duplicate negations of
Ashbery. His newest work, *The System*, is couched in the clichés
of devotional and pseudo-devotional writing. "One may be
depressed by reading the fine print in the 11th edition of the
Encyclopedia Britannica, with long prose passages in eight point
type, and feel as if one is drowning in a sea of unintelligible
print—and yet that this is one's favorite ocean, just as drowning is
said to be delicious when one stops struggling." Ashbery repro-
duces that delicious sensation. His poetry starts with a sensation,
as does Valéry's, and ends with "a riot of perfumes."

One must also mention that new ways of writing were
opened for Ashbery by *Hebdomeros* of di Chirico, another instance of what he regards as neglected work of high quality. Ashbery was admittedly moved by the interminable digressions and
flourishes of di Chirico's prose, which tends to burst out in terribly long sentences that go on for pages, and which are novels of
one character. The skene may change several times in di Chirico's
sentences, as in Ashbery's, and the course of this sentence is as a
cinematic flow, under which the writer is pushing further and further ahead, though camouflaged by one of those "urgent masks,"
which may be, for example, Sir Thomas Browne.

John Ashbery's work is much concerned with, and has a true
solicitude for, "the bitter impression of absence," and this poetry
that speaks of the "fundamental absence" of our day should certainly be more sufficiently celebrated. With their fluorescent
imagery, disjunction, collages, two-dimensionalisms, innovations
in traditional forms and "simultaneous" use of an aggregate of
styles, John Ashbery's poems today constitute a revitalization in
American poetry. He is not merely a prestidigitator of devices, but
a poet of the stature of Wallace Stevens.

Note: Observations in quotes are from extensive conversations and interviews
with the author from 1964-71.

(1971)

Galway Kinnell

POETRY, PERSONALITY
AND DEATH

In this little poem by Stephen Crane, I find an image which stands as the portrait of us all:

> In the desert
> I saw a creature, naked, bestial,
> Who squatting upon the ground,
> Held his heart in his hands,
> And ate of it.
> I said, "Is it good, friend?"
> "It is bitter—bitter," he answered;
> "But I like it
> Because it is bitter,
> And because it is my heart."

The poetry of this century is marked by extreme self-absorption. So we have even a "school" of self-dissection, the so-called confessional poets, who sometimes strike me as being interested in their own experience to the exclusion of everyone else's. Even Robert Lowell, in *Life Studies*—that rich, lively book which remains more fascinating than all but a few of the books of its time—puts me off somewhat by the strange pride—possibly the pride by which the book lives—that he takes in his own suffering.

I was on a bus some years ago, when a man suddenly spoke up in a loud, pained voice: "You don't know how I suffer! No one on this bus suffers the way I do!" Somebody in the back called out, "Rent a hall!" Someone else said, "Do you want to borrow my crutches?" and actually produced a pair of crutches and offered them across the aisle. The man tapped his knee and looked out the window with an exasperated expression, as if to say, "I wish there weren't so many nuts riding the busses." What I would like to find in poetry, as on that bus, is one who could express the pain of everyone.

Robert Bly's poems often seem liberated from this self-absorbed, closed ego. In his first two books Bly avoids specific autobiographical detail almost entirely. Though he speaks in the first person about intimate feelings, the self has somehow been erased. The "I" is not any particular person, a man like the rest of us, who has sweated, cursed, loathed himself, hated, envied, been cold-hearted, mean, frightened, unforgiving, ambitious, and so on. Rather it is a person of total mental health, an ideal "I" who has more in common with ancient Chinese poets than with anyone alive in the United States today. This would be a blessing for all of us if Bly had really succeeded in "transcending" personality in his poetry. But I think he has not. He simply has not dealt with it. He has been vehement about getting rid of old poeticisms, and this he has done: his poetry is, indeed, contemporary; it is his role as poet he has borrowed out of old literature.

This borrowed self, this disguise, may be deliberate, the consequence of a theory of impersonality. It seems to spring, too, from a compulsive need for secrecy, from the poet's reluctance to reveal himself in his poems. Consider this poem, "The Busy Man Speaks":

> Not to the mother of solitude will I give myself
> Away, not to the mother of love, nor to the mother of conversation,
> Nor to the mother of art, nor the mother
> Of tears, nor the mother of the ocean;
> Not to the mother of sorrow, nor the mother
> Of the downcast face, nor the mother of the suffering of death;
> Not to the mother of the night full of crickets,
> Nor the mother of the open fields, nor the mother of Christ.
>
> But I will give myself to the father of righteousness, the father
> Of cheerfulness, who is also the father of rocks,
> Who is also the father of perfect gestures;
> From the Chase National Bank
> An arm of flame has come, and I am drawn
> To the desert, to the parched places, to the landscape of zeros;
> And I shall give myself away to the father of righteousness,
> The stones of cheerfulness, the steel of money, the father of rocks.

The individual lines are strong; yet the poem as a whole leaves me unsatisfied, as do all poems which divide men into two kinds. Someone less unwilling to reveal himself might have reversed the positives and negatives. But if Bly had said, "To the mother of solitude will I give myself/ Away, to the mother of love . . . ," then he would, perhaps, have been obliged, in the second stanza, to say, "And yet I give myself, also, to the father of righteousness. . . ." Speaking in his own voice, the voice of a complicated individual, he would have been forced to be lucid regarding his own ambiguous allegiances. Bly stumbles as if through fear into setting up this simplified *persona*, the "busy man."

A *persona* has its uses, and also its dangers. In theory, it would be a way to get past the self, to dissolve the barrier between poet and reader. Writing in the voice of another, the poet would open himself to that person. All that would be required would be for the reader to make the same act of sympathetic identification, and, in the *persona*, poet and reader would meet as one. Of course, for the poem to be interesting, the *persona* would have to represent a central facet of the poet's self; the kind of thing Browning's dramatic monologues do very well, prose fiction does much better.

In the voice of J. Alfred Prufrock, Eliot expressed his own sense of futility and his own wish to die. Without the use of the *persona* Eliot might not have been able to express this at all, for isn't it embarrassing for a young man to admit to feeling so old? The *persona* makes it OK. For the same reason, it is an evasion. As he develops his character, even Eliot forgets that this sense of futility and this wish to die are his own, as well as Prufrock's. The *persona* makes it unnecessary for him to confront the sources of these feelings or to explore their consequences in himself. It functions like the Freudian dream, fictionalizing what one does not want to know is real.

The problem is similar in James Dickey's "The Firebombing," the most famous *persona* poem of recent years. In his attack on the poem—an attack almost as famous as the poem—Robert Bly says:

> If the anguish in this poem were real, we would feel terrible remorse as we read, we would stop what we were doing, we would break the television set with an axe, we would throw ourselves on the ground sobbing.

Oddly enough, Dickey, in the poem, accuses his *persona* of just that indecent coldness of which Bly accused Dickey, and in much the same terms:

> My hat should crawl on my head
> in streetcars, thinking of it,
> the fat on my body should pale.

Over and over in the poem, Dickey makes clear the moral limits of his *persona*, that ex-firebomber whose aesthetic relish in his exploits was a function of his lack of imagination, his inability to conceive of the persons he killed, and who lives ever after in confusion and unresolved guilt.

The poem is not about the pleasure of war, but about the failures of character which make war, or mechanized war, possible.

And yet, Bly's criticism is not irrelevant. I, too, find something in this poem which makes me uneasy, something which has to do, I think, with the evasions permitted by the use of the *persona*.

In an essay James Dickey wrote on the *persona* in poetry, he says,

> A true poet can write with utter convincingness about "his" career as a sex murderer, and then in the next poem with equal conviction about tenderness and children and self-sacrifice.

This is true. Even a poet who does not write "dramatic" poetry, who writes only about himself, must experience all manner of human emotions, since he uses the words which express these emotions. As Whitman says,

> Latent in a great user of words, must be all passions, crimes, trades, animals, stars, God, sex, the past, might, space, metals, and the like—because these are the words, and he who is not these, plays with a foreign tongue, turning helplessly to dictionaries and authorities.

I admire James Dickey for exposing the firebomber within himself—particularly since the firebomber does appear to be a central facet of Dickey's makeup. It is a courageous act. Few poets would be as willing to reveal their inner sickness, and we can be sure that many poets seem healthier than Dickey only because they tell us less about themselves.

Yet revelation alone is not sufficient. In the same essay on the *persona*, Dickey has this curious sentence—curious for what it fails to say:

> The activity [of poetry] gives the poet a chance to confront and dramatize parts of himself that otherwise would not have surfaced.

Between "confront" and "dramatize," aren't certain crucial verbs missing? If Dickey does feel as close to his *persona* as he seems to, if he feels within himself a deadness of imagination regarding those whom he hurts, if he himself even vicariously takes aesthetic pleasure in killing, can't we expect him, as a poet, to explore this region of himself—not merely to dramatize it as though it belonged to another? We don't ask that he suppress the firebomber within; on the contrary, we want him to try to find out what it means in his own life. Thoreau said, "Be it life or death, we crave only reality." Dickey does not accept the risk of this search, the risk that in finding reality we may find only death; that we may find no sources of transfiguration, only regret and pain. Instead, he uses a *persona* as a way out, in much the same way Eliot does.

In *Earth House Hold*, Gary Snyder points out that

> The archaic and primitive ritual dramas, which acknowledged all sides of human nature, including the destructive, demonic, and ambivalent, were liberating and harmonizing.

Neither liberation nor harmony can result from "The Firebombing," for the drama it enacts has no protagonist: now it is the poet, now it is someone else invented to bear the onus the poet does not care to take on himself. As a result, this poem trying to clarify the sources of war adds to our confusion.

* * *

We can't understand this phenomenon in poetry—this closed, unshared "I"—unless we look at its source, the closed ego of modern man, the neurotic burden which to some degree cripples us all. I mean that ego which separates us from the life of the planet, which keeps us apart from one another, which makes us feel self-conscious, inadequate, lonely, suspicious, possessive, jealous, awkward, fearful, and hostile; which thwarts our deepest desire, which is to be one with all creation. We moderns, who like to see ourselves as victims of life—victims of the so-called "absurd" condition—are in truth its frustrated conquerors. Our alienation is in proportion to our success in subjugating it. The more we conquer nature, the more nature becomes our enemy, and since we are, like it or not, creatures of nature, the more we make an enemy of the very life within us.

Alchemy, the search for the philosopher's stone, was, on the surface, an attempt to master nature, to change base metals into gold; secretly, however, it was a symbolic science, and its occult aim was to propitiate the sexual, creative forces in nature, and to transfigure the inner life. When chemistry finally overthrew alchemy, in the seventeenth century, it was a decisive moment, among all the other decisive moments of that century. Overtly a quest for pure knowledge, chemistry derives its enormous energy from the desire to subdue and harness.

This is the case, of course, with the whole scientific and technological enterprise. The fatal moment was when the human

mind learned the knack of detaching itself from what it studied,
even when what it studied was itself. The mind became pure will:
immaterial, unattached, free of the traumas of birth and death.
Turned on any natural thing, the eye trained to scientific objectiv-
ity and glowing with the impersonal spirit of conquest, becomes a
deathray. What it kills is the creative relationship between man
and thing. In the science fiction stories that scientists sometimes
write on the side, they often reveal the fantasies of cosmic hostil-
ity which lurk unobserved in their learned treatises.

Not long ago it was commonly supposed that the scientific
spirit would solve our social ills. We heard talk of a "cultural lag,"
according to which we had gained control over nature but not yet
over ourselves. Science was to cure that. We now know that science is the trouble. I cannot forget how, in those days when our
involvement in Vietnam was just beginning, so many social scientists blithely stepped forward to defend our madness. They were
not bloodthirsty men; for the most part they were polite, mild, and
well-meaning. But they saw Vietnam in geo-political terms, as an
objective, technological problem, to be dealt with by technological and social-scientific means. The United States undertook this
most stupid of wars, during which so many have died, die, and
will die for nothing, in exactly the same spirit in which it under-
takes the exploration of space—as a challenge to our technology:
Can we do it? Did I say, "die for nothing"? That is not quite it.
They die for science.

One might have thought the Americans would be more likely
to die for material gain. But no, America is not a materialist country. Perhaps there has never existed a people who cared less for
material. We despise it. The effort of our technology is to turn us
into nearly immaterial beings who live in a nearly immaterial
world. Our most pervasive invention, plastic, is an anti-material;
it puts up no resistance, it never had its own form, it is totally subject to our will, and relative to organic materials, which return to
the life-cycle, it is immortal. We spend billions of dollars trying
to render our bodies acceptable to our alienated condition: as
odorless, hairless, sanitary and neutral as plastic. Americans who
are white feel that the black man with his greater physical grace,
spontaneity, and "soul" resides closer to nature, and therefore
regard him as a traitor to mankind, and fear him.

This attempt to transcend materiality is, of course, a world
wide phenomenon, involving all countries and all races. It is only
that the white American has taken the lead. He is the one marked
and transfigured by the technological age—and I mean "transfig-

ured" literally. What else can one make of the changes that have
come over the European face after it migrated to technological
America? Contrast the ancestral faces one still sees in Europe,
contrast the faces in old paintings and photographs. Is it just in
my imagination that the American chin has thickened, its very
bones swollen, as if to repel what lies ahead? And those broad,
smooth, curving, translucent eyelids, that gave such mystery to
the eyes—is it my private delusion that they have disappeared,
permanently rolled themselves up, turning the eyes into windows
without curtains, not to be taken by surprise again? And that the
nose, the feature unique to man, the part of him which moves first
into the unknown, has become on our faces a small, neat bump?
Maybe only healthily large teeth cause the lips to protrude, giving
the all-American mouth its odd, simian pucker.

That the human face has changed at all is, of course, a question. I have perceptive friends who assure me the American face
differs in no way from its European sources. These things are all
guesses, and guessing itself can make it so. But Max Picard so
loved the human face, so carefully meditated on it, that I have to
believe something of his sense of its fall. He writes—and I choose
a passage from *The Human Face* almost at random:

> In our day, it seems sometimes that were eternity but to touch it,
> the face of a man must fall apart, even as a ghost collapses at the
> touch of holy reality. . . .

> In such a face there is a fear that it may be the last. It is timorous,
> lest from it be taken, and it cowers within itself, it holds itself
> tightly, it becomes sharp and shiny. Such a face is like polished
> metal. It is alike a metallic model: cold. It is fashioned to endure,
> but not based upon eternity as were the faces of olden days. Such
> a face watches constantly over itself. It even fears to rest at night,
> so mistrustful is it of its very own sleep.

I spent a year not long ago in Southern California. There I
saw men with these changed faces willing to do anything—pol-
lute, bulldoze, ravage, lay waste—as long as it made money. That
seemed in character. What surprised me was that they were willing to do it even if it didn't make money. California matters
because it represents the future of the rest of us; it is a huge mirror set up on the western shore of what we shall become, just as
the United States mirrors the future of the world. The Asians, too,
appear to adore our technology—some of them doubtless wor-
shipping it even while it burns them to death.

* * *

Yet one sees signs around us of the efforts to reintegrate ourselves with life. One sees it in poetry, perhaps particularly in
poetry. For poetry has taken on itself the task of breaking out of
the closed ego. To quote from Gary Snyder again:

> Of all the streams of civilized tradition with roots in the paleolith-
> ic, poetry is one of the few that can realistically claim an
> unchanged function and a relevance which will outlast most of
> the activities that surround us today. Poets, as few others, must
> live close to the world that primitive men are in: the world, in its
> nakedness, which is fundamental for all of us—birth, love, death;
> the sheer fact of being alive.

The first important poem of this new undertaking is Allen Ginsberg's "Howl." It is the first modern poem fully to break out, fully
to open itself. It is a poem which consists of autobiography, just
as confessional poetry does; yet at the same time it transcends
autobiography and speaks on behalf of everyone. "Howl" has
become the most famous poem of its time less by its "style" or
"subject matter" than by this inner generosity.

"Howl" suffers the self, it does not step around it. It gets
beyond personality by going through it. This is true of much of
the interesting poetry of today. It is one reason that Robert Bly's
prose-poems are so moving. For the first time in his poetry, Bly in
The Morning Glory speaks to us—and for us—in his own voice.
As one reads, the "I" in the poem becomes oneself.

> I am in a cliff-hollow, surrounded by fossils and furry shells. The
> sea breathes and breathes under the new moon. Suddenly it rises,
> hurrying into the long crevices in the rock shelves, it rises like a
> woman's belly as if nine months has passed in a second; rising
> like milk to the tiny veins, it over-flows like a snake going over a
> low wall.
>
> I have the sensation that half an inch under my skin there are
> nomad bands, stringy-legged men with firesticks and wide-eyed
> babies. The rocks with their backs turned to me have something
> spiritual in them. On these rocks I am not afraid of death; death is
> like the sound of the motor in an airplane as we fly, the sound so
> steady and comforting. And I still haven't found the woman I
> loved in some former life—how could I, when I loved only once
> on this rock, though twice in the moon, and three times in the ris-
> ing water. Two spirit-children leap toward me, shouting, arms in

the air. A bird with long wings comes flying toward me in the dusk, pumping just over the darkening waves. He has flown around the whole planet, it has taken him centuries. He returns to me the lean-legged runner laughing as he runs through the stringy grasses, and gives back to me my buttons, and the soft sleeves of my sweater.

The poem is personal yet common, open yet mysterious. For the moment of the poem, I, too, have loved "only once on this rock, though twice in the moon, and three times in the rising water."

We move toward a poetry in which the poet seeks an inner liberation by going so deeply into himself—into the worst of himself as well as the best—that he suddenly finds he is everyone. In James Wright's "The Life," whatever is autobiographical—and the reference in the first stanza must have its origin in something very personal and particular in Wright's life—is transmuted, opens out as the inner autobiography of us all:

> Murdered, I went, risen,
> Where the murderers are,
> That black ditch
> Of river.
>
> And if I come back to my only country
> With a white rose on my shoulder,
> What is that to you?
> It is the grave
> In blossom.
>
> It is the trillium of darkness,
> It is hell, it is the beginning of winter,
> It is a ghost town of Etruscans who have no names
> Any more.
>
> It is the old loneliness.
> It is.
> And it is
> The last time.

That poem, and the following passage from John Logan's poem, "Spring of the Thief," are among the great, self-transcending moments of contemporary poetry.

> Ekelof said there is a freshness
> nothing can destroy in us—
> not even we ourselves.

> Perhaps that
> Freshness is the changed name of God.
> Where all the monsters also hide
> I bear him in the ocean of my blood
> and in the pulp of my enormous head.
> He lives beneath the unkempt potter's grass
> of my belly and chest.
> I feel his terrible, aged heart
> moving under mine. . . can see the shadows
> of the gorgeous light
> that plays at the edges of his giant eye . . .
> or tell the faint press and hum
> of his eternal pool of sperm.
> Like sandalwood! *Like sandalwood!*
> *the righteous man*
> *perfumes the axe that falls on him.*

The selflessness in these passages is the result of entering the self, entering one's own pain and coming out on the other side, no longer only James Wright or John Logan, but all men. The voice is a particular recognizable voice; at the same time it mysteriously sheds personality and becomes simply the voice of a creature on earth speaking.

If we take seriously Thoreau's dictum, "Be it life or death, we crave only reality," if we are willing to face the worst in ourselves, we also have to accept the risk I have mentioned, that probing into one's own wretchedness one may just dig up more wretchedness. What justifies the risk is the hope that in the end the search may open and transfigure us. Many people feel one shouldn't poke under the surface—that one shouldn't tempt the gods or invite trouble, that one should be content to live with his taboos unchallenged, with his repressions and politenesses unquestioned; that just as the highest virtue in the state is law and order, so the highest virtue of poetry is formality and morality—or if immorality, then in the voice of a *persona*—and on the whole cheerful, or at least ironic, good humor. In Tacoma, Washington, once, after a reading in which I read certain poems that exposed my own wretchedness, a woman came up and handed me a poem she had written during the reading. There was a little hieroglyph for the signature. Under it, it said, "If you want me, ask." The poem went like this:

> Galway Kinnel
> Why
> Are you in love with blood?
> What
> Dark part of your soul

Glories so
To wallow in gore?
Deep in your mind there lies
Despair, disgust, disease.
When
Did the beauty of life
Go from your desolate soul?
How
Can life be sweet to you
Who hold a wondrous gift
And use it for
Depravity?
Your voice too is false
Your comments cruel
As the depths of your heart
Exalt in ugliness
And dwell
In death
Here
In the midst of life
You
Are a sickness.

I laughed later that night, when I read it. But the laughter died quickly. For a long time I kept the poem pinned to the wall above my desk, as a *memento mori*. It is a risk: it is possible we will go on to the end feeding, with less and less relish, on the bitter flesh of our heart. The worst is that we ourselves may be the last to know that this is how we spent our life.

* * *

If much stands to be lost, however, it is true that everything stands to be gained. What do we want more than that oneness which bestows—which *is*—life? We want only to be more alive, not less. And the standard of what it is to be alive is very high. It was set in our infancy. Not yet divided into mind and body, our mind still a function of our senses, we laughed, we felt joyous connection with the things around us. In adult life don't we often feel half-dead, as if we were just brains walking around in corpses? The only sense we still respect is eyesight, probably because it is so closely attached to the brain. Go into any American house at random, you will find something—a plastic flower, false tiles, some imitation panelling—*something* which can be appreciated as material only if apprehended by eyesight alone.

Don't we go sightseeing in cars, thinking we can experience a
landscape by looking at it through glass? A baby takes pleasure in
seeing a thing, yes, but seeing is a first act. For fulfillment the
baby must reach out, grasp it, put it in his mouth, suck it, savor it,
taste it, manipulate it, smell it, physically be one with it. From
here comes our notion of heaven itself. Every experience of
happiness in later life is a stirring of that ineradicable memory of
once belonging wholly to the life of the planet.

Somehow it happened that the "mind" got separated from the
rest of us. It got specified as the self. In reality, the mind is only a
denser place in the flesh. Might we not just as well locate our center in the genitals, or in the solar plexus? Or even in that little
shadow which Hesse describes, that goes from the shoulder to the
breast? We have to learn anew to take delight in the physical life.

> If I worship one thing more than another it shall be the spread of
>   my own body, or any part of it,
> Translucent mould of me it shall be you!
> Shaded ledges and rests it shall be you!
> Firm masculine colter it shall be you!
> Whatever goes to the tilth of me it shall be you!
> You my rich blood! your milky stream pale strippings of my life!
> Breast that presses against other breasts it shall be you!
> My brain it shall be your occult convolutions!
> Root of wash'd sweet-flag! timorous pond-snipe! nest of guarded
>   duplicate eggs! it shall be you!
> Mix'd tussled hay of head, beard, brawn, it shall be you!
> Trickling sap of maple, fibre of manly wheat, it shall be you!
> Sun so generous it shall be you!
> Vapors lighting and shading my face it shall be you!
> You sweaty brooks and dews it shall be you!
> Winds whose soft-tickling genitals rub against me it shall be you!
> Broad muscular fields, branches of live oak, loving lounger in my
>   winding paths, it shall be you!
> Hands I have taken, face I have kiss'd, mortal I have ever touch'd,
>   it shall be you.
>
> I dote on myself, there is that lot of me and all so luscious. . . .

The great thing about Whitman is that he knew all of our being
must be loved, if we are to love any of it. I have often thought
there should be a book called *Shit*, telling us that what comes out
of the body is no less a part of reality, no less sacred, than what
goes into it; only a little less nourishing. It's a matter of its
moment in the life-cycle: food eaten is on the cross, at its moment

of sacrifice, while food eliminated is at its moment of ascension. There is a divine madness, remember; and if you dismiss the exuberance of self-love, you may be left with an impeccable reasonableness, but a dead body.

In the tale of Dr. Jekyll and Mr. Hyde, the vicious, animal half of the man escapes the control of the civilized, rational half and destroys it. The story is a Victorian fantasy which plays out the dread of nature; it is also a true myth of repression and its consequences. I wonder if the tale shouldn't be rewritten, with a happy ending? How would it be if, in his nightly cruising, Mr. Hyde should discover the possibility of tender love? What would happen if he came back to the fearful, overly mental, Puritan, self-enclosed Dr. Jekyll and converted him, so that they went out cruising together; or else, if he came back and seduced him? This conjectural version of the story would assume that the blame for their disharmony lay more with Dr. Jekyll than with Mr. Hyde, and it would look primarily to Mr. Hyde for their salvation.

Many ancient stories tell of the mating of man and animal—the Dr. Jekyll and Mr. Hyde of nature. It seems always to be a female human and a male animal who mate, never the reverse. Of course, around farms men have always copulated with animals, and it would be difficult to render this act into an instructive myth, since the men use the animals, if not rape them. In Cohn Wilson's *Encyclopedia of Murder*, he records the case of a man who preliminary to killing someone would fuck a goose, or after fucking a goose would kill someone, however you like to look at it—the basic pathology is clear. But the basic reason is that women—at least in the imagination of men—reside closer to nature, feel less threatened by it, are more willing to give themselves up to it. Leda undoubtedly knows terror as she lies under the swan—for in matings between beings so alien there must be an element of rape—but she also knows exaltation, as she gives herself to the natural life. Therefore men always depict the Muse as female; and in this sense the poet knows himself to be of a more feminine disposition than the banker.

> Muses resemble women who creep out at night to give themselves to unknown sailors and return to talk of Chinese porcelain— porcelain is best made, a Japanese critic has said, where the conditions of life are hard—or of the Ninth Symphony—virginity renews itself like the moon—except that the Muses sometimes form in those low haunts their most lasting attachments.

So wrote Yeats. If one chooses, one can think of the muse in less fanciful terms, as Gary Snyder does:

Widely speaking, the muse is anything other that touches you and moves you. Be it a mountain range, a band of people, the morning star, or a diesel generator. Breaks through the ego-barrier. But this touching-deep is as a mirror, and man in his sexual nature has found the clearest mirror to be his human lover.

Let me turn for a moment, then, to that widely used—or perhaps not so widely used—sentence, "I love you." Who is the "I"? Who is the "you"? Everyone except people who make scientific studies of love admits that love is a force of a kind which transcends person and personality. Wasn't Gatsby's most devastating put-down of the love between Tom and Daisy to say that it was "only personal"? Plato was eloquent in persuading us that love is a transcendent force, but in his dream, the loved person, and indeed the whole realm in which love takes place, turn into rubble. For the Christians, too, love transcended person and personality; it was not the man or woman, but the image of God in the person, that one loved. The Christians, unfortunately, were unable to permit this love to include sexual love, for it was too much for them to conceive of God as having sexual intercourse with himself through the instrumentality of his images.

D. H. Lawrence wrote an odd little poem on the subject:

I wish I knew a woman
who was like a red fire on the hearth
glowing after the day's restless draughts.

So that one could draw near her
in the red stillness of the dusk
and really take delight in her
without having to make the polite effort of loving her
or the mental effort of making her acquaintance.
Without having to take a chill, talking to her.

It isn't always easy to know when Lawrence is serious and when he is joking. As a rule of thumb, probably serious. But this union deeper than personality, as Lawrence of course knew, is not to be had that way. As with poetry, so with love: it is necessary to go through the personality to reach beyond it. Short of a swan descending from heaven, the great moments of sexual love are not between strangers, but between those who know and care for each other, and who then pass beyond each other, becoming nameless creatures enacting the primal sexuality of all life.

It is curious that sexual love, which is the only sacred experience of most lives on this earth, is a religion without a Book.

Even the *Kama Sutra* is too much like a sex manual. It is a religion that has many poems, though, and I would like to quote two of them, the first D. H. Lawrence's "River Roses," a matchless account of the casting off of selves:

> By the Isar, in the twilight
> We were wandering and singing,
> By the Isar, in the evening
> We climbed the huntsman's ladder and sat swinging
> In the fir-tree overlooking the marshes,
> While the river met with river, and the ringing
> Of their pale-green glacier water filled the evening.
>
> By the Isar, in the twilight
> We found the dark wild roses
> Hanging red at the river; and simmering
> Frogs were singing, and over the river closes
> Was savour of ice and of roses; and glimmering
> Fear was abroad. We whispered: "No one knows us.
> Let it be as the snake disposes
> Here in this simmering marsh."

The separate egos vanish; the wand of cosmic sexuality rules.

The following poem, section 5 from "Song of Myself," though not ostensibly a love poem, obviously has its source in a love experience. It is the kind of poem Dr. Jekyll would write, after his seduction by Mr. Hyde.

> Loafe with me on the grass, loose the stop from your throat,
> Not words, not music or rhyme I want, not custom or lecture, not
> even the best,
> Only the lull I like, the hum of your valvèd voice.
>
> I mind how once we lay such a transparent summer morning,
> How you settled your head athwart my hips and gently turn'd over
> upon me,
> And parted the shirt from my bosom-bone, and plunged your
> tongue to my bare-stript heart,
> And reach'd till you felt my beard, and reach'd till you held my
> feet.
>
> Swiftly arose and spread around me the peace and knowledge that
> pass all the argument of the earth,
> And I know that the hand of God is the promise of my own,
> And I know that the spirit of God is the brother of my own,
> And that all the men ever born are also my brothers, and the
> women my sisters and lovers,

And that a kelson of the creation is love,
And limitless are leaves stiff or drooping in the fields,
And brown ants in the little wells beneath them,
And mossy scabs of the worm fence, heap'd stones, elder, mullein
    and poke-weed.

* * *

The death of the self I seek, in poetry and out of poetry, is not
a drying up or withering. It is a death, yes, but a death out of
which one might hope to be reborn more giving, more alive, more
open, more related to the natural life. I have never felt the appeal
of that death of self certain kinds of Buddhism describe—that
death which purges us of desire, which removes us from our
loves. For myself, I would like a death that would give me more
loves, not fewer. And greater desire, not less. Isn't it possible that
to desire a thing, to truly desire it, is a form of having it? I suppose nothing is stronger than fate—if fate is that amount of vital
energy allotted each of us—but if anything were stronger, it
would not be acquiescence, the coming to want only what one
already has, it would be desire, desire which rises from the roots
of one's life and transfigures it.

This Navajo night-chant, which is no more than an expression of desire, gives whoever says it with his whole being, at least
for the moment of saying it, and who knows, perhaps forever,
everything he asks.

Tse'gihi.
House made of dawn.
House made of evening light.
House made of the dark cloud.
House made of male rain.
House made of dark mist.
House made of female rain.
House made of pollen.
House made of grasshoppers.
Dark cloud is at the door.
The trail out of it is dark cloud.
The zigzag lightning stands high upon it.
Male deity!
Your offering I make.
I have prepared a smoke for you.
Restore my feet for me.
Restore my legs for me.
Restore my body for me.

Restore my mind for me.
This very day take out your spell for me.
Your spell remove for me.
You have taken it away for me.
Far off it has gone.
Happily I recover.
Happily my interior becomes cool.
Happily I go forth.
My interior feeling cool, may I walk.
No longer sore, may I walk.
Impervious to pain, may I walk.
With lively feelings may I walk.
As it used to be long ago, may I walk.
Happily may I walk.
Happily, with abundant dark clouds, may I walk.
Happily, with abundant showers, may I walk.
Happily, with abundant plants, may I walk.
Happily, on the trail of pollen, may I walk.
Happily may I walk.
Being as it used to be long ago, may I walk.
May it be beautiful before me.
May it be beautiful behind me.
May it be beautiful below me.
May it be beautiful above me.
May it be beautiful all around me.
In beauty it is finished.

(1971)

Adrienne Rich

POETRY, PERSONALITY AND WHOLENESS:
A Response to Galway Kinnell

To the memory of Paul Goodman

Galway Kinnell's essay ("Poetry, Personality and Death") seems to me, like his recent poetry, a truly serious enterprise, an attempt to look at fundamentals that we are all going to have to examine if poetry, or personality itself, is to have any future. Instead of counselling us to try a certain kind of image or poetic structure, he asks us to think about our lives, the full weight of our existence as it is brought to bear on the act of writing. It doesn't surprise me that this essay comes from the man who wrote *The Book of Nightmares*. In that book, and in this essay, Kinnell's struggle with essentials gives me a certain kind of hope.

Yet in reading the essay I have the curious sense of a blind spot floating between the writer and his subject, —an almost-yet-never-quite-touching of a painful lesion that I believe Kinnell and other poets will have to begin probing sooner or later. At almost every point the essay seems to edge away from its true subject, or perhaps I should say, from the point where the curing of the lesion, the solution of the problem, might begin.

Kinnell's concern is with the "I" or self in poetry as it is being written today.[*] He traces the movement of certain poets "beyond personality"—that is, beyond mere confession—to a *persona* (as Dickey in "The Firebombing") or a kind of abstract, oversimplified "I" (as Robert Bly in "The Busy Man Speaks"). He feels (and I agree with him) that this movement in such poets has been an evasion; that it has neglected the real exploration of self, the real inward work, which would authenticate the "I" rather than set up an ideal "I" or, alternatively, a *persona* onto whom the poet can unload anything in himself which he rejects. Kinnell believes, and I believe with him, that we desire a poetry in which the "I" has become all of us, not simply a specific suffering personality, and not an abstraction which is also an evasion of the poet's own specificities.

---

[*]Although I paraphrase his argument in responding to it, I hope readers of this piece will return to Kinnell's essay, which deserves close reading on its own.

272

* * *

Kinnell goes on to try to probe the sources of what he calls "this closed, unshared 'I'" in poetry, "the poet's reluctance to reveal himself in his poems," locating it in "the closed ego of modern man, the neurotic burden which to some degree cripples us all." In his analysis of this ego he has written some accurate and important paragraphs: here he is moving close to the lesion itself. He describes man's approach to nature as to a problem to be solved, a force to be harnessed, rather than as something to be lived with, inwardly and outwardly. He calls science and technology to task for their fatal detachment from what they study, their depersonalization in the name of conquest. In these sentences he describes that split between man and what Paul Goodman has called his "only world," which has given him over to isolation and despair.

It is in poetry that Kinnell sees some hope of an effort toward reintegration—poetry in which the poet would speak to us in his own voice, but having gone "so deeply into himself . . .that he finds he is everyone." And Kinnell lingers over the idea of going that deeply into the self, as a possible risk that "one may just dig up more wretchedness"—also, perhaps, a risk of total solipsism. But even more, I think what is dreaded is a risk of some deeper exposure than had been counted on. And perhaps that *is* the terror—of finding that one *is* "everyone," not a *poète maudit* with one's own dark and dazzling guilt; that there has been an enormous failure—not a curse, not a doom, but a failure, a history of bad faith and willfulness—by that part of the human race which calls itself masculine and which exists sometimes, painfully enough, in the form of a poet. It is significant that the rest of Kinnell's essay is spent touching on sexuality.

* * *

Kinnell says that man is separated from his animal nature, and cites the story of Dr. Jekyll and Mr. Hyde, the Victorian myth of this separation and repression. He goes on to say that "many ancient stories tell of the mating of *man* and *animal*" but that—the nouns become perplexing here—"It seems always to be a *female human* and a *male animal* who mate, never the reverse" (italics mine). (He dismisses actual acts of copulation by men with animals as irrelevant to the myth, "since the men use the animals, if not rape them.") Women mythically mate with animals because "Women—

at least in the imaginations of men—reside closer to nature, feel less threatened by it, are more willing to give themselves up to it." We seem here to be peeling those strange onion-layers of the myth, the reading of the myth, and the uses of that reading to explain as primal or natural what may be simply social or political.

Women are less alienated from nature, according to Kinnell (and this may be true, if only as a result of their historic lack of participation in man's world of struggle and conquest); certainly they are so "in the imaginations of men." But then, in man's imagination, is woman "human" in the generic sense, or is she "nature"—part of that same nature from which man has severed himself through objectification and domination? Obviously, when perceived as a womb, a cunt, a piece of ass, a chick, or in any of the age-old masculine terms, she becomes part of that non-human, natural world from which the male has detached himself, and which he seeks to subdue, to know only for the purpose of using. At the same time, masculine poetry attests that man has also imagined her as an eternal mystery, therefore unknowable as humans are supposed to want to know each other. Masculine ambivalence toward nature consists, on the one hand, in reducing it to the object of his desires, seeking to possess and dominate it at the cost of real relationship to it; and on the other hand, mythifying and frequently sentimentalizing it, e.g. in terms of the mystery of womanhood, the purity and innocence of childhood. Neither of these attitudes—domination and idealization—leads to that state of being which is named, in *The Book of Nightmares*, "Tenderness toward existence." The contradiction between these attitudes lies not only beneath the white American's oppression of blacks, as Kinnell has pointed out, but more universally beneath man's historic ill-faith toward woman.

* * *

In the case of the male artist, I can only imagine that the split, the contradiction, is especially painful and especially destructive. On the one hand, woman is Muse, Goddess, Life Force; on the other, she is simply an accessory to *his* life, whose presence helps make his creation possible in a thousand purely practical ways: she is expected to satisfy his lust, bear children for whom he can have patriarchal feelings, cook his meals, hush up the children when he is working, uproot herself to follow him where his fate may take him, accept his sexual strayings, type his manuscripts, be sympathetic—but not too sympathetic—to his friends, sit as his model—in other words, to make her life an accessory to his own. Now, all of this may be true, in other modes, of the sexual relations of the factory worker or the corporate executive. But it is a contradiction which the artist can continue to evade only at his peril. On the one hand, the male artist is a man with a special relationship to his own femininity (or, as Kinnell says, "the poet knows himself to be of a more feminine disposition than the banker")—a man for whom the split from the natural life has more immediate and obvious dangers than it does for the banker, in terms of his very identity. On the other hand, he has frequently evaded his own femininity, or projected his hatred of it, through an ordinary *macho* relationship to women.

I have to ask myself whether it is because I am a woman that the idea of the Muse seems so uninteresting to me. Kinnell quotes Gary Snyder on the Muse as "anything other that touches you and moves you . . . Breaks through the ego-barrier . . . . Man in his sexual nature has found the clearest mirror to be his human lover." I do not know whether the male artist really feels that the mysterious woman he is in bed with is a mirror to him; I doubt that the woman, at her deepest level of consciousness, feels like a mirror. This is idealization and over-simplification; it simply omits too much social reality. However, it is perfectly plausible that the male artist uses and can make use of his "human lover" in this way. For woman in her sexual nature the Muse cannot be the human lover (as man) because it is man and man's world which makes it especially difficult for her as artist. Man may at various times exist for her as teacher, idol, guru, master, all dominating roles; he may also exist as a friend with whom she struggles in all the warmth and friction of her affections; but he is definitely not the Muse (unless indeed, the anti-Muse, the demon lover, like Sylvia Plath's "Daddy"). Emily Dickinson's Muse, if any, was her own soul—*the* Soul. Edna St. Vincent Millay was no more than a graceful and conventional poet when she addressed her sonnets to some mythified lover; her best work (and least-known) is the sonnet sequence she wrote about a woman in a house in New England, watching over the last illness of a husband she had previously left and now no longer loves: "Sonnets From An Ungrafted Tree." For Emily Brontë, nature itself is the creative energy behind her work; and nature is identified with *her* nature:

> Often rebuked, yet always back returning
> To those first feelings that were born in me . . .

I'll walk where my own nature would be leading:
It vexes me to choose another guide . . . .

As woman's "human lover" man is still the male, with masculine
expectations of the role she will fulfill for him, the accessory,
"feminine" part she will play—all while she is trying to do an
artist's lonely and independent work. Possibly the idea of the Muse
is man's way of projecting and objectifying his own feminine principle—along with his negative feelings about that principle (see
the quotation from Yeats on the Muse that Kinnell also supplies).

* * *

"In the tale of Dr. Jekyll and Mr. Hyde, the vicious, animal
half of the man escapes the control of the civilized, rational half
and destroys it." Then Kinnell proceeds to his own fantasy, which I
at first found rather attractive, of the conversion of Dr. Jekyll by
Mr. Hyde, so that "they went out cruising together; or [Hyde] . . .
came back and seduced him." What Kinnell forgets is that Dr.
Jekyll expressed his animality by raping and murdering women. I
cannot submit to the idealism which imagines that in this state of
affairs Mr. Hyde would "discover the possibility of tender love,"
whether homosexual or heterosexual. I think I understand what
Kinnell is trying to say; what I want to elucidate is that the terms of
his thought are out of focus; they neglect a terrible central core to
the whole problem.

Kinnell ends by quoting several poems, one of which, a
prose-poem by Robert Bly, uses women and children in a con-
ventionally mythic way: woman-sea, source of all life; "the
woman I loved in some former life" (I believe Bly more when he
describes death as being "like the sound of the motor in an airplane
as we fly, the sound so steady and comforting"). James Wright's
poem, "The Life," is a fine Wright poem in its delineation of "the
old loneliness"—but it is precisely beyond that old loneliness that
I believe Kinnell is saying we can move, in our poetry and in our
lives. (It is the *acceptance* of that loneliness as being fated or
metaphysical rather than a result of the closed-in ego of man, that
I believe shadows the poetry of some of the best male poets alive.)
In the second of two Lawrence poems quoted ("River Roses")
Kinnell sees the true shedding of personality and the true absorption into universality through sex; his phrase for this (echoing the
line, "Let it be as the snake disposes") is: "The *wand of cosmic
sexuality* rules" (italics mine). In none of these poems is there any
imagination of what a real woman might be feeling.

The problem for Kinnell, I believe (and if I single him out in this essay it is not because I think his blindness is greater but his potential for vision more)—the problem for Kinnell is the problem of the masculine writer—how to break through the veils that his language, his reading of the handed-down myths (and, I am forced to say, his very convenience), have cast over his sight; and what that will cost him. To become truly universal he will have to confront the closed ego of man in its most private and political mode: his confused relationship to his own femininity, and his fear and guilt towards woman.

* * *

The lines from "Song of Myself" which Kinnell quotes ("Loafe with me on the grass. . .") rightly call us back to that poet, that American, who of all his brothers was most able to accept himself in his bisexual wholeness. For him, as for Dickinson, there is no Muse: only his Soul. Whitman's homoerotic poetry does not represent a flight from woman but a recognition of woman, and of the being in himself and in his beloved that is capable of tenderness, vulnerability, mutuality. ("Out of the dimness opposite equals advance.") It is worth noting that Whitman really does accept woman's lust as a good and natural part of her being, rather than as a devouring force or a self-destructive drive. The opening lines of the section quoted are:

> I believe in you, my Soul, the other I am must not abase itself to
> you,
> And you must not be abased to the other.

It is possible (I am thinking in particular of some of the new poems of Kenneth Pitchford) that we are on the brink of a new bisexuality in poetry written by men, which in claiming its own wholeness would be able to greet wholeness in woman with joy instead of dread. But no such poetry will be made out of theories; it will be born out of personal and collective struggle, and many costly recognitions.

* * *

At the end of his essay Kinnell says, "The death of the self I seek, in poetry and out of poetry, is not a drying-up or a withering. It is a death, yes, but a death out of which one might hope to be reborn *more giving, more alive, more open, more related to the natural life"* (italics mine). Reading these words I am reminded of a notebook in which I wrote down parts of a conversation I had been having with a much younger woman, of great clarity and beauty of mind, a political radical and a feminist, of whom I asked the question, "What do you see becoming of men?" Her answer was, "I have two visions. One: that men will become more open, more concerned with feelings, more gentle, less power-seeking, than they have ever been. The other: that, given new methods of reproduction in the future, the sex will simply die out."

I believe that Galway Kinnell is concerned in his work with a death which is not that dying-out of a self and sex that has ceased to have any vital energy—having misconstrued energy not as Eternal Delight but as Pure Will. I have thought that the sense of doom and resignation to loneliness endemic in much masculine poetry has to do with a sense of *huis clos,* of having come to the end of a certain kind of perception. What I would like to offer here is a clue to a way onward, a way that will of necessity dredge up much wretchedness, but that will, I believe, be finally transfiguring.

(1972)

Charles Wright

CHARLES WRIGHT AT OBERLIN

In November, 1976, Charles Wright spent a week at Oberlin as part of a series of residencies sponsored by Oberlin's Creative Writing Program and supported by the National Endowment for the Arts. At two evening seminars with students and staff who had been reading his work, he responded to both general and specific questions. Discussion centered on Bloodlines *(Wesleyan, 1975) and on the nearly completed manuscript of* China Trace *(Wesleyan, 1977), which he had shared with us in a mimeographed version. This is an edited transcript of the proceedings.*

We began by suggesting that Wright say something about himself and his background.

Well, I was born on the 25th of August in 1935, on my father's birthday, in Hardin County, Tennessee, in a place called Pickwick Dam. We lived in Oak Ridge during the Second World War. After the war we moved to Kingsport, Tennessee, where we stayed. It's in the upper wedge of Tennessee, eight miles or so from where the Carter Family lived, all-time great American poet-singers. In the tenth grade I was sent to a school that had eight students, a place called Sky Valley, outside Hendersonville, N.C. My last two years of high school were at an Episcopal boarding school with the unlikely name of Christ School, in Arden, N.C., known to its students as "Jesus Tech." Both these schools, Sky Valley and Christ School, made profound impressions on me and gave me a lot to write about later, mostly in *Hard Freight* and *Bloodlines.*

After high school I went to Davidson College, which turned out to be four years of amnesia, as much my fault as theirs. Probably more. Then I went into the Army for four years, three of them spent in Italy. After the Army I went to the University of Iowa for two years. Oh, this is ridiculous. I did grow up in East Tennessee and Western North Carolina, which had a lot to do with my poems. Place has a lot to do with everyone's poems. I now live in California in a little town called Laguna Beach, and have lived there for the last ten years. It's a good place for a writer because it's so boring there's nothing to do but write.

My biography is pretty much the biography of almost everyone here. I happened to be in that place and you were probably
somewhere else. We all went through more or less the same
things. I discovered poetry when I was sitting under an olive tree,
like Ferdinand. Or was that a fig tree? Anyhow, it's true. I got
interested in poetry rather late in my life. I was a history major in
college, for reasons I'm still unsure of, and which were probably
wrong. Amnesia period.

I suppose my original impetus for writing came from my
mother because she was, I started to say, a failed writer, which, in
a sense, I suppose she was. So she tried to encourage writing in
me. It didn't take hold until very late. Until I was in the Army,
though I had tried my hand at some stories while at Davidson—
the less said of that the better. Anyhow, I was given a book, *The
Selected Poems of Ezra Pound*, when I was living in Verona, Italy,
and I was told to go out to Sirmione, on Lake Garda, where the
Latin poet, Catullus, supposedly had a villa. That's the legend,
anyhow, and it doesn't matter if the legend is true or not, it should
be, like all legends. It's still one of the most beautiful places I
have ever been to, or expect to go to. Lake Garda in front of you,
the Italian Alps on three sides of you, the ruined and beautiful
villa around you, and I read a poem that Pound had written about
the place, about Sirmione being more beautiful than Paradise, and
my life was changed forever. No kidding. I was at that time twen-
ty-three or twenty-four. You can't get more romantic than that,
can you, unless you're Gauguin?

I went to Iowa when I was twenty-six. I didn't even know
what an iambic pentameter line was, so Iowa was good for me. It
may not always be good for everybody, but it was good for me because I didn't know a damned thing. I even got in because I
applied in August and no one happened to read my manuscript.
So I shut up for two years and listened. And that's my bio.

*Did you have any teachers during that time, the Iowa time, who
meant a lot to you?*

Donald Justice and Paul Engle were teaching there at that
time. Justice had a major effect on my life. For several years,
everything I knew about poetry I knew through him or because of
him. He was an incredibly fine teacher and poet. He still is. And I
was very fortunate, I feel, to have started out with him instead of
someone else, because the things he taught me about language
and style and care and precision are things you really have to

learn first, and not pick up later on, as you probably *won't* pick them up later on as you might, say, pick up other things that become necessary. Because I'd started in the middle, don't you see, and had to begin back at the start. And Justice knew what the right tracks were. Actually, the best thing that happened to me was when I went into the Army. I signed up for the Army Language School and learned a little Italian and got sent to Italy for three years. It cost me two years of my life but it has repaid many times over. I lived in Verona for three years, a beautiful city; I discovered poems there, and painting and eating well and, indirectly, it got me to Iowa where I got serious about writing.

Have you been back to Italy since?

Yes, for a year. I was teaching at the University of Padua, in 1968, and I lived in Venice. It's only about a twenty-five minute drive from Venice to Padua. I lived in Venice for a year and I benefitted from it greatly. It's everything everybody has always said it was, unique in the world, absolutely gorgeous, just decadent enough for me.

Did you write about Venice while you were there?

No, but only because I tried desperately not to. It's like writing a poem about snow while the snow is falling. You try not to. Now that I think back, I did write a couple but not as many as I could have. I wrote a poem called "In the Midnight Hour," a Wilson Pickett title. I also wrote a poem about Frederick William Rolfe, "Baron Corvo," who was a fascinating Englishman. The rest of the poems I wrote there really didn't have that much to do with Venice as such. But I've written a lot since then that sort of seems influenced by the city. In a way, all the poems I've written since then have been influenced by Venice to a certain extent. There is a connection, a lushness connection, in my mind between my East Tennessee foliage and the Venetian leafage, gold leafage, that seems to have stayed with me ever since, and it keeps coming out in my poems. And the presumptuousness of Venice and the sumptuousness of Venice have somehow sneaked in. I tried to knock some of it down but it kept coming back. I think Venice has a lot to do with—now, now this is terribly embarrassing for me, sitting up here talking about how my work is changing, my work has done this, how my work has done that, so please bear with me—I think it did, the city I mean, have something to do with how, as they say in music, I went up a step. I picked it up a step. From "streamlined" to a somewhat lusher energy. It had to do with Venice and it had to do, as I've just mentioned, with reaching back into my childhood, as it were, a place called Hiwassee, North Carolina. Which is where a poem called "Dog Creek Main-line" came from. It was a place that was carved out of the wilder-ness, one of those TVA dams. A type of back wilderness that is very lush and large and that encroaches on you continually. There was, and is, some strange balance for me between Italy, and Venice especially, and the wilderness of East Tennessee and west-ern North Carolina. I still haven't figured it out completely. I haven't got it straight, but it keeps on coming up.

I'm really curious about Pound. I'd like to know how you'd sug-gest reading him and how valuable he was to you in terms of your work.

Apart from my teacher, an influence that everyone has to some degree or other, there have been two major influences on my work. Pound was one and Eugenio Montale was the other. Pound was a tremendous influence, he was the first poet I ever read seriously. I think if the first poet you read seriously is a good or a great poet, then you're stuck with him forever. I figure I got lucky. I think he really had the golden ear. There's no doubt about it: everything they say about his ear is true. Everything they say about his politics is also true. They were very bad. I've been teaching for ten years, and I've never had the nerve to try to teach his poems. He was such a learned man. At least, he knew a little about a lot of things. And he knew a lot about some things. He's easy to read if you've read all the books that he's read and have remembered the same things from them that he did. It helps to be a Pound freak, and to be interested in anything he did, just because he did it.

How about Montale and his influence on you? Did that come through translating his poetry?

Well, he taught me a little about Hermeticism, which I'm not at all sure is a good thing, but I am (was) fascinated by it. Hermeti-cism is a kind of poetry I don't think I write. I try not to. But the way he went about writing his poems when he was in his "Her-metic" period made him able to write hard-edge images, a type that Italian poetry hadn't seen much of before and hasn't seen much of since, though I am no expert on Italian poetry, I assure you. And if you're able, I think, to get out of the hermetic mold and to still keep the vividness, the freshness, the newness of the imagery that he was able to write because of it, then I think you can learn something, and I think I was able to learn a lot from Montale. As in most translating, I think that the translator is the one who gets the most out of the translation, no matter how good the translation turns out to be. The reader of the translation is not going to get what the translator got out of it, even though he may get a lot.

Did you ever work with Montale?

No. He was called "Il Taciturno," Montale, and he really doesn't like to talk very much and I can certainly understand that. So I didn't want to disturb him. Also, he lived in Milan and I was living in Rome. Still, I should have gone up. I handled Pound equally brilliantly. I'd follow him around for days in Venice. I'd even follow him to his restaurants. But I could never just walk up to him and say "hello." Anyhow, what are you going to say to a man like that, "I like your poems"? This really isn't a good answer to the Montale question, because you'd have to be able to read Montale and be able to see what steals I've made and used. I feel I did learn something about how to manipulate lines. How to move a line, how to move an image from one stage to the next. How to create imaginary bridges between images and stanzas and then to cross them, making them real, image to image, block to block. And compression from Pound. Condense, compress. And those are the two people who do those things as well as anyone.

The "Mottetti" must be one of your favorite Montale poems; maybe you should say what that is.

It's a group of twenty poems. Not only that, they're the first things I ever translated by him. The twenty poems are twenty love poems to an unnamed woman, and I still don't know her name, even though I studied with a woman when I was at the University of Rome when I had my Fulbright who had been working on Montale for about twenty or thirty years, something you don't do with an existing writer in Italy, you have to wait till they are very dead. But she had been doing this and she still didn't know the woman's name, but she said she was a Canadian whom Montale had had an affair with, even though he was very much in love with his wife, too. But these Motets were to this particular woman, and

they were love poems. Neither of my twenty-part poems are love
poems but, yes, twenty became a number, a magic number for me,
because of the Motets. I think the Motets are fantastically performed. They are also discrete poems. Each one exists in itself,
whereas I should like to think that my twenty-part poems are single poems, or rather that one is a single poem and the other is a
sequence. The first Motet is a great poem. They are all short, I
don't know what the longest one would be—fifteen, sixteen, seventeen lines, something like that. They were, as I say, the first
things I translated. Then I translated an entire book called *La
Bufera, The Storm*, which has a 15-part sequence called "Flashes
and Dedications," travel poems about places in England, the Middle East, about different places in Italy.

*There seems to be an important formal precedent for you and oth-
ers in Montale's sequences.*

It's a different kind of idea of a sequence. I gather M. L.
Rosenthal is writing a book on the sequence in modern American
poetry. His theory is, I think, that the sequence is the modern
answer to the long poem and he's probably right. I guess they do
hook together. It's wonderful to see Pound's attempt at this,
which comes from Dante. You see something in the first two or
three Cantos and then you see it in the one hundred and whatevers
too. I mean he keeps going back and forth, Pound does, even
though he says, "I cannot make it cohere," he's probably right, in
the end, when he says, "It coheres, all right, even if my notes
don't cohere." That's an approximate quote. It all cohered in his
head somehow. It's the fourth anniversary of his death today. He
died on the first of November, "Tutti Santi," All Souls' Day. There
are recurring themes, and threads, let's say threads. It is a grab
bag. It's the most beautiful grab bag in every sense. I believe
Pound will be the chapter headings, and not the footnotes, of this
century's poetry in English. I think he's probably our most important poet, but I have been wrong before. He has stuffed our grab
bag century the way it is, fragmental and disorganized and cruel
and with great flashes of beauty, the same way his Troubador century was, his Dante century. He is our "broken bundle of mirrors."

Could you talk a little more about Hermeticism?

Hermeticism meant a poem that was almost impossible to penetrate the meaning of. I don't think it was ever true. Oh, it may have

been temporarily so at the time they were doing it, during the thirties or the forties. In the same way, those things may not seem tremendously hermetic now. We make associations now, as readers, more readily and without so much fuss. And if we can come to think in associations, then we won't have to worry about strict logic, and Hermeticism will be clear as air. But that is originally what it meant. It probably also had something to do with Mussolini and disguising what you were saying. It became sealed, hermetically sealed.

I notice you use a lot of words that either are made up or are very rare. Even in the ones that are made up it's almost impossible to mistake what you mean. What comes to mind is the word "shevelled"; as far as I know that's not a word.

Everyone knows what "dishevelled" means so "shevelled" would mean the opposite. That's the kind of word I'm interested in making up. I always try to be as clear as a lake. And even though I do have this business in my system now, that's still what I always try to do, be clear.

Which business?

This language business, you know, you have got to try everything that's available to you. I'm extremely interested in sound at the moment. I'm not interested in a flat line, or the flat language that has been fairly popular in the last, say, ten to twelve years. One person writing it extremely well, maybe two or three, and everyone else writing it extremely poorly. But I really like sound. I like musical sounds a lot.

Which sounds do you like?

Oh, lots of sounds. Not noise, sounds. Mostly I like the sound of words. The sound, the feel, the paint, the color of them. I like to hear what they can do with each other. I like layers of paint on the canvas. I also know after I'm tired of lots of layers on the canvas, I'm going to want just one layer of paint and some of the canvas showing through. But I'm not quite to that point yet. I'm still trying to do whatever I can with sound. My mother's family is all very musical. Everybody could play something, except me. I was the only one who could play nothing. If you notice the dedication in *Bloodlines*, it's to my brother, Winter Wright. I don't know if they are famous enough for you to know them or not, but Johnny and Edgar Winter, the rock musicians, are my first cousins, and that whole family is musical, they all play something. Edgar plays everything. But that's where this sound thing comes from, I guess; I take it out in words. Repressed music. My father's family can't even carry a tune. Somehow I was the one of them that shook loose. I wanted to play the banjo, not write poems.

Do you think you can trust the musical impulse in poetry?

To a certain degree, yes. You also have to be careful it doesn't overwhelm the poem. I'm a fan of Father Hopkins, Gerard Manley Hopkins. Sometimes I think his sound patterns are so strong that you miss what he is saying. And what he's saying is about as crucial a thing as you can say. But his sound patterns are too strong. My favorites are the Terrible Sonnets, where everything seems to fit together just right, even though some of the more Baroque poems, like "Spelt From Sibyl's Leaves," are among his greatest.

In your long poem "Tattoos," do you think of the notes as if they were another section of the poem?

No. I would have given anything not to have used the notes but I also wanted it to be very clear that each one of these was an actual situation, that it had not been made up but had actually happened, that it became a psychic tattoo in my life that would always be with me. I knew that later I would write something that would be conceptual, that I was going to play off the conceptual and theoretical poem against "Tattoos," and I wanted the actual thing to be as specific as possible. That's why they have dates on them and that's why they have notes. I thought that if I didn't, the hook-up would be lost. The reason I put them at the end of the poem instead of at the bottom or under the title of each one was that I also wanted the reader to go all the way through and try to figure out what was going on and then when he came to the notes say, "Yeah, they really are real things. Let me go back and read it with that in mind, and then read them again." And, as I said, "Skins" was conceptual. I wanted to balance it, and "Skins" is about such things as truth, beauty, the eventual destruction of the universe, metamorphosis, that kind of thing. They are supposed to be abstract and musical against the actual.

Were you able to plan "Tattoos" before you wrote the individual sections?

To a certain extent. I didn't know what I was going to write about. I didn't know what the situation would be. I just knew it was going to be a situation. I wrote the first one, the one about the camellias, reminding me of the Mother's Day business with the red rose and the white rose. That started me back into that whole period of my life. I wrote another one, and I kept thinking, or trying to think, of things that had made a great impression on me over the years. And some things go back to when I was five years old.

I didn't have them all in mind when I wrote the first one. Particularly the one about the janitor. I hadn't remembered that in thirty years. Another thing I did was I played nothing but country music on the radio and record player almost every day for six months while I was writing the things trying to put myself back in that time period, because that is what I grew up listening to.

Was there a connection between the snake-bite section and the blood-poisoning section?

No, it wasn't a bite. I didn't get bit. It was just something I saw. A snake-handling ceremony. That's what they do. The blood poisoning, that was a nail in the foot. For some reason the nail went in the foot but the blood poisoning was in the arm, and my brother somehow got blood poisoning at the same time and his came out of the stomach. He was swaddled up on the lower bunk of a double-decker bed. I was six and he was four. He had these big towels around him and I had my arm out also got up in wet towels. I was six when this happened and both of my parents were dead by the time I wrote the poem and I have to say, "was it really like this?" That's how I remember it, but who knows? The point of all this is that anyone can pick out twenty incidents in his life and do that. I would like to think there are at least twenty that one will never forget. I tried to pick from the ones that seemed important enough to make a thread go through a single poem. Whereas "Skins" is not a thread, it's a ladder. I'll read one of the "Tattoos" and if there are no questions I'll read the second one and then go for three.

> Necklace of flame, little dropped hearts,
> Camellias: I crunch you under my foot.
> And here comes the wind again, bad breath
> Of thirty-odd years, and catching up. Still,
> I crunch you under my foot.

Your white stalks sequester me,
Their roots a remembered solitude
Their months of snow keep forming my name.
Programmed incendiaries,
Fused flesh, so light your flowering,

So light the light that fires you
—Petals of horn, scales of blood—,
Where would you have me return?
What songs would I sing
And the hymns . . . What garden of wax statues . . .

                                                        —1973

Obviously this is a set-up poem for what's coming after. Where I
used to live in Laguna Beach, before I moved this summer, there
is a giant camellia bush. I mean a giant camellia bush. I mean as
big as from that couch to that couch. Every February it would
come into bloom and drop its blossoms. This is what started the
whole poem. The dropped flowers, red and white. Thinking of St.
Paul's Episcopal Church. What song would I sing? What garden
of wax statues? "Programmed incendiaries" because they're programmed to fall off as soon as they bloom. Thirty-odd years
because I was thinking back to when I used to do my church number. Should I go on? This next one was written about the death of
my father in 1972.

The pin oak has found new meat,
The linkworm a bone to pick.
Lolling its head, slicking its blue tongue,
The nightflower blooms on its one stem;
The crabgrass hones down its knives:

Between us again there is nothing. And since
The darkness is only light
That has not yet reached us,
You slip it on like a glove.
Duck soup, you say. *This is duck soup.*

And so it is.
            Along the far bank
Of Blood Creek, I watch you turn
In that light, and turn, and turn,
Feeling it change on your changing hands,
Feeling it take. Feeling it.

                                                        —1972

My father's favorite expression when I didn't understand something was that it was duck soup, incredibly simple. That darkness is only light which has not yet reached us, I understand, is a physical fact. That is what's happening. There is light coming behind all the darkness if it ever gets down. Not in our lifetime. For my taste, now, it's a little too metaphorical in the last stanza. I don't think I'd write it that way now. Blood Creek is a renaming of a creek called Reedy Creek in Kingsport. Which on one side was the country and the other side was more or less town. "Blood Creek" is too metaphorical, I think.

So that's an exception? Most of the place names are actual places?

Almost everything. All of them have references in my life to real places. Real things.

Why the crabgrass in the first stanza? And what is the night-flower?

There is a lot of crab grass in the lawns. Crab grass is very big down South. I don't know if it's as big up here. If you can't get the crab grass out of your lawn, the lawn gets eaten up by crab grass. My father's mature life was one continuous battle against crab grass and rose diseases. Crab grass is almost indestructible. You can't stop it. It's something small. Nightflower is a metaphor. The death flower, and one wishes one had not said it three years later. But that's the story of almost everything. One tries to be as exact as possible at the time. I believe in trying to combine passion and exactness in language in poems and it's always hard to do. It's easy to be passionate or it's easy to be exact. If you're just exact it's boring, if you're just passionate it's formless, and probably boring too. If you can get the two together, you've got something memorable.

How do you react to poems after you finish writing them as opposed to later on?

I'm like everyone else—they're always better right after writing them. I'm not too embarrassed now, I guess, because I do think "Skins" and "Tattoos" are probably the two best poems I've done up till now. I don't think "Tattoos" is as ambitious as "Skins." But taken together, I think they are very ambitious. Too

ambitious for what I was able to handle at the time, or might ever
be able to handle. I also think that if you don't try to write something that you can't handle, then there is little point in it.

Something to do with satisfaction?

Yes, I feel some satisfaction in them. I wish they were better
but I feel more satisfaction about these two poems than anything
I've done up to what I'm working on now.

What would you change in those poems?

Nothing, probably, because at the time that was the best I
could do. And I disagree with Auden, presumptuous as that is. I
don't think you should keep going back and changing and changing stuff that you wrote when you were thirty when you're sixty.
You've become a hard-line Anglican, you used to be a Socialist. I
think that's foolish. He wants us not to have "September 1st,
1939" because the line "We must love one another or die" is false:
we're going to die anyhow. Well, sure, but how can he deny us the
poem when he's already given it to us? He can't do that. Well, of
course, he can, he did. I mean he tried to. No, I probably wouldn't
do anything better. This is even better than I could have done at
the time. It's like when you're playing pool and you're doing fantastically. Everything's dropping. You're playing so far over your
head you can't believe it. And in certain moments in "Skins" I
think I was over my head. There were certain moments when I
found my level, too.

Did you have any sections that you left out of "Tattoos"?

Yes, I did. Five of them. I didn't have any from "Skins" that
I threw out, but I had five from this one. There were several that I
considered writing about and didn't. Reasons now I'm not sure of
and they may have fitted into the scheme just as well as these do.
But at the time I didn't think so.

*You say you wrote the first one first (but the others are not in
chronological order) and that gave you the five-line stanza. Was
that comfortable to work with?*

It was very comfortable and that's why I changed it in
"Skins" to one fourteen-line stanza, it was so comfortable. I'd

used it a couple of times in *Hard Freight* and liked it. Three stanzas is a good form for me and fifteen lines is a good length for me. The basketball players all have their favorite spots on the floor to shoot from, so many feet from the basket. Well, I feel comfortable at fifteen lines or thereabouts. Also, three stanzas is good because you can present something in the first, work around with it a bit in the second and then release it, refute it, untie it, set fire to it, whatever you want to, in the third. And that's its main problem for me. I felt I'd explored enough of what could be done, so I changed it for the next poem. Unfortunately, I didn't realize until I was about halfway through that I was using what Lowell was using in his *Notebooks*. Of course, it's no more his than mine; it's been around for hundreds of years. Still, his *Notebooks* was fairly current, and if I'd thought of that when I started I probably would have continued on with the five-liners, the three five-line stanzas. But these bothered me, in addition to what I've just said, because of *The Dream Songs*, which are in three six-line stanzas. You can't win. Whatever you do you can't win. To get away from this I went to that and found out I'd screwed up there too. Still, I do like them being different.

Shall I go on? This is the one about snake handling. It takes place outside of Asheville, North Carolina.

> Body fat as my forearm, blunt-arrowed head
> And motionless, eyes
> Sequin and hammer and nail
> In the torchlight, he hangs there,
> Color of dead leaves, color of dust,
>
> Dumbbell and hourglass—copperhead.
> Color of bread dough, color of pain, the hand
> That takes it, that handles it
> —The snake now limp as a cat—
> Is halfway to heaven, and in time.
>
> Then Yellow Shirt, twitching and dancing,
> Gathers it home, handclap and heartstring,
> His habit in ecstasy.
> Current and godhead, hot coil,
> Grains through the hourglass glint and spring.

—1951

It helps to know that the configurations of the copperhead are dumbbell shapes or hourglass shapes. It also helps that a copperhead, even though poisonous, won't kill you unless you're

already rather sick. It will sure make you sicker. It'll send you to
the hospital, but it won't kill you unless you're in trouble anyway.

So most of the snakes that they pick up will be copperheads.
But they pick up those big-ass rattlers too, and if they bite you it
doesn't mean you shouldn't have, it only means that you didn't
have enough faith. Also they stroke them when they pick them up,
on the stomach, so as not to disturb the rather drowsy state they,
the snakes, are in. The people believe that there is a passage in
scripture that tells them they will handle snakes. Which is where
godhead and that business comes from. If you believe enough you
will be able to handle the snakes. Shall I keep on doing these?

> Hungering acolyte, pale body,
> The sunlight—through St. Paul of the 12 Sorrows—
> Falls like Damascus on me:
> I feel the gold hair of Paradise rise through my skin
> Needle and thread, needle and thread;
>
> I feel the worm in the rose root.
> I hear the river of heaven
> Fall from the air. I hear it enter the wafer
> And sink me, the whirlpool stars
> Spinning me down, and down. O. . .
>
> Now I am something else, smooth,
> Unrooted, with no veins and no hair, washed
> In the waters of nothingness;
> Anticoronal, released. . .
> And then I am risen, the cup, new sun, at my lips.

—1946

I don't know how many of you people are associated with the
Catholic Church or the Episcopal Church, but it's practice not to
eat before taking communion. When you're ten or eleven years
old you're always hungry and you're always fainting at the altar
because you're hungry. That's sort of what happened. Mr. Kent
gave me the wine to bring me around. That's why the cup is at my
lip because he gave me the sacramental wine to wake me up. It's
in here not just because it's amusing that I fainted at the altar but
because I think it's symptomatic of the sparring match that I had
for about ten years with the Episcopal Church, in which I was
raised, in which I was tremendously involved for a short amount
of time and from which I fled and out of which I remain. But it
had a huge effect on me. If nothing else, from Sunday School I
learned all those stories in the Bible which were very important

and which I would never have known otherwise. It's a very strange thing about being raised in a religious atmosphere. It alters you completely, one way or the other. It's made me what I am and I think it's okay. I can argue against it, but it has given me a sense of spirituality which I prize. I just don't want it all so bleeding organized.

Do you think that the ritual of the church has affected the sense of form in your poems?

Yes, I like the ritual, that's the part I like the best about it. I think it has something to do with the form, the continuing formality that I find. I can't quite get away from a certain amount of formality in my work. I think ritual is a part of life, and here's a ritual that goes on in people's lives. There are people who wouldn't want that to affect their poems. I realize that, but, yes, it still does have an effect on my life, the ritual does. And I'm glad for it.

Will you say something about how you came to write "Skins"?

It started with those two lines in #1: "There comes that moment/ When what you are is what you will be. . . ." Even though I had it in mind as an extension of, or continuation of, or an overlay to, the "Tattoos," even when I was still writing "Tattoos," that statement is what the poem itself took off from. Because I realized I had reached that point (I think I was thirty-eight), and by then—long before then—there does come a time when, as Metropolitan Life says, "The future is now." There you are. You are what you're going to be. One hopes one can make the best of it. Now, each one of these "Skins," just as the "Tattoos" did, has a very specific reference, although each one of these is, as I've said before, conceptual, abstract, and I suppose theoretical. And I can give them to you if you wish. They are so outrageously pretentious that I didn't include notes for them. But just for the fun of it, I'll tell you what I had in mind. The structure of the poem is a ladder. Ten up, ten down. It starts at Point A, and comes back to Point A. Number 1 is the Situation: what you are is what you will be. After that, I said, what the hell, let's go for it. So this is the one in which I decided to really over-reach myself. Number 2 is Beauty. Number 3 is Truth. Number 4 is the Beginning and Eventual Destruction of the Universe. Number 5 is Organized Religion. Number 6 is Metamorphosis, in this case the metamorphosis of the mayfly. Numbers 7, 8, and 9 are the four elements and combinations thereof. 7 obviously is water; 8 is air/earth; 9 is earth/fire. 10 is the fifth element, Aether, the air above the air. The Greeks called it the fifth element. That's the top of the ladder. It ends with a colon, and then it comes back down. All of this is trying to make some sense out of one's situation. "Tattoos" was me in relation to the past. "Skins" is me in relation to the present. *China Trace* is me in relation to the future. There's the seed of a mad plan going on here. It is even more involved: *Bloodlines* is the center of the three books *Hard Freight*, *Bloodlines* and *China Trace*. "Tattoos" hooks up with *Hard Freight* and the past, and "Skins" hooks up with *China Trace* and the future. All three are supposed to work together in a smudgy sort of way and are part of an idea I started out with about seven years ago and that I'm just about to finish with in *China Trace*. . . . Anyhow, number 11 starts five poems of things that are rejected: number 11 is Primitive Magic. Number 12 is Necromancy. Number 13 is Black Magic. Number 14 is Alchemy. Number 15 is Allegory—all rejected. And then the next four are acceptances: and they are of course again what I've gone up the ladder with: earth, air, fire and water. Number 20 is the Situation again, point A. Pretentious, perhaps, reaching, surely, but I was trying to keep it all in terms of natural objects. Even though the situations and concepts are large, I hope the meanderings will come close to home. Now that was the hardest to do in the five rejections, in the magic part, where you get into Alchemy. And in the one on allegory it's impossible to keep allegory from coming in.

Would you go through from 11 on again?

Yes. Number 11 is Primitive Magic. It's a matter of reverse signs. The first two lines set up the situation. The next six lines come from a documentary movie I saw on TV, the best one I've ever seen, about a South American Indian tribe, "The Tribe That Time Forgot." It's a description of some of the images in the film. The last six lines are my own. That's Primitive Magic. Number 12 is Necromancy, the summoning of and speaking to the dead. That comes from a book on magic and superstition, the title of which escapes me—it's a red and black book I read some four or five years ago. This is the way one was supposed to do it: you took this many paces, at that particular time, in that direction: straight description of how it was supposed to be done. Number 13 is Black Magic: the Hand of Glory is actually something in Black Magic, a hand, bones of a hand, and it was done in that particular manner. And all those things like man-fat and wax and ponie and sesame were all part of the ritual. Number 14 is Alchemy, that is, base metal into gold. Number 15 is Allegory, the seven-caved mountain and the serpent on the cross, all those things. The Slaughter of the Innocents, and so on. Echo is something I've used before: I used it in "Delta Traveller": it's another euphemism for Whatever's Out There . . . . In *China Trace* I use it even more: I get to the point of calling it a wind. It's just another euphemism for the word that no one knows. Number 19 is Earth again, which is what I believe in, the earth. Number 20 is the same situation I started out in. It's where I started out, the physical point, though that point is never the same. You have to say it's Point A, though Point A isn't Point A again after you've left it. But it's not Point B either, or even Point A and a half. I suspect that "Skins," and "Tattoos" as well, is overwritten to a certain extent. It's a lushness I used because the book concerns my background. A growing up that I consider lush, one that really prepared me for nothing except imagination. And the whole book was rather like going into the dark and the unknown and making a lot of noise against the darkness and scaring away the evil spirits to keep up your own courage. Like that. I can write as flat a line as the next guy if I want to. And I've done so, and not always on purpose. Also, I think of my growing up in this way because in East Tennessee and western North Carolina the landscape was always bursting out. Or at least it is in my memory. It was jam-packed full of leaves and trees and flowers and all that. This isn't something one has to know, but it was on my mind when I was writing the poems. In *China Trace* there are several alliterative, lushy kind of poems. Again, they are the ones that seem closest to my past autobiography, rather than moving away from me toward my future one.

In thinking about China Trace, *and in taking sections 1 and 20 of "Skins," that is, the Situations, it seems to me that* China Trace *is a pilgrim's book. In the sense of what has happened in "Skins," and the way that the voice is a consciousness, or that you oriented yourself to the present, and then returned to the situation, and this seems to be a kind of journey, trip or movement. It's really not answered in any of the poems that come after "Skins." But it seems that* China Trace *comes out of that need.*

It does. At least, I meant for it to take off from "Skins" instead of, say, the last three poems in *Bloodlines*. It was the one of the three books, as I said, that was supposed to relate to the future. Of course, one can't really write about the future. But it also might be called The Book of Yearning. But, then, any book could, I guess. In a way it's another parabola back to Point A, but it wants to act as a parabola on to Point B.

I should back-pedal, and say that I don't think *China Trace* is quite as yearny as "Skins" is. It's called *China Trace* because it's an attempt, or a hope, to write a book of Chinese poems that don't sound like Chinese poems and aren't Chinese poems but are like Chinese poems in the sense that they give you an idea of one man's relationship to the endlessness, the ongoingness, the everlastingness of what's around him, and his relationship to it as he stands in the natural world. I'm trying to talk about things that I don't know anything about, because I haven't been there, in terms of something I do know something about, because I'm standing in the middle of them. This is, of course, hardly an intellectual breakthrough, but it's been workable before. Whereas in "Skins" it's all more theoretical and conceptual. *China Trace* is really more down to earth, even though it might look more cosmic. That's why there are so many dates, hours of the day, phases of the moon, all of that business where you locate yourself in a particular time and place and are sort of just washed over by the complete everlastingness of it all, that feeling that everyone feels, and has been feeling ever since we stopped beating with sticks on the ground. *China Trace* is a more ambitious book than *Bloodlines* is, as *Bloodlines* was more ambitious than *Hard Freight*. An increase in intensity all down the line. It's also more ambitious in that I'm trying to do all this with everyday objects. At one time I was going to call the book *Quotidiana*, which is the title of one of the poems in the book. The first half was at one time called "Colophons," redoings of themes I had tried in the first two books. The second half was to be called "Medallions" and would take off in the direction in which I hoped to move. They still work in that way, the two sections, but they're not titled anymore.

There's a journal-like quality to many of the poems, and I'm interested in whether they're arranged in chronological order.

They absolutely are, with perhaps one or two exceptions in each section. It was conceived of as a book from the first poem on, even though each poem is discrete, I think, and has its own entity and doesn't have to depend on any other, as most of the "Tattoos" do and all of "Skins" does. But it was conceived of as a book in the way that *Bloodlines* was. Now all this structure and intertwining isn't of itself necessarily good, but there it is, and it runs through the three books. Obviously I didn't know, back when I got going on *Hard Freight*, that I was going to write a book called *China Trace* that was going to be made up of poems all twelve lines or less, which is, in fact, what I've done. I did that because *Bloodlines* is a book of ten poems, two of them very long, and the first poem I wrote after finishing it was a short poem, "Childhood," the first poem in *China Trace*. So I decided, rather arbitrarily, that no poem was going to be longer than twelve lines. In the first section 1 wanted to have an example of each length of poem from one to twelve lines but I couldn't write a four-line poem. It was the hardest thing. They always came out sounding like a stanza that needed another stanza, or two more stanzas. I finally got one, entitled "Guilt," in the second section. And so I do have an example of each of the twelve line lengths in the book, if not in the first section.

There's something I wanted to ask about when you were beginning to talk about Pound as an early influence. Or how that influence has carried over into this book, what you wanted for the character of the poems, the sense of emblem or the sense of sign. Because it seems to me that the language seems always to be trying to break into a third dimension, always trying to become very graphic, very physical, in the way that the Chinese characters are.

Well, I know nothing about Chinese ideograms, but I would hope that some of the language would be compressed enough, vivid enough, so there could be some kind of transference, transferral, between the words. I don't know enough to even talk about that. I know that I agree with Pound: it must be a wonderful way to write, to be able to see, physically, what you're saying. In one poem, the title, "Spider Crystal Ascension," is supposed to be ideographic. The title is three separate words that are supposed to give you an idea of what's coming in the whole poem. I did have the idea of compression, which is maybe as close as we can get to the ideogrammic method. To compress the language and the thought to such a point that it stops being small and starts to enlarge. I don't quite know how to explain this, but it gets past a certain point, and goes out the other side and gets larger. It expands. Which is to say, rather than writing a lot to get larger and larger, you write less and less. And I don't mean Concrete poetry. I don't mean Imagism, though there is an element of that.

Just regular writing, imagery and metaphor, compressed to such an extent that it goes out the other side. That is so theoretical I can't back it up at all, but it did seem possible to me. Again, that's one of the reasons I wanted to write very short poems. The black hole might be an example. In the black hole, as I understand it, the gravity is so great that it pulls everything in to such an extent that light cannot escape and has to exit out the other side. And that there is possibly another universe back there. You could take a handful of matter, if it were possible, from a black hole and stand up out of your chair and drop it, and it would go right through the earth.

Is that going on in the whole book?

I hope it's going on in both halves. The second half is certainly getting down to the nitty-gritty of my wishes, which would be to be saved, but there's no such thing. I keep trying to say that all the way through, in different aspects, in different guises, and in the last five poems I say it even more so. The last poem ends up with the person of the poems, who is most often called "I," but sometimes "You" or "He," as a constellation in the sky. That's as close as he gets. Cut up in little stars. That also contains, of course, an allusion to Verona, Italy, which is the place where I first began to read poems, and where I first began to try to write them.

Why is it that you use the epigraph twice?

Well, for one thing, I've never seen it done before, using the same epigraph for both halves of a book. And I wanted to make sure it wasn't forgotten by the time you got to the second half. I knew the second half of the book would be very different from the first half. In tone, density, imagery, and even in language, I knew the second half of the book would be different. Otherwise there seems little point in doing fifty of the poems, you'd just do twenty-five of them. I wouldn't have done it if I didn't think there was a real reason behind it. It wasn't just to be cute.

Could you talk about the poem "January"?

Well, I wrote it in Iowa City. And it was colder than hell. I don't know what to say about "January." This may sound presumptuous, but I think the poems in *China Trace* are extremely self-explanatory. In a way that "Skins" and "Tattoos" may not be. I don't know what to say about "January" except that at the time I wrote it I believed the first stanza very much. I believe it because, in some other life, the face I look on I won't be able to recognize, because it's going to be a leaf or a piece of grass. Or it's going to be a rock or dirt or something. It's not going to be anything I would recognize because it would be insens . . . insensate. . . .

You won't have a nervous system.

Yeah, right, I won't be able to figure it out. "Snow" sets up what I really believe in the book. And I think that all the poems, in various disguises, show it all the way through the book. Coming back is something we don't know about. The last three lines in "January," the spider is "he" because the spider is usually "she." Black widows, one always thinks of. This is a black widower. I was just trying to reinforce what I said in the two previous books as quickly and as graphically as possible. Say what you have to say, then beat it. The one thing about *China Trace* is that I'm extremely emotionally involved in all these poems, to the extent that I'm putting it right out there for anyone who wants to see it. It's what I think. I'm saying it again and again, obsessively, as I tend to do. I'm still so close to it I can't judge it, but I'm sticking with it to the end.

And "Captain Dog"?

Captain Dog is what some of my students used to call me about eight years ago. And "dog" keeps popping up in these poems. "Captain Dog" is a poem of process, which explains itself and its processes as it goes along. Jump-cut. Jump-cut is what each stanza is doing. There's no logical movement from stanza to stanza. And dog because a dog is a dog. And a Captain Dog is pretty high up in the hierarchy of dogs, I guess. There is also the reverse spelling of dog. . . . I have always been very fond of the phrase Captain Dog, and I like titles with dog in them: *Andalusian Dog*, *Portrait of the Artist as a Young Dog*, *Dog Yoga*. . . .

What about the vision of death in "California Twilight"?

The poems can be mutually exclusive, as I've said. Things are dead, but there are processes in the book by which things change. And I am not talking about reincarnation at all. At all. At all.

Would you say something about "Nerval's Mirror"?

The person in the poem is the speaker, not Nerval. The "I." And the mirror means that he was not mirroring what had happened to Nerval. That in Nerval's mirror you had to be Nerval to see what he saw, naturally. It takes more than trappings and emulations. Nerval was an incredible spirit, who really was mad, and he wrote this beautiful prose piece about walking up to the stars. "Aurelia," it's called. And I think I meant in the poem that this is the mirror image of what would happen to the "I" of this book now, were he to try and be Nerval. I meant for the title to explain why he says what he says. It was a reversal, as all mirrors are.

There's a sense of witness: what the mirror saw. And that's a sense that runs through the other poems.

Yeah, and it's what the mirror sees also in me, that even if I'm edgy and anxious, I'm safe and well-fed, and would probably not have the snap or whatever to make that break that Nerval did. And would never want to, not needing it because my cold nights are down here and don't have to be in the stars. There's a sense of an incredible vision Nerval had then that this person will never have. And from which there is no return. This book is for a condition of return. Or of staying here and not snapping. And the book is about not dying, right? All poems are about not dying, in a way.

Would you read, then comment on the poem, "Reunion"?

> Already one day has detached itself from all the rest up ahead.
> It has my photograph in its soft pocket.
> It wants to carry my breath into the past in its bag of wind.
>
> I write poems to untie myself, to do penance and disappear
> Through the upper right hand corner of things, to say grace.

This is the poem I expect to get the most flak about, for that transition in the second stanza, and for that bald statement. I meant the transition to be totally unexpected. This "I" is the most jarring and wide-gulfed transition in any of the poems. It's the closest I got to "salvation," since salvation doesn't exist except through the natural world. In any poem, it's the closest I can get to making a hook-up with my religious background.

Would you also read and talk about "Stone Canyon Nocturne"?

Ancient of Days, old friend, no one believes you'll come back.
No one believes in his own life anymore.

The moon, like a dead heart, cold and unstartable, hangs by a
  thread
At the earth's edge,
Unfaithful at last, splotching the ferns and the pink shrubs.

In the other world, children undo the knots in their tally strings.
They sing songs, and their fingers blear.

And here, where the swan hums in his socket, where bloodroot
And belladonna insist on our comforting,
Where the fox in the canyon wall empties our hands, ecstatic for
  more,

Like a bead of clear oil the Healer revolves through the night
  wind,
Part eye, part tear, unwilling to recognize us.

"Stone Canyon Nocturne" is a central poem in the book. Stone
Canyon is a canyon in Los Angeles. The poem contains things
that I believe very deeply. At Stone Canyon, there's a strange
physical sensation brought about by extra-bodily substances.
There are fossils in the canyon which can come into your hands
very easily.

How close is China Trace *to* Bloodlines *in its use of sequence?*

I wanted these to have a journal-like, everyday quality.
That's not like *Bloodlines* at all.

It's that sense of meditation, too, that's going through the book.

At one time in the poem, almost every time you see the word
"you," I had the word "pilgrim" in there. But it seemed too much
like a minor league *Pilgrim's Progress*, so I took it out.

*Could you talk about composition? Do some of these poems, the
shorter ones, write themselves pretty quickly?*

No, no. The one you don't have—the last poem in the book,
called "Him"—took five weeks to write: it's eight lines long. And
I worked on it every day, threw out and added, threw out and
added. Some have been quicker than others. The only one I've

written in a day I wrote two days ago, here in Oberlin. Naturally they don't take as long to write as "Tattoos" or "Skins," but for me they're much harder to write than a normal, say, sixteen- to thirty-line poem. Because one can get into an exposition there where you can cut and add and expand. There isn't an hour in the past two years and three months—even in the middle of my classes, when I'm teaching—it's terrible, I'll blank out and start thinking about the one I'm trying to write. The one-line poem was cut down from many lines, and took, oh. . . . I don't know. Most of the twelve-line poems started out as twelve-liners.

Do you think you're using the line differently in this book?

I think it's a longer, more relaxed line. For example, the line "All day they have known what we will know when the time comes." A much longer, flowing, less frenetic line. Also, the lines are physically longer. I'm trying to write longer and longer lines. The one I'm most proud of is a nineteen-syllable line that doesn't break down into smaller units. It's in "Spider Crystal Ascension." It's a longer, prosier line, but what I'm interested in doing is writing a long *packed* line, which is really next to impossible. But I figure if I can write the long easy line I can get to the packed long line. The line I do write, I think, takes off from the iambic base, stretching it or shrinking it in the way that Eliot spoke of when he talked about free verse. I count every syllable and every stress.

You say you count every syllable and every stress. But at what point? Early on?

Immediately. I'm always conscious of this. I can see a seven-syllable line through a wall. All my lines are extensions of seven-syllable lines, or contractions. I try to elude the stanza thing. Stanzas are so much of the retentive side of my personality that I. . . . Of course stanzas are a great help a lot of times, but I try to stay away from them, and that's hard for me to do. Very hard. I don't like blocks in poems, I like breathing space. What I try to do is to get uneven lines in stanzas, which is also very hard for me to do as I tend to want to even everything up. I do try to use the white space of stanza breaks.

But since it is hard for me to avoid blocky stanzas in my poems, I've tried to use them as units almost autonomous in themselves. I did this mostly in *Hard Freight*, where I would write the poems in stanzas. That is, a stanza at a time, and only one stanza at a time, at the most two. So when I'd go to do the following, or next, stanza, some time would have passed, a day or two or sometimes more. And there would be some slight logic gap that I would try to retain, and so each stanza would begin to take on a little life and isolation all to itself, though, as it were, still plugged into the life-support systems of the overall parent body. I did this partly from the painter-idea I talked about earlier, using stanzas in the way a painter will build up blocks of color, each disparate and often discrete, to make an overall representation that, taken in its pieces and slashes and dabs seems to have no coherence, but seen in its totality, when it's finished, turns out to be a very recognizable landscape, or whatever. Cézanne is someone who does this, in his later work, to an almost magical perfection. I'd like to be able to write poems the way he painted pictures. And who wouldn't, you might well ask.

And I love the space, the white space, in poems, and I've tried to use it more in *China Trace*. Space has everything to do with the line, it's what the line lives in and breathes in, if it is to breathe at all. Space, and the line in it, is what's starting to tweak me now. Space is what's always new, it's what's always happening. Well, this is long-winded and not exactly an answer to your question, but, yes, I do count all my syllables and stresses.

And yet it doesn't take up the foreground of your attention as you write?

If you write enough, you just become aware of it. Some people have spent a lot of time trying to get away from that completely. And day after tomorrow I may decide: No more of that trash. But not yet. Mostly, it has to do with the "music" of poems, whatever that is. Everyone hears it differently, of course. I tend to work in stress groups. I am, like most people who write poems, inordinately fond of my own ear, and trust my ear maybe more than I should. As Woody Allen says, "It's my second favorite organ." (He was referring to something else.) I'm a primitive poet, I think. I trust my ear, I trust my instincts because I'm not particularly well-read or learned. I trust my ear and instincts to make the jumps, what sounds right, the way someone who can't read music can play music. By ear.

You're very conscious of technical matters. Are you as conscious of content? Or is it a matter of "I don't know what I'm saying but I'm saying it"?

No, I'm very conscious of it, particularly in this book. In fact, from the poem "Dog Creek Mainline" on, I've been very conscious of content. Before that, in *The Grave of the Right Hand* and the first third of *Hard Freight*, I was much more interested in just putting the poem together. Now I'm interested in putting it together the best and most interesting way I can and also saying whatever it is I have to say. I really don't think the content has to shape the form, and I don't think that the form necessarily shapes the content, though I suppose both can. And that's all right. One quote I like is by Philip Larkin, the English poet who works, for the most part, in rhyme and meter: "Form means nothing to me, content is everything." Maybe not an exact quote, but close enough. And I'm sure he means it. Fascinating. Two other quotes, slogans, which should settle the question, but won't, are both by Pound: "Only emotion endures" and "Bad technique is bearing false witness." Now I think probably both of these are true, but I do think one is truer than the other.

There seems to be a contradiction. You're trusting your impulses, and yet fully conscious of what you're doing. You must surprise yourself sometimes.

Well, that did happen in "Reunion." Yes, that did surprise me. That jump surprised me, and I kept on with it. But I guess what I'm trying to say is that once I get involved in what I'm doing, my instincts and impulses are going to follow what's the right thing. . . . I don't know what else to say. You write your poems in the way that best pleases you and that's all you can do. Well, form and content. I admit that one manipulates, I admit that I have certain things in mind I want to say, but I still think I'm trusting my instincts in *how* I say it.

Can you remember any changes you made in "Spider Crystal Ascension"?

What I did was I got those first two lines, and held onto them for about four days, without knowing what to do with them. I was trying to describe the gigantic movement of the Milky Way through the Montana sky, as seen from a place twenty miles from the nearest house, absolutely pitch-black, when the Milky Way is an incredible thing, in the dark of the moon, radiating out, and it really does look like a spider. . . . I didn't know what to do with it. And then I got that long line—"All morning we wait for the white face to rise from the lake like a tiny star." That came from the ascent. But that still wasn't enough. I waited another couple of days, and I was walking along thinking about the poem and the phrase "And when it does . . ." suddenly came to me. That's my favorite part of the poem. "And when it does," what? "We lie back in our watery hair, and rock." That's what. You know we're down there too, and one of us is going up. . . . So those five lines took about eight days, back and forth, back and forth, writing, crossing out, trying to get it to sound right and to say the right thing. I wanted the idea of being electrified up there, so I finally got "juiced." Then I still didn't have a title for it, so I decided to take the three biggest words in the poem and put them together.

I have something I want to read. A letter Rilke wrote to his wife about Cézanne. . . . "The convincing quality, the becoming a thing, the reality heightened into the indestructible through his own experience of the object. It was that, to him, that seemed the aim of his innermost work. . . . The painter, the artist, whatever, should not become conscious of his insight. Without taking the way around through his mental processes, his advances, enigmatic even to himself, must enter so swiftly into the work that he is unable to recognize them at the moment of their transition. For him, alas, to watch them . . . delays them; to him they change like the fine gold in the fairy tale which can no longer remain gold because some detail went wrong." That does not contradict counting syllables or anything else of that sort. One last thing I want to read is by Ambroise Vollard, Cézanne's friend and dealer. "Very few people had the opportunity to see Cézanne at work because he could not endure being watched while at his easel. For one who has not seen him paint, it is difficult to imagine how slow and difficult his progress was on certain days. On my portrait there are two little spots of canvas on the hand which are not covered. I called Cézanne's attention to them. 'If the copy I'm making at the Louvre turns out well,' he replied, 'perhaps tomorrow I will be able to find the exact tone to cover up those spots. Don't you see, Monsieur Vollard, that if I put something there by guesswork, I might have to paint the whole canvas over, starting from that point?'"

(1977)

Sandra McPherson

SECRETS: BEGINNING TO WRITE THEM OUT
Revelation, Confession, and Ethics; Discretion and Diplomacy; Health and Art

In a humorous and sympathetic poem about a flasher on a city traffic island, Judith Moffett concludes:

> How many of us
> struggled not to brandish forth
>
> some hard truth: "People don't respect me, I'm scared
> all the time," or "When I touch my wife I can feel
> her flesh crawl. Not a one of the kids is mine."
> Sham, shame. Whatever.
> The one home truth most private, most
> unspeakable, hardest and truest. That very one.

This essay (originally a talk presented at the Aspen and Napa Writers Conferences, summer of 1985) will begin to explore issues that come up when we're afraid to write about that "one home truth most private": that is, what we're afraid to write about, why we are, and what happens when we write about it. I've chosen this topic because a man says our Oregon workshop has helped him to write about his mother's suicide attempt which he witnessed as a child and which was never explained to him; and because a woman says she had postpartum depression for four years and finally wrote about it but is afraid the poems will cause her son undue guilt feelings; and because both men and women I know suffered too long in silence as victims of incest; and even because in living with my daughter and in having lived with a husband I find I need to continually make choices as to what I can or must (for my sanity) or must not (for their well-being) say about either of them.

That husband's mother burned his first book because it told some family secrets. A good friend, whose secret of giving up her child I wrote about, felt "used" and tore up my first three books page by page and threw them into the fire.

So many people have brought similar dilemmas to me that I decided to interview some friends and students in return. Is there anything you would *not* write about? we began. And for what reasons would you refuse to write about it? fear, shame, honor, etc.? One woman explained she would not write about her former husband's insanity and violence. She does not wish to expose her children to things that she has come to terms with. She does not want to destroy her children's mostly happy memories of their father. She does not want to show them the depths of his degradation for she feels it's not meant to be part of their life, they shouldn't have to live with it. Whereas most of the rest of this talk will deal with choosing to bring experiences like hers out into the open, she spoke eloquently and justly in defense of remaining silent. She said she *will* write about the tragedy she lived, but perhaps as a theater piece. Remember that you have that option—to use characters to speak lines which are really your own. My friend, whose children are in their 40s, said that even though she may choose not to write directly about the tragedy in her life, it is one reason she is moved to write, there is depth in her writing because of it.

My second question was, Have you at some time written about a subject or event that you withheld for a long time, or your family withheld, even for much of your life? If so, describe what you went through to get it on the page. The most illuminating answer was from a 43-year-old woman. Her war-veteran husband had beaten her frequently. She said she had not coped with this before she came to poetry. She had been taught in school that poetry was only written in *universal* terms. Further, her church and her parents had advised her just to remain quiet and "take it." When told in workshop that what had happened to her was worth saying, she couldn't stop writing. Poetry, she said, gave her a place with dignity to cope with it. She feels that not all audiences are willing to deal with her subject, but she will persist. A woman counseling Vietnam veterans' wives asked to see the material, then quickly turned it down even though it is the only poetry on that subject that I have seen. My friend assumed few people are interested in acknowledging the wife's struggle.

All interviewed agreed they did not write with the intent to hurt someone. They were concerned with accuracy of representation of another's character; they abhorred lying, ruthlessness, exaggeration, even blame.

The goal here is not to get a person to write about things he or she doesn't want to write about; I don't wish to be an evangelist for the confessional. But poets need especially to feel confident about the decisions they have made for themselves—to reveal or not to reveal. Here we can study how some writers came to make that choice. Maybe one of the cases will mirror the reader's own and help in his or her questioning.

To tell the truth about his mother and others in the family, W. D. Snodgrass (that pioneer of what we, though not the poet himself, call confessional poetry) had to publish a small, nearly unobserved and long unreprinted collection of poems struggling with conflicts in his family, under a pseudonym, S.S. Gardons, which he says is "Snodgrass spelled sideways." In "The Mother" he writes: "If evil did not exist, she would create it/ To die in righteousness. . . ." In a poem about his equivocal, mistrusting or paranoid father, Snodgrass expresses disgust with the way his father pretends to be friends with people he hates—then uses that friendship to gather evidence of the unworthiness of these "friends." The father never speaks his mind. As the poem mounts you can see Snodgrass's contempt for his father's wishywashi-ness, for his lack of commitment to truth.

Since his other books are equally personal and direct, how did he choose to conceal these particular poems? Was he more afraid of his family than of the former wives, lovers, and lovers' husbands written about in *Heart's Needle* and *After Experience*? Aren't we most intimidated by our families? In response to my query, Snodgrass writes:

> Since these poems say, in effect, "My mother devoured my sister" I didn't want the poems to fall into my mother's hands—they would merely make her more unhappy and hate-filled than she already was and so make her behavior perhaps even worse. That was specially to be avoided because I still had a brother and sister who lived in her vicinity, but I wouldn't want to hurt and/or dam-age her anyway. She obviously couldn't help what she had done and it was clearly too late for her to make any changes in her atti-tudes.

(Then parenthetically he adds "The first of those poems that was published was identified as a translation from Kozma Prutkov, a hoax poet made up by Count Alexei Tolstoi.") Where Auden kept modifying his borrowing from Nijinsky ("We must love one another or die"), Snodgrass states with certainty and proves with details from his life

> Without love we die;
> With love we kill each other.

Snodgrass writes that since both of his parents have passed away, the book, *Remains: A Sequence of Poems,* is now available again, published in 1985 by BOA Editions.

For conflicts of candor we can look to Cavafy. Although Cavafy suppressed in his lifetime several love poems found in a file called "Passions," he noted that it was important to him that even when the events in the poems became no longer "applicable any more in my life . . . they will be applicable to feelings of other lives." He felt that any poem of his "based on a truth" must have found a truth that "may repeat itself in another life." "Indeed the probabilities are that it must." The loyalty to truth remained, even though he did not make the results public; he had to speak the truth if not publish it.

To himself he kept poems regarded as "too personal . . . too explicitly sexual, or too progressive for the taste of his particular community of readers." "Hidden Things," written in 1908, reads

> From all the things I did and all the things I said
> let no one try to find out who I was.
> An obstacle was there transforming
> the actions and the manner of my life.
> An obstacle was often there to silence me when I began to speak.
> From my most unnoticed actions and my most veiled writing—
> from these alone will I be understood.
> But maybe it isn't worth so much concern
> and so much effort to discover who I really am.
> Later, in a more perfect society,
> someone else made just like me
> is certain to appear and act freely.

If the silencing agent was homosexuality, his prophecy at the end has, seventy years later, been true enough to permit a large body of unveiled gay literature. But not every writer feels free to be open. The conflict to be so must be re-argued in each individual writer. Cavafy seems to say that the truest core of himself is that one thing he won't openly write about. In Moffett's words: "The one home truth most private, most/ unspeakable, hardest and truest."

We should place our work in history. There has to be a first time for each issue to appear in a literature. In our century there is still so much that needs to be added, and you might be the person to initiate the subject. I don't think parenting has often been dealt with frankly in poetry. Look at the life your mother or father lived: is there a poetic literature of their experience? I mean, not written *about* them but *by* one of their own? In the case of my

family and their peers: suicidal Christians, post-menopausal
sense of worthlessness, aging without the expected sense of fulfillment—and the opposite, finding new sources of life at that
time—these are subjects that need more poems. There could be
more poets who have struggled to speak of their family's poverty.
John Haislip reveals his strain to do so even in the title of his
poem "Fewer Than Necessary Rhetorical Stanzas For The Poor."
"Do not forget," he begins, though one can see from the reticent
tight style in these excerpts that he does not enjoy remembering
the humiliation and bitterness he was formed in.

> My father doomed, alone at four, given
> As an orphan to his uncle; never freed
> Until he married, sold the farm and moved.
> But locked outside the town without a job,
> He set his heart a rock against the place.
> . . . .
> My mother rode the trolley into town,
> Worked by waiting tables for the rich.
> I walked the tracks with shopping sacks of food
> From town to home alone to save the dime:
> . . . .
> If this is touched with pity for myself: well,
> The thirties made an ugly kind of drunk.

And just before that a curious line: "Do not forget them with an
angry poem." He tells me this is the same as "Remember them
with an angry poem." Anger as a helper of memory. As an affir-
mative step and as a memorial to the dignity of the impoverished.
He is saying that angry remembering can overcome the feeling of
the shame of poverty.

Sometimes even remembering anger taxes the poet. Joan
Swift wrote two series of poems, 13 years apart, about a rape by a
stranger who forcibly entered her house. She came to regard,
years after she wrote "The Line-Up" (from the first series), her
motherly attitude toward "her" rapist as not representing the complexity of her feelings—and she began to write a new series of
poems moving closer to the truth. Here is "The Line-Up" (written
in slant-rhymed couplets):

> Each prisoner is so sad in the glare
> I want to be his mother
>
> tell him the white light will go down
> and he will sleep soon.

No need to turn under eyes
to shuffle   poor soldiers   boys

in a play
to wear numbers   obey.

They have hands as limp as wet leaves
the long fingers of their lives

hanging. They cannot see
past the sharp edge nor hear me

breathe. O I would tell each one
he will wake whole again

in some utterly new place!
Trees without bars   sun a sweet juice

a green
field full of pardon

The walls come in. I am
captured like him

locked in this world forever   unable to say   run

be free
I love you

having to accuse
and accuse.

And here is most of "Another Witness" from her new series published spring of 1985 by Dragon Gate Press in the collection *The
Dark Path of Our Names*. The rapist she sent to San Quentin had
been released and was being tried for the rape and murder of a
woman named Joan Stewart, who lived just a few doors from
where Joan Swift lived at the time of her own rape:

The prosecutor wants me to open
my memory like a trunk,
pull out the dress of India cotton,
green and yellow print
. . . .
The jury sees me running up the stairs—
I think the mailman has a gift.

                        But it's you,

. . . .
I almost say *hello,*
but you're too quick.
You grab my throat.
The lost crystal world of the chandelier
sways above my head.
No one hears the scream
I swallow when your hand
shuts over my mouth.
The other grips my hands behind me.
                                    And I am so light
with fear you push me down the hall easily,
so light I float above the bed.
You pull me to my knees,
mutter an incantation behind my back.
Two gloves fly over my head.
You lift my dress.
Something feathered, a wren or winter thrush,
stirs between my breasts.
                          Now I must say it.
The word *sodomy* forms on my tongue,
dissolves like a wafer, forms again
to hang over the court reporter's desk.
A juror coughs.
I say *no.*
Oddly, you obey.
I think you have a knife.
When you enter the other place
I feel tears start.
The whole courtroom is silent.
Beyond the windows, Lake Merritt
shines in the sun
and joggers color its shore.
But I run back through time
until my thighs are sticky with you.
Don't tell, you say.
Thirteen years later
                    seventy-five people
turn toward the witness stand.
They see your limp hands on the bed,
a shred of noon light.
I kiss one knuckle. I don't know why.
The skin is sad and black.
A vein splits into two separate rivers.
I love you, I say into that air
                                and this.
Your palms stroke my face,

vanish like birds into a tree.
Don't move, you say.
Surely the blade poises
over my back now.
I wait to die.
Don't move, you say again.
The door shuts
     and you are here
listening to how I wash my legs and face.
I change my dress, put on another,
rose and blue.
Outside, the street is a ribbon
tied to anywhere.
I drive an hour. Two.
I drive all the way to a telephone booth,
the police station, a lineup,
to another district attorney.
I drive to a different state
and back again
     while you break rock in prison.
"Is the man you describe in the courtroom today?"
the prosecutor asks.
"Yes," I say.
"Will you point to him, please?"
When we face each other
     she becomes visible,
the woman you murder twelve years
after me.
Her name is the same as mine.
Rain nets the hills.
Wind hurls a tree to ground
and lines sag without power.
She walks near that house
I left years ago, white shutters
and bricks unchanged.
One of us must lift her now
from the wet grass,
sponge clean her bloody throat,
     I who spoke love,
     you who killed for that lie.

  The full terror of her experience is recounted here—even the "I love you" which she has told me surprised, embarrassed, and repulsed her. In this poem she has reclaimed her true emotions, not the trained ones of maternal attitudes no-matter-what. What pushed the poet to tell, in this new series of poems, more truth than she felt she did in the first series is partly that they are based on a trial format. She took an oath to tell the whole truth in the courtroom and she used trial transcripts in composing the sequence. As the end of "Another Witness" shows, the poem is in part about exposing a lie.

Swift's poems on rape have been gratefully received by most readers, but I heard one voice the opinion that she should split her book royalties with the rapist. As if she were getting career mileage out of a sensational story. This person said it was her duty to rehabilitate the rapist, not to exploit him in poetry! That person should note another motivation for writing the series: the end of "Another Witness" says, of the victim Joan Stewart, "One of us must lift her now." Joan Swift chose to be the one to carry the memory of this kinswoman more gently into history.

To write about painful memories, we need to learn to ask questions about what we don't see and to be good observers of what we do see. In "North American Time" Adrienne Rich says

> Suppose you want to write
> of a woman braiding
> another woman's hair—
> straight down, or with beads and shells
> in three-strand plaits or corn-rows—
> you had better know the thickness
> the length the pattern
> why she decides to braid her hair
> how it is done to her
> what country it happens in
> what else happens in that country
>
> You have to know these things

To understand, to grasp history, to see fully, we must ask the right questions. Rich's poem "Mother-in-law" addresses this issue. "Tell me something," the mother-in-law repeatedly asks. Rich asks back

> Some secret
> we both know and have never spoken?
> Some sentence that could flood with light
> your life, mine?

But the mother-in-law buffers the truth with Valium, responds with platitudes of domestic wisdom ("A cut lemon scours the smell of fish away/ You'll feel better when the children are in school"). Yet she continues nagging "tell me something true/ tell me something" until Rich answers

> Your son is dead
> ten years, I am a lesbian,
> my children are themselves.
> Mother-in-law, before we part
> shall we try again? Strange as I am,
> strange as you are? What do mothers
> ask their own daughters, everywhere in the world?
> Is there a question?
> Ask me something.

A journalist is instructed to inquire who, what, when, why, how, and where? and make stories of those facts to inform or do investigative journalism to expose. The poet, unlike the journalist, may be struggling to survive a story of much personal anguish. We must ask for things we may not want to hear but which we crave because they are true. Who? may be the son whose birth brought on postpartum depression; how? may be what instruments did your father use to physically abuse you? The where? might be a list of places your mother hid bottles of gin. You don't want to publish these facts in a newspaper; you don't want to air them on *60 Minutes*; but you may have in mind a small audience which includes yourself and your abusive father and your alcoholic mother and your innocent son.

We must do it without tattling, or without the tone of tattling, gossiping, or blabbing. Patricia Hampl has a poem in her first book about a family secret, her mother's epilepsy. Having worked for years as a librarian without telling any of her colleagues of her condition, the mother certainly wasn't about to celebrate the publication of the following poem, "Mother-Daughter Dance":

> Because it is late
> because we fought today
> because it was hot
> and heat is an excuse
> to be alone,
> I sit in this chair stuffed
> with old sun, leftover heat.
>
> Our fight. The subject as always was history.
> You made me look over my shoulder.
> Mother was back there, speaking
> to us in epilepsy, that language

she learned on her own,
the one we encouraged her to use
at the dinner table.
In my mind, I fell down, writing,
trying to make history repeat itself,
burning with translations of guilt
for the men in the family.
Father forced a yellow pencil
between Mother's teeth, like a rose:
you die if you swallow your tongue.

All afternoon you yelled at me
as I slithered nearer to her.
We were doing the mother-daughter sweat dance,
salt dance, sexy Spanish rose dance.
You were yelling from the English language,
that fringed island I swim toward at night.
"The pencil," you were screaming in your language,
"Take the pencil from her mouth.
Write it down,
write your message down."

The advice to write is urgent. The poem's point about history should not be missed: any private story is human history, not just your own. It can help someone else to live. Someone else who is perhaps feeling hopeless.

Years before, Hampl had told me that her mother thanked her for unburdening her of the secret of her epilepsy. But when I asked her about that story again recently, she realized that the story wasn't finished. She wrote to me:

> I told my mother that if she demanded it, I would not publish the poem—but that it was a strong poem, that others thought so too, and that my collection would be less strong without it. In other words, I gave her the power of decision but I loaded the situation with guilt for her. Soon after, she came to me and said go ahead with the poem because she could see it was a good poem and that was more important . . . As I write this to you, I realize I *do not know* for sure if my mother . . . ever really *was* grateful for this poem. . . .
>
> I broke off here for a moment and called my mother to ask her, point-blank, if she had ever felt pleasure or relief about the publication of the poem or if she had only let me publish it as a favor. Her answer didn't miss a beat, "I only did it for you." "Did you ever feel good about the publication?" "No," she said. She continues to feel fearful about public misinformation and bigotry

regarding epilepsy. She likes, however, a new poem I wrote about her mastectomy—something which, as she put it, "is accepted."

The interesting thing here is that . . . we can talk of [the poem] as if it were something beyond the control of either of us. My mother is attached to me-the-writer. I suppose that she somehow accepts that it can't be helped if she gets hit in the cross-fire from time to time. But then, I'm usually careful about where I aim.

. . . I recognize in this situation a constellation of motivations, beliefs, wishes and events which makes both of us unreliable witnesses to our own past.

Where Swift gives testimony under oath, Hampl's letter gives voluntary testimony to the Memory divided between "ruthless" devotion to recovery of truth—"surgical accuracy"—and the Imagination devoted to creation of a shaped and possibly "more useable" truth.[*]

When we come to make this difficult decision alone, we can begin by asking ourselves the right questions:

—are we most afraid of the poems which could harm ourselves?

—in what ways could this happen?

 • political risk?

 • disinheritance? discomfort in the family?

 • loss of literary esteem?

—if we don't write about it, are we "sinning against ourselves"?

—against others who could benefit by the issue coming out in the open?

—isn't there a self-portrait implicit in the poems of each of us? isn't the self in the best truthtelling poems often anguished? and if that portrait is of someone searching for honesty and relief of suffering, won't this new material be respected even by those whose lives are spoken about in it?

The usually dazzling critic Christopher Ricks told me in conversation that Sylvia Plath's journals don't do anything for her reputation. But maybe we should ask, when do we stop writing "for our reputations"? When do we stop excluding, censoring, and begin to include for the sake of honesty and wholeness and

---

[*]See Hampl, "Memory and Imagination," in *The Dolphin Reader* (Houghton Mifflin, 1985).

for the sake of extending the art? Do we write as people with reputations to keep up or do we write as whole people?

A student of mine, 21, a talented writer, said of a poem she'd
brought to workshop, "My mother made me take that line out."
The line was about her alcoholic doctor father at a family Christmas party. We have to ask that student and ourselves, "How many
lines is your mother going to make you take out?"

One woman expected her violent military ex-husband to appear with a gun at one of her poetry readings because she took *no*
lines out. But she persisted in writing about him, believing we
shouldn't have to get security clearance to write our poems.

Whose terms of secrecy are we going to accept? The abusing
parent's or mate's? Or are we going to present the secret in a
poem and alter those terms so that the abuser is now the one invit-
ed to accept the openness of the victim's community? Give the
secret of openness to that person, or else they may forever keep it
from themselves.

A poem recreates the secret, replays it. The only thing added
is the victim's response. That is what is spoken out loud for the
first time. Freed and freeing speech. Permission to respond.

Confidante, priest, psychiatrist—those sworn to secrecy are
like the poem in that you do confide in a poem, confess in the
poem, probe the conscious and unconscious layers of your history
in the poem. And telling the truth in a poem, just like telling the
truth to people who play these roles, usually leads to genuine
changes in your life. Yet confidante, priest, and psychiatrist are
sworn to secrecy and a poem seems so public. But we could ask
ourselves, isn't the poem itself a secret? No matter how public it's
made, doesn't it retain the qualities of a secret partly because
writing a poem is an intimate act?

Its likeness to a secret is in the verb *keep*: the poem seems to
keep for us all the details in lifelike condition, actually in a life of
their own. And a more resolved life than the writer may have lived
when silent.

I'd like to let Joan Swift have the last words, from her letter
describing the writing of her two rape series.

> In the . . . 1970 . . . sequence of rape poems . . . I was able
> to write only from my own point of view. I felt tremendous guilt,
> the female collective unconscious kind, and besides that, guilt for
> being responsible for his getting caught and thus for his life. I . .
> . [chose] a series of metaphors . . . to hide behind. . . . I cer-
> tainly wasn't able to come right out and say that I'd told him I
> loved him. . . . There isn't much anger in those poems, only

compassion. . . . No actual trial was held, only a preliminary hearing, since he later changed his plea to guilty. I was the only witness; . . . no one else's story was told. I was confessing, in a way, but hiding behind a lot of devices.

What I chose to reveal in the . . . 1983 . . . sequence, including the poem "Another Witness," results directly from sitting in the courtroom during the trial and later reading transcripts. There was a whole complicated story to be told, involving a number of people, among them a murdered woman. The best way to tell everyone's part in the story was through their own words. During the preliminary hearing, I had omitted the "I love you" from my testimony, and when I told [the prosecutor] I had said that, he immediately decided to use it in the trial, presumably to show that I had saved my life with the words. From my point of view, I was again responsible, this time for a woman's death, and I had to confess more openly. In front of God, the judge, and everybody. . . . No hiding places.

I did want to protect [the victim's husband] because he had gone through so much hell already. And . . . the only real name I've used is Charlie Red, and he can come and get me if he can read. I tried to be as candid as possible. . . . I put off writing my own testimony as long as I could, then decided to just say it the way it was. . . . I guess it took courage to write the poem. It certainly took courage to say it in court. And, yes, I am afraid what people will think. It's not a feminist approach. People will think I'm a cringing coward. . . .

I guess I worry mostly about how my mother will react. I'm enclosing an article which appeared in the North End edition of the Seattle Times a couple of months ago. When I sent it to her, she said, "Well, I guess everyone in Edmonds knows now that you were raped." When I told her that the paper had gone out to about 100,000 people, not just Edmonds, she didn't know what to say.

I believe good poems come from telling the truth. That's best. Tobias Wolff says a good writer has "the willingness to say that unspeakable thing which everyone else in the house is too coy, or too frightened, or too polite to say."

I think poems in themselves are a way of saying things discreetly.

I would add only that the poem is discreet because no matter how much you feel you are blurting out the truth, you the writer must, by the very nature of the art of poetry, *discover* that truth, the truth of what you feel, *while* writing. You may be victim or witness, but you are historian and artist. And you are telling other people's stories when you tell your own.

(1986)

Laura Jensen

LESSONS IN FORM

FIRST LESSONS

I don't remember being born. Books tell us it is after our births that we each begin to discover our self. This self is a human being's prior knowledge. The human lives within the skin of that human self; it senses itself.

> We think by feeling. What is there to know?
> I hear my being dance from ear to ear.
> I wake to sleep, and take my waking slow.
>
> Of those so close beside me, which are you?
> God bless the Ground! I shall walk softly there,
> And learn by going where I have to go.
> Theodore Roethke, "The Waking"

To this prior self we must return for identity's sake. Selfish senses are there to declare us ourselves. In sleep we return. We return when we find a corner chair and eat potato chips or read an old children's book—we return to our prior self, to that one self within the skin of a human being.

We must return, because it is from within that skin that we look outward to attend to human myths. We learn the pattern around us, we learn how we fit in. We do not know these are our lessons in form. We know it as knowledge of the real world. When I first made words with a pencil the word *form* to me was only the way I misspelled *from* on my earliest envelopes of notes to the family. The patterns of letters were the real way words were done. But spelling was really a lesson in form, only one pattern of the many human patterns, only one language.

When I was a child my mother and uncles performed in their Gord Family Orchestra, a dance band for Scandinavian music. I watched my uncles on accordion and banjo and drums and my mother on piano, heard the feet of the dancers stamp on the floor at the end of the schottische. A holiday dance for the Scandinavian brotherhood they belonged to, or one of their songfests, or a family wedding—there was always a holiday. There was always a holiday at my grandmother's house, where the kitchen window looked down at the bay—Thanksgiving. Christmas. Or Sunday.

Or weekday afternoons when cranes moved among piles of boards at Dickman's Mill below us, the boards like sugar wafers on Grandmother's cookie plate. Machinery noises, then the whistle as the train passed. These high holidays structured a calendar of expectation for me. There were always other children. My sister, my cousins.

The calendar's most important holiday was the day school began. Those first days were very warm and the sky brilliant blue outside the panes crossed by cream-colored framework. One day a new boy came to meet our kindergarten class as we sat in the large window seat filled with sun. He met us by feeling our faces because he could not see. He would be in our school in the fall, and when I sat near him that fall I saw technology—his Braille typewriter and cream-colored Braille sheets. At six I learned he could use technology to transcend, that technology was wonderful. But more than that, this meeting told me that I could see.

The holidays always to come—those were my first lessons in form.

TEACHING FORM

Grown up, we continue good lessons. One lesson is meeting ourselves again in other new children. The poet Daniel Halpern looks from a window to the beach and wants to advise the child there:

> When you think too much about all there is
> you begin to lose what you have.
>
> "Child Running"

The child cannot hear him and is listening to something Halpern cannot hear.

In 1985 it snowed for two weeks and the house where I lived was covered with icicles—icicles like the teeth of a monster or Scheherezade's swords hanging from the tin roof outside the kitchen door. I asked some children who were marching the neighborhood with a shovel to clear the back steps—after I paid them the oldest boy seized one icicle sword and brandished it away with him, flourishing it happily, as I stood diminished and surprised. In the summertime a hummock of earth a block away was covered with daisies, bachelor buttons, cosmos. Once children had run through it, crushed parts of the flowering just to spend a moment in daisies higher than their heads. I had looked forward to their daisies. But these lessons in meeting children's creative urges give us back something that was our own when we were children.

TRANSFORMATION

We feel that surge to form as poets:

> And I can't get rid . . .
> Of the urge to impose a form on what I don't understand,
> Or that which I have to transform because it's too grim as it is.
>   Carolyn Kizer, "Singing Aloud"

I ride the bus in Pierce County and often encounter the mentally ill. Western State Hospital is in Pierce County and most of those discharged remain there. One day I came out of the rain while waiting for a bus to spend a couple of minutes inside the dry drugstore. "Are the kids bothering you?" asked the clerk. "I don't have any kids," I answered. But I knew she meant the mental patients waiting for the bus. These are not kids; to call them kids is to refuse to acknowledge them, to call back an image of the Bethlehem Hospital that brought the word "bedlam" to our language. The image does not acknowledge that the purpose of care is improvement. These are not children, but adults whose mental hell and traumatic real experiences could happen to anyone. According to Richard Warner in *Psychology Today,* many symptoms of schizophrenia may be the common psychological effects of long-term unemployment. The schizophrenic rate rises and falls as the job market falls and rises; the schizophrenic who recovers is the one who finds a job. By working the person transforms the life. In a way the word "Kids" comes close to being correct—like children, all adults need to form and transform.

One day I rode home from Seattle from visiting a friend and I listened to a rider talking. The ride was not dismal; her words transposed the ride, took it up a few notes into another key. Her face had a scrubbed look. Her child looked like an angel. She was explaining things to the other young mother, not as though she needed to be understood, but as though her life were beautiful. But what was the beauty about? Housework for her sister once a month? The Bumbershoot Arts Festival crowd and her boyfriend's band there? Or her kind intonation of *helicopter* for her son, his hands on the bus window? The helicopter rose heavy above a smoky industry. But she had transformed a sister's housework, an Arts Festival, a rock band, and a helicopter.

In spring we see black branches transformed to a flowering fruit tree. It seems like magic. But most transformations are subtler, are transpositions or variations, just enough to entertain the senses, not so much that form is completely altered.

TO FORGET FORM

Last year I saw the world take on new form—a form that was a kind of formlessness. The world was delayed, then sudden—unpredictable, filled with barricades and messages left for others that I could not ignore; these confused me. Much information bore no resemblance to the truth, much true information was not about the topic that interested me. The old world was unfamiliar and inappropriate. The world was too loud, too dangerous, too heavy—it weighed a ton and a half. Noise screamed past ignoring me. The news was of hard times, violence. Sirens, alarms alerting me that once again dreadful things had happened I could never know the truth about. No word for it.

I may be describing a world turned incoherent as an essay, for Composition is incoherent when all the information is old information. For coherence Composition recommends a mixture of the old and new.

I may be describing grief. For at the time my god-mother had died. My mother was very ill. I worried, but worked hard because I was of a mind to work hard.

I may be describing a world of mixed feelings, for while this formless world repelled so, it still had my attention.

I may be describing a world without enough money, a world of financial insecurity, for I was using food stamps, not for the first time, and its uncertainties alarmed me.

I may be describing the world Benjamin Péret views as a world of unthinking activity. His alternative is to dream and to meditate. To never separate day and night.

But I think I am describing a feeling: I am at the park, waiting for the runner with the torch:

> . . . I say it is like
> a cover from an old
> Saturday Evening Post by
> Norman Rockwell—the blue
> sky roped by stars and stripes,
> the old brick restaurant,
> the green canopy over us,
> the old people in hats and mesh

chairs. After some serious
waiting, a number
of false here they ares,
the children release
their balloons as rehearsed,
and from back of the crowd
I see the runner dimly,
and clearly above him the torch.
He tells me each
keeps the torch he ran with.
And we walk and wheel
back to the ducks.
Where the shadows of a willow
reflect, he tells me
I'd become an alcoholic
if I had a glass like that
to drink from.

Laura Jensen, "Possessions"

A traditional scene and an ambiguous comment on it. The words mean that the little scene will not be enough. The words sound disillusioned. I think I am describing disillusion—in which we forget form.

FALSE FORM

For Plato, the teachers of false forms were the Sophists. They created illusions and led Greek youths into false beliefs. Should we believe a false thing, to be disillusioned is a great Truth. These Sophists could be recognized in three ways—they treated the student as prey, they used a method of argument that was contentious, and they performed their teachings strictly on a monetary basis.

My mother had a money box with a coin till under the lid. She counted bills and coins at the kitchen table, did addition and subtraction. The money had to last. But there was a savings account for college, so there was hope. The first time I bought clothing for myself, a sweater, when I was very young, I knew I could buy the sale sweater and bring home something from the larger bill my mother had given me. In high school I worked at the public library twenty hours a week for two years and had the privilege of saving every check for college. I learned that everything costs money. But there was a savings account for college, so there was hope.

I think a world where there must be a money box is an illusion only if our thoughts dwell only on the money box.

FORMULATION

Poetry is our lesson in poetry.

That mind forming has an accuracy in view. *Accuracy* is a word with mundane connotations—typing class, measuring cups in kitchens. But our accuracy is not an accuracy to a model or a recipe, our accuracy is a future accuracy, an accuracy of what has not yet been. It is an accuracy of vision, an account of now, an account of a memory or a vision, an account of a dream, of a fiction totally imagined, described, accurately and exactly to our best ability beyond misstatement, beyond misshaping any shape in our Idea. In our practice as poets, to be Inaccurate becomes a real Lie. All our attention is on the page. We cannot account for the hours spent—we have only the page. A radar screen watcher works a high vigilance profession. Our attention is so intense that it is a vigilance too.

Some of us find that what we hear must be in accord with our vision. We can become very critical of life. Matthew Arnold wrote that poetry is a criticism of life. So to refrain from turning to the page can be a real Lie. I think poets become critics because to allow misunderstanding about that important matter at hand, a poem, would be a real Lie.

But we know it is a lie to brow-beat with truths beyond our listeners' endurance. A lie to betray their willingness to attend. To be unceasingly accurate until their illusions vanish is a lie, for cruelty is a lie about mercy. Hence the minimalist less is more. Hence a merciful several stanzas are often more memorable than a cruel several hundred pages. Hence our devotion to poetry as the truest language art of all. Willa Cather reportedly said that the real secret of form is to know what is not necessary, to know what to leave out.

To the writer the word *form* has mostly to do with the verb *to form*. And that has to do with the hand and page and eye.

PLATO'S FORMS

Plato and other philosophers contemplate the Idea. In daily life people deal with things, imperfect realizations of the Idea. Shelley, mourning the death of Keats, writes:

> The One remains, the many change and pass;
> Heaven's light forever shines, Earth's shadows fly;
> Life, like a dome of many-coloured glass,
> Stains the white radiance of Eternity,

Until Death tramples it to fragments.—Die,
If thou wouldst be with that which thou dost seek!
Follow where all is fled!—Rome's azure sky,
Flowers, ruins, statues, music, words, are weak
The glory they transfuse with fitting truth to speak.

In the autumn I was reading Francis Cornford's translation of
Plato and found the words from Shelley chosen for illustration.
Artists are also concerned with the Idea. Artists make things ap-
pear to represent Ideas with no existence in the particular room.

When I talked to a friend, Dan Blachly, he told me he was
waiting for his trial. Others had pleaded guilty and been excused,
but he and another had not hesitated. They had pleaded not guilty
to jumping the fence at Fort Lewis when they came there to
distribute their fliers. Because of their plea they could state their
political case in court, and did state their case. They were fined
five hundred dollars, not a small amount for a jazz piano player
who also does moving and hauling with a battered truck. But they
did not hesitate and made their point. If in responding to events,
we do not hesitate, we create an activist. If in responding to the
empty page, we do not hesitate, we create a writer. In what we do
not hesitate to do, we create a pattern, a form for our lives. The
activists stayed on my mind.

I looked up and saw an extra sky. I saw Shelley's domed sky
singing the theory of forms, the theory of ideas. What I saw surprised me. I saw a panel of sky that is total disarmament. It
showed the nuclear complex as an illusion waved before us by
Sophists. Meaningless activity exhausts us into acceptance of
what exists as a truth. But is not something that can destroy us not
true, but false? I was born in 1948. For the first time in my life I
looked up at sky and saw total disarmament. I had never seen that
before.

(1988)

BODY AND SOUL:
THREE POETS ON
THEIR MALADIES

1.

Charles Simic

MY INSOMNIA AND I

I would not have been the same man if I had been able to sleep well in my life.

It all started when I was twelve. I fell in love. I lay in the dark trying to peek under her skirt. I thought her name was Maria, but it was really Insomnia.

In a life full of troubles, Insomnia kept me company against the fear of the dark.

We were like young lovers. I had no secrets from her. Our silences were as eloquent as speech.

Most of the time, I resisted the impulse to toss and turn. I didn't blink. I tried not to swallow. I didn't even move my tongue.

My mind was like Ulysses. We took long sea voyages. We were often in South Seas and China. In nineteenth century London and St. Petersburg we were afraid. In Belgrade bombs still fell.

Mostly, though, it was quiet. Like Noah's crow we reconnoitered the empty universe. Acrobats of the abyss, face to face with the Great Nothing.

We had many conversations with dead philosophers, mystics and prisoners:

"I'm awake because I don't wish to be surprised by my future," said one.

"There's freedom only for the awake," said another.

Horror of consciousness, everybody's favorite home movie.

I often felt like a schoolboy writing the same word or two over and over again on the blackboard.

My shoes with their broken and reknotted laces stayed in the corner.

Time vanished. Soused with melancholy, eternity came to breathe on me.

My fleas didn't sleep well either.

Occasionally, I climbed my own private stairway to the dark heavens. It was like an empty nightclub with a tragic menu on each table.

O soul, nowhere awaited!

The child I was often came to visit me. He wanted to show me things in a theater with mice-eaten red curtains. I went reluctantly, since, of course, he didn't exist. It was like walking backwards on a tightrope with eyes closed.

In the woods one Sunday we came upon a couple lying on the ground. Hand in hand, ourselves fearful of losing our way, we saw what we first surmised was a patch of snow. In a spot rarely visited, we came upon the embraced ones, the two clutching each other naked on the cold ground. . . . In the woods that already had a bit of purple shade, some bird chirping and falling silent as we stole by.

At 3 a.m. I always believed the worst. Lying stiffly, counting my heartbeats to a thousand and one!

I pretended to believe in the future, but even so, fits of doubt. Even when I slept I dreamed I was awake.

My conscience knew its business. I was continuously under surveillance. I had a theory: God is afraid of insomniacs, but not the devil. I imagined labyrinthine cities where I would elude my guilt.

My love read Russian novels at night while I read mysteries and history books. The rustle of our pages being turned made the mice in the walls tremble, the angel of death put on his glasses and peeked over her bare shoulders.

So many judges, so little justice in the world! Murder is a folk art, it occurred to me. They keep perfecting it without ever being pleased with the results.

I already had my own gallows. "Long live the brotherhood of the sleepless!" I shouted with the noose tightening around my neck, but all anyone else heard was the old bedsprings creak.

And then, just as the day was breaking, I smiled to myself as I felt my love leaving me.

(1994)

2.

Shirley Kaufman

BACKACHE, POEMACHE, AND *BOTZ*

What's disgusting about backache, of course, is that it's not serious enough. On a suffering scale of 1 to 10, it's most likely 10. You begin to feel ashamed. Not that you want something worse to complain about. Your friends, with their smash-ups, losses, incurable cancers, autistic children, are too nice. They even bring you soup when you can't get out of bed. All you have to say is, "My back's killing me," and fifteen people immediately tell you what to do. The whole world has a backache. That's probably what's wrong with it. All those decisions being made in the wrong chairs.

"My poem is killing me." Six of my poet friends study the lines to tell me what's wrong. We meet once a month to "help" one another. After all these years. Everyone has a different cure. Take this out. Switch this around. What you need is . . . . End it here. No. End it there.

It's clear that from the time we crawled out of the slime, we were never meant to stand up straight on our two little feet. Bunions, corns, ingrown toenails, fallen arches. The curved posture of apes seems much more natural, the way they lope along with their long arms, using both hands and feet. Hubris got us where we are. We should have been happy walking on four paws like the other animals, sniffing the earth or the water under the earth, all the senses alive as they are when the words start coming.

Most of us walk backward into our lives, unable to free ourselves from the past we keep looking at. Mothers. Fathers. Old poets. We go on being their children. How vulnerable our backs must be, out there on their own, having to feel things first, to bump into the future alone like that, without knowing where they are headed. A poet's condition.

So I try what they tell me. I try what they don't tell me. I use ancient remedies. I listen to testimonies. I get over it. (I finish the poem.) Months pass. Sometimes years. And then the next time comes. To relieve me of certainty, to make sure I know about the uses of memory. To remind me I'm not yet bodiless.

Now it's the next time. I bring the pain to the Dead Sea. The lowest spot in the whole world. No living organism grows in these mineral waters. A good place to dump pain. I can drive down the hill on the Jericho road and get there in less than an hour. Walk over the solid brine, step into that sulfur-scented, calm, oily water, let my feet slip from under me, stretch out on my back, and float. Like an inflated rubber raft, little air-filled bulges. Little word-filled stanzas. No. The sea is the raft, holding me up. And I'm in it, and on it. Until I *become* it (the great maternal cliché).

> . . . . Sunlight
> peeling off the old skin.
> Not wondering how it happened.
> So that the surface floats
> on its warm back, smiling.
> So that the body loosens itself
> to kindness. The one thing
> we're ready for.

Almost 2,000 years ago Hadrian chained a row of slaves and threw them into the Dead Sea. He wanted to prove that men could drown but not sink in those dense waters. I can float, and not drown. Sometimes writing is a kind of floating. When you give yourself to it, when you let yourself look up at the clear, unlimited blue, and hear what it tells you.

And then there's the mud. Black, greasy, stinking mineral soup from the bottom of the Dead Sea. You can slosh it over your skin at beaches along the shore. Or go to a place where cheerful experts welcome your aching flesh. They heat the stuff in buckets, as hot as you can bear, spread it like honey all over your shoulders, arms, legs, and back, a comforting poultice of mud. They ease you down on the table. You lean into it, sink in the hot porridge. They wrap you tight in plastic sheeting, wrap you tight in blankets, a bound mummy. You feel the mud suck at your sore back. You feel the pain ooze out of your spine, trickle out of your pores and into the cushion around you, lose itself in the mud. You stand in the shower after and wash it away. Clean towel. White page. This is where I begin.

The word for mud in Hebrew is *botz*. *Botz* is also a kind of coffee Israelis like to drink. It started during WWII when there were no instant varieties, and coffee was scarce. For *botz* half a teaspoon would do. Before filters and drips and French vacuums. Before acupuncture, shiatsu, Alexander, Feldenkreis, and prose poems. It's simply coffee, ground very fine, stirred into a cup of boiling water, and allowed to settle at the bottom into dark brown mud. The crucial muck where all the words are. An unrefined version of Greek, Turkish, or Arab coffee brewed in a pot. Delicious. Just so you drink the dark essence and stop when you taste the bitter dregs, before you get to the bottom.

(1994)

3.

Lee Upton

THE CLOSEST WORK

When Louise Bogan wrote of lingering childhood memories she remarked that "such memories, compounded of bewilderment and ignorance and fear, . . . we must always keep in our hearts. We can never forget them because we cannot understand them, and because they are of no use." Perhaps only in the conventional sense was she referring to the "use" that we make of certain memories; perhaps we feel ourselves to be used by memories, particularly those that, once dormant, rise before us with surprising new strength.

When I entered grammar school I did not know the alphabet, and I was perhaps very slow to learn to read. But once I began to read it was as if I were within the room of the book, entering without having heard the door open before me or close behind me. To be absorbed: the phrase has a specific resonance for me, for it was as if I had been admitted wholly into reading and writing. Repeatedly I would read the often mediocre books that we were given in grade school, discovering that speed and concentration determine certain effects. And when I went on to study books that were beyond my capacity I felt a sense of gratitude, as if the books sent me forward into the wonderfully strange.

Reading and writing, done with pages less than an arm's length away, were activities accomplished in a small space removed from the more hazardous bewilderments of childhood. Otherwise, outside of the book and the papers on my desk, I experienced a sensation of stopping short—a zone, a range of distance—that I avoided and feared.

Then, so much of the world was unreliable. How long it would take me to learn to tell time, to play games on the playground. In some situations, I simply could not understand what other children seemed to understand easily. I accepted my own bewilderment as inevitable, and I came to rely on my reading and my writing. Poems, what little I knew of them, were the best sort of matter for the intense reading I depended upon, and they offered intimations of a way of being that much of the world refused me. Poetry was an efflorescence, an inky apparition. Poets were their words. They were the matter of their books. Somehow, I believed, poems materialized after the poets' deaths. I came home from school with words written on my hands as if my words were my skin.

A vague air of insult traveled about the mid-Michigan farm community in which I was raised. To write poetry meant to affront insult through presumption, for poetry was the most presumptuous thing to which I had been introduced. It repudiated our slights and elevated our value. And it came to me, often enough even in its doggerel form, as the most particularly impossible thing around me.

A year before I secretly pledged myself to poetry, a photographer taking my picture (I am a seven-year-old in my First Communion dress) remarks: "One of her eyes droops." I am not offended but feel grateful for his close attention. In the photograph I am seriously trying to be Mary the Mother of God. Because my prayer book has been forgotten, I am staring at a blank sheet of paper at the level of my breastbone. The paper is folded to resemble a book.

By the time it is discovered that I cannot see writing on the blackboard at school, not even from the front row, that I cannot read the numerals on the clock on the wall, that I have panicked secretly when attempting to recognize the faces of my playmates as they ran about on the playground, I am nine years old. I have learned to read and to write and have promised myself a secret and seemingly impossible ambition—and all this has been conditioned by my being a child like many others, simply enough, commonly enough, a myopic child.

A preoccupation with perception and scale—a sensitivity to distances: these emerge in some measure in my poetry from my experience with early work close to the page. If I prefer to repeal certainties, if often the work seems to draw up short before diverse panels of meaning, it is because I would duplicate an atmosphere of both absorption and resistance. To point to the subjectivity of any vision, to move from opacity to contingent moments of clarity: these have been customary for me.

My repetition of the sensation of working close to the page, of looking up from miniature figures into vague distances, occurs in my poetry as an endeavor that is marked by repetition. In the very act of repeating a sensation from the past I am inevitably touching the pulse of much poetry, for of course many poetries are devoted to repetition, most commonly repetition of word, of phrase, of sound, of image, of conception. In turn the poem lives through repetition; it is measured by its ability to lure readers to repeat the poem over an individual life and over the lives of generations. The poem *bears* repetition and may grow from the poet's compulsion to repeat, paradoxically, because it does not repeat itself twice in the same way. In our individual lives the poem continues to reveal to us new filaments of meaning as if we may only partially see, only partially hear, the poem in each reading. "The words of a dead man/ are modified in the guts of the living," Auden wrote, his imagery suggesting that it is the body that consumes the poem, the body that modifies it for us.

The drive to repeat in the poet—the compulsion emerging from latent sources in the memory and in bodily sensation and, often enough, in the conscious will to intervene in repetitive patterns of language—is in turn affected by the desire to reveal a phantom at the borders of consciousness. The unnamed force that we recognize in some poems (I think immediately of Emily Dickinson's spiritual intimations) issues a ghost light, flickering and dissolving but providing us with a glimpse of other orders. However briefly, a sense of immense depths and incredible breadths is ours. This sensation of freedom may repeat itself while we write poems and while we read the poems of others—perhaps if we are patient, if we are determined to see and to listen most fully, to allow our fallible senses to move against their limits.

As a child, when I at last wore glasses, it became clear to me that by having my near-sightedness corrected I also gained new vulnerabilities. The feelings of other people suddenly seemed unbearably close, as if I were being violated in some inchoate manner. To see clearly meant it was now possible to feel in a new way and thus to experience others' repugnance or irritation or dismay. There were more colors in people's faces, and the colors took on sharper edges. Yet it was difficult to make any edges appear around myself. When I become a teenager I disliked wearing glasses and tried at times, miserably, to go without them—out of vanity and out of the self-protection that young people so often desire.

The temptation to look away from what has the potential to harm is a common temptation that the poet must labor to overcome. The poet must make felt and seen what we would instinctively avoid. Louise Bogan writes of an experience of this order in "A Tale," a very early poem which she reprinted in most of her collections. In a desolate landscape a young person encounters the monstrous: "something dreadful and another/ Look quietly upon each other." These two unknown monstrous beings are locked together by their gazes as if to see, however "quietly," means to risk identification and, in such sustained proximity, paralysis. As her autobiographical prose informs us, Bogan was blind for two days in childhood as a result of apparently repressed trauma, most likely involving violence and her mother. She writes of the return of her vision: "I remember my sight coming back, by seeing the flat forked light of the gas flame, in its etched glass shade, suddenly appearing beside the bureau. What had I seen? I shall never know." Surely the recesses of her poetry, her attention to invisibilities, her extreme challenge to conventional comprehension, to "making sense," were profoundly influenced by such an early experience.

My own problems with sight were surely in no way tragic but common and correctable. I was fortunate to have been given the experience of the contingency of vision. It is perhaps good to know something of how inevitably we adapt ourselves to the strangeness of even a small and frequently experienced difference. To realize at a relatively early age how resistant the world was to understanding is not, perhaps, poor training for anyone who would write poetry. It guarantees that one sees the world as if one lingers at the edges of the gulf between one's self-knowledge and the world's knowledge of selves. The poetries that I come to most often are recalcitrant to measure and sensitive to the margins of experience.

In the small compass of the personal, I have been referring to vision, but I wish now to discuss the speech that may seem necessary in response to another sort of sensory boundary. If proximity, being close to the page and finding there a quality of intimacy, has been significant for me (as it has been for many others) still other proximities affect my work. I am interested in thinking at the edges of perception, thinking of the poem at the boundaries of comprehensibility. I mentioned, earlier, the ghost light, the abraded perception, that one finds in certain poetries as if the poem must not only point to the senses but show the labyrinthine ways in which the senses meet their limits. I have had the fortune to be close to a life in which understanding was shown to be no guarantee of value and in which compressed, uncommon language was not only respected but desired.

Among my most memorable experiences were those of repetition in which I must be careful to speak distinctly and to repeat myself. As my father's ability to hear became poor, he taught himself to watch faces intently, to move his lips with our lips as we spoke to him. To be heard by him meant that all of us in our family must weigh our words. This speaking required a rapid foreshortening. We reduced our remarks to make them pointed and to make repetition somehow easier for ourselves.

In his partial deafness, my father cared for words deeply, especially those that were memorable and odd, whatever words might resist our enemies. He would have been pleased with very little, I believe now, but I felt then that he wanted something from his children toward which he could immediately respond. He wanted a stubborn quirkiness of sentiment that answered his own sense of the stubborn quirkiness of things. It was characteristic of him to most admire people who worked hard (just as he did as a farmer) and yet he was most fond of remarks that reflected, however difficult it was to make such remarks, an irreverent ebullience, a relief from care and labor.

At times I would be tired even before I spoke to him, as if it would be too much of an effort for me to repeat myself and to make words strong enough for him. I was ashamed, then, because he was so obviously patient with me. I knew too that speaking with him could be a wonderful event—his face reflecting a tender surprise and a stoic foreknowledge of the ways of the world. Yet it was also somehow a painful event, as if too much feeling threatened to fill me at once. To be listened to with such hope, from someone so eager for laughter, eager for the jarring dislocations of meaning that create laughter: How fortunate I was, and how readily his fullest responses made whatever was anaesthetized and reluctant to feel within me break open and thaw painfully.

In my early work a tone of voice may be heard that is, I have only recently come to realize, derived from a training in inflection and repetition that I received from my father, when even the most innocent words bore the potential to baffle and harm—or to meet the undisguised yearning in his face.

It is a commonplace to speak of the sensuous nature of much poetry. Yet some of us seek the sensuous which reflects blight, a pock mark, and erosion. The senses reveal shifts, decay, limitations, for the senses live while we live. They may abandon us as they respond to time and to trauma. To chart the contours that perception may afford us has been of particular interest to me in my earlier work, for the body does not give the same message to us all. To finger the contours of sensory abridgement, to press at the nature of the seen and the heard—these are possibilities that may, for some of us, at least for some time, prove sustaining. One gains, inevitably, a sense of one's boundaries. And one gains the hope of trespassing against such limits, to know better the range of a common struggle.

(1994)

NOTES ON CONTRIBUTORS

Margaret Atwood is the author of more than 25 books of poetry, fiction, and non-fiction. Her most recent novel, *Alias Grace*, was published in 1996.

Marvin Bell lives in Iowa City, Iowa, and Port Townsend, Washington. His thirteen books of poetry and essays include *The Book of the Dead Man* and, in 1997, *Ardor (The Book of the Dead Man, vol. 2)*.

Robert Bly's new book of poems, *Morning Poems*, was published this year by HarperCollins. His most recent book of prose is *The Sibling Society*.

Russell Edson, the leading American prose poet, is the author most recently of *The Tunnel: Selected Poems* (1994).

Günter Eich, one of Germany's preëminent postwar poets, died in 1972. His selected poems are available in *Valuable Nail* (1981).

Jean Follain (1903-71) wrote subtle, expressive poems in both verse and prose, many of which are available in expert translations by W. S. Merwin (in *Transparence of the World*, 1969) and by Mary Feeney and William Matthews (in *A World Rich in Anniversaries*, 1981).

John Haines, who divides his time between Alaska and the continental United States, is the author most recently of *The Owl in the Mask of the Dreamer: Collected Poems* (1993).

Donald Hall lives in New Hampshire as a freelance writer. His twelfth book of poems was *The Old Life* in 1996 and a new volume titled *Without* will appear from Houghton Mifflin in 1998.

Miroslav Holub, Czech poet and immunologist, has most recently published *Intensive Care: Selected and New Poems* (1996). His new book of essays is *Shedding Life* (Milkweed Press).

Laura Jensen lives in Tacoma, Washington, and is the author of several books of poems, including *Shelter*, *Memory*, and *Bad Boats*.

Shirley Kaufman has published six volumes of her own poetry and several books of translations, including Abba Kovner (from

Hebrew) and Judith Herzberg (Dutch) in the Field Translation Series. Her most recent book is *Roots in the Air: New and Selected Poems* (1996). She lives in Jerusalem.

Galway Kinnell's most recent book is *Imperfect Thirst*. He teaches in the New York University graduate writing program.

Denise Levertov's most recent books are *New and Selected Essays* (1992), *Tesserae* (memoirs, 1996), and *Sands of the Well* (poems, 1996).

Larry Levis' posthumous collection of poems, *Elegy*, will be published by University of Pittsburgh Press in the fall of 1997.

William Matthews is the author of ten books of poems.

Sandra McPherson's seventh and eighth full-length books are *Edge Effect: Trails and Portrayals* and *The Spaces Between Birds: Mother/Daughter Poems 1967-1995*, both published by Wesleyan in 1996. She teaches at the University of California at Davis.

Adrienne Rich's most recent books are *What Is Found There: Notebooks on Poetry and Politics* (1993) and *Dark Fields of the Republic: Poems 1991-1995*.

Dennis Schmitz is the author of several books of poetry, including *About Night: Selected and New Poems* (1994).

David Shapiro is the author of 20 volumes of poetry and literary/art/architectural criticism, including the first book on John Ashbery's poetry and on Mondrian's flowers (Abrams). He was nominated for the National Book Award for poetry in 1971.

Charles Simic directs the writing program at the University of New Hampshire and has published many books of poems and translations, most recently *Walking the Black Cat* (1996).

Gary Snyder is a poet, essayist, and watershed activist. His most recent books are *Mountains and Rivers Without End* (a book-length poem sequence) and *A Place in Space* (new and selected prose). He teaches part-time at the University of California at Davis and lives in the northern California Sierra.

William Stafford (1914-93) was one of this country's presiding poetic spirits. *The Darkness Around Us Is Deep*, his selected poems, was published in 1993.

Alberta Turner is Professor Emerita of English at Cleveland State University. Her selected poems, *Beginning with And*, was published in 1994.

Lee Upton's third book of poetry, *Approximate Darling*, appeared from the University of Georgia Press in 1996. Her second book of criticism, *Obsession and Release: Rereading the Poetry of Louise Bogan*, appeared in the same year from Bucknell University Press.

David Walker teaches modern literature and creative writing at Oberlin College. He is the author of *The Transparent Lyric*, a study of the poetry of Wallace Stevens and William Carlos Williams, and of many essays and reviews of contemporary poetry.

C. D. Wright's most recent poetry collection is *Tremble* (Ecco, 1996). She lives in Rhode Island where she teaches at Brown University and is the State Poet.

Charles Wright has published many volumes of poetry, including *Country Music: Selected Early Poems* (1982), *The World of the Ten Thousand Things* (1990), and most recently *Black Zodiac* (1997). He teaches at the University of Virginia.

James Wright (1927-80) helped reinvent American poetry at mid-century. His complete poems, *Above the River*, appeared in 1990.

David Young is Longman Professor of English at Oberlin College. He has published eight books of poetry, including, most recently, *The Planet on the Desk: Selected and New Poems, 1960-1990* (Wesleyan, 1991) and *Night Thoughts and Henry Vaughan* (Ohio State, 1994).

ACKNOWLEDGMENTS

Every effort has been made to obtain permission to reprint the selections in this collection.

Margaret Atwood: "Poetic Process?" first appeared in FIELD #4 (Spring 1971): 13-14. Reprinted by permission of the author.

Marvin Bell: "Noun/Object/Image" first appeared in FIELD #24 (Spring 1981): 29-33. Reprinted by permission of the author.

Robert Bly: "Reflections on the Origins of Poetic Form" first appeared in FIELD #10 (Spring 1974): 31-35. "Recognizing the Image as a Form of Intelligence" first appeared in FIELD #24 (Spring 1981): 17-27. Both selections reprinted by permission of the author.

Russell Edson: "Portrait of the Writer as a Fat Man: Some Subjective Ideas on the Care and Feeding of Prose Poems" first appeared in FIELD #13 (Fall 1975): 19-28. "Image and Language" first appeared in FIELD #24 (Spring 1981): 28. Both selections reprinted by permission of the author.

Günter Eich: "Some Remarks on 'Literature and Reality'" was first published in German in *Akzente*, Jahrgang 3, 1956, No. 4. Copyright © 1956 by *Akzente*. Reprinted by permission of *Akzente* and the Estate of Günter Eich. This translation first appeared in FIELD #3 (Fall 1970): 54-55. Reprinted by permission of the translator.

Jean Follain: This translation of "Meanings of Poetry" first appeared in FIELD #15 (Fall 1976): 58-61.

John Haines: "Further Reflections on Line and the Poetic Voice" first appeared in FIELD #9 (Fall 1973): 79-82.

Donald Hall: "Goatfoot, Milktongue, Twinbird: The Psychic Origins of Poetic Form" first appeared in FIELD #9 (Fall 1973): 38-49. "The Line" first appeared in FIELD #10 (Spring 1974): 84-86. "Notes on the Image: Body and Soul" first appeared in FIELD #24 (Spring 1981): 13-16. All selections reprinted by permission of the author.

Miroslav Holub: "Poetry and Science: The Science of Poetry/The Poetry of Science" first appeared in FIELD #21 (Fall 1979): 76-95. Reprinted by permission of the author.

Laura Jensen: "Lessons in Form" first appeared in FIELD #38 (Spring 1988): 15-23. Reprinted by permission of the author.

Shirley Kaufman: "Some Thoughts about Lines" first appeared in FIELD #9 (Fall 1973): 83-84. "Here and There: The Use of Place in Contemporary Poetry" first appeared in FIELD #23 (Fall 1980): 44-65. "Backache, Poemache, and *Botz*" first appeared in FIELD #50 (Spring 1994): 55-57. All selections reprinted by permission of the author.

Galway Kinnell: "Poetry, Personality and Death" first appeared in FIELD #4 (Spring 1971): 56-75. Reprinted by permission of the author.

Denise Levertov: "Work and Inspiration: Inviting the Muse" first appeared in FIELD #1 (Fall 1969): 24-40. Reprinted by permission of the author.

Larry Levis: "Some Notes on the Gazer Within" first appeared in FIELD #19 (Fall 1978): 28-49. "Eden and My Generation" first appeared in FIELD #26 (Spring 1982): 27-46. Both selections copyright © Estate of Larry Levis, and reprinted by permission.

Sandra McPherson: "The Two-Tone Line, Blues Ideology, and the Scrap Quilt" first appeared in FIELD #44 (Spring 1991): 22-33. "The Working Line" first appeared in FIELD #8 (Spring 1973): 54-60. "Secrets: Beginning to Write Them Out" first appeared in FIELD #34 (Spring 1986): 19-36. All selections reprinted by permission of the author.

William Matthews: "A Note on Prose, Verse and the Line" first appeared in FIELD #10 (Spring 1974): 87. Reprinted by permission of the author.

Adrienne Rich: "Poetry, Personality and Wholeness: A Response to Galway Kinnell" first appeared in FIELD #7 (Fall 1972): 11-18. Copyright © 1972 by Adrienne Rich, and reprinted by permission of the author.

Dennis Schmitz: "Gorky Street: Syntax and Context" first appeared in FIELD #38 (Spring 1988): 39-47. Reprinted by permission of the author.

David Shapiro: "Naked Masks: An Introduction to John Ashbery's Poetry" first appeared in FIELD #5 (Fall 1971): 32-45. This slightly revised version reprinted by permission of the author.

Charles Simic: "Some Thoughts about the Line" first appeared in FIELD #11 (Fall 1974): 62-63. "Images and 'Images'" first appeared in FIELD #23 (Fall 1980): 24-26. "My Insomnia and I" first appeared in FIELD #50 (Spring 1994): 53-54. All selections reprinted by permission of the author.

Gary Snyder: "Poetry, Community, & Climax" first appeared in FIELD #20 (Spring 1979): 21-35. This revised version was included in his *The Real Work* (New Directions, 1980) and is reprinted by permission of the author.

William Stafford: "A Way of Writing" first appeared in FIELD #2 (Spring 1970); 10-15. Reprinted by permission.

Alberta Turner: "Not Your Flat Tire, My Flat Tire: Transcending the Self in Contemporary Poetry" first appeared in FIELD #13 (Fall 1975): 78-89. Reprinted by permission of the author.

Lee Upton: "The Closest Work" first appeared in FIELD #50 (Spring 1994): 58-63. Reprinted by permission of the author.

David Walker: "Stone Soup: Contemporary Poetry and the Obsessive Image" first appeared in FIELD #13 (Fall 1975): 39-47. Reprinted by permission of the author.

C. D. Wright: "A Taxable Matter" first appeared in FIELD #40 (Spring 1989): 24-26. This slightly revised version reprinted by permission of the author.

Charles Wright: "Charles Wright at Oberlin" first appeared in FIELD #17 (Fall 1977): 46-85. Reprinted by permission of the author.

James Wright: "A Response to 'The Working Line'" first appeared in FIELD #8 (Spring 1973): 61-64. Reprinted by permission of Edith Anne Wright.

David Young: "The Bite of the Muskrat: Judging Contemporary Poetry" first appeared in FIELD #7 (Fall 1972): 77-88. "Language: The Poet as Master and Servant" first appeared in FIELD #14 (Spring 1976): 68-90. "Second Honeymoon: Some Thoughts on Translation" first appeared in FIELD #11 (Fall 1974): 78-88. All selections reprinted by permission of the author.